D0140205

BRIEF GROUP TREATMENT

PRACTICAL TRAINING
FOR THERAPISTS AND COUNSELORS

BRIEF GROUP TREATMENT

PRACTICAL TRAINING
FOR THERAPISTS AND COUNSELORS

Jerrold Lee Shapiro, Ph.D.
Santa Clara University

Lawrence S. Peltz, Ph.D.
Private Practice

Susan Bernadett-Shapiro
Santa Clara University

WARNER MEMORIAL LIBRARY
EASTERN COLLEGE
ST. DAVIDS, PA. 19087

BROOKS/COLE PUBLISHING COMPANY
I(T)P® *An International Thomson Publishing Company*

Pacific Grove • Albany • Belmont • Bonn • Boston • Cincinnati • Detroit • Johannesburg
London • Madrid • Melbourne • Mexico City • New York • Paris • Singapore
Tokyo • Toronto • Washington

11-12-98

Sponsoring Editor: *Eileen Murphy*
Editorial Assistant: *Susan Carlson*
Marketing Team: *Deanne Brown,*
  Romy Taorima, and Jean Thompson
Production Editor: *Mary Vezilich*
Design Editor: *Roy R. Neuhaus*
Interior and Cover Design: *John Edeen*
Interior Illustration: *John and Judy Waller*
Art Editor: *Lisa Torri*
Manuscript Editor: *Patterson Lamb*

Cover Photo: *Quilt courtesy of Judy Boisson*
*American Country. Published in **The World***
***of Amish Quilts,** © Good Books. Used by*
permission.
Typesetting: *Bookends Typesetting*
Printing and Binding: *R. R. Donnelly & Sons,*
  Crawfordsville
Cover Printing: *Phoenix Color Corporation*

Copyright © 1998 by Brooks/Cole Publishing Company
A Division of International Thomson Publishing Inc.
I(T)P The ITP logo is a registered trademark under license.

For more information, contact:

BROOKS/COLE PUBLISHING COMPANY
511 Forest Lodge Road
Pacific Grove, CA 93950
USA

International Thomson Editores
Seneca 53
Col. Polanco
11560 México, D.F., México

International Thomson Publishing Europe
Berkshire House 168-173
High Holborn
London WC1V 7AA
England

International Thomson Publishing Japan
Hirakawacho Kyowa Building, 3F
2-2-1 Hirakawacho
Chiyoda-ku, Tokyo 102
Japan

Thomas Nelson Australia
102 Dodds Street
South Melbourne, 3205
Victoria, Australia

International Thomson Publishing Asia
221 Henderson Road
#05-10 Henderson Building
Singapore 0315

Nelson Canada
1120 Birchmount Road
Scarborough, Ontario
Canada M1K 5G4

International Thomson Publishing GmbH
Königswinterer Strasse 418
53227 Bonn
Germany

All rights reserved. No part of this work may be reproduced, stored in a retrieval system, or
transcribed, in any form or by any means—electronic, mechanical, photocopying, recording,
or otherwise—without the prior written permission of the publisher, Brooks/Cole Publishing Company,
Pacific Grove, California 93950.

RC 488 .S456 1998
Shapiro, Jerrold Lee.
Brief group treatment

Printed in the United States of America
1 2 3 4 5 6 7 8 9 10

Library of Congress Cataloging-in-Publication Data
Shapiro, Jerrold Lee.
    Brief group treatment : practical training for therapists and
counselors / Jerrold Lee Shapiro, Lawrence S. Peltz, Susan Bernadett-
Shapiro.
        p.   cm.
    Includes bibliographical references and index.
    ISBN 0-534-35554-4 (pbk.)
    1. Group psychotherapy.   2. Group counseling.   3. Brief
psychotherapy.   I. Peltz, Lawrence S.   II. Bernadett-Shapiro,
Susan, [date]   III. Title.
RC488.S456 1997
616.89'152—dc21   97-37797
                                                             CIP

To my sister, Linda Shapiro, who shares my history with love and understanding
JLS

To my father, Joseph Peltz. May his example of loving kindness live on in all of us
LSP

To the Bernadett family—sisters Ann & Kathy Jo; brothers Tino, Andy, Mike, & Dan; mother Pat; and late father Faustino—my original group experience
STBS

and
to all of our students and colleagues in the group training sequence at the University of Hawaii and Santa Clara University

CONTENTS

PART 1

BASIC GROUP PROCESS   1

1 AN INTRODUCTION TO BRIEF, CLOSED GROUPS   3

Groups as the Treatment of Choice   3
Short-Term Groups   5
Some Realities of Managed Care   7
Summary   9

2 GROUP PROCESS PHASE I: PREPARATION   11

Group Commonalities and Differences   11
Stages of Group Models   12
Value of Predictable Process   14
Phase I: Preparation   16
Summary   40

3 GROUP PROCESS PHASE II: TRANSITION   47

Phase II: Transition   49
The Two Major Tests of Leadership   64
Transition to Treatment   78
How It's Supposed to Go Versus Real Life   78
Summary   79

4 GROUP PROCESS PHASE III: TREATMENT   80

Phase III: Treatment   80
Therapeutic Intervention   88
Summary   96

5 GROUP PROCESS PHASE IV: TERMINATION   97

Preparation for Termination   97
Phase IV: Termination   100
Termination in Open Groups   107
Follow-Up   109
Summary   110

6 THE GROUP LEADER   112

The Group Therapist   112
Characteristics of the Group Therapist   115
The Ideal Personality for a Group Therapist   116
Personality and Method   119
Types of Leadership   120
The Multiple Roles of Group Leadership   126
Information Systems of Group Leaders   135
One Piece of Group Process   141
Leadership and Group Process   145
Summary   145

7 ETHICS   158

Professional Issues in Group Leadership   158
Ethics   158
Safety Precautions on Entering Groups   164
Summary   168

8 GROUP LEADER TRAINING   169

Training   169
A Model Training Program   174
Summary   179

9 CO-THERAPY   180

Co-Therapy   180
Summary   185

PART **II**

GROUPS FOR SPECIFIC POPULATIONS   *187*

Nominally Homogeneous Groups   188
How to Use This Section   189

10   ADULT CHILDREN OF ALCOHOLICS   *190*

The (Invisible) Elephant in the Living Room   190
Unique Characteristics of This Population   191
Preparation   194
Transition   196
Treatment   197
Termination   198
Summary   199

11   ADOLESCENTS   *201*

Characteristics of Adolescents   201
Adolescents and Group Treatment   202
Adolescent Groups and the Brief Treatment Model   204
Preparation   205
Transition   205
Treatment   207
Termination   209
Summary   209

12   INDIVIDUALS WITH EATING DISORDERS   *211*

Types of Eating Disorders   211
Preparation   216
Transition   217
Treatment   218
Termination   219
Summary   220

13 COUPLES   *221*

History   221
Characteristics of the Population   223
Preparation   223
Transition   226
Treatment   227
Termination   229
Premarital Groups   229
Cross-Cultural Couples   233
Summary   233

14 GROUPS FOR PERPETRATORS AND SURVIVORS OF DOMESTIC VIOLENCE   *235*

Domestic Violence   235
Two-Stage Process   236
Anger Management Groups   236
Advanced Groups for Perpetrators   237
Treatment for Survivors of Family Violence   240
The Children   242
Summary   243

15 SINGLE-GENDER GROUPS: WOMEN'S GROUPS, MEN'S GROUPS   *244*

Women's Groups   245
Men's Groups   248
Summary   254

16 WHITHER BRIEF GROUP TREATMENT?   *255*

Historical and Recent Trends   255
Into the Millennium   257
Professional Issues in Groups of the Future   259
Summary   264

REFERENCES   *265*

INDEX   *281*

SENIOR AUTHOR'S PREFACE

This text represents its authors' long professional and personal association. The three of us met and worked in Hawaii during the 1970s. Both of my co-authors first entered my life as graduate students at the University of Hawaii: Lawrence in counseling psychology in 1973 and Susan in the graduate nursing program in 1978. Our professional and personal collaboration has continued to the present. I have provided this personal account to explain our personal and professional frameworks and their impact on our work.

I have been involved in the practice of group therapy, group counseling, and growth groups since 1965. However, my interest in groups and other multiperson therapies did not begin auspiciously.

As a student intern, my first exposure to groups was a current events group that met several days a week at the VA Outpatient Center in Boston. The group was used essentially as a holding area for patients (primarily with dual diagnosis or ambulatory schizophrenic diagnoses) and was charged with "getting the men to talk about current events." The predominant therapeutic tool was the morning edition of the *Boston Globe*. Although I was never convinced that any learning or meaningful discussion about current events ever occurred, something interesting happened over the three-month duration of our group.

Despite no apparent lessening of the patients' symptoms, attendance was fairly stable, and I grew to like several of the group members. Meanwhile, two floors away, a psychologist and social worker held a discharge planning group that I was allowed to observe through a two-way mirror. Members of this group seemed to experienced rapid, marked amelioration of their symptoms. My longing to do similar work remained unrequited during that training. I had similar experiences in internships at Downey VA Medical Center in Illinois and again at the Boston VA Outpatient center in 1965 and 1966.

As in intern at Hawaii State Hospital in Kaneohe in 1966 and 1967, I was given my first "therapy" group. At that time, it was common practice in psychology to provide interns with patients *they could not possibly harm*. This group met on Monday, Wednesday, and Friday morning from 7:45 to 9:15. The members were six men of Japanese descent, all of whom were diagnosed "chronic undifferentiated schizophrenic." The shortest hospitalization stay of any of the members was 19 years. My supervisor observed all sessions of this group from behind the ubiquitous one-way mirror, and we discussed the sessions immediately after they ended. I have three very clear memories of this group: (1) the discrepancy between my initial tolerance for silence (approximately 23 nanoseconds) and that of the patients (approximately 23 hours); (2) my never discovering whether three of the patients spoke any

English, pidgin English, or Japanese (my co-therapist was a Japanese-speaking psychiatric nurse); and (3) my undying gratitude for the federal government's mandate that certain holidays were to be observed on Mondays or Fridays.

A second group, which I led during my intern year, was a Tuesday-Thursday afternoon group of acting-out adolescents.

It is no small wonder to me that, for the next three decades, this background led me to devote much of my clinical and research interest to group processes. Between 1965 and 1997, I have been directly involved with more than 500 growth, therapy, counseling, and industry groups as a leader, member, researcher, supervisor, and consultant. Since 1969, I have also taught courses and developed vertically integrated training programs in group counseling and therapy in graduate programs in New York, Hawaii, and California—most recently at Santa Clara University.

All this involvement has convinced me that group treatment should be the cornerstone of any major mental health treatment program. I believe there are many advantages of group treatment that go far beyond the obvious economic benefits. Research and clinical writings also support this contention. I am also aware of the most unfortunate continuing aspect of group leadership in institutional, organizational, and treatment centers: *Very few of the people who lead groups are formally trained in group process.* Many group leaders are well-trained individual counselors or therapists who have been assigned to groups without completing even one course or supervised practicum in group work. Even with the best intentions, such leaders tend to do individual therapy with an audience rather than use the most powerful and dramatic effects of group process and influence.

This book is based on a crucial supposition: *Group leaders must be aware of group process.* The book represents an attempt to provide a road map for graduate students and new group leaders. However, it is not an attempt to chart every street, road, or lane. The point of view presented here is my belief that interventions in any successful group (or any other type of treatment) depend a great deal on timing. If I don't know where the group is at any given moment, I am far more likely to take wrong turns in my attempt to get where I want to go.

The inexorable generic process provided in this book is designed to serve the leader as a signpost and reference map. It is as theory-free and objectively descriptive as my colleagues and I could make it. We have spent many hours observing and consulting with leaders whose perspectives are widely divergent; the process described gives substantial attention to their approaches.

Our personal approaches to counseling, therapy, or task groups are closely related. Dr. Bernadett-Shapiro's primary orientation is object relations. Both Dr. Peltz and I describe ourselves as existential, with his approaches tending toward the American cognitive end of that realm and mine tending toward the European dynamic end. We are sure that the illumination shed by our varying perspectives will leave important areas of the landscape in shadows. Certainly leaders of groups with widely different theories, goals, and populations may have to adapt portions of the process for their maximal personal use.

We apologize for the fervency with which some of this book was written. The apparent certainty we exude is not intended to sell something to the unwary. Rather, it expresses the enthusiasm of practitioners who have embraced group process for 30 years and extol its virtues as an old friend and lover. Even after all these years and hundreds of groups, each of us enters each new group with anticipation, excitement, and hope. We are all active clinicians, currently leading brief treatment groups. Dr. Bernadett-Shapiro has taught group leadership at two universities and is the consultant-supervisor for the experiential groups in the graduate counseling psychology program at Santa Clara University. Dr. Peltz is co-leading couples groups and adult groups, and he and I regularly co-lead men's groups in the community. I also teach introductory and advanced group classes throughout the year at Santa Clara University.

Although much of this book was written for our students in counseling and clinical psychology and in social work, we hope that experienced group practitioners will also find something new in it or remember an older precept of value that has drifted away.

As you read this text, you may notice that many of the references may seem dated. Wherever possible, we have used the most comprehensive source. Thus, many of the outcome research references date back to the 1970s, a time of great interest in and prolific research on group outcome and process. Similarly, much of the salient work with adult children of alcoholics was done in the 1980s, and work on adolescence came out in the 1970s and 1980s. We refer to several recent studies that have added to our knowledge of group therapy and counseling. However, when a recent study primarily replicates older data or observations, we have chosen to cite the primary source in order to honor the pioneering work in the field.

We would like to acknowledge many wonderful people who have guided our learning about group therapy and counseling over the years. In particular, we want to thank all of our students in the group training classes and advanced leader training programs at the University of Hawaii Counseling and Guidance Program (1970–1978), School of Professional Nursing and Social Work (1976–1981), and Santa Clara University (1982–present). Many of these students have become professional group leaders and teachers, and we take great pride in our small part in their success.

We are grateful to Lloyd V. Dempster of Texas A & M University–Kingsville, Aaron W. Hughey at Western Kentucky University, Brenda Freeman of the University of Wyoming, and Ann Puryear at Southeast Missouri State University for their insightful comments and reviews. We also wish to thank several people at Brooks/Cole: Eileen Murphy, our editor, met tight deadlines and provided inspiring, energetic, and straightforward assistance. In addition, editorial assistant Susan Carlson, production editor Mary Vezilich, and design editor Roy Neuhaus provided excellent, timely support.

Jerrold Lee Shapiro

BASIC GROUP
PROCESS

CHAPTER 1

AN INTRODUCTION TO BRIEF, CLOSED GROUPS

This text is designed for leaders of counseling, therapy, and growth groups who wish to bring a time-honored, proven, effective, ethical approach to treatment groups in an era in which cost containment and economic concerns are regarded as being at least as important as therapeutic and ethical considerations. The therapeutic approach is based on the following assumptions that are supported by research data, clinical observations, and the economics of managed health care.

- Groups are the treatment of choice in a brief therapy model.
- Treatment groups are most effective if they are closed, short term, and process centered.
- Thematic groups with somewhat homogeneous membership will be most effective in the short term.
- When groups are led properly, there is a genetic, predictable process.
- Multiperson treatments such as groups require different therapist skills from those used with individual modalities.
- Training for leaders in group methods is necessary if group treatment is to be effective.

These assumptions provide the backdrop and the *raison d'être* for this text.

GROUPS AS THE TREATMENT OF CHOICE

In a special edition of the *Journal of Specialists in Group Work*, Shapiro and Bernadett-Shapiro (1985) argued that the beginning of the 21st century would be marked by extensive growth in group treatments. More recently, experts commenting on managed care treatments such as Budman (1992), Budman and Gurman (1988), and Norcross, Alford, and DiMichele (1992) have echoed that forecast.

Although we believe group treatment will be prominent in the future, we acknowledge its long and successful past. Since the turn of the 20th century and

Pratt's (1906; 1907; 1908; 1911) early attempts at alternative group treatment for tuberculosis patients, groups have been used for virtually every patient population known (cf. Lubin & Lubin, 1987). Throughout this century, the use of groups and research on their effectiveness has varied as practitioners of each major type of mental health treatment (medical, psychotherapy, family therapy, group therapy) have alternated in viewing group treatment with enthusiasm or relative disinterest. At the present time, primarily because of financial considerations, medical-biological treatments are ascending in popularity as are group counseling and psychotherapy approaches.

The unique advantages of group treatment are listed below:

1. *Cost.* Research (e.g., Shapiro, 1978) has indicated that group psychotherapy has been as successful as each other form of treatment in comparable or shorter time periods. Economics, however, are not the sole advantage of group treatment.

2. *Connectedness.* Groups provide opportunities for socialization, a sense of shared experience, and a corresponding reduction of feelings of isolation. Many groups also lead to continuing care by way of post-group support systems.

3. *Reality Testing.* The group environment provides opportunities for learning and practicing new behaviors in a setting that closely resembles the real world. Feedback from other group members will be different from the reactions of an individual therapist, whose contract is to understand the client from the client's personal perspective.

4. *Vicarious Learning.* In a group, each member has the opportunity to learn by observing others. For many people, learning is best accomplished when the individual is not on "the hot seat."

5. *Minimization of Pathology.* Not all the therapy that occurs in a group comes from the leader. Much help is offered by members to each other. When someone receives assistance from another who is "just a member like me," the receiver sees that his or her problems are not impossibly serious or unmanageable. The result may be development of a more positive and hopeful outlook.

6. *Altruism.* A common source of problems for individuals seeking mental health treatment involves low self-esteem. When members act benevolently toward their peers or provide insight or caring for other group members, they normally feel quite good about seeing the results of their efforts and about the act of helping itself. Feelings of altruism are incompatible with low self-esteem. A group setting in which one member can assist another offers possibilities for enhancement of self-esteem.

7. *Experimentation.* Group members are encouraged to experiment with novel behaviors and reactions and are motivated to request feedback within a nurturing environment. The group is a setting in which members might rehearse new behaviors and/or get advance reactions to an anticipated event without the risk inherent in the event itself. They may then plan their behavior accordingly in preparing for the real occasion.

8. *Dilution of Transference Relationships.* Although the primary and most powerful transference occurs between group members and group leaders, there is

inevitable projection onto other members of the group as well. This shift allows all members to be more aware of such projections and eases the working through of problems because the intensity is somewhat distributed throughout the group.

SHORT-TERM GROUPS

Evaluating outcome research on time-limited groups is complicated by a host of factors; not the least of these is defining *brief treatment*. Koss and Butcher (1986) considered brief treatment to involve groups that met for fewer than 25 sessions. Budman, Demby, and Randall (1980) used 15-session groups. Shapiro (1978) and his colleagues (Diamond & Shapiro, 1973; Shapiro & Diamond, 1972) reported on 30-hour groups and 20-hour groups (six 2-hour sessions and one 8-hour marathon). Foulds (1971) and many other group leaders who practice in university settings ran groups for an academic semester or quarter. Another complicating factor for empirical comparisons is the experience of leaders. Often groups are regularly led by trainees or inexperienced group therapists.

Reviewers of the time-limited group literature (Dies, 1992; Budman, Simeone, Reilly, & Demby, 1994) concluded that these groups, when led by experienced professionals, are effective in alleviating symptomatology and fostering growth. In comparison to waiting list control groups, time-limited group members show significant improvement (for example, Piper, McCallum, & Hassan, 1992). However, Piper et al. have also indicated that such groups may not be as powerful or comprehensive as longer-term therapies or individual work of equal duration.

The upshot of these data is that brief treatment groups must be *carefully geared to specific limited goals, conducted by trained professional leaders, and structured to maximize factors such as cohesion, altruism, and the other unique group treatment advantages by employing a process focus.*

Closed, Short-Term, Process-Oriented Groups

Many leaders prefer ongoing groups in which members enter and leave as doing so is personally appropriate (e.g., Yalom, 1995). Arguments that this more closely simulates real life are undeniably compelling. As members enter and depart the group, individuals have the opportunity to work with their personal issues of separation and individuation, fears of intimacy, dependency, and rejection. They can weigh their own considerations about when "it is time." Certainly such groups have a valuable place in therapy.

However, there are also compelling advantages for groups to begin and close together, such as the time involved in incorporating a new member or the adjustment to the loss of a senior one. In open groups, with each change in the group population, there is an inevitable regression to earlier stages of group process. The developmental process is a core component in group effectiveness. Interruptions of the process may inhibit the natural unfolding of the group progress and the impact it has. In a brief therapy environment, the team synergy of a closed group is particularly healing.

The focus on process is particularly central to group members' learning about themselves and their impact on others. A process focus provides a developmental psychological map of the interpersonal terrain. With this as a guide, the leaders may highlight more clearly the current reality of the group and the impact of individuals within that framework. A focus on process also trains individuals to explore the context and consequences of their actions as well as the content and apparent motivation. More than that, a *process focus* creates a unique setting for personal learning. A frequently disconcerting fact in the life of parents and teachers is that our children and students learn only when they are ready to learn. Repetitions alone, even those with the most compelling multimedia delivery systems, are insufficient if the receiver is unprepared. A process focus sets the stage for learning in two ways: (1) It provides a focus on self and on the here-and-now interactions between self and others, eliminating distractions; (2) because it is socially unusual, it adds a certain amount of functional anxiety and vigilance, both of which facilitate learning.

Thematic/Relatively Homogeneous Groups

For short-term treatment, group members must be able to affiliate with each other fairly quickly. Doing so is easier when they feel commonalties between their abilities and needs and those of their peers. The most important homogeneity in a group is levels of ego-strength or its converse, levels of pathology. Although groups have been shown to be effective with almost every level of pathology, they are overly impacted by discrepancies. To a large degree, the most pathological individual in a group has the greatest influence in restricting the group's trajectory. Thus, a group of people with acute concerns are best not mixed with clients whose problems are chronic.

Content themes are of value for both attracting members to work on a predictable concern and also for centering the discussion around consensual issues. Broad themes in which each member sees part of himself within the purview of the group are most effective. A theme is best utilized as a catalyst to group formation and development rather than as a definition or defense of member personalities.

Predictable Generic Process

The first section of this manual is dedicated entirely to an observable process model. The model has emerged from 25 years of research and clinical work (Shapiro, 1978). It coordinates well with the work of other researchers and clinicians (e.g., Corey, 1990; Corey, Foulds, & Hannigan, 1976). A four-phase, 30-stage model is detailed. Leaders are trained to observe the natural development of the group process. Effective interventions are tied directly to specific points in the evolving process. For example, different leadership actions are necessary when the group is in Phase 2 (Transition) or Phase 3 (Treatment) than when it is in Phase 4 (Termination). Leadership challenges and the methodology to employ them effectively for the group's benefit are necessary to provide the transition to treatment.

Premature attempts to intervene therapeutically and directly before these challenges emerge may actually deter the group process.

Group Treatment, Individual Treatment, and Family Treatment

Group treatment requires a number of unique skills that are different from those necessary in individual or family modalities. Of particular note is the sophisticated ability to intervene at three different levels: intrapsychic, dyadic, and group. In individual work, the latter two are somewhat irrelevant except in addressing the transference or personal therapist-client interactions. In couples or family therapy, the therapist must be aware of the system that exists among the clients outside the therapy hour. Interventions are best geared to addressing this ongoing system. In group, the system that develops is present only during the group itself. Each individual is best served if he or she receives from the group interactions important personal information that is transferable to life outside the group.

Training in Multiperson Therapies

Although formal group treatment has an almost century-long history, the majority of group leaders today have been trained primarily or solely in individual and family therapy methods. This book is designed for those who have some schooling or practice in group treatment. It is no substitute for a rigorous training program or supervised experience. A model of minimal training requirements and basic skills is provided in Chapter 7.

SOME REALITIES OF MANAGED CARE

The evidence is mounting that health care in America will be addressed more and more by an economic model (DeLeon, VandenBos, & Bulatoa, 1991). Health maintenance organizations (HMOs) promise cost containment and full health care from womb to tomb in return for a moderate regular premium and control of risk by spreading it across large populations. The dollars saved, however, may come at a high price. Members of such an insurance plan normally have less discretion about the type of treatment they may receive for any given ailment and, to some extent, whether their plans will authorize any treatment at all. The bottom line for any business such as an HMO is the difference between dollars received in premiums and expenses incurred from providing treatment. Maintaining and expanding profit margins often means restricting and limiting "expensive" care and procedures.

Among the considerations for a patient's care are the cost of treatment, actuarial information, likelihood of spontaneous recovery, patient's usage of services, availability of providers, and specific plan contract provisions. For example, not all mental health care plans include hospitalization. Others allow hospitalization for emergencies (homicide or suicide potential) only. Many plans include few or no outpatient services. When they do include outpatient therapy, authorization is required for services beyond a specified number of sessions (often as few as two or three). The therapists who may provide these sessions and their fees are limited, and certain treatments are favored. For mental health, the favored treatments are medication and time-limited group therapy.

According to a series of articles that appeared in the *Wall Street Journal* (Hymovitz & Pollock, 1995; Pollock, 1995) and professional literature (e.g., Shore, 1996), the currently evolving system of managed care and capitation[1] has caused both consumers and providers to suffer a degradation in treatment. Providers must work for substantially lower fees to belong to these organizations and they must subscribe to regulations that place cost consciousness on a par with quality of care standards. Providers who receive lower fees per patient hour must increase their practice volume to maintain their personal standards of living. Consumers are restricted to certain providers for their care and in many situations to the type of care available. For a specific number of psychotherapy sessions to be attached to a diagnostic code, for example, would not be unusual. In some plans, the type of treatment is also prescribed (i.e., for depression, Prozac first; cognitive behavior therapy second).

A harsh reality is that mental health is not a high priority in such systems. Like other "lower-status" medical specialties (e.g., pediatrics, obstetrics), practitioners have had to fight for the diminishing pot of dollars available. As a result, the quality of care inevitably suffers. Indeed, rewards, such as bonuses and promotions, are commonly given on the expense end of the equation rather than the care end. "Successful" providers are those whose computer track record shows that they see clients for the fewest sessions. Saving money by withholding treatment is often cherished within managed care organizations. Primary care physicians or triage personnel receive bonuses for referring the fewest patients to expensive treatment.

Managed Care and Group Treatment

What are the implications of these trends for your practice? Your clients will have fewer sessions. They may be resentful in group because they were denied more costly individual psychotherapy or counseling. They may exhibit more pathology because less severe "problems in living" are addressed at the primary care physician level and not referred or may not be covered by the insurance plan. They are less

---

[1] Capitation is a system of managed health care in which a provider organization is paid a certain monthly dollar amount for each covered participant. The contracting group agrees to provide all services necessary to the entire group of insureds. Thus, if the contract capitates 10,000 lives for mental health services for .90 per life per month, the provider organization will receive $9,000.00 per month. It will then provide necessary therapy services and pay for overhead, quality assurance, utilization review, a tracking computer system, and designated hospitalization with those funds for the entire 10,000 participants as needed.

Capitation is contrasted with a "fee-for-service" arrangement in which providers are compensated only for specific services rendered.

likely to be "YAWVIS"[2] patients and more likely to have Axis II diagnoses, borderline personality traits, or primitive defensive structures. They will already have been medicated or will have tried medication that was not successful. As a group leader, you will have less ability to screen your clients effectively.

Dealing in such brief intervals with groups of patients having such a wide range of needs requires adjustments to your normal practice or leadership style. Normally, when time is short, a leader's natural tendency is to speed up to try to cover everything before time expires. Unfortunately, accelerating treatment in counseling and therapy frequently has a paradoxical effect. Increasing pressure to find solutions is routinely met with greater patient resistance to change.

This paradox provides a prime reason to use a process-oriented model. With this model, patient resistance is coalesced and can be dealt with ontologically. By viewing resistance as an important part of the "readiness-to-learn" phenomenon in group, the existential process model actually increases the pace at which members approach desired outcomes by judiciously moderating speed at certain crucial junctures, early in the group. By focusing directly and in predetermined ways on the developmental stages of resistance, group members who are beginning from a point of lower motivation have greater opportunity to become open to healing.

It is important to understand that whatever theory or techniques you customarily use will be effective with some segment of the population in your groups. The process model is designed as a substrate in which your particular theoretical perspective may be maximally effective. On this foundation, psychodynamic, behavioral, and psychoeducational groups can all be enhanced.

In much of the literature, these theories are juxtaposed as competing approaches. By contrast, the current approach was designed by observing the commonalties of successful groups of every type. Similarities are most dominant early in the group process. In the treatment phase, the different approaches demonstrate clear distinctions. Thus a Gestalt-oriented leader and a cognitive behavioral leader will seem to share more commonalties in approach in the transition phase and far less during treatment. The ensuing brief treatment model is sensitive to cost containment, is adjustable across theoretical orientations, and is likely to maintain quality care at least within appropriately defined limits.

SUMMARY

Group psychotherapy is a modality particularly well suited to emerging needs within mental health delivery systems for informed and proficient care. The group context encourages individuals to explore the consequences of their actions as well as the meaning and underlying motivation. A group process model is proposed as an efficient means of participant learning and behavioral change.

---

2 YAWVIS is an acronym for the traditional patients who get the most care and highest interest from practitioners. These patients are young, attractive, wealthy, verbal, intelligent, and sexy.

Leadership training in group process is essential. The most effective leadership interventions are tied to this predictable model of developmental generic group process. In addition, the leader must attend to three levels of process and intervention: intrapsychic, interpersonal, and group level.

Certain participant and treatment variables have been shown to affect group treatment outcomes. The ideal group is closed, time limited, homogeneous, and process focused. Groups with specific limited goals, led by trained professional leaders using interventions geared to increase cohesion and altruism among members, are most productive.

CHAPTER 2

GROUP PROCESS
PHASE I: PREPARATION

STAGE 1   DETERMINATION OF GROUP GOALS AND POPULATION

STAGE 2   LEADER ANNOUNCES GROUP LOGISTICS

STAGE 3   MEMBERS APPLY FOR THE GROUP

STAGE 4   SCREENING

*"While I know each group is unique,
I frequently have a sense of* déjà vu *in
every group I lead."*

This casual lunchtime comment between two group leaders in Hawaii one day in 1970 spurred a 25-year intensive study of groups, beginning with a survey of local and national experts on group process. The results of the survey and of group leadership literature indicates that experienced group leaders see distinct differences in their groups as well as commonalties that make them all appear similar.

GROUP COMMONALITIES AND DIFFERENCES

This seeming contradiction is present in all forms of therapy to some extent. Most theorists point to commonalities in recommended treatment approaches that stress the individuality of every patient. Nowhere is the apparent incongruity so sharply expressed as in group therapy.

Yalom (1995), among others, notes the seemingly infinite variety of content issues and problems addressed in groups. Specific material discussed, therapeutic interventions, and conflict resolution are unique to each group. Because each group comprises several different personalities at a particular period of time, singularity of expression and novel experiences are to be expected.

Despite the variance in specific content and content themes between groups, the *process* or pattern of interaction within different groups is remarkably similar. In an effective and successful group, certain stages normally occur in a reliable sequence.

STAGES OF GROUP MODELS

As Table 2.1 shows, several authors have described predictable stages in group development—developmental schema in which successive stages are built on completion of previous ones. As early as 1936, Wender described four such stages for patients in neo-analytic group therapy. His process description included (1) intellectualization, (2) transference between patients, (3) catharsis, and (4) group interest as patients moved through emotional difficulties to emerge with effective interest in their social sphere and society in general.

Battegay (1989), working with a similar framework 53 years later, formulated a very similar five-stage developmental sequence: (1) exploratory contact, (2) regression, (3) catharsis, (4) insight, and (5) social learning. Battegay clearly states that such stages may well be limited to *closed, long-term, analytically oriented groups.*

Dreikurs (1951) employed an Adlerian perspective, focusing more on the educative process in groups. He perceived four stages: (1) establishment of relations, (2) interpretation of dynamics, (3) patients gaining understanding, and (4) reorientation.

Tuckman (1965) and Tuckman and Jenson (1977) described their five stages as (1) forming, (2) storming, (3) norming, (4) performing, and (5) adjourning. Schutz (1973), whose work centered primarily on growth groups, described "an inevitable sequence" of three stages: (1) inclusion, (2) control, and (3) affection. Members work through their conflicts of belonging to the group, establishing and maintaining their roles in the group pecking order, and exploring their closeness to other members.

Yalom (1995), in the latest revision of his classic group psychotherapy text, sees an initial stage, characterized by orientation, hesitant participation, search for similarities, search for meaning, and dependency. This is followed by the second stage, characterized by conflict, dominance, and rebellion. The third stage for Yalom involves the development of cohesiveness. These are quite similar to Schutz's formulations. However, Yalom describes several qualifying factors that can dramatically affect his indicated sequence: leadership qualities, patient qualities, additions to and deletions from membership, and attendance. Yalom also suggests that discrete stages can be described reliably only early in a group's development. As a group develops over time and experiences subgrouping, it becomes more differentiated from other groups. One crucial factor in Yalom's model is that it is based almost entirely on open-ended groups. Authors whose research is on closed groups are able to describe an extended process because of the essential nature of their groups.

Table 2.1 Several Conceptions of Predictable Group Stages

Author and Date	Stage 1	Stage 2	Stage 3	Stage 4	Stage 5	Stage 6
Wender, 1936	Intellectualization	Transference between patients	Catharsis	Group Interest, social interest		
Dreikurs, 1951	Establishment of relations	Interpretation of dynamics	Gaining understanding	Reorientation		
Schutz, 1973	Inclusion	Control	Affection			
Tuckman, 1965 Tuckman & Jensen, 1977	Forming	Storming	Norming	Performing	Adjourning	
Shapiro, 1978	Introduction	Learning the rules	Therapy proper	Termination		
Henry, 1981	Initiating	Convening	Formation	Conflict	Maintenance	Termination
Dies, 1985	Preparation	Early group sessions	Transition	Working	Termination	
Corey & Corey, 1987 Battegay, 1989	Initial stage Exploratory contact	Transition Regression	Working Catharsis	Ending Insight	Social learning	
MacKenzie, 1990	Engagement	Differentiation	Working	Termination		
Yalom, 1995	Orientation, hesitant participation, search for similarities, search for meaning, and dependency	Conflict, dominance, rebellion	Cohesiveness			

Shapiro (1978), describing a core group process for both therapy and encounter groups, formulated four inevitable process phases: (1) introduction, (2) learning the rules, (3) therapy proper, and (4) termination (transfer of training).

Corey and Corey (1987) used a similar paradigm, based on their own considerable work with closed groups in a college population, and described (1) an initial stage, (2) a transition stage, (3) a working stage, and (4) an ending stage. MacKenzie (1990) calls his stages (1) engagement, (2) differentiation, (3) working, and (4) termination.

The chronological process analysis presented in this text conforms to the whole group model espoused by Corey and Corey (1987), Fiebert (1963), MacKenzie (1990), and Shapiro (1978). Clearly, open-ended groups such as those described by Yalom, will conform to this model only to the extent that there is stable membership over time. Without question, predictability of process diminishes as membership changes.

Group process in closed groups is presented in four interlocking phases (see Figure 2.1). Each phase comprises a number of identifiable stages and tasks. The four phases are

Preparation

Transition

Treatment (working; intervention)

Termination

The process presented is descriptive of a *well-screened, optimally functioning, time-limited closed group, led by an accomplished leader with therapeutically viable clients in a counseling, therapy, growth, or encounter format.*

This process is envisioned as both *inevitable* and *ideal*. It is inevitable in the sense that successful completion of each previous stage is considered prerequisite to engaging in and coping with subsequent stages. To some extent, however, this model is also an ideal. Many groups fail to complete all the stages. Hence, one aspect of the success of any group can be measured by progress through the process sequence prior to termination.

VALUE OF PREDICTABLE PROCESS

Group leadership shifts with group process. Leadership behaviors that are effective at one stage in a group are often deleterious at other stages. It is axiomatic that group members such as patients in psychotherapy need to know where they are and the extent of their resources prior to developing new life paths. Thus in the words of a recent group participant, "If I don't know where I am when I start out, in an hour I could be two hours from my desired destination." It is essential that an effective group leader appraise the lay of the land before heading off to explore new directions. All change-based interventions described in this text are geared precisely to the existing process in the group.

Figure 2.1 **Phases and Stages of Normal Group Process**

Phase I: Preparation
 Stage 1:   Determination of Group Goals and Population
 Stage 2:   Leader Announces Group Logistics
 Stage 3:   Members Apply for the Group
 Stage 4:   Screening
Phase II: Transition
 Stage 5:   Leader Specifies Ground Rules
 Stage 6:   Introductions
 Stage 7:   The Initial (Short) Silence
 Stage 8:   The Short Silence Is Broken
 Stage 9:   Discussion of There-and-Then Topic
 Stage 10:   Natural Death of Discussion
 Stage 11:   The Long Silence
 Stage 12:   Members' First Sortie
 Stage 13:   Opening of the Discussion
 Stage 14:   Group Leader Focuses on Here-and-Now Process
 Stage 15:   Debriefing the Leadership Tests: Focus on Feelings
 Stage 16:   Leader Encourages the Expression of Emotion
Phase III: Treatment (Working; Intervention)
 Stage 17:   Internal Focus
 Stage 18:   Norms Are Solidified
 Stage 19:   Minority Members Identified; Inclusion Revisited
 Stage 20:   Intensity Increases
 Stage 21:   Leader Employs Therapeutic Skills
 Stage 22:   Problem-Solving Orientation Practiced
 Stage 23:   Expression of Feelings about the Process and the Group
Phase IV: Termination
 Stage 24:   Leader Announces Imminent End of Group Time
 Stage 25:   Invitation to Work
 Stage 26:   A Trust Boost
 Stage 27:   Transfer of Training
 Stage 28A: Good and Welfare
 Stage 28B: Closing Ceremonies
 Stage 29:   Leader's Closing
 Stage 30:   Aloha

The process analysis described in this text represents the results of the author's 10 years of research with group leaders and 30 years of personally leading, supervising, and observing groups and group leaders in a host of clinical settings. It is designed as a map to get the novice group leader to the right neighborhood. The unique streets, roads, lanes, and blind alleys must be individually discovered.

Despite best efforts to remain eclectic, any such formulation will represent several biases in theory, perception, and description. It behooves the reader to use this process formulation as a guide that must be adapted to personally relevant theories and populations. Differences in approaches to specific populations are described in the final part of the book. The primary theory that underscores this work is a *dynamically oriented existential psychotherapy*. Therapists with related theories (i.e., Gestalt, psychodynamic, and object relations) will have little difficulty applying the principles. A greater bridge must be constructed to accommodate behaviorally based or psychoeducational theories. However, the core principles and process are claimed to be universal. Divergences between approaches will occur primarily in Phase III (Treatment), where specific interventions will be more differentially based in the practitioner's theory.

PHASE I: PREPARATION
STAGE 1: Determination of Group Goals and Population

A group begins as a concept. Leaders normally respond to an identified need in a particular community. Once the need is recognized and a group intervention chosen, the leaders must then reach the target population with information and enticement to apply for inclusion in the group. Establishing and maintaining a productive treatment group is no easy task, especially in a private practice setting. Careful planning and effective, ethical marketing are essential.

Within a managed care or capitated environment, the needs of the patients will be assessed by an agent of the responsible third party payer. Leaders may be establishing groups based on patients' coverage and economic demands as well as their clinical needs. The inherent ethical concerns will have to be addressed continually, both with potential group members and with the preferred provider organization (PPO), health maintenance organization (HMO), or insurer (cf. Rosenberg & Zimet, 1995). For example, a particular HMO or PPO might cover its members for substance abuse but not for marital difficulties. Under other circumstances, a group might be free to focus on both or either. In a limiting environment, the treatment may have to be focused primarily on the importance of substance abuse in family discord, and membership may be restricted by use of diagnostic codes that involve drug or alcohol problems.

Among the multitude of factors that will influence the group membership makeup are cost, location, time of day, length and number of sessions, leader characteristics and credentials, population, cultural factors, and the desired mix of clients. Only when these factors are carefully evaluated can the leader move to an invitation for members to apply. Each logistic criterion set by a leader will narrow the range of applicants and the heterogeneity among members.

FEES The fee charged for group sessions will have a powerful impact on membership. Some fees are clearly too high for many potential patients. By contrast, some fees will be too low to draw certain populations.

Fees can range widely in a given area. A brief informal survey in the San Francisco Bay Area conducted by the senior author in 1991–1993 revealed that average charges for outpatient fee-for-service groups were between $20 and $40 per hour per patient. A typical 90-minute group session, with one or two leaders, would cost $30 to $60. Most surveys indicate that groups for adolescents or children have slightly lower fees. Many such groups require monthly commitments of members or payment for the entire period (e.g., 10 sessions) at the outset. Members of a PPO or capitated contract might be required to make a fixed co-payment, with the leader billing a set amount to the insurer or subcapitated organization for the balance.

The San Francisco survey showed that lower fees were normally available for groups conducted in church, school, or community settings. Several groups conducted in community agencies used sliding scales that ran from $1 to $15 per session. Health maintenance organizations and employee assistance programs (EAPs) offered specific theme groups for members at no or nominal out-of-pocket cost.

Many group leaders have found to their surprise that fee setting is quite peculiar. High fees will eliminate certain portions of the population, but very low fee or "free" groups will do the same thing. As one potential participant at a free clinic stated, "If it's free, it ain't worth nothin'." A curious trait of American society seems to be the perception that something that is free is not as good as things that cost a lot. One way to solve the dilemma of offering groups to people who cannot afford to pay for treatment is to make the group have an *apparent* price. Thus, for one series of "free" groups at a community mental health center, patients were required to pay 50 cents per session. However, each member was given 50 cents worth of bus tokens at the end of each session. The groups had far higher attendance than comparable "free" groups.

Setting fees may be complex for a professional. If the fee is not determined by the referring entity, such as the clinic or managed care organization, several factors must be balanced. Among these are the therapist's experience and training, customary rates in the region, and needs and resources of the client population, as well as the therapist's need for income.

LOCATION   The most common locations for groups are community agencies, clinics and hospitals, churches, schools and colleges, private offices, and hotel meeting rooms. The specific group meeting site should be consistent with the desired participants. The specific site for a group meeting will dramatically influence group composition. Some people are so uncomfortable with certain settings that they would not consider attending any meeting held in these places. Community agencies, for example, will attract some folks and repel others. A neighborhood community center might limit the number of applications from people who want anonymity or who live in different neighborhoods.

Distance and travel time are also significant factors in the viability of a particular group setting. Many groups seem to meet in the early evening hours. Getting across town at these times in most major cities can be a traffic nightmare. In addition, some group members want the security of their home community for the meeting place, whereas others prefer to travel further for anonymity.

Distance and commute time make up one factor, but this is not the only determinant of participation. In Honolulu, a group held at the Kalihi community center (a poorer neighborhood) would not draw many potential group members from nearby Aiea or Pacific Heights. Almost every community has districts that are threatening to people from other locales. These discomforts range from fears about physical safety to a sense of estrangement with people from different cultures or socioeconomic strata. For example, a group held in a poorer neighborhood on the south side of Chicago would have a completely different composition from that of a group held in a wealthy northern suburb such as Winnetka. Similarly, a university setting may be very comfortable and familiar for college graduates but much less so for those who do not have college experience. Some potential members will avoid a church meeting place because of the denomination. Others will feel safer because of the presumed sanction of a religious setting.

Another factor is that some members prefer a group that is distant from their home or work sites to better safeguard confidentiality. Others prefer the close proximity to reduce travel time. Often within EAP programs, the work site is proffered and flex time provided by the employer. This arrangement will obviously suit some potential members better than others.

TIME OF SESSION   In some ways, the time of the session can be the most critical factor in enrollment. It must be acceptable to the desired population. Groups that meet in the morning are very unlikely to draw many working people. Similarly, dinner-hour groups will be less attractive to members with families, and Saturday evening groups are anathema to singles. For many years, group leaders who wanted male participants traditionally avoided Monday evenings in the fall on the premise that these men would not forgo Monday night football on television. By contrast, it was an especially desired time for women's groups. Groups for young mothers may be held successfully during the middle of the day if they provide a playroom and child care. In general, most therapists hold group meetings in the late afternoon or early evening.

Within a managed care program or HMO, groups are often provided only during normal office hours. Patients who cannot attend at designated times are simply discouraged. Unlike a consumer-oriented private practice situation, HMOs and capitated care environments may be reticent to accommodate a wide range of patient scheduling needs. Their financial compensation will not be impacted directly by lower enrollment. Of course, failure to service the needs of the contracting agency could cause them to lose the next contract.

Group leaders must also consider their own diurnal energy levels. Some leaders have their best energy for group work in the evening whereas others are fading at this time. Co-leaders of marathon groups often try to match their own periods of highest energy with their partner's lower times.

LENGTH OF GROUP   The total number of sessions and the extent to which groups are open or closed also affect potential participation. Some members will choose a closed group with a predictable fixed number of sessions; others prefer the flexibility of the open environment. Closed groups that have more than 10 or 12 sessions (or 30 hours) may be too large an initial commitment for some potential members. Open groups may also appear foreboding in length. Some people will be threatened by a group that appears too short to accomplish much without great intensity. In general, closed outpatient groups are commonly 6 to 20 sessions in length, with the vast majority in the 10 to 12 session range.

PUBLICITY   The manner in which members are sought is also a powerful factor in group success. Advertisements posted on telephone poles or supermarket bulletin boards pull different populations from those attracted by a professional note circulated among local individual therapists. Many clients are unwilling to commit their time or psyches to any methods that in any way sound unprofessional, yet an equal number shy away from the established health care provider in search of something more meaningful. It is incumbent on the leaders to predetermine which of these populations they wish to tap. Typically, groups that are oriented toward growth or education can be drawn with publicity that is more open and general. By contrast, therapy group members are often referred by informed colleagues.

LEADER CHARACTERISTICS AND CREDENTIALS   Potential group members often show great interest in the qualifications of leaders. Some will be interested in working only with licensed professionals with advanced degrees. Some will be attracted to leaders with a particular theoretical approach. By contrast, people who are distrustful of traditional medicine may be attracted to self-help leaders who are themselves dealing with issues similar to those of the members.

In addition, cultural factors may be significant. Potential members will be reluctant to apply for inclusion in a group if they think the leader is unable to understand their ethnic or cultural concerns. For example, in a recent group offered for Japanese Americans whose parents were interned in camps during World War II, one leader had a Japanese surname and one had a European surname. It is doubtful that this group would have had much success if the leader with the Japanese surname and appropriate cultural experience had not been available.

One of the most successful and continuous group therapy programs in the country has been housed in the Vet Centers, meeting places of an organization designed to assist Vietnam-era veterans. One of the major advantages and appeals of such centers is that they are staffed by veterans (combat and noncombat) as well as civilians.

STAGE 2:   *Leader Announces Group Logistics*

The announcement and statement of critical logistics is very important in determining who will apply for the group and what may happen once sessions begin. Such factors as where and how the group is publicized; cost; meeting place; number of sessions and time of sessions; group goals; leader's reputation, theoretical background, and age; potential clients' perception of the professionalism and warmth of the leader will all substantially affect the subsequent group membership.

The following figures are examples of characteristic announcements that have appeared in major cities around the United States. Names and identities or other distinguishing characteristics have been changed for professional reasons.

Figure 2.2 is an announcement for an awareness and movement group. It was advertised by flyers sent to people on a selected mailing list. An advertisement like

Figure 2.2   Sample Group Announcement (Smith and Jones)

A Weekend Workshop

Awareness and Movement

Led by Bill Jones, Ph.D., and Jean Smith, M.A.

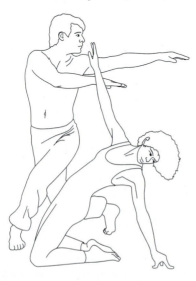

Bill is a certified clinical psychologist and a Gestalt therapist. He has been practicing psychotherapy for over 10 years in his community. He is also on the Ethics Committee of the State Mental Health Board and works as a program developer for the state's mental health services.

Jean is an advanced practitioner in Rolfing and a dance and yoga instructor. She teaches creative movement and has done substantial work in integrating movement techniques.

We will work with the group to help members integrate the different components of their beings. Through a series of movement exercises and individual and group work, members will have an opportunity to come to a better understanding of self and of the body as a source of energy and expression.

Dates: February 6 & 7, 1995

Schedule: Friday, February 6, 8–11 P.M.
                   Saturday, February 7, 10 A.M.–6 P.M.

Fee: $45.00; students $35.00

Location: Central Church
                   6245 Halekulani Lane
                   Honolulu, Hawaii 96823

this is likely to draw such participants as students in mental health–related professions, mental health professionals, dancers, and college-educated, somewhat sophisticated, middle-class working people. It is unlikely to draw severely disturbed or poverty-level participants. Members of such a group (in the encounter/workshop format) would typically be functioning adequately and would be interested in experimenting with growth activities.

For comparison, examine Figure 2.3. This is a similar advertisement sent to people on a similar mailing list, but the location and fee are quite different.

Dr. Van Wheeler, whose announcement appears in Figure 2.3, is clearly positioning herself to attract a wealthy clientele. Cost, location, and presentation all are

Figure 2.3   **Sample Group Announcement (Van Wheeler)**

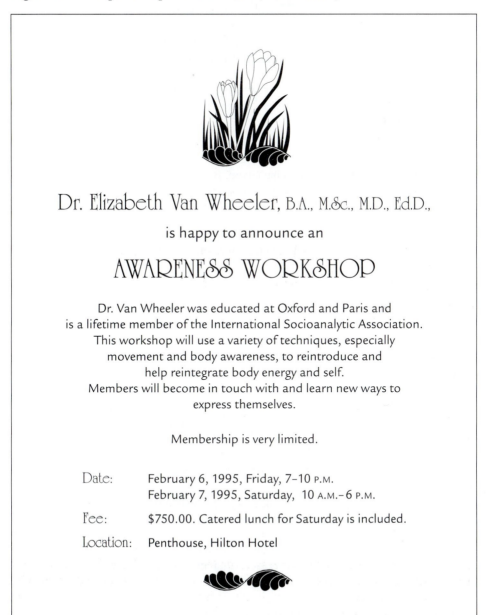

Dr. Elizabeth Van Wheeler, B.A., M.Sc., M.D., Ed.D.,

is happy to announce an

AWARENESS WORKSHOP

Dr. Van Wheeler was educated at Oxford and Paris and
is a lifetime member of the International Socioanalytic Association.
This workshop will use a variety of techniques, especially
movement and body awareness, to reintroduce and
help reintegrate body energy and self.
Members will become in touch with and learn new ways to
express themselves.

Membership is very limited.

Date: February 6, 1995, Friday, 7–10 P.M.
           February 7, 1995, Saturday, 10 A.M.–6 P.M.

Fee: $750.00. Catered lunch for Saturday is included.

Location: Penthouse, Hilton Hotel

Figure 2.4   Sample Group Announcement (Guru Shana Rakar)

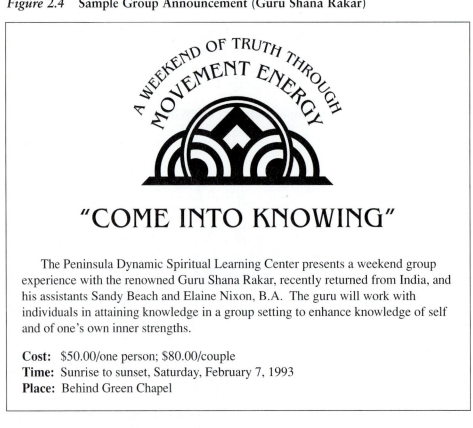

A WEEKEND OF TRUTH THROUGH MOVEMENT ENERGY

"COME INTO KNOWING"

The Peninsula Dynamic Spiritual Learning Center presents a weekend group experience with the renowned Guru Shana Rakar, recently returned from India, and his assistants Sandy Beach and Elaine Nixon, B.A. The guru will work with individuals in attaining knowledge in a group setting to enhance knowledge of self and of one's own inner strengths.

Cost: $50.00/one person; $80.00/couple
Time: Sunrise to sunset, Saturday, February 7, 1993
Place: Behind Green Chapel

geared to eliminate patients and students in the middle and lower socioeconomic levels. Although this therapist is offering services that seem to be similar to those described in Figure 2.2, a very different participant is likely to apply for her group.

Another flyer type of advertisement for group members has recently appeared on university campus bulletin boards. It is unlikely that Guru Rakar, whose group session is presented in Figure 2.4, will compete for the same populations that Dr. Van Wheeler will attract.

Another means of inviting members is with memoranda such as the one in Figure 2.5.

The next four announcements are also for professionals, but presented in different ways. Figure 2.6 announces an entire season of scheduled groups developed by a group therapy center. In Figure 2.7, an individual psychotherapist establishes the relocation of her practice by announcing two new groups to her colleagues, asking for referrals. Figure 2.8 is a notice of a group developed for and by psychotherapists. The last, Figure 2.9, is a request for referrals from the director of a state mental health clinic.

Figure 2.5   Sample Group Announcement (Quincy Mental Health Clinic)

MEMORANDUM

March 19, 1991

To: Selected Psychotherapists in Private Practice; Selected Psychotherapists in
        State Mental Health Centers
From: Quincy Mental Health Clinic (QMHC)
Re: Referrals of nonpsychotic patients

This is to inform you that Dr. Joe Smith and Dr. Elaine Brown will be conducting
weekly group therapy sessions on Tuesday evenings, 7–10 P.M., commencing
May 1, 1991, for 12 consecutive Tuesday evenings. The group membership will
consist of 8 to 10 patients who are diagnosed with neurotic or situational adjustment problems. The focus of this group is interpersonal, and it is seen as an excellent adjunct to ongoing individual therapy. If you have any nonpsychotic, Axis I
patients who you feel would benefit from this group, Joe and Elaine would appreciate your referring them. Sessions will cost $20 per participant per session.
Sliding scale applies.

We will screen all members carefully for "goodness of fit" in the groups. Please
contact Joe and Elaine at QMHC, (617) 555-9590.

SEMIVOLUNTARY GROUPS   In a managed care environment or in certain geo-
graphical areas in which choice is limited, members may be offered a particular
group or a small choice of available groups. The example in Figure 2.10 is from a
large managed care operation in a metropolitan area. It is an internal note to the
triage personnel regarding patient intake.

Other managed care providers use similar referral systems. In one local HMO,
for example, group therapy is continuous. All patients are assigned for a specified
number of sessions to a large group run by staff who rotate into and out of the
group. When one group has 15 members, a second group is started. The group
goals are assessment and treatment. No patient is offered any other outpatient
treatment except medication.

Finally, a third managed care system provides a menu of services for clients.
These clients, in consultation with their primary care physician or mental health
triage personnel, may choose a theme group (addiction, adult children of alcoholics,
past trauma, stress management, women's issues, couples, etc.) or a general ongoing outpatient group.

Because these groups are all part of the same network and are administratively
and financially linked, screening differs from that in unrestricted outpatient environments. Patients who wish to use their prepaid insurance coverage often do not
have as wide an assortment of choice for group or individual forms of treatment.

Figure 2.6   Sample Group Announcement (Kentucky Center for Group Therapy)

THE KENTUCKY CENTER FOR GROUP THERAPY

Proudly Announces Its Lineup
of Groups for the Winter 1995 Season

Men's Group   for males 21+. Led by Martin Reilly, Ph.D., and Bill Bernstein, M.S.W., this group will meet on Thursday evenings from 7:30 to 9:30 for 10 weeks. The themes for the winter groups are friendship, communication, and balancing work and home life.

Women's Group   for females 21+. Led by Maggie Cotton, Ph.D., and Jen Cohen, Ph.D., this group will meet on Wednesday evenings from 7:30 to 9:30 for 10 weeks. The themes for the winter groups are balancing work, relationships, and home life, and communication skill building.

Friday Night Couples Group for Married and Committed Couples will continue for another term. There is space for two or three new couples in this ongoing group. The group focuses on communication within and between couples as well as issues of security and freedom. It stresses male–female dialogue. The group meetings are from 7:30 to 9:30 for 10 weeks and are led by Dr. Myra Stone and Dr. Will Stone.

Therapist's Growth/Supervision Group   will be open this winter for four to six new members. This group, which meets from noon to 2 P.M. on Fridays, accepts licensed therapists in any discipline who wish to explore transference/ countertransference issues and professional/personal concerns. The leaders, Martin Weiss, Ph.D., and Cindy Swarz, M.D., work from a psychodynamic framework.

Anxiety and Phobia Group   for adults will begin on January 9 and run for eight consecutive Mondays, 2:30 p.m. to 4:30 P.M. Dr. Cecily Brown will lead this group.

All groups meet in our second floor group room, Ste. 200, 2222 Bardstown, Louisville.

PROFESSIONALS AND REFERRALS ARE WELCOME TO ALL THESE GROUPS.

PLEASE CALL OR FAX 555-5000 TO SCHEDULE A SCREENING INTERVIEW OR TO REQUEST FURTHER INFORMATION.

Figure 2.7   **Sample Group Announcement (Karple)**

Sandra A. Karple, Ph.D.
Individual and Group Psychotherapy
Offices in Palo Alto and San Francisco
(415) 555-4414

Member, American Group Psychotherapy Association
Northern California Group Psychotherapy Society
Advanced Certification: Maritime Society of Group Psychotherapy

Dear Colleague,

I am announcing the relocation of my private practice with the following two groups beginning in January. I would appreciate referrals of appropriate clients.

Women with Eating Disorders
An eating disorder is a symptom associated with issues intertwined with female psychological development. This group will provide an environment in which members can focus on

    (1) Origins of problem eating vis-à-vis feelings of powerlessness in the family of origin or society in general
    (2) Food as a means to express unconscious and/or unspoken needs
    (3) The promotion and practice of strategies for enhanced self-care in a nurturing, protective environment

Meets on Friday mornings 7:30 to 9:00 A.M.

Psychotherapy Group for Women
This group is a resource for women who wish to explore issues of identity, family dynamics, and relationships with friends, work associates, and society-at-large.

Meets on Wednesday evenings 6:30 to 8:00 P.M.

I will personally meet individually with prospective members to assess whether the group will be an appropriate resource for their change and growth.

The monthly fee for each group member is $160. There is no charge for the screening interview. Membership is limited to eight participants.

I have been a licensed clinical psychologist in Massachusetts and California for eight years. My research on the psychology of women has been published in professional journals.

I welcome further contact from you.

Figure 2.8   **Sample Group Announcement via FAX (Anderson and Ellman)**

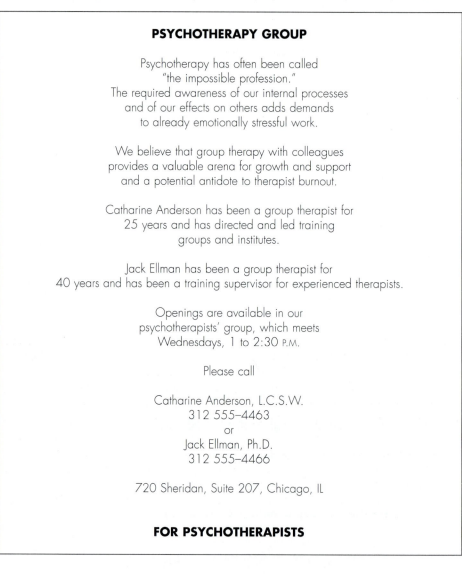

PSYCHOTHERAPY GROUP

Psychotherapy has often been called
"the impossible profession."
The required awareness of our internal processes
and of our effects on others adds demands
to already emotionally stressful work.

We believe that group therapy with colleagues
provides a valuable arena for growth and support
and a potential antidote to therapist burnout.

Catharine Anderson has been a group therapist for
25 years and has directed and led training
groups and institutes.

Jack Ellman has been a group therapist for
40 years and has been a training supervisor for experienced therapists.

Openings are available in our
psychotherapists' group, which meets
Wednesdays, 1 to 2:30 P.M.

Please call

Catharine Anderson, L.C.S.W.
312 555–4463
or
Jack Ellman, Ph.D.
312 555–4466

720 Sheridan, Suite 207, Chicago, IL

FOR PSYCHOTHERAPISTS

Similarly, practitioners are more likely to accept a wider range of clients in a group because they have "a right" to treatment, according to the list of benefits in their medical insurance coverage. Alternatively, a therapist who is a full-time employee of an HMO and who is not subject to profit-sharing or bonus pressure, may be more circumspect in including a member in a particular group than an outpatient therapist who is "hungry" for patients.

INVOLUNTARY GROUPS   A major factor in the composition of groups is the extent to which they are voluntary. In the groups advertised above, group member-

Figure 2.9   **Sample Group Announcement (State Mental Health Clinic)**

June 1, 1993

Intradepartmental Memo

To: All Therapists
From: Director, State Mental Health Clinic
Re: Available Spaces in Couples Groups

This fall, two of our psychology interns and two psychiatric residents will lead couples groups in the evenings. One resident and one intern will jointly lead groups on Tuesday and Wednesday evenings. The groups are designed to help couples in conflict learn more effective communication patterns and to help reduce our waiting list rolls. Please make referrals directly to Dr. Hong, intern training coordinator. We will need at least eight couples to fill both groups. All costs will be covered by my office, and services to patients are free. I trust you will consider need as one factor in selection.

ship was by application and selection. Such is not always the case. Figures 2.11 and 2.12 present two examples of a nonvoluntary group assignment. Such introductions to group membership carry with them potentially destructive elements.

The membership of institutional groups, such as those for hospitalized patients, the military, prisoners, students, graduate students, business or management representatives, or court-directed participants, is frequently by assignment rather than choice. In these cases, a primary leadership responsibility is to address effectively the resentment and resistance that members often bring to the group. Completing any real therapeutic work will be difficult until the group members are at least nominal volunteers. The probability for positive results is slight unless members are willing to see what they can achieve even though they are in an involuntary or mandatory group.

STAGE 3:   *Members Apply for the Group*

Application for group membership can take several forms. Potential members can personally apply by telephone or complete an application and mail or bring it to the growth center, mental health clinic, or leader. They can also approach the group by referral from appropriate sources, such as other therapists, physicians, clergy, parents, schools, former clients, or spouses.

It is essential that leaders and members are clear at this stage that members are *making application* to the group. There is no guarantee of participation. Mandatory groups, of course, may guarantee attendance, if not full participation.

Figure 2.10   **Sample Internal Memo Regarding Groups Available to Patients**

Directions to Triage Nurse
After medication options are considered and patients have medication consults if necessary, it is strongly encouraged that they be referred to the outpatient group network in the system. Please refer to your Group Openings Worksheet published each week by the Center. Please note that group treatment is far less costly than individual outpatient treatment. It is also better for most of our patients.

July Group Schedule
All adult patients who work or reside in cachement area one should be referred to the outpatient group conducted by Millie Greenstock, M.S.W. The group leader for patients in cachement area two are to be referred to Mark Willow, M.F.C.C. The group leader for cachement area three is Juanita Lopez, Ph.D. Patients who live or work in cachement area four should be given a choice of the most convenient group session. No groups will be started in area 4 until Sept. 15. Any patient wishing a different group location or time is free to choose one, but "group hopping" will not be possible.

Specialty Populations
Patients with addiction problems are to be referred to local 12-step programs and the groups for recovering addicts. Grace Lee, M.S.W., will be conducting a group for recovering addicts in the southern region on Saturday mornings. Either Bob Wilson, M.D., or Maggie Kane, M.D., will be doing the Wednesday evening addiction group. No members who are currently "using" are appropriate for these groups. They are designed as post-detox groups.

The Adult Children of Alcoholics group will be available in August at the central office. Contact Marie for scheduling. The group therapist will be named.

The singles group is also taking referrals this month. Contact Dr. Bernstein at 555–5465. A new men's group will be available in August and Dr. Farraday is signing up members now. Finally the women's groups are being led by Dr. Clark (southern area). Felice Roll and Candy Martin are doing the central region group.

All referrals are to be made directly to the group leader.

STAGE 4:   *Screening*

Screening is one of the most critical components of the entire group process. A poorly screened group is assuredly one with extra handicaps. Some screening errors can be so serious as to almost guarantee failure. Selection for inclusion is most often made by the leaders or the institution sponsoring the group, although Vander Kolk (1985) notes that occasionally members are involved in, or make, the decision. In open higher-functioning groups, members who are added often have to pass some

Figure 2.11   **Notice of Mandatory Attendance Groups,
Sent to Parents of Schoolchildren**

Dear Mr. and Mrs. White:

Your son/daughter has been reported to the school principal repeatedly for smoking in the school lavatories. In lieu of punishment, he/she has been assigned to a group guidance session with Miss Young, the school counselor. The sessions will occur every Monday, Wednesday, and Friday from 10 to 11 A.M. We have found that these sessions are helpful to students and do reduce future infractions of school policies. Attendance is mandatory for one month with your consent. If you accept these terms, please complete and sign the attached permission slip.

If you would prefer to discuss this matter with me personally, please call for an appointment.

Sincerely,

John Edwards
Principal

Figure 2.12   **Notice of Mandatory Attendance Groups**

MEMO

To: Inmates Black, White, Brown, Green, Redd
         Charlestown Penitentiary
From: J. E. M. Cauliflower, Warden

You have been assigned to group therapy with psychology students S. Johnson and J. Jackson. The group commences 0900 Wednesday, May 1, and will terminate at 1030. The group will last for 15 weeks or until your release. It is expected that you will learn social skills necessary for your upcoming release from this center. On-time attendance is mandatory.

screening by members. Lifton (1966) and Hansen, Warner, and Smith (1980) provide guidelines for timing and approaches to such additions.

There are differences in populations and goals between growth and therapy-type groups. Members must therefore be screened accordingly. Mixing psychotherapy patients and growth-oriented clients will limit the learning of both. Group progress is often dependent on agreements or compromises—sometimes unconscious—about the type of material and the psychological language system the group will use and the goals it will pursue. The sooner these agreements can be made, the further the group can progress in the allotted time. A group with widely divergent goals cannot make these agreements readily and will spend an inordinate amount of time in Phase 2 (Transition), leaving far less group time actually to work on change.

In some ways, the group's progress is most limited by the pathology of the lowest-functioning member. A poor mix of members can make progress beyond the earliest stages of the process laborious and painful. Indeed, inadequate screening is the most likely cause for a group to become bogged down or produce casualties.

When one considers the very significant ramifications of ineffective screening, this stage is curiously minimized by counselors, therapists, and group leaders. Screening errors are most probable when leaders are too eager to fill their groups, when they underestimate psychopathology (especially in growth-oriented groups), or when they overestimate the effectiveness of the natural screening of the market-place. The ethical guidelines of the Association for Specialists in Group Work (1989) recommend individual prescreening interviews by the leaders of the group. The Guidelines of the American Association for Counseling and Development (1988) require member counselors to

> screen prospective group members, especially when the emphasis is on self-awareness and growth through self-awareness. [The group leader] must maintain an awareness of the group members' compatibility throughout the life of the group. (p. 3)

Capuzzi and Gross (1992), Carroll and Wiggins (1990), Corey (1990), Shapiro (1978), and Yalom (1995) are among the authors who have underscored the primacy of screening for effective groups. They have identified two major screening questions in a group setting:

1. Is this group appropriate for the client?
2. Is the client appropriate for this group?

HOMOGENEITY OR HETEROGENEITY?   Some leaders favor homogeneous membership to emphasize participants' shared experiences, understanding, and altruism and to instill hope by providing encouraging examples of success within the group setting. Others favor heterogeneous membership for its diverse feedback possibilities, higher levels of interest, and models of novel approaches to problem solving.

Many questions arise regarding this issue:

- Should people with different problems be in the same group?
- Do you have to share a particular problem personally to understand fully the emotional ramifications of that problem?
- Should members who know each other (e.g., from work, school, neighborhood) be in the same group? What are the implications of a prior acquaintance for the involved members? What are the implications for the members who do not know anyone in the group from past association?

■ What are the ramifications of loss of confidentiality in employee assistance program (EAP) groups offered in the workplace?
■ What is the appropriate age range for members?
■ Which age groups fit together and which don't?
■ When do you include both genders and when do you have independent men's groups and women's groups?
■ Should people with addictions be in groups with nonaddicted peers?
■ Which diagnostic categories are best kept apart?

With the increasing growth of 12-step groups, based on the Alcoholics Anonymous model and a host of other self-help programs, large numbers of group participants have had experiences that lead to certain expectations of a group with a designated leader. Groups that are geared to a 12-step model and consistent with its philosophical underpinnings can accommodate such members quite successfully. However, mixed groups with alternative theoretical perspectives may not fare as well. The time required to reindoctrinate all members to a novel method of group work and a new psychological language system could drastically reduce the time and energy needed to progress through the normal group process. By contrast, members with prior experience in 12-step meetings and individual therapy often adapt quickly and utilize well what a group has to offer.

EGO STRENGTH   As a rule of thumb, the most salient screening question has to do with a potential member's ego strength. Generally, heterogeneous membership with regard to anamnestic information is desired. People of different ages, races, cultures, and walks of life often become a very productive group. However, the group is best served when members are roughly similar in ego strength. People with essentially equivalent levels of pathology will work together better than groups with wide-ranging differences. Thus, a mix of people whose needs for support and growth differ dramatically will work less well. One example of this occurred in an outpatient clinic. In a group of eight members, diagnoses of participants included schizophrenia, bipolar disorder, borderline personality disorder, adjustment disorder, dysthymia, and posttraumatic stress disorder. By the third session, only three members had come to all three sessions. In such a group, the neediest person would exert the most control on the direction of the process.

ISOLATES   Another screening issue involves group isolates. Common examples of isolates in a group include one person of a different gender, a person addicted to alcohol or drugs in a group in which addiction is not an issue, or an individual isolated by a wide age gap.

A 17-year-old high school senior was referred to the senior author after two years in a particularly trying group therapy experience. This group, led by a locally well-known therapist, consisted of nine members—the teenager and four couples aged 29 to 45 who were having marital problems. Suzanne simply did not belong in this married couples group. Not only did she misunderstand many of the conflicts between the couples, but she emerged with an especially pessimistic view of marriage and heterosexual relationships. Subsequent consultation with the group therapist confirmed that in his opinion, Suzanne did not get much out of the group, and several of the other members were reticent to discuss some of their sexual problems in front of a "17-year-old child." This was a clear case of poor or absent screening based on the simplistic notion that because all nine of these people could benefit from group treatment, they could function well together.

In another situation, an experienced group trainer was asked to consult with an ongoing women's awareness group in a small community. The group was stalled and making no progress. He reported,

> As a male, I was surprised to receive this request and reticent to accept. This surprise was minor to the shock I experienced on entering the group room. In addition to four single women (Mary, Kathy, Ann, and Peggy) and three married women (Martha, Linda, and Sandy), there was another group member by the name of Edward. Ed was a social worker, the former husband of Linda and Kathy and the current lover of Peggy. The rationale of the group was that because Ed was being discussed so much in the group, it seemed only fair to have him present. The block in this women's awareness group was that, dynamically, the group process centered around a *man*. I recommended an immediate "Edectomy." He and I left the group together to the relief and benefit of all concerned.

MORE SEVERE PATHOLOGY   Potential group members with Axis II disorders can be very well accommodated in groups that are specifically geared to their developmental relationship needs (see Finn & Shakir, 1990). Similarly, groups are commonly employed for treatment of patients with psychotic and severe addiction problems. The crucial screening factor is the limitation to relatively homogeneous membership and a generally longer time frame for the group to function.

POOR ALIGNMENT OF POPULATION, GOALS, AND RESOURCES   Screening difficulties based on the presence of isolates are easier to foresee than differences based on symbiotic pathological systems, level or type of problem to be discussed, or readiness and motivation for the group experience. In groups with heterogeneous membership held in an outpatient setting, several types of members can be extremely counterproductive for group progress. Brain-damaged, mentally defective, severely psychotic (especially withdrawn and paranoid) patients, psychopathic individuals, nonrecovering drug or alcohol addicts, suicidal clients, and very assaultive patients are all bad risks in an outpatient group and have no place at all in growth groups. Not only will these members benefit little or even regress personally, but they will also severely limit the gains by other members of the group. These clinical observations have long been confirmed in the group therapy literature by Slavson (e.g., 1951), Yalom (1970), Rosenbaum and Hartley (1962), and Corsini and Lundin (1955). Certainly, any member whose pathology would lead him or her to be insensitive or in extreme instances to prey on other members is a poor risk (Dinkmyer & Muro, 1971).

SYMBIOTIC COMBINATIONS   Certain combinations of group members also can cause grief for the group leader and inhibit the group process, particularly in growth groups where the group contract often has no allusion to pathology. People who have outside-of-group relationships (particularly secret ones) may be a problem. Vander Kolk (1985) and Capuzzi and Gross (1992) also indicate the potential dangers of mixing suicidal patients of different levels of lethality. Another potentially disruptive combination involves a person who uses hysteric or borderline defenses and an authoritarian personality type who tends to avoid intimacy by "protecting" (fathering, mothering) others.

An example of this predicament occurred during introductions in an intern-led growth group for graduate students in a mental health training program. Three members of the group had already given their names and described their personal expectations when a fourth said,

> My name is Christine . . . I don't know if I should be here . . . I get scared easy and I'm afraid of you two especially [she indicated two of the men in the group]. When people start getting upset and emotional I freak out. I even tried suicide three times.

As quickly as an "Amen" to a particularly moving prayer, Dan, one of the men in the group, responded in a crisp, booming voice,

> Well, you don't have to worry here, sweets; anyone who tries to get you upset will have to answer to me first.

During his response he extended his index finger in an arc pointing toward each member of the group.

This symbiotic relationship interrupted group process for several sessions. Whenever other group members began to discuss anything emotional, Christine would begin to shake, cower, and express a need to run from the room. Dan would then respond by verbally intimidating the person who was expressing the high levels of emotion. In this way, the principals allowed one another to express the feelings that they were personally unable to express directly. Christine never had to deal with her "unacceptable" anger, and Dan never had to deal with his anger-covered fear. They effectively kept the group from getting to deeper (more frightening) levels of interaction.

The co-leaders had their hands very full with this relationship until the fourth session of the group. At that meeting, a breakthrough occurred when Christine tried to provoke the group by being absent after having been seen in the hall outside the group room minutes earlier. Without her presence, the group leaders progressed swiftly to confront members' feelings of being threatened by her fragility and by Dan's intimidation. By the next session, when she returned, Dan had sufficient courage to refuse to save her from her anxiety. Only then could the group move forward.

THE EXTRA-GROUP RELATIONSHIP
Another combination of members that causes great difficulties is two members who have had a serious prior relationship. This is especially powerful when the group is composed of others who do not know one another well. The case of Denise and Billy provides a clear example.

The group was designed to help people learn to relate more comfortably and effectively to members of the opposite sex. Because of this theme, there was a prerequisite that members did not know each other beforehand.

As the group progressed, it became clear that each time Billy spoke, Denise made the next statement and "put him down as a typical male." Similarly, whenever Denise spoke, Billy accused her of "being sexually provocative, but denying it verbally" (a pejorative perception that nevertheless subsequently turned out to be accurate). The other group members and leaders confronted them several times with this pattern, with no apparent behavior change.

Their interaction became so dominant that the group leader finally confronted them with the following statement: "You two sound like a married couple deciding to get a divorce and wanting to gain some measure of revenge." This was followed by a pregnant silence during which both Denise and Billy got very pale. Finally, they admitted that they *had* been married for four years and were competing to seduce opposite sex group members. The group continued only after they agreed to drop out and seek individual psychotherapy.

SECRET MOTIVATIONS   One other type of person who makes group work especially complex is the person who has "something to sell." These individuals come to groups essentially to convince others to join with them in some belief system or value. They are either sufficiently insecure, well defended, or convinced enough of their own righteousness to be unaccepting of others members' values, beliefs, or language systems. Recent converts to religious, spiritual, or pop psychology sects can frequently spend much of the group's time attempting to induce other members to accept verbatim their own elitist, myopic approach to understanding their experience and their own singular jargon. In the process, they reject all others as unsophisticated or insensitive. Such members often seduce other members and unsuspecting leaders into expending vast amounts of time attempting to "work with them and be fair."

Denny was one such participant in an otherwise high-functioning outpatient group of helpers in mental health fields. He was a supportive and contributing member of the group for several sessions. In the fifth group meeting, a question of an unwanted pregnancy came up in the group. Marion volunteered that several years ago, she had had an abortion, an act that entailed making a very painful and difficult decision. While she was weeping, Denny became increasingly agitated, finally bursting out of the room screaming at her, "Anyone who has murdered a child should be put to death herself!" After he left, the group turned its attention to supporting Marion.

At the next group meeting, he arrived with "Right-to-Life" literature and pictures and railed at the group and at Marion in particular for a lengthy period before the leaders finally demanded that he stop, whereupon he again left the session. His belief and feelings about abortion (although not his position on the death sentence policy) was likely shared by others in the group. What made his group participation problematic was his vehemence, his unwillingness to consider others' opinions or feelings, and his "judge, jury, and executioner" stance. He literally shouted down others who tried to support Marion or discuss the unwanted pregnancy with the man who originally brought it up for discussion. The leaders, admittedly caught off guard by this series of actions, permitted it to progress far beyond what might be appropriate or healthy for the group.

THE COST OF INADEQUATE SCREENING   The screening stage of group process is critically important in setting group tone and eliminating unnecessary problems. Errors of omission and of commission come back to haunt group leaders in a variety of ways. Poor screening can seriously limit group outcome. A leader who attempts to do bargain basement screening will pay for it several times over during the life of the group.

One example of incomplete screening will make this point clear. Nine members were enrolled in a one-day marathon group in 1973. On the last day before the group was to meet, one co-leader was talking casually to a colleague regarding his disappointment about the lack of a tenth group member. The colleague replied that he had a person on his waiting list, suggesting that the co-leader call her. Because it was so late, a very brief, inadequate telephone screening was done. Tina, a mental health professional, seemed motivated and pleasant on the phone and was invited to come to the group the following day. The co-leader wrote,

> I rationalized: There's not enough time to do a personal in-office screening; she was "screened" by a colleague; she's been on a waiting list for a group, so she couldn't be in urgent need of help; she's a professional person in a mental health profession—a psychiatric nurse. These justifications were used in the absence of the typical appropriate face-to-face interview.

Tina was the fourth member to introduce herself the next day. Her speech was exceptionally fast and pressured, and her eyes seemed to glaze and defocus every few seconds. A short excerpt of her eight-minute self-introduction follows:

> "Well, my name is Tina, but it isn't really Tina that's only since it happened, before that is was different but really the same—Sally or Rudy but that was before the man-husband-father rolled over the kids with the steam roller-crusher-flat but not really only but they were dead but I didn't so now they cry but it seems no he didn't exist—they are. God punishes them but I save-savior-saved. . . ."
>
> During this the other group members appeared terrified and seemed to be trying to enlarge the size of the group room by pressing their backs against the walls of the room. The group co-leader had a look of shock, surprise, and what could be most kindly described as a "How could you do this to me?" look on his face. I expect that my own face took on the customary countenance of a person who has recently been kicked in the stomach by a horse. (Shapiro, 1978, p. 76)

Once Tina was through with her introduction, and before the remaining members introduced themselves, the leaders called a break and contacted a colleague. They arranged for emergency treatment and reconvened the rather shaken group members once she had departed. The group wrestled with Tina's pathology for approximately two hours before they were able to refocus on their own personal concerns.

SCREENING MEMBERS INTO THE GROUP   Screening is best employed for inclusion rather than exclusion (e.g., Yalom, 1995) and necessitates finding a good mix of people: similar enough to understand one another, yet different enough to be able to learn innovative viewpoints, behaviors, and solutions to problems from one another. One or two appropriate members can bridge a gap between two otherwise discrete subgroups of people within a single group. Group membership also needs to coincide with the ability and level of functioning of the leaders. Groups simply cannot progress beyond the leaders' ability to effectively cope with any particular level of process.

One example of screening in members with special abilities to bridge gaps occurred in a recent outpatient couples group. Three couples were ready for the group: a married couple in their mid-twenties with two small children; an unmarried couple without children in their mid-twenties; a couple in their late thirties with a blended family. The leaders added a couple in their thirties with no children and a couple approaching 40 with two young children from the current marriage and two adolescents from her prior marriage. These two last couples helped provide additional support and connections between members.

In a group conducted in a local church, the counselor added two recovering alcoholic members to a group whose prior enrollees were parents of children who were abusing alcohol and nondrinkers who had excessive emotional dependence on institutional authorities.

Members may also be screened in to a group to fill out the age range or to balance other characteristics. A group of five members in their twenties and thirties and one aged 55 has a potential isolate, but adding a few members in their forties could minimize that possibility. Similarly, in a group of graduate counseling students, two males were added to balance a group of five women and two other men.

The screening interview form shown in Figure 2.13 is the one we commonly use. It is not necessarily appropriate for any particular group setting but may be used as a model. No legal ruling has been made regarding use of this form.

Once the logistics are set and group members screened, Phase I of the group process is complete. When the group convenes, Phase II begins.

PREGROUP PREPARATION   Prior to the first actual group meeting, some leaders prefer a pregroup meeting for orientation and preparation. Egan (1976), who conducts "human relations training" groups from a skills training perspective, prefers a structured approach with considerable training to orient members for maximum work in the group once it actually begins. Corey (1990) focusing primarily on university level counseling groups, favors a fairly elaborate preparatory session in which the leader explores with the members their

> expectations, fears, goals and misconceptions; the basics of group process; psychological risks associated with group membership and ways of minimizing them; the values and limitations of groups; guidelines for getting the most from the group experience; and the necessity of confidentiality." (p. 93)

Corey also uses this initial session for extended screening and obtaining a commitment to continued membership. In these sessions, he discusses with participants the importance of their own preparation for group work; stresses the importance of their personal level of investment; examines with members their reasons for being in the group, expectations, hopes, and fears about participating; and helps them better crystallize their personal life issues and level of disclosure. In addition,

Figure 2.13   **Screening Interview Form**

SCREENING INTERVIEW FOR GROUPS

Jerrold Lee Shapiro, Ph.D., A.B.M.P.
OHANA Family Therapy Institute

This is a generic model.
Please adjust for specific groups as appropriate.

Part 1

To be completed by group leader prior to interview.

Type of Group: Therapy _____ Growth _____ Counseling _____ Other _____

Population: _____

Dates & times for group meetings: _____

Special Considerations: _____

_____

*Specific population requirements, etc.

Part 2

To be completed by group leader while interviewing prospective members.

Name: _____ Sex: _____

Address: _____

Phone: _____ Age: _____ Marital status: _____

Ethnicity/culture: _____

For therapy groups: Detail results of psychological assessment and/or mental status exam. Viability for group treatment?

(continued)

Figure 2.13   *(continued)*

For all groups:

1. How did you hear about this group? (referral source or ?)

2. Reasons for applying for group.

3. Describe prior counseling/therapy experience (situation and evaluation)

   Individual:

   Group:

4. Please list any current psychiatric or medical conditions and treatment.

5. Relevant medical history
   (some leaders prefer a medical history checklist)

6. Alcohol and drug history (any dependence/addiction etc.)

7. Relationship/sexual history (especially interpersonal difficulties)

8. Any particular problems with the law?

Figure 2.13   *(continued)*

9. To what extent is your current situation a crisis?

10. Some estimate of self-esteem (i.e., How satisfied are you with the way you are? What do you need to change?)

11. When events become anxiety producing, do you tend to become more quiet or more talkative? (examples)

12. What role do fate, luck, or chance play in making your life what it is?

13. Do you tend to trust others quickly or slowly?

14. What do you hope to get out of this group?

15. What do you expect to get out of this group?

16. Is there a particular best way for others to relate to you? (example)

he impresses members with the importance of thinking between sessions about what they wish to address and of keeping a journal.

At least one controlled research effort established the value of a preparatory session in increasing subsequent member interpersonal interactions (Yalom, Houts, Newell, & Rand, 1979). The authors also claimed that patients' faith in the process improved, maximizing any potential placebo effects. Yalom (1985) later described a fairly extensive preparation including an exploration of misconceptions and expectations; description of his existential theory of group work; prediction of stumbling blocks; discussions of trust, self-disclosure, extra group socialization, confidentiality, and goals; exploration of risks inherent in group therapy; and an examination of how members can best grow from the experience. Vinogradov and Yalom (1990) particularly encourage the use of such sessions to reduce negative expectations. In their review of pregroup participation, Orlinsky and Howard (1986) concluded that a majority of studies strongly favor role preparation procedures as measured by self-reports of members, observers and leaders, and paper and pencil indices. Piper and Perrault (1989) were less enthusiastic about the value of pregroup training in their subsequent review of outcome measures. However, they did indicate that the cost in time for any benefits was minimal. In general, if the group leaders are more comfortable with a "prepped group," the preparation is probably worth doing.

At Santa Clara University, the handout reproduced in Figure 2.14 is mailed to counseling psychology graduate students, prior to the initial session of their mandatory training groups. Regardless of whether pregroup sessions or instructions are employed, the screening and preparation end with the first session of the group.

SUMMARY

Similar to human development in general, each group is both unique and shares universal process and stages. The authors use four stages of group process: preparation, transition, treatment, and termination.

The preparation stage includes determination of the group goals, population, logistics, and screening criteria. The logistics of the group will follow rationally and will depend on the specific goals and population. Screening group members involves finding a therapeutic fit between member and group. Ego strength is identified as the most important screening factor in creating a therapeutic group. Screening is both an inclusive and an exclusive process as the leaders attempt to bring together people who are similar enough to be able to empathize yet different enough to expand their repertoire of problem-solving behaviors.

Figure 2.14   **Pregroup Instructions**

Please read the following information carefully. If there are any questions that your group leaders cannot answer, please contact Dr. S.

These groups are a required, nongraded, cost-free component of the CPSY Master's degree program. They are intended as a preparation to CPSY219 (the course on group leadership). The groups serve several functions and it is important that you understand these. It is the intent of the faculty that you have the opportunity to talk about and deal with personal aspects of yourselves that are likely to impact on your training and future counseling. We expect that you will be as open and honest about your personal self as you feel appropriate in these group settings. These groups are designed to be confidential and the faculty of the program will not be privy to any *content* discussed in the group with two exceptions (outlined below). Although the leaders and faculty will do all they can to maintain confidentiality, it is incumbent on you as an individual to use common sense and good judgment about what you choose to talk about in group. It is essential that each of you also be very careful about confidentiality of your fellow members.

It is important to recognize the difference between content and process. Issues of process have limited confidentiality. When a group member, for example, reveals, hypothetically, that he or she was a "recovering heroin addict," that communication (the content) is protected. However, in a discussion of this student's capacity as a counselor, the professional group leader may discuss issues with respect to how this individual deals with others, how this student relates to others, how this student relates to conflict and coping: all experiences that the leader may have had with the student in group. Under rare circumstances, these *process* issues may be discussed by the faculty. Thus, it is confidential if you say you are a recovering addict. It is not necessarily confidential if you ridicule someone else who discloses that he or she is one.

EXTENDED CONFIDENTIALITY

Additional requirements are imposed on group members and the co-leaders that are not or may not be typical of a clinical setting. First, confidentiality continues beyond the end of the group through the duration of your experience at Santa Clara and beyond. (Explanation: While you are a student here, the group member who revealed he/she was a "recovering heroin addict" must have that communication protected as long as the person remains in the program, as long as you remain in the program, and into the future, even if you were only a group member and not that individual's therapist.)

Second, extended confidentiality means extreme awareness to third party sensitivity. (Explanation: Let us say that I report a "Samoan nun I once knew in group revealed she was an alcoholic." As a teacher or supervisor, one can clearly use experiences in group for exemplification in class as long as the *identity* of the person is withheld. As a practicing counselor, one can refer to experiences and "cases" with colleagues, at workshops, and so on. However, in this case I have withheld the name, but is that sufficient protection of this individual? Is it appropriate for me to say a "Samoan nun" or is this statement already too revealing? After

(continued)

Figure 2.14   *(continued)*

all, how many Samoan nuns are there in the Santa Clara program. Could you walk down the hall and identify several Samoan nuns or just one?

If you assume that each of the 10 members of your group has 3 close friends in the program, that makes 30 people! It is likely that for the duration of your graduate classes at least one of these 30 people (unknown to you) will be in class with you. If you make a reference to information about this person, even though you have withheld the name, that information may be enough for this individual in your class to know whom you are *referencing*. If he or she can surmise the identity, you have violated the original person's confidentiality. This is something of a burden when you think about it, but the purpose of this introductory set of values is simply to remind you of your responsibilities.

It is our experience that confidentiality is rarely violated. If such a violation does occur, it may be unintentional or accidental. However, if confidentiality is violated by clear lack of responsibility on the person's part (or an innate tendency to gossip), this behavior is grounds for the person to lose his or her MFCC license once he or she has become a professional, and it is also grounds to question a person's ability to succeed in this field.

EXCEPTIONS TO CONFIDENTIALITY

The legal and ethical standards of mental health professionals require a "breach of confidentiality" in the event that a group member is determined to be a danger to himself or herself or to the person or property of another, or in the case of child or elder abuse. In addition, if, in the group leaders' assessment, a student member is in need of individual psychological or medical intervention in order to practice safely as a mental health professional, the leaders will consult with the training group supervisor. If the supervisor concurs with the assessment, a faculty member will become involved in interviewing the student. As a result of this interview, a plan will be developed with the student for her or him to receive assistance and intervention when appropriate.

This is a rare occurrence (twice in the past 10 years), and it is intended for the benefit of the students and the program. It is not intended as a way to remove students from the program. Rather, it is used to identify special needs and to try to correct problems before they become serious. The faculty is generally much more concerned with students' reactions to others' vulnerabilities than to any specific content or things you may disclose about yourself.

The training group leaders and advanced student co-leaders are required to attend weekly group supervision. It is important for student group members to know that while the process and content of group dynamics are discussed, individual student identities will not be revealed except as discussed above.

ACADEMIC VERSUS THERAPEUTIC STATUS

A second goal of the faculty is to give students an opportunity to understand in a fuller way what it is like to be a client. This is an essential part of training and we expect you to learn a great deal from it. Some programs make personal therapy

Figure 2.14 **(continued)**

a mandatory part of the student training. We do not have such a requirement (except for this very short pregroup). However, we strongly recommend that all students avail themselves of personal therapy during and after their training as preparation for success in the field.

Group experiences in which members work with their own emotional, cognitive, and value-based reactions are generally seen as an integral part of any graduate training in human services work. Often students remember the work in groups with peers as the most meaningful of all their graduate school experiences. We hope you will use the group in this way and gain a great deal from your participation.

This experience has both academic and experiential/therapeutic aspects. The extent to which you use the group for your own understanding and therapy is up to you.

The group itself is a hybrid: part therapy and part academic. There is an expectancy, for example, that the people in this group are not significantly pathological, that they are essentially "normal" and may be expected to do things typical "clients" might not be expected to do, for example, (1) accept the termination of the group at six weeks without a need to be weaned away from this encounter in a more therapeutically thought-out manner; (2) attend the process because attendance is required (even though if you were a client you might simply skip this week because you needed to "resist" important psychological issues that you were gradually beginning to confront. These points of divergence between what is academic and what is therapeutic may get confusing; when in doubt, assume that you are in a basically academic setting and that you are attempting (for the purposes of clinical training and experience) to *simulate* the therapeutic milieu. The closer you get to it, the better the learning experiences will be; the more you try to act and feel like a client (not a student), the better the group will be. The more you trust in your leader and the therapeutic process (rather than be a grade-conscious student), the better will be your education experience. Remember: If you participate, you will get credit; *you do not have to perform.*

ATTENDANCE

Attendance is required. There are several reasons for this requirement, the most important of which is that everyone in the group becomes a "significant other" as time progresses. When one or two significant others are absent, the whole group suffers from it, losing pace over it, slows down, needs to recover, and so on. To experience fully the processes of change and evolution of a group (packed into six weeks), we need to count on each other's presence.

Groups meet for six 2-hour weekly sessions. There will also be one 8-hour marathon session, *generally* between the 3rd and 4th session.

Students must attend the marathon and are expected at all sessions. A single absence may be permitted by the group leader. Missing more than one session or the marathon will require repetition of pregroup.

(continued)

Figure 2.14   *(continued)*

If you will have to miss group once in the quarter and you know this in advance, *please defer enrollment in pregroup until a subsequent quarter.* Look at your schedule and sign up for this pregroup only if you are sure you will be able to make these meetings.

Please note: You will be asked to participate at a level appropriate to your own personality style and demands of the field (there is a difference between nonverbal participation and a clear indication that you are only passing time with no intention of being a group member).

Students must keep a journal of their reactions during the group sessions. Criteria for what is required in the journal follows:

These journals will be used as part of the CPSY219 (Group Counseling) course. Therefore, it is important to keep the journal accurately, and to hold on to the journal until you take the Group course. *Please note: You will not have to turn in any part of the journal unless you decide it is appropriate.* During the group course, you will be asked to compare your group with the theoretical models presented.

The journal should include three components:

1. Entries from each session in which the events of the session are described.
2. Your feelings about and during the events. Remember that feelings are emotional reactions.
3. Your thoughts about these events and the session. Include perceptions of your fellow members and the leaders.

The leadership teams from each group consist of a senior leader who is a licensed mental health professional with experience in leading these kinds of groups, and a co-leader who is an advanced student in the program. Senior leaders are normally in private practice in the community.

How should I behave in Group? What is expected? What should I avoid doing? I've just started the program, and I don't know what is expected of me.

Answers to these questions are not easy. However, there are some positive attitudes that make group work easier and allow you to have a better experience. Think about adopting them and try to be reasonably experimental.

1. Be careful about your expectations. These groups are not in-depth psychotherapy such as personal individual psychotherapy. They focus more on interactions and on problems that can reasonably be addressed in the seven sessions. They are also not like classes. The group leaders will

Figure 2.14   *(continued)*

not structure the groups like a class. The members will have to create much of the structure and build it with increasing trust during the group.

2. Be courageous and as time goes on, try to "give" the group some personal issues you might not otherwise share publicly. Communicate these issues and you will probably be quite surprised how effectively the group treats them and/or you with them.

3. Try to take small "risks" and reasonable chances.

4. Assume that your feelings have validity. If you feel something about someone in the group, try to put that into words that communicate and get those feelings out. Rather than call the person an S.O.B., maybe you can get that anger out in a more effective confrontation. Try it. However, consider the difference between feelings and judgments. Feelings are emotions. They occur in your body and express a personal reaction. Judgments are opinions about another's behavior. There is a considerable difference. The expression of the following feelings, "I feel angry when you dismiss my ideas," will potentially open a discussion. That is not the case when you judge: "Of course you don't understand; you are stupid."

5. Listen to feedback you are getting. Watch how others listen to feedback they are getting.

6. Give feedback. Be forthcoming.

7. Avoid these if you can:
   a. Avoid "intellectualizing" too much; try to stay at a feeling level as much as you can.
   b. Avoid absolutes: Everything is OK in group. If someone tells you that "storytelling" is bad or "asking questions" is bad, forget these absolutes. Too much storytelling is bad. Too much question asking is bad. Too much confrontation is bad. Too much kindness and reassurance are bad, too. Look for a nice balance and help steer the course of the group as if it were a great spaceship that needed frequent mid-course corrections to properly get it to its destination.
   c. Avoid withholding: The group will get nowhere if you withhold. We won't know what you are withholding; we won't know you very well if you do, and you'll feel alienated from the process and the group if you hold back too much.

8. Be aware of yourself. Are you talking too much, dominating too much, being too much of one thing? How are others seeing you? Seek feedback and try out novel behaviors.

9. Finally, if you have done therapy before, been in groups before, have a great deal of experience . . . try to recapture your innocence; try not to fall into the role of healer–helper–therapist, but try, once again, to find the client in you, the person who is struggling with issues. Concentrate on your "clienthood," your neediness. As the group progresses and

(continued)

Figure 2.14   *(continued)*

matures, your skills as a listener and helper, even some of your interventions, will be encouraged and will even come spontaneously to you, and we will all profit from them. But to enter the group with an attitude of being an auxiliary, stand-by therapist-on-call does disservice to the growth of the group. Be a client first and foremost and the opportunities to "lead" or help or try out some interventions will present themselves. Don't compete with the leader or co-leader. It just inhibits the group and minimizes your personal learning in the group.

I have read and understand all of these pregroup instructions.

_____   _____

Student Signature   Date

CHAPTER 3

GROUP PROCESS PHASE II: TRANSITION

STAGE 5   LEADER SPECIFIES GROUND RULES
STAGE 6   INTRODUCTIONS
STAGE 7   THE INITIAL (SHORT) SILENCE
STAGE 8   SHORT SILENCE IS BROKEN
STAGE 9   DISCUSSION OF THERE-AND-THEN
           TOPIC
STAGE 10   NATURAL DEATH OF DISCUSSION
STAGE 11   THE LONG SILENCE
STAGE 12   MEMBERS' FIRST SORTIE
STAGE 13   OPENING OF THE DISCUSSION
STAGE 14   GROUP LEADER FOCUSES ON
           HERE-AND-NOW PROCESS
STAGE 15   DEBRIEFING THE LEADERSHIP
           TESTS: FOCUS ON FEELINGS
STAGE 16   LEADER ENCOURAGES THE
           EXPRESSION OF EMOTION

It's not about making *the horse drink;*
It's about giving the horse a salt lick
on the way to the trough.

The predominant task of Phase II [Transition] is to prepare the group members for treatment or intervention. It is natural for members to be fearful of and resistant to change. The core function of the transition period is to make the upcoming treatment more palatable. During this group phase, members are encouraged to build trust and confidence in themselves and the other members, develop group cohesion, learn group norms, reduce anxiety about personal introspection and revelation, and become a bit more experimental. These conditions are accomplished by allowing the natural group process to unfold and helping members understand and come to grips with their internal feelings and certain inevitable dilemmas that emerge (see Dies & Dies, 1993). During this period, the leaders provide support and encouragement for the members' struggles and growth. They also help the group members learn how to focus on the here-and-now process in the group.

The early stages of group process have some therapeutic value, but their greatest impact is in teaching the members the language, focus, ethics, and process of the group. These stages can be quite lengthy, taking several sessions, or quite brief, as with a group consisting of graduate students enrolled in a class focusing on group process. During this stage, members need to feel that they are included and that the group will offer them something.

Corey and Corey (1982) write,

> Before groups progress to a working stage, they typically go through a transitional phase. During this phase, groups are generally characterized by anxiety, defensiveness, resistance, the struggle for control, inter-member conflict, conflicts with or challenges to the leader, and various patterns of problem behaviors. (p. 121)

MacKenzie (1987) characterizes this period as one of rebellion and struggle for differentiation, emphasizing issues of control, dominance, and anger. Members question how well they fit in the group, whether the confidentiality is real, and what will happen if they disagree with others. In addition, two specific major tests of leadership must take place: (1) discovering the limits of the leader's skill, emotional strength, and competence (the group's ceiling), and (2) becoming aware of matters beyond the leader's abilities (the group's floor). The extent to which these matters are managed and resolved will substantively determine the extent of work that can be addressed later in the treatment phase of the group.

A perceptive group leader can glean a great deal from pregroup behavior. Do members linger outside the group room or come directly in? Do they speak to others socially or keep to themselves? Are they early, on time, or late? How have they dressed for the group? Where do they sit? Do they continue to chat after the group leader announces the commencement of the group?

No leader will make final or absolute judgments about group members based on such nonverbal behavior, but he or she can develop hypotheses that can be subsequently tested as the group process unfolds. For example, the leader may make tentative assumptions about members, based on where they sit in the group. Typically, participants tend to sit next to people from whom they feel support, across from people to whom they're attracted, and at right angles to people who seem threatening. Such information can help a group leader make early estimates of interpersonal reactivity and comfort among members.

If you make the heuristic assumption that people do not choose their seats accidentally, you can formulate hypotheses readily about members' feelings of affinity or expectations of support. These assumptions may be used later in orchestrating dyadic interactions between members. For example, when Sarah described considerable anxiety about speaking in the group, the leader turned to Darrell, who was sitting next to her. His statement that he was also anxious helped normalize Sarah's experience, and helped reduce her anxiety to more manageable levels. Because they had chosen to sit in adjacent seats, the leader's choice of Darrell was a reasonably safe bet for a supportive reply.

PHASE II: TRANSITION
STAGE 5:   Leader Specifies Ground Rules

SETTING THE TONE   The entire tone for the group may be set by the leader's introductory remarks. The manner in which the group leader presents herself and the ground rules will be the first cue members have for learning how to behave and talk in the group. One of the most critical factors to be determined is the level of anxiety that will be employed. It seems clear that as the level of ambiguity (or the lack of structure) increases, anxiety increases, and this affects everyone's level of performance. Figure 3.1 illustrates the relationship of performance and anxiety.

In most of American culture, anxiety is roughly linearly related to ambiguity. As can be seen in Figure 3.2, as ambiguity rises, so does anxiety. Conversely, when the opposite of ambiguity (structure) increases, anxiety goes down commensurately.

The group leader can effectively manage the level of anxiety in the group setting by maintaining control over the amount of structure present in the group at any one time. We know that optimal learning in any setting occurs when anxiety is at moderate levels. Therefore, a group leader can enhance the effectiveness of the group process by maintaining levels of structure that engender moderate levels of anxiety. When members of the group appear too anxious to be productive, the leader can add structure to bring the anxiety to more productive levels. Conversely, when there is too little arousal in the group, the leader can reduce the amount of structure. This is most easily done by making clear to members that they are to do

Figure 3.1   **The Relationship Between Performance and Anxiety**

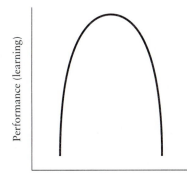

Performance (learning)

Anxiety (arousal)

Figure 3.2   **A Rough Estimate of the Relationship of Ambiguity and Anxiety**

something, but providing few cues as to what specifically is expected of them. In the vernacular, members can then get "psyched up" for the session.

SPECIFYING GROUND RULES   Each group and each group leader will have certain idiosyncratic rules and preferences about group participation. The specifics of such instructions seem less important than the level of structure they convey. Therapy groups, children's groups, and classroom groups generally have more restrictive and structured ground rules than do encounter, T-, and growth-oriented groups. Some representative ground rules are included in the sample introduction given below:

> *Susan (Leader):*   Hello; my name is Susan. I'll be co-leading this group with Jerry [*indicates co-leader*]. Our goal in this group is for open, honest communication between members. We will stress becoming aware of and expressing feelings because that's something we all share and understand. We will be focusing a great deal on the "here-and-now," or what's going on within this group in the present, because we can all look at that much more effectively than we can examine a "there-and-then" memory. We will also work toward congruence in integrating thoughts and feelings.
>
> Needless to say, "here-and-now" feelings about "there-and-then" events are very much grist for our group mill. Jerry, would you like to add anything?
>
> *Jerry (Leader 2):*   Thanks, Susan. I'd like to begin by underscoring what Susan has already said. I'd also like to bring up a few other ground rules. First and foremost is confidentiality—what is said in this group must remain within the group. If something really important happens to you in the group, we encourage you to bring that back home to important people:

spouses, family, friends, and others, but we ask you not to share anyone else's words or experience or to identify anyone else. Is that OK? [*Pauses*] A second form of confidentiality involves whether members of the group can meet outside the group—say, over coffee—and discuss group events. How do you feel about that?

If desired, discussion follows until a group decision is reached or it seems clear that one will not be reached at this time. Many leaders, including Yalom (1985), presume that the members will inevitably talk outside the group. They request that whatever conversations occur are subsequently shared with the group during sessions.

> *Jerry:*   Another ground rule for this group has to do with the expectancies that people often bring into the group with them. Unlike popular magazine articles or other sensationalized accounts, there will be no nudity, sexual touching, or violence within this group. Also, since this is an enclosed room and the air is recirculated, we ask you to refrain from smoking for the two-hour session. We also ask that you not eat or drink during the session. [*These rules are optional and clearly depend on leaders' preferences.*] Also, please do not come to future sessions either drunk, high, or stoned.

> Let us add that if you do not wish to do something or talk about something, all you need to say is "I don't want to do or talk about that," and we won't push you, nor will we allow the group to push you. However, if you say "I can't—generally an avoidant reaction—we'll gently nudge you.

> Are there any questions?"

> *Susan:*   Two additional points. This is a place for you to bring up and discuss things that are bothering you. It's a safe place to take risks and talk about your real problems. Finally, you've probably noticed the videotaping (audiotaping) equipment in the room. These sessions will all be taped. These tapes will be available only to members and leaders in the group. Their purpose is to help us better understand and remember what went on in the session. The tape of each session is kept only until the next session. [*Taping sessions is most common in training and growth groups and least common in therapy groups. It is clearly dependent on a leader's preference as to whether any taping takes place and how the tapes are used.*] Any questions, comments, issues?

Even in this short opening, several ground rules are established, and yet the level of ambiguity is still high. Briefly, these rules were initiated: First names used; leaders identified; co-leadership equality established; open, honest communication stated as goal; focus on feelings stated; expression of feelings stressed; here-and-now defined; taking one's experience home suggested; confidentiality identified as foremost group rule; no nudity, sexual touching, or violence; no smoking; no eating;

no one to attend while drunk, high, or stoned. In addition, members were cautioned to say they *won't* talk about something, not *can't* talk about it. They were told the group could discuss issues and make group decisions, and that they should bring up their own problems. Despite all this information, the group members' anxiety is likely to be somewhat high because they really do not specifically know what is expected of them personally.

A much less structured, less common in the 1990s, yet still extant, opening for encounter groups leads to a very different level of anxiety: "Hello; my name is George, and this is my co-leader, Pam. The only rules for this group are that there'll be no homicide or screwing."

This minimal structure normally will produce greater levels of anxiety for group members. For that reason, such limited directions are considered insufficient even for growth groups consisting of higher-functioning members. Clients who can tolerate higher levels of tension are best served by some predictable structure and a focus of attention on the anxiety they do experience. Always essential is that the level of structure and anxiety be group specific and balanced to produce maximal growth possible for the members.

In theme-centered and psychoeducational groups, ground rules are necessarily more specific. Often, handouts or reading assignments are provided for members' discussion. The leader may begin with a structured exercise that is related to the group theme or composition. For example, in a couples group, each couple may be asked to describe how they happened to get together. This is an endeavor that normally is not unique, focuses on happier days, and is enjoyable to most couples. The leader may then follow with a suggestion that each couple present together discussions of what and when things changed. Vastly greater structure may also be employed, as in the following two examples.

Bob: Hello. My name is Bob. I am a Gestalt therapist, and this will be a Gestalt group. As I mentioned to you in the interview sessions, I like to work with one member at a time, individually. I use the "hot seat," with which many of you may be familiar. When any of you is ready, the hot seat is available. I will work intensively with you and your concerns. If I am able to do so at that time. While you have the hot seat, I ask that others refrain from commenting unless absolutely necessary. If you choose to speak at that time, we'll have to see what will happen.

When you take the hot seat, I expect you to focus on the totality of your experience at the moment—what you are experiencing, feeling, thinking, and so on. I will ask you to focus on many nonverbal aspects of your ongoing experience. Gestalt therapy works to find integration, a whole that is greater than the individual parts of experience. The goal here is for you to come to your senses as a way of fully living your life.

I'll fill you in on more theory later. Let's begin the group now. Who would like to be the first to take the hot seat?

In this example, members may have great anxiety about being in the hot seat, but the rules are crystal clear. There is little anxiety for a member who determines that he will not be taking that special seat. The high level of structure gives members a sense that they have control over what will be expected of them and an ability to limit the depths of the unknown. Behaviorally oriented psychoeducational groups also have a greater amount of structure:

> ***Sandra:*** Hello. Welcome to the group. As we discussed in the pregroup sessions, each of you has come to the group wanting to become more confident in your relationships. As you know, confidence is built slowly, success by success. This group will provide each of you the opportunity to have successes in relationships and to learn how to continue a positive pattern in your relationships. Mark, could you continue?

> ***Mark:*** Thank you, Sandra. First, I want to tell you that I am a graduate of a group like this. I never believed I could lead a group, yet here I am. So if I could build my confidence, anybody can.

> Each of our 12 sessions will have a theme and a series of exercises for all of us to practice and progressively work toward a more confident self. The more you can bring yourself to try new behaviors, the more feedback you can get and the more progress you will make. We will not embarrass you, nor will we criticize your attempts. You will be given honest feedback as to what works well and what could be improved. All of us will make practical suggestions to help you.

> ***Sandra:*** Two more things. Nobody will be forced to try anything. It's up to you how much you choose to do or how far you would like to go. We'll just help you and give you the opportunity to learn in a safe setting. Second, there will be homework that we all ask you to do each week. Some of it will be easy; some may be a little difficult. All the homework will be similar to the practicing we do in the group.

> To begin now, I'd like each of you to introduce yourself. Tell your name, describe what brought you to this group, and say what greater confidence will do for you. [*Turning to her right, she continues*] Would you be willing to begin? What is your name?

This highly structured group introduction is geared for low ambiguity, low anxiety, and greater leader influence on process.

Regardless of the specific introduction, as the rules are given by the group leaders, the level of ambiguity and hence the level of anxiety are set. In this way, a basic tone for the group is determined: the less structure, the more ambiguity, the more anxiety, and the greatest amount of freedom for members. The leaders must balance security and freedom for members by considering the population, their needs, and their ego strength.

STAGE 6: *Introductions*

Each member of the group is asked to introduce himself or herself. The three most important components of this process are *entry, becoming accustomed to sharing information about oneself,* and *open communication of expectancies.*

Leaders frequently ask members to give their names, describe what they hope to gain from their group participation, and state what they fear might happen in the group. Such an introduction allows members to enter the group by participating. Generally, providing this information is relatively nonthreatening, as members have already rehearsed it during the screening procedure and in their heads while thinking about the group. Talking on instruction, about fears and expectancies, is also excellent basic training for later group participation. Hence, from the outset, the leader's expectancy that members will discuss such things in the group are being made clear and members begin practicing.

One interesting phenomenon that occurs in many groups is that members are so busy rehearsing what they'll say when their own turn comes that they do not remember the names or introductions of other members who precede them. Often the first member to introduce himself learns the most about the other members. In pointing this out, the leader begins to establish the principle that the topic for discussion is members' behavior within the group.

It is important to finish the whole round of introductions before any major issues are allowed to develop. Frequently, a group member has been thinking about a problem and waiting to share it for so long that simply giving his name is a cue for a rush of affect and a plea for assistance. The leader's task is to help everyone become at least nominally included in the group before any issues occur that could shut members out. One example of this, already cited, was that of Tina, the improperly screened member.

Another, less bizarre example occurred in an encounter group led by two supervised student group leaders. One of the leaders introduced himself (the fifth person to do so), and a member who had also introduced himself began engaging the leader in a fairly intense manner—asking for help, advice, and so on. The leader mistakenly began to do therapy, and this piece of process lasted almost an hour of the two-hour session. During this time, the group members who had not yet been introduced and the other co-leader maintained a watchful, anxious silence. Only after this "therapy" ended were they able to join the group. Not only did they report feeling like outsiders, but they also said they felt like latecomers to the group. Furthermore, the co-leader who was left out felt that her effectiveness as an equal co-leader had been permanently diminished. Her status as a leader was in fact lower than his for several sessions, even though she was the more experienced of the two.

Sometimes not everyone is present during the initial introductions. This is obviously true in groups with open membership or an open membership period. Some groups employ an inner (active) circle and an outer (observer) circle. Other groups, such as the advanced training groups led by Shapiro and Peltz, have two members operating video cameras at all times. It is essential that any originally unincluded members are provided an opportunity to introduce themselves as soon as they enter the inner group circle. In the training groups with the video camera operators, the leaders ask the operators to leave their cameras in their turn and take part in the introductions along with the other members.

STAGE 7:   *The Initial (Short) Silence*

After introductions have been completed, members typically turn to the leader with the expectation that he or she will provide some structure. When the leader does not do this, a short silence ensues. This silence lasts typically less than two minutes.

STAGE 8:   *The Short Silence Is Broken*

For leader-centered groups, in which responsibility for change rests with the group leaders, the silence will probably be ended by a leader suggestion for some type of group activity. This may be a structured exercise, reflection on the group theme, some type of warm-up technique, or a request for an agenda.

Most counseling, therapy, and growth groups are member centered and process oriented. In these groups, it is important to impress upon members that they are responsible for their personal changes. The leader will normally refrain from ending the short silence as a way of underscoring this learning by members. In member-centered groups, the short silence is ended by one or more members in one of the following ways:

1. Request for information
2. Demand for leader structure
3. Expression of frustration or discomfort
4. Nonverbal signs of anxiety

In our culture, silence in a group setting that is not precipitated by a special request for it (e.g., "Let us pray") or by particular situational demands (e.g., library, funeral parlor) seems to be anxiety provoking. The ending of this short silence (often only microseconds) appears to be an attempt to eliminate the increasing anxiety.

REQUEST FOR INFORMATION   Because the silence is ended as a way of reducing the anxiety provoked by its existence, the manner of its termination often appears less than rational. Requests for information can run the gamut from "Tell me what to do now" to "What do you think of the situation in the Near East?" to "Can the Giants catch the Dodgers this year?" One fascinating instance occurred in a group led by a therapist whose husband was a locally famous therapist and whose father-in-law was an internationally known author. The request for information proceeded as follows:

> *Member 1:* You said your last name was _____ ? Was your husband in the paper last week?

> *Therapist:* Uh-huh.

Member 2:   Are you related to _____ (*father-in-law*)? Oh, wow. I've read a lot of his stuff.

Member 3:   Me, too; he's brilliant.

Member 4:   Well, his philosophies are intriguing from a Western point of view, but hardly complete when considering Eastern approaches.

This request for information served the function of reducing anxiety and distracting the group from its primary *here-and-now* focus and attendant anxiety. Because such *there-and-then* discussions are unlikely to be fruitful in the long term, the leader needs to be careful not to encourage their continuance. However, the therapist is able to collect valuable diagnostic information about members' styles of responding and the methods each one uses to manage anxiety, even from this brief, early episode.

In groups that have been given an out-of-group assignment such as journal keeping or assigned homework, the request for information usually centers around the extra group task. Here are some typical examples:

"In this journal, do we have to remember everything in the group? Wouldn't it be better if we took notes during the meetings?"

"Do we have to turn in the journal? The whole journal or parts? Do you want it typed?"

"Are you both on staff here?"

"What happens if we can't get all the assignments in on time?"

DEMANDS FOR LEADER STRUCTURE   Sometimes, members' anxiety is expressed in apparently discrepant demands for leader action. Frequently they consist of such comments as these:

"O.K., you're the leader; what do we do now?"

"Do you have any starting (ice-breaking) exercises? I hear that's a good way to start a group."

"What are you going to do now?"

"Well, are we just going to sit here?"

One impressive example of this type of demand occurred during a human relations training workshop with administrators from a community college. The actual length of this short silence was approximately *90 seconds* and was broken with these comments:

Member 1:   Look, I just can't stay here all day, I've got work to do.

Member 2:   Time is money.

Member 3:   What's the matter with you?

Member 4:   Look if *you* don't want to teach this class, one of us can.

Each of these statements, directed at the leader, was uttered with increased intensity. Incredible as it may seem, four years after this 90-second silence, one group member recalled his experience of the entire group as the "agony of nobody never saying nothing."

EXPRESSION OF FRUSTRATION OR DISCOMFORT   In some groups the anxiety is expressed directly:

> "I just can't stand it when it's so quiet."

> "Somebody say something!"

> "I'm starting to sweat, and my heart is thumping, and I feel really shaky and hot."

NONVERBAL EXPRESSIONS OF ANXIETY   Some of the common ways members express anxiety without words include shaking, constant shifting of positions, leg jiggling, crying, giggling, dropping or spilling something, whispering something to another member, and whistling.

It is important for the leader to recognize the discomfort and use that recognition to begin orienting members to focus on their internal experience. Each leader and theory has a different way of reflecting back to the clients what is being heard. It is also a time for leaders to be making mental notes about the members' different abilities to contain and use their anxiety and to notice coalitions, support, and antagonisms already present in the group. *It is not a time to make the group safer by "fixing the anxiety problem"* (Bernard & McKenzie, 1994).

STAGE *9:*   *Discussion of There-and-Then Topic*

Once the silence is broken, members of the group will frequently pick up any topic for discussion with a there-and-then focus. This discussion of some external commonality seems to be

1. An effort to stimulate group activity
2. A hedge against another (painful) silence
3. An early attempt to establish a sense of belonging in the group

The topic is frequently interesting and most often safe, objective, and something the majority of members can share. This is especially true for groups who have out-of-group activities in common and, of course, natural groups.

This there-and-then discussion of seemingly irrelevant topics demarcates a time that is both difficult and rich for therapists. During these conversations it is imperative that the group leader *not* become involved in the *content* of the discussion. No matter how interesting the topic, the leader's task at this juncture is primarily diagnostic. The therapist may make a few process comments during stage 8, but by far the most important task for her or him is to observe the group members developing their "pecking order" and establishing their various roles in the group.

A better way to facilitate the group is for the leader to make process comments. In one 1994 group, the members were discussing the O. J. Simpson murder case. When asked for her opinion, the leader intervened by commenting, "This group has found a topic that includes most members and is apparently safe at this time." If the leader does not get embroiled in the content of the there-and-then topic and hence does not keep it alive, this conversation will die a natural death.

STAGE 10:   *Natural Death of Discussion*

After a time, members begin to drop out of the there-and-then discussion—perhaps from boredom, perhaps from hearing the process comments of the leader, or perhaps the anxiety is lowered enough to facilitate movement to less safe (more here-and-now) topics. In any case, the discussion pales and finally terminates. In some groups of highly anxious, highly verbal people, the group therapist may have to be gently directive in terminating this discussion, especially if group time is limited. Normally, leader references to group process will be sufficient to encourage the demise of this discussion.

STAGE 11:   *The Long Silence*

With the death of the there-and-then discussion, a longer period of silence often commences. Members now have some sense of what they are not supposed to discuss but are unclear regarding the kind of work that is possible in this group. The silence can last from 30 seconds to a few minutes to (in rare cases) over an hour, depending on the leaders' orientation, theory, personal tolerance for ambiguity, and the level of members' ego strength. The period is characterized by nervous fidgeting, lack of eye contact, avoidance of physical contact, maintenance of social distance, and increasing anxiety.

Some group leaders will break the silence as certain optimal levels of anxiety are attained. They may, for example, comment at the group level by giving voice to the anxiety present in the room, or they may focus on an individual member or piece of the process. Others will rely on group members to end the long silence. Some leaders argue that if the therapist ends the silence, group members will learn to rely on her or him to continue to do so in the future. This is a responsibility they prefer to leave with group members. These leaders are most likely to hold to that standard in long-term depth-oriented groups, groups with experienced members or mental health professionals, or high-level growth groups. They may take the time of silence to observe the members' nonverbal behaviors for later use in the therapy phase of the group process.

By contrast, leaders of groups with completely inexperienced group members, groups with severe time limitations, or themes that are not benefited by the silence find it best to terminate the silence as a way to keep group anxiety from becoming dysfunctionally high. They then assist the group to focus on the anxiety that such silence arouses and help members to increase their self-observation.

In short-term groups mandated by managed care coverage, the silence may seem to leaders as an inordinately slow or obtuse way to get members to learn how to focus internally and be more fully present. Many leaders in such groups will terminate the silence by requesting that a particular member refocus on a personal matter, or to ask the group members in general to consider how they would like to attain their stated goals in the group. One leader of theme-centered groups often asks how the current silence fits with the theme.

WHY SILENCE?   The use of silence and ambiguity in a group setting has been one of the most misunderstood and misused aspects of group treatment. Clearly, it may have quite wide-ranging results. To create a group in which members will gain optimally from each progressive group stage, the leader must prepare the members for the next stage of the group process. However, to be effective, the leader must not do everything for the members of the group. Like a good parent, the leader must let the members experiment and sometimes stumble in the learning process. However, it is always a good idea to take appropriate safety precautions to avoid having those under your care fall on their heads.

To be effective, the silence in a group needs to serve as a clear indication to members that each of them is responsible for their own anxiety and how they accommodate it. The leader wants to send a message that the members are capable and do not need to be bailed out. Normally, a well-timed silence gets that message across effectively and expeditiously. However, in a group in which members are not yet prepared to exercise some rudimentary responsibility for their own feelings, a lengthy silence may be both premature and detrimental.

What this means to the practitioner is that the silence is a valuable tool in the group. Like all tools, it can be used effectively or ineffectively. To effect or proliferate a silence without a specific process or therapeutic goal in mind is inappropriate. In using ambiguity, leaders are advised to consider the members' sophistication, ego strength, and readiness; timing of interventions; and leaders' tolerance.

LEADER ANXIETY   Because silence in a group setting is anxiety producing, group therapists must discover their own tolerance for such anxiety and work to increase their own thresholds for silence. Lengthy silences can be very difficult for leaders to withstand and can have dramatic effects on members. Shapiro (1978) described the longest silence in his personal group leadership career:

> I was co-leading a one-day marathon group with _____ . Since most of the group members knew me already, it was agreed that my co-leader would take the lead during the early phases of the group. . . . The silence lasted for 46 minutes and 22 seconds (but who was counting?), punctuated only once by one member of the group remarking after 21 minutes, "I bought a Toyota yesterday. . . ." The laughter release was immense for most of the members and myself. (My co-leader took the opportunity to slowly swing the toothpick in the lower right corner of his mouth all the way over to the lower left.) . . . After the entire silence, one woman began to discuss a very serious problem and the group really took off from there. . . . There couldn't have been

another 20-second silence for the duration of the 15 hours. . . . It seemed almost as if nobody was going to risk another massive silence like the last one. . . . In retrospect it was one of the most powerful groups I've ever been involved in. Most members used the experience to make decisions they wanted to make, and the transfer of training was immense. . . . Sometimes I think a large part of the power of that group was the members' working on real problems out of fear of another silence occurring as painful as the first. (p. 87)

WHEN SILENCE DOESN'T EQUAL ANXIETY   Silence is not always a generator of anxiety. In almost every group, there are members who use the quiet to "center" themselves, rid themselves of daily stress and pressure, or just cherish the moment of respite from a preschooler's or boss's ostensibly endless questions or demands. These members may welcome the very silence that others find painful and difficult. Discussions that break and process the silence may help members face some of the intrinsic differences that exist in the group.

ONE RULE OF THUMB   In deciding how long to maintain a silence, leaders must first be aware of their personal level of psychological comfort with a given silence. Once they are clear that the silence is not pushing their own personal limits of tolerance, they would do well to monitor the members' nonverbal behavior. As a general rule, it is unimportant to break a silence when the first member shows anxiety by psychologically leaving the room. However, about the time the second or third member seems to be "spacing out" as a way to control his or her level of anxiety, it is wise for a leader to intervene by asking an individual who is sitting adjacent to this member to describe what he or she is feeling. In a singles group of people in their twenties and thirties, the following interchange occurred:

After discussing the "bar scene" for a lengthy time, the discussion drifted away into silence. In less than a minute, Mark had left his body in the room but not his consciousness. A few minutes later, Sallie became more physically agitated and seemed to be getting ready to shut down as well. Sallie was sitting between Jim and Louise.

> *Larry (Leader 1):*   [*noticing Sallie's agitation*] Jim, what's happening with you right now?
>
> *Jim:*   I am really feeling anxious. I don't like this quiet.
>
> *Larry:*   So this is troubling for you. How about you, Sallie?
>
> *Sallie:*   I am really anxious. I do not care for silence. It's the way my mother used to punish me. She would just ignore me. It's also what my old boyfriend did. He'd get icy cold and completely quiet and I was supposed to figure out what to do.

Sallie was brought back to the room by the leader's intervention with Jim. She was not singled out at a time when she was showing clear signs of agitation. She was very ready to talk about her own anxiety once the silence was broken. She also provided some important information about her needs and issues in this group.

It is not important that the member who is called on has a "right" answer. What might have occurred if the leader had addressed Louise instead of Jim?

Larry (Leader 1):   [*noticing Sallie's agitation*] Louise, What's happening with you right now?

Louise: I am just feeling the peace and quiet. This is the first moment I've had to meditate and focus on myself. It's great.

Larry: So I've managed to interrupt your moment of tranquility. Do others also need the time to come to quiescence? How is the silence for you, Sallie?

Sallie: I am really anxious. I hate silence. It's the way my mother used to punish me. She would just ignore me. It's also what my old boyfriend did. He'd get ice cold and completely quiet and I was supposed to figure out what to do.

Such an intervention has several advantages. It elicits information from several members (Jim, Sallie, Louise). It sets an expectation that the leader will ask members about their feelings. It also gives Sallie an opening to talk about her fears without being singled out or put on a hot seat at a time when she is showing so much anxiety nonverbally.

STAGE *12:*   *Members' First Sortie*

Whether the leader encourages a participant to speak or a member volunteers, one member will express himself or herself in an attempt to define his or her role in the group. The member can do this by

1. Asking for group help in problem solving
2. Asking for group attention
3. Trying to win the affection of the group or of a particular member
4. Meeting some perceived group expectancies
5. Obtaining leadership of the group

It is axiomatic in systems theory (e.g., Haley, 1963) that each time members of the group speak, they are simultaneously conveying information and defining or redefining the relationships between themselves and other members of the group at that moment. In a recent group, Sandra talked about her feelings and then asked Fred to describe his reaction to what she said. In so doing, she was conveying information and asking a question. *She also redefined the relationship between herself and Fred* and perhaps other members of the group. Thus, she established that she had a right to share information about herself, that she had a right to ask questions of Fred and an expectation that he respond to what she had said. Fred's response,

"I felt very sad when you were talking," gave her a content answer to her question and by its occurrence, conveyed his agreement to her assumptions about their relationship.

This concept seems quite applicable to the silence breaker in a group. Frequently the person who speaks first and thus terminates the long silence predisposes the other group members and leaders to perceive him or her in a particular way. This person may be defined as the identified patient: "Well, I've got this big problem I need help with," or nonverbally, he or she may indicate a desire for group attention by crying, flirting, fainting, getting up and moving around, and so on. Of course, verbal expressions of almost any type will also call group attention to the speaker. In addition to requesting group help in solving a problem, a member might ask the group to share in other feelings he or she may be experiencing. A group member may express comfort or discomfort with the silence and look to other members for confirmation or support:

"I really get uptight when it's so quiet."

"I wish someone would say something."

"Wow, this is the first relaxing moment I've had all day."

"Is this what's supposed to happen?"

Such interactions can help determine a member's role in the group, gain attention, meet perceived expectancies, or win affection from the group or a particular member. Indeed, a moderate amount of problem sharing at this stage may win a member the role of "star" patient and potentially exempt him or her from subsequent pressures to work in greater depth in the treatment phase of the group.

INTRODUCTION TO THE LEADERSHIP CHALLENGE   One common pattern following the silence breaking is an early form of what is commonly referred to as a *leadership challenge*. This event, which occurs almost universally in growth groups and frequently in therapy groups, often occurs at this point in the group process.

The leadership challenge is a crucial and mandatory component of group process. Until the group confronts the ability of the leader to withstand adversity and personal discomfort, members will have difficulty trusting the leaders' abilities to handle the members' serious personal dilemmas, problems, and concerns. A leader who acts defensively and ignores or attacks a member who issues a challenge is an unlikely source of support for members' most sensitive feelings.

If the challenge is to occur at this point in the group process, it is normally characterized by questions regarding the leader's competence, training, background, or methods regarding how the group may proceed:

"Exactly how many groups have you actually led?" (typically asked only of novice leaders)

"Are you a psychologist or a real doctor or what?"

"How old are you?"

> "Well, if nothing is going to happen, why don't you [*directed to the leader*] suggest a technique or exercise? If you don't know any, I could suggest a few. . . . I hate wasting time like this; why don't we try _____ ?"

Another example, spoken angrily and forcefully, might be

> "O.K., let's get this show on the road; obviously they [*addressed to leaders*] aren't going to do anything. Why don't we elect a chairman to bring up topics or something?"

In addition to delivering their challenges at high volume, some group members intersperse Anglo-Saxon terms commonly denoting sexual intercourse between or even within other words. Unless the leader is prepared to deal with this type of language and delivery, the group can become rooted at this stage for an excessive time. Leadership challenges as crucial tests are addressed later in the chapter.

If the leader does not succumb to the pressure to be the expected authority figure by instituting the requested action (exercise, explanation, etc.) and responds instead to the process extant in the group, other members may begin to respond to the silence-breaking member. An understanding can then begin to emerge that members will be responsible for their own growth and change.

A leader may at this point focus on the process of the individual member:

> So you would like me to structure this situation by suggesting topics for discussion. Is there a particular topic that you would like to discuss?

The focus may also be on the group:

> John is expressing some discomfort at the silence. What are other people feeling?

Note that it is usually preferable to ask *what* emotion is being experienced to help focus the members on their internal reactions. The use of the word *how* (are you feeling?) commonly elicits the automatic reaction, "Fine; how are you?"—much less fruitful therapeutically. Of course, the leader may decide to remain silent.

STAGE *13:*   *Opening of the Discussion*

If the leadership challenge is not instituted here, or if the members are relatively comfortable with the way the leader responds, the first member's personal disclosures will help encourage others to risk entering the group discussion.

As soon as the first member breaks the speaking barrier, other members also let their thoughts and reactions be heard. Often at this point, rather judgmental reactions are expressed, with members agreeing with the statements of the first speaker or being critical. Occasionally, criticism for breaking the silence is leveled. In other groups, the attempt to win attention is rejected or the problem that has been brought up may be viewed as inappropriate.

During all this discussion, the leader must not join in or take sides. His or her task is to use this interaction to train the group participants in beginning to explore the process of their group. Ultimately, members will be responsible for instituting discussions and examining their internal processes that govern the way they interact.

STAGE 14:   *Group Leader Focuses on Here-and-Now Process*

While the entire interchange regarding the first speaker's communication unfolds, the leader must continually focus the group's attention on the ongoing process. Instead of joining in on either side of the issue, the leader-therapist must make statements that answer the unasked question, "What's going on between us, at this time, in this room?"

A leader's interaction at this point might be like the following sample:

> What I'm aware of is that Greg was saying he was dissatisfied with what was happening and requesting that the leaders put in an exercise. Then Joan and Marie expressed their anger with him for doing that and pointed out that they didn't want to do an exercise.

Another response might be this:

> I saw Greg asking for help with his problem of making positive sounding statements and somehow getting people angry with him, and now it seems like Joan and Marie are angry with him. Seems like whatever you do on the outside to get people angry is happening right here. I wonder what's going on?

Similar leader interactions, all focusing on the *here-and-now,* continue throughout this period of the group. In essence, the group members are being trained to scrutinize their behavior *as it occurs.* Changes will be more likely once members receive feedback on the impact and consequences of this behavior from their fellow members and the leaders.

As the leaders continue to make here-and-now process comments, members begin to open up or "unfreeze" some of their less threatening but still important concerns.

THE TWO MAJOR TESTS OF LEADERSHIP

As the group begins to open up, the potential for greater depth and vulnerability increases. Before progressing to these more sensitive areas, members must develop trust for each other and especially for the leaders. One way to establish greater security is to be fully aware of the potential limits in a situation.

In every group, two limits of the group leaders' skills must be ascertained: an estimate of their strengths (how much they can handle), and an estimate of their limitations (what they cannot handle). Often the establishment of the weaknesses come first.

The First Leadership Challenge: Setting the Floor

A common challenge to a leader is the "unsolvable problem." This problem occurs in some form in every change-oriented group and in most task groups. It provides an opportunity for the group to experience the leader's work with a seemingly important yet relatively "safe" topic. After all, a leader's failure to help with a problem that is not solvable is ultimately not very threatening.

The challenge usually begins when one member begins to talk about a personal problem (frequently a marital or relationship problem) that occurs outside the group yet presumably affects his interactions in the group as well. The presentation of the problem and accompanying indecision about what to do are lengthy, time-consuming, and frequently accompanied by sadness, crying, anger, frustration, or fearfulness. Often the problem area—marriage, separation, divorce, parenting, affairs, sexual inadequacies, aggression, substance abuse—is one that affects or interests many group members. A spirited discussion ensues, with the presenter discussing the problem and expressing feelings in more and more detail.

As the discussion continues, other group members attempt to help by giving advice, recommending alternative solutions, and offering guidance, assistance, and support. Frequently members will share their own similar experiences in this area, expressing how they handled or mishandled similar situations in their own lives. This advice is freely offered and usually presented with caring, concern, and support for the individual, but it falls on seemingly deaf ears.

ALL THE SUGGESTIONS FAIL TO RESOLVE THE PROBLEM (THE CLASSIC "YES, BUT" RESPONSE)
Despite the concern, support, and caring with which the advice is offered, it is all rejected. The problem is maintained in full force in spite of a wealth of alternative suggestions. This refusal to try a resolution is reflected in several ways:

1. A failure to move on: The patient holds on to the problem and the discussion of it.

2. A lack of change in the expression of feelings: This member's affect remains the same despite the input or ostensible catharsis.

3. Active rejection of or disagreement with the advice: The member refuses to admit that the problem could have a solution.

The following vignette excerpted from a training group illustrates this process:

Marty: I wonder if it's O.K. to talk about this problem I'm having with my wife.

Leaders: [*nonverbal signal to go ahead*]

Marty: Well, I don't even know where to start—my marriage is really bad now. I don't know, it was, you know, good for a while, but now . . . it's like I don't know any more . . . seems like she's angry at me all the time and I'm angry at her all the time . . . I just dread going home even . . . I really feel guilty about that [*nonverbal signs of sadness, frustration*].

Val: How long has it been like this?

Marty: Almost two years.

Val: Have you done anything about it?

Marty: I feel like I'm at my wits' end . . . like I've tried everything . . . nothing seems to work.

Sue: You know I went through that for six years before I finally got a
divorce. Have you thought about that?

Marty: I think about it all the time, but then I think I just haven't tried
hard enough. You know, I always believed that if I really worked at it, I
could be married to anyone . . .

Mel: That sounds self-defeating to me.

Sue: Yeah, when do you know you've tried enough? I went back and
forth like that for years before I finally walked out one day—never to
return.

Marty: Well, you know, I've thought about divorce, but I've just been
brought up to think divorce is wrong . . . failure.

Flo: You know, when George and I had problems like that, we had a baby.
That really changed our lives for the better.

Mel: Whoa, that seems it'd really compound the problem if things didn't
get better.

Marty: I always wanted kids, but now I'm afraid of being even more
entrapped. Maybe I just ought to drop it; nothing seems to help.

Val: What about counseling?

Marty: She won't go. She says that since I'm a counselor professionally,
the counselor and I would just gang up on her.

Peter: What about your minister, or a friend of the family—someone she
trusts?

Marty: That's a good idea, but she's really a loner, you know; I don't think
she'd trust anyone.

Sue: It just seems like nothing will work . . . really frustrating.

Marty: Yeah, I feel like that, too, but I keep hoping and believing there
must be some way out of this mess.

Sue: Do you do anything together? Maybe if you took up a hobby or a class together . . .

Marty: You know, I thought that was it, too. We took this aerobics class together, and I really got into it, even though it was her suggestion. But then she began resenting my being better than she was and she dropped the course, so I dropped it too. I was only doing it to be with her.

[The interaction continued this way for approximately 20 minutes.]

Peter: [*after a silence*] I'm really frustrated.

Gail (Leader 1) [*addressing a member who appears bored*]: Sandy, where are you?

Sandy: Bored and frustrated.

John: Me, too; I just feel guilty saying it, but there's no way to help him.

Cliff (Leader 2): What I see happening here is Marty presenting a real problem, many people offering advice, and the advice being rejected, and several people becoming frustrated and feeling helpless.

The leaders' role in this example was to focus on group interaction and describe the group process. If we keep in mind the importance of this piece of group process, the reasons for the leaders' behavior is clear. In terms of group process, the leaders must pass a test: They must demonstrate to the group the kinds of problems they cannot fix. The problem in this group context is unsolvable and it serves the group by remaining so. If the leader gets involved in advice giving or doing therapy with the help-rejecting complainer, this stage can be maintained indefinitely.

It is important for the leader to wait until the group members become frustrated, bored, or angry before pointing out the help-rejecting nature of this interaction. Thus, the leader's job at this stage is to be patient; then, at the optimal time, he or she is to describe the process as Cliff did in the example above: presentation of the problem, several offers of advice, a rejection of the advice, a lack of resolution, an emergent group sense of frustration.

Leaders can also use this piece of group process to underscore the importance of congruence between verbal and nonverbal expression of the issue. Despite its evident seriousness and personal nature, the "unsolvable" problem is often presented in a detached, summarized, analytical fashion. In one group, a member talked about his rejection by his parents and twin sister following his public announcement that he was gay. Although his feelings about this rejection would seem noteworthy, most of his presentation involved analysis of how his family were victims of social pressures and prejudice. He said he felt that his twin's reaction was understandably defensive. He psychologized that if he were really emotionally female, then his twin must be afraid of her own masculine tendencies.

Herb: I think my sister is truly afraid of her own homosexuality.

Will: What are you afraid of?

Herb: Nothing. I've already come out. She's just headed for trouble unless she comes to grips with her inner psyche.

Martha: Maybe she doesn't have any homosexual feelings. I don't, and I don't think that makes me screwed up.

Sallie: I've never had attraction, sexually, for other women, but I sure get off on men [*directed at the male co-leader, an issue that was to become dominant a short time later*].

Herb: Well, I think if she looked deeper, she'd see that she's repressed all those feelings.

Martha: So you think I've repressed mine also. [*Herb was silent at this point, but he had an expression on his face that could have been translated, "If the shoe fits, wear it."*]

Ailene (Leader 1):   Martha, what are you feeling now?

Martha: Well, he just called me a queer.

Ailene: So, you're feeling . . .

Martha: I'm pissed at Herb. He as much as said that you're either a *homo* and know it or you're *homo* and repress it.

Roger (Leader 2):   Herb, what do you hear Martha saying?

Herb: Oh, she's just uptight.

Roger: What do you hear in her anger at you?

Herb: She's threatened and feeling scared of her inner tendencies.

Roger: What are *you* feeling?

Herb: Oh, I know how she feels. I was there once, too.

Roger: What are *you* feeling?

Herb: Oh, well, what she's rea— . . .

Roger: WHAT ARE YOU FEELING?

Herb: I don't know. I'm pissed at you for jumping me like this.

Roger: Good. I am pressuring you and I'd be angry too if I was on the receiving end. What are you feeling toward Martha?

Herb: Mad. I hate words like *homo* and *queer.*

Roger: They put you down.

Herb: Yeah.

Roger: What's happening now?

Herb: I don't know.

Roger: Focus on your body. What feelings come up?

Herb: Funny feeling in my stomach . . .

Roger: What emotion do you usually feel in your stomach?

Herb: When I'm afraid.

Roger: Afraid of?

Herb: The group won't accept me, because I'm gay.

Roger: Anyone in particular?

Herb: Joe . . . [*indicating a young male in group*]

Joe: Wow, that really scares me.

Ailene: That could mean . . .

Joe: Yeah; I really don't know how to take that.

Ailene: I can see you're shaking.

Joe: Well, I'd like to be close to Herb, but it really scares me to think of sexual . . .

Ailene: Can you tell Herb what kinds of feelings you're experiencing and what limits you have?

Joe: Yeah.

Ailene: Go ahead.

Notice how both leaders consistently focus on the here-and-now group process and on feelings. The group has come a long way—from discussing Herb's twin sister and her purported problems of repression (outside of the group) to the impact of a relationship between two males when one has described himself as a homosexual. It is too early in the group process for the group members to stay with this level of interaction for very long. However, such pieces of process occur regularly during this time period. The leaders' refocusing the problem—from speculation about someone who is outside the group to members' feelings—provides the group with valuable information about what the leaders can and cannot do.

The most important leader virtue during this time is patience. The leader can focus on the presenting individual and request feelings only after the discussion has progressed long enough for most members to have some feelings about the presenter and the problem.

Typically, this is a long, drawn-out, difficult procedure, but the leader's interventions are designed to assist members in identifying, clarifying, and understanding their emotions as primary motivators of their behavior. Leaders will ask members to describe and pay attention to their emotions as a way to keep a here-and-now focus in the group. Remember: This is not a time for treatment; the leaders' job is to train the members to be maximally available for the treatment they will receive later in the group. There is tremendous pressure for group leaders in short-term groups to try to hurry through this stage and get to the "really important" treatment phase. However, pushing the members at this point usually will have a paradoxical effect. They will work more efficiently when they are more fully trusting of the group leadership and the other members. It is best to encourage these types of tests and to work with them rather than treat them as a barrier to some subsequent work presumed to be more important. The leadership test is the primary work at this stage.

Novice leaders often ask how to distinguish between unsolvable problems and workable requests for assistance. In addition to clues in the content of the expressed concern, three parameters are common to "unsolvable" problems.

1. Normally, the problem occurs outside the group.
2. It has a long history.
3. There is some discrepancy between the intensity of the problem and the amount of emotion the presenter displays in the group.

Problems with content clues include requests for miraculous cures:

- In one group, a woman tearfully told the group that she wanted an amputated limb to be restored and healthy.

■ A man wanted the group to convince his ex-wife to come back to him after 18 years of divorce.

■ A 12-year-old wanted his deceased grandmother returned to life.

■ A college sophomore wanted better food at the dormitory.

■ A woman wanted the group to get help for her husband's alcoholism.

Discrepancies between expressed affect and content of the predicament are frequently an obvious sign of the "unsolvable":

■ In an outpatient group, a woman spoke of the recent sudden death of her husband as if she were describing his going to the corner to buy a loaf of bread.

■ In a military group, a young airman spoke unemotionally about a "Dear John" letter from his wife, although other men in the group became tearful at his description.

■ A 50-year-old administrator talked about being laid off from a job for incompetence after 27 years with the same company, yet he complained only about age discrimination.

■ A graduate student in a training group spoke with anger about her husband for not being more understanding about her infidelity.

Such detached discussions of issues that would seem traumatic are cues for the therapist to attend to group process or to focus on the missing *affective* components in the here-and-now.

The Second Leadership Challenge: Finding the Ceiling

The second challenge for leaders (although not necessarily in that order) represents the group's testing the leaders' strengths. During the leadership challenge, leaders will be pushed to set limits on members' behavior. By setting these limits, a leader provides structure and consequently reduces anxiety in the group. Until the leaders demonstrate their ability to handle a difficult challenge, the members will be less trusting and treatment will be less effective.

The leadership challenge is a most threatening time for leaders, especially those who are novices in group treatment. For this reason, many leaders attempt to avoid or deny the challenges that do occur. Such avoidance will create fertile ground for additional challenges, decrease trust in the leaders' abilities to help members, and effectively place limits on potential growth in the treatment phase of the group.

The leadership challenge may occur around the silences or at any time during the group. If it is resolved when it first appears, it may not recur. However, many leaders report that some small leadership challenge may be part of every session as a test that the group remains a safe place for members' vulnerability.

Leadership challenges that occur during this stage of the group are often quite strong, especially when they are the last step before the group moves into the treatment phase. The strength of the challenge often symbolically represents the level of members' security needs. These challenges take two forms, each requiring slightly different responses:

1. Attacks on the leader as an authority figure
2. Personal or ad hominem attacks

As a rule of thumb, leaders generally respond as authorities when they are challenged as authorities; they respond personally when the challenge is personal. The response is mitigated, of course, by their personal values, abilities, and theory.

CHALLENGES TO LEADER AS AUTHORITY FIGURE   Prior to trusting any authority figure, individuals need to be reassured that the authority will use his or her power fairly and protectively. The group members will find ways of challenging a leader to prove that the group will be a safe place. The challenges to leaders' authority can come in myriad ways.

Questions about the leaders' experience, competency, age, training, background, or methods are commonplace, as are requests for them to take an active role in setting an agenda for the meeting. By facing up to and dealing with the challenge, a leader shows that he or she can handle attacks, demonstrates that expressions of negative feelings are not necessarily wrong or inappropriate, and shows that individuals will not be rejected for expressing their anger or fears. The leader should indicate, however, that members will be asked to express their fear directly rather than through the cover of anger.

When leaders' authority is challenged, they should respond from the position of authority. They should treat the challenge as resistance. They then should interpret, reflect, and encourage the expression, examination, and exploration of the intrapsychic basis of the members' discontent and discomfort over the lack of customary leadership.

In response to a demand that the leader do something to give her direction, one member asserted, "A proper leader would have an agenda and a direction for us. How are we to possibly do it right without any plan or method?"

The leader replied, "I understand that you would like me to be more directive. What is your discomfort with the apparent lack of structure?" This response invited the member to begin exploring personal reactions and influences. The following interaction ensued.

> *Debbie:*   Dammit. I asked you for direction and you just threw it back on me. I don't know what to do. That's why I politely asked you to do your job. You are the one getting paid for this, aren't you?

> *Kate (Leader):*   I do understand that you would like me to structure this situation much more for you. Why is not knowing what's happening so much of concern?

> *Debbie:*   Yes! It is important. I paid good money for this and now I have to do all my work and all yours also.

Kate: Focus on your work. What would you like to happen for you right now?

Debbie: I don't know what I want. I just know that I'm upset.

Kate: There's good reason for that upset. I am apparently not living up to your expectations, and you are quite upset because of a lack of direction. Where else in your life do you feel this way?

Debbie: I don't feel this way anywhere else. I keep things in control.

Kate: That must take a lot of energy. So this is a unique situation for you?

Debbie: Yes!

Kate: What would happen if you experimented by seeing what Debbie is like without the structure?

Debbie: I could do that by myself.

Kate: Yes you probably could. Are you willing to try it now? Just take a moment to focus on what's inside you rather than what I am doing or not doing.

Defensive responses by the leader will normally lead to exacerbations of the test. For example, if Kate had responded to Debbie's challenge by taking it personally or responding at the same level, the challenge might have been intensified or gone underground to emerge with greater vehemence later. The next example demonstrates a defensive response.

Debbie: Dammit. I asked you for direction and you just threw it back on me. I don't know what to do. That's why I politely asked you to do your job. You are the one getting paid for this, aren't you?

Kate (Leader):   I don't particularly like your tone. If you are prone to anger, you might want to explore your need to deal with that and to project it onto authority figures.

Debbie: I just want you to do your job. I don't want to sit around and waste time.

Karl: Yeah. I agree with Debbie. Why don't you suggest some way that we can get this show on the road?

Kate: Karl. Please wait. Now Debbie, where outside do you get so angry? Who are you really angry with? If it's all authority figures, perhaps someone from your past? Your parents?

Debbie: No. It's just you. You're the "teacher" here. I thought you'd present something for us to work on. I don't have any issue with my parents.

Debbie might maintain her combative stance or she might be defeated, but the group leader has so far informed the group that there is little maneuvering room here. In a sense, the floor and ceiling are quite close together. Further tests of leadership, perhaps more vehement ones, are inevitable if the group is to move into any realistic treatment.

Another way for leaders to handle the problem is the approach favored by Bernadett-Shapiro. Her method has three components:

1. *Crystallizing the resistance.* Utilizing the catalyst[1] leadership role, the leader focuses on the member's negativity and anger and clarifies the expression of anger.

2. *Working with the anxiety.* When the initial leadership challenge occurs, the anxiety level in the group rises significantly. As the leader remains in control in the face of the anger, the anxiety in the group begins to subside. She then moves to requesting feelings and perceptions from others in the group. This normally elicits a combination of criticism and support for the leader.

3. *Working through.* The leader then "orchestrates" to assist the group members in discussing their different reactions with each other. The ability to contain these feelings and give the group an experience of safety in the face of negative emotions sets the ceiling in the group. Members now know how far they can go into exploring difficult emotional matters with this leader. They also begin to understand that they can agree to disagree without the occurrence of disasters.

Bernadett-Shapiro notes that this process may have to be repeated several times during a single session during the Transition Phase.

PERSONAL CHALLENGES TO LEADER   Sometimes the challenges are directed not toward the leader's authority as much as to the leader's person. These questions attack a leader's character more than his or her abilities as a leader. Such challenges may take many forms, but all seem to be related to some form of active transference.

■ One man in a group accused the leader of doing the group only for the money, suggesting he had no interest in the group members.

---

[1] In later chapters, five key roles of leadership are defined and explicated. In addition to serving as group *catalyst,* leaders also are *orchestrators, information disseminators, environmental manipulators,* and *participants.*

■ In groups of professionals, frequently one member believes that he would be a better leader than the person actually leading the group.

■ A woman accused a male group leader of rejecting her by the way he looked at her and accused him of refusing to acknowledge the obvious sexual connection between them.

■ In another group, the same leader was criticized for looking at a woman in the group with what one member described as "bedroom eyes."

■ In a mandatory group, leaders were verbally attacked for "forcing" inmates of an institution into the group against their will.

The leader's personal appearance or office are frequent targets.

■ A leader was chastised for being overweight and told that if he couldn't take care of his personal life, he could never be helpful to a member.

■ One female leader was asked repeatedly how old she was and then informed that she was too young to understand mature adults' problems.

■ In one group of parents, the leader was repeatedly told that having children's drawings on the wall was "unprofessional" in a setting for adults.

Leaders need to be able to respond to these challenges and confront the challenger in a beneficial way. Leaders who are too sensitive about such personal matters should take care to work them through, at least to the point that they can use the challenge therapeutically. In general, certain groups and group members seem able to ferret out a leader's personal weakness with the unerring precision of a laser beam. These include clients who are manic (bipolar disorder), have borderline personalities, or who are adolescents.

How will a leader deal with a personal challenge? The general rule of thumb is to respond personally. However, the group reins need to be temporarily handed over if the leader is to work with the challenges most effectively. *Having someone to take over temporarily when such situations arise is one of the primary advantages of having a co-leader in the group.* If there is a co-leader, as is strongly recommended in this text, a leader might indicate nonverbally that the co-leader is to take over, or he or she might make a statement to the challenger and other group members such as this:

> I want to respond to you personally, but it would be inappropriate to do so in the role of leader. Russ [*indicating the co-leader*], would you be willing to be in charge of the process while Debbie and I talk about these concerns?

The challenged leader will then deal directly with the member in question. In one group, for example, a member refused to do an exercise suggested by the leader and indicated that she was refusing because she "felt" the leader was "not a real person." After temporarily stepping into the membership role, the leader began to talk directly with that member:

Joann (Leader): What is it about me that makes me feel so unreal to you?

Arlene: Everything about you. You are just always asking questions? "How are you *feeling*? "Go with that!" "What does that remind you of?" Well what are *you* feeling?

Joann: Well, right now I'm feeling anxious in the face of your anger.

Tony (Co-leader):   Arlene, you seem surprised by Joann's answer. What's going on inside for you?

In a group of group therapists, the leader was angrily challenged by a member at the beginning of the second session:

Bill: You know, I am just sick of this shit. You don't seem to realize who is in this group, and you're jerking us around with this elementary nonsense. Either get with the program or get out, I am sick and tired of wasting my time with an amateur.

Michael (Leader) [*After glancing at the co-leader and nonverbally indicating that she should assume sole leadership for a while*]:   You really seem enraged at me. What am I doing that's bringing up such strong feelings?

Bill: Well, that's the point, you stupid asshole. You don't even know how inept you are. [*He followed this with a vituperative outburst of barely contained rage, peppered with questions about the leader's parentage and making several derogatory oedipal references in less of a literary than a street-language hyphenated format.*]

Michael [*In an angry voice*]:   You know, Bill, I am not willing to have you dump like this. If you have an issue with me, let's deal with it; if not, back off. I am really angry at what seems like an unprovoked attack on my character.

Bill: Unprovoked! You ask for it just by the way you sit there . . . so uptight and arrogant.

Peggy (Co-leader):   Bill, you seem absolutely enraged at Michael. What do you want from him at this time?

Although Bill continued his outpourings of feelings, dismissing Peggy as well, the rest of the group was able to view his behavior as unreasonable and came to the support of the leaders, confident that they were strong enough to stand up to even such an extraordinarily powerful challenge.

Much later in the group, during Phase III (the Treatment Phase), the issue of Bill's anger at Michael reemerged. This time the group was prepared for it. They had sufficient trust in the leaders and far less fear of conflict in general to be totally disconcerted by the attack. By then, the group had a history of resolving conflicts.

At that time, Bill was able to describe his attraction for Peggy and his inaccurate assumption that she and Michael were involved sexually. With the group's help, he was able to become aware of both his process of making assumptions and his self-inciting internal process as well as his primitive (and self-defeating) method of aggressive confrontation.

However, at the time of the initial challenge, neither of the co-leaders had any sense of what was going on inside Bill. They could only deal with the personal attack in a personal way. Michael, to whom the challenge was directed, responded initially by requesting that Bill focus on his anger and subsequently with a direct expression of his own anger. Peggy appropriately maintained the leadership by orchestrating the conflict.

If there is no co-leader, the leader may ask a member to play the mediating role during the conflict. Although this is not optimal, one positive side effect is to indicate to the group that they have the resources in the membership to deal with difficult and unsettling interchanges. Second, the member who is chosen normally has quite an ego-building experience.

In some groups, no member could be expected to serve as temporary co-leader. In such situations the leader must play multiple roles simultaneously: supporting the challenging member's attack, dealing with and expressing her personal feelings at the time, interpreting what is going on for the group, and monitoring the other members. Most group leaders have developed the skill to do this over time, or they focus solely on the principal goal of the leadership challenge test: giving the group members a sense of how much she can tolerate—providing a ceiling. *Remember: Leadership challenges are to be embraced rather than avoided. The successful resolution of leadership challenges allows the group to enter treatment successfully.*

Two final words on leadership challenges: Normally, the leadership is challenged in a way that is manageable. Challenges are usually by members of the same sex as the leader and at a level at which the leader is not out of her depth. The goal of the challenge is for the group to find leader strength so they can establish a safety zone. It is not about defeating the leader. In fact, despite our considerable fears, the group will not allow the leader to be overthrown. Nobody would know what to expect in such a situation. It is simply not safe for the members to allow a revolution.

STAGE 15: *Debriefing the Leadership Tests: Focus on Feelings*

After the leader has focused on the here-and-now feelings of group members and has identified the feelings of helplessness, anger, and frustration, group members begin to express a variety of emotons. They may express frustration about the situation, anxiety about talking, fear that the group really cannot help anyone, anger at the leader for not being a good therapist (as indicated by the inability to cure the problems of the help-rejecting complainer), fear at becoming a target of a member's or leader's anger, empathy with other members, boredom, pressure to bring up their own problems. This expression must be supported.

STAGE 16:   *Leader Encourages the Expression of Emotion*

No matter how negative the verbally expressed emotion may be for the leader, he or she must support its expression. Members must learn that the group is a safe place to say even difficult things. The leader's encouragement of the discussion of affect is crucial for the development of group trust (Rogers, 1969) and cohesion (Yalom, 1995)—two central components of the therapeutic outcome of the group process.

At this point the final major group norm is established: the open honest expression of feelings. This marks the end of Phase II. Members now know what it takes to be a group member. They still need to practice these skills and to try them on for comfort and suitability; but by this stage in the group process, all the information as to what's expected of members is available. The group is now prepared to proceed to the business of change.

TRANSITION TO TREATMENT

The successful resolution of the two tests of leadership ushers in the Treatment Phase of the group. At this point, four group norms are established: (1) a focus on here and now, (2) a focus on feelings, (3) an open expression of feelings (and personal thoughts), and (4) an avoidance of judgments of others in the group. These norms will occur within the range of trust determined by the leadership tests.

Some additional transition may occur, especially if the tests come early or after some particularly deep therapeutic or emotional work. Members will need to reassure themselves that the group remains a safe place. Smaller leadership challenges may occur throughout the group. Some groups seem to mark every progress in the group with an additional test of leadership. When members are particularly anxious, or when the membership includes borderline personality types or borderline defense structures, leadership challenges may come even during termination. Also, the group may stray from a process orientation from time to time when the anxiety level rises in the room. Whenever these events occur, the leader's job is to refocus the group's attention on the process, to encourage them to focus on and to express their feelings.

HOW IT'S SUPPOSED TO GO VERSUS REAL LIFE

Readers should understand that each of the stages is depicted here as if it occurs discretely in the actual group process. A text must present them this way for descriptive purposes. In the real-life group situation, however, the movement from stage to stage is less clear-cut. Often stages need to be repeated, and because a group is working on Stage 11 during a given session is no guarantee that it will begin the next session at Stage 11 or 12. Indeed, it may regress to Stage 9 or 10. Furthermore, some members may persist through subsequent stages in displaying behaviors customary at earlier stages. Similar to other changes involving people, the distinctions between stages are often less discrete in an actual group than are the broader-based phases of group process.

SUMMARY

The second phase of group process is the *transition* phase, which normally occurs during the first one-third of a time-limited group. In this phase of the group process, members learn to trust themselves, the leaders, and other members in the group. Members learn how to help one another by sharing their personal feelings and experiences with each other. Each member must preserve personal boundaries while participating in intrapsychic, interpersonal, and group-level dialogue.

The transition phase requires the leader to embrace challenge and conflict within the group actively to demonstrate safety and boundaries for treatment. Successful negotiation of the two major tests of leadership—establishing the leader's skill and competence, and recognizing that there are matters beyond the leader's abilities—results in cohesion and development of an environment that encourages members to confront intrapsychic and interpersonal change.

CHAPTER 4

GROUP PROCESS
PHASE III: TREATMENT

STAGE 17 INTERNAL FOCUS
STAGE 18 NORMS ARE SOLIDIFIED
STAGE 19 MINORITY MEMBERS IDENTIFIED;
INCLUSION REVISITED
STAGE 20 INTENSITY INCREASES
STAGE 21 LEADER EMPLOYS THERAPEUTIC
SKILLS
STAGE 22 PROBLEM-SOLVING ORIENTATION
IS PRACTICED
STAGE 23 EXPRESSION OF FEELINGS ABOUT
THE PROCESS AND THE GROUP

To be effective, group leaders must have the therapeutic abilities and timing to direct members into appropriate insights and behavior change. Leaders' functioning is crucial during the Treatment (III) and Termination (IV) phases, which will determine whether members are to derive any lasting therapeutic benefit from the experience.

PHASE III: TREATMENT

Much has been written about the "instant intimacy" of the here-and-now group. Such intimacy has certain therapeutic as well as entertainment value, but it is only the means to an end if the group is truly designed for relatively permanent behavior change. The professional leader understands that group members must be prepared to learn before they can learn. As described earlier, several hours of group time are spent preparing members for the therapy to follow. At the conclusion of the last chapter, we noted the members' readiness for the treatment available in group therapy once they have learned the group norms and have begun to operate within the purview of these norms. In short, once the group members are comfortable within the tested parameters of a group and are willing to be open to change in the here-and-now, they are prepared to learn how to make desired adjustments in their lives at home.

Learning in group therapy occurs just as it does in all other settings. The group leader is responsible for providing an environment in which members may safely experiment with new behavior and learn by trial and error, receiving immediate feedback and reinforcement for desired behaviors. Members must be allowed opportunities to gain insight and understanding and to experience vicarious learning through the behavior of others by identification and imitation. They must be able to explore their own expectancies and to test these under conditions in which they are assured of honest feedback.

The Paradoxical Environment: Higher Intensity, Lower Danger

A curious aspect of the group environment is that it is both safer than other contexts and simultaneously more anxiety provoking. In a group that is functioning well, the emotional intensity is often artificially high. Much of this intensity—and also much of the group members' learning—is a result of members' experimentation with new behaviors and thoughts in a situation that limits the consequences of such trial and error learning. Group members may experiment with expressing their fears without concern for the repercussions of such admissions. They may learn from other members' feedback how much of this fear they can handle and how it can be expressed effectively.

This is quite different from other situations. In a work environment, for instance, direct expressions of any emotion, particularly fear, sadness, or anger, may be unacceptable. The ramifications of such emotional outbursts could be severe. However, by becoming *aware* of the fear through the group and receiving feedback from other members, an individual might find an effective way to express his or her experienced affect in other settings.

The group is uniquely designed to allow people to have emotional experiences and to learn *during* the experience. The intensity created in group sessions actually creates opportunities for members to wrestle with difficult issues and interactions and to observe themselves while they are reacting.

In the description of the group process that follows, notice how group members participate in each others' problem solving and in giving and receiving reinforcement. Under these circumstances, learning is enhanced both in amount and in speed of acquisition. The group's reputation as a "psychological pressure cooker"—a place where behavior change can occur more rapidly than in normal social situations, with less loss of energy—is well earned.

Solvable Problems

Remember Marty, the "Help Rejecting Complainer" who had an unsolvable problem with his wife in Phase II? Let's look at how Marty might deal with the same issue during the Treatment Phase of the group.

Marty: I wonder if it'd be O.K. to talk about this problem I'm having with my wife.

Leaders: [*Nonverbal signal to go ahead.*]

Marty: Well, I feel really stuck. We are not getting along at all, and I am just not sure what I am doing to keep the conflict going. I'm afraid that I started a fight last weekend for no good reason. It makes me worry a lot.

Gail (Co-Leader):   What would lead you to do that?

Marty: This feels embarrassing, but I think it was a time when we could have been close, and I got anxious.

Val: That's really sad.

Marty: Yeah, it's almost like I don't want it to work, but I really think I do.

Val: Sometimes I think my husband picks fights with me when he's afraid of something or needs to be more in control.

Sue: I do that.

Marty: You pick fights?

Sue: Sometimes, I know I'm being unreasonable, but I just press matters until it ends in a fight. I have an excuse though. I always blame it on PMS. [*smiling.*]

Cliff (Co-Leader) [*smiling*]:   I guess that won't work for you, Marty. Why do you think you picked this particular fight? What was going on?

Marty: Well, it was Saturday night and we were free. The kids were off with my in-laws and we had planned a nice dinner. Then her sister called just as I was finishing the special meal I was preparing and Linda just talked to her for a long time. I just got more and more burned. I thought the meal would dry out and I just got more pissed off by the minute. When she got off the phone, I started in with provocative comments about her sister. I just kept ragging on her until she lost it. Blew the entire night.

Cliff: So what made you wonder about your motives?

Marty: Well, Linda didn't know the meal was done and *I didn't tell her.* I just assumed she should know. I also know she is very sensitive about her family and as much as she rags on them, I know I shouldn't.

Cliff: So what advantage did the fight have for you? It sounds like the consequence of your actions was distance instead of closeness. Could that have been an unconscious goal?

Marty: You know, I hate when you do that [*smiling and looking down*]. That's what bugs me! This is very embarrassing. I even knew when I did it that I could ruin the evening. I think I was so afraid that I'd get my hopes up for a great romantic evening and sexual fulfillment for a change and if it didn't happen I'd feel rejected. So, I just made sure it wouldn't happen.

Cliff: It was worse to take the risk of rejection than to arrange for the rejection under your own control.

Marty: That sounds dumb, but true.

Mel: If I were Linda, I'd be really frustrated.

Marty: She is. The thing is that she is really trying now. She has her stuff too and she's not that easy to live with at times, but just because she has an open gas tank doesn't mean I have to light matches and drop them around.

Gail: Sue, you're having a strong reaction right now.

Sue: Well, it's two things. I do the same thing to my boyfriend. I pick fights to test his loyalty and how much crap he'll put up with to make him prove he loves me.

Gail: . . . and the second?

Sue: I was wondering if Marty had done that to me at the beginning of this session.

Gail: Do you want to ask him?

Sue: Did you pick a fight with me about the directions because you wanted to push me away? I felt really pushed away.

Marty: I did. I find you very attractive and I need to focus on my marriage now, so I tried to make you less appealing by making you wrong.

The leaders were then able to get Sue and Marty to work on the interaction in the group. Once they learned how to resolve such issues in other ways, they were asked to refocus on the relationships at home.

This interaction is quite different in tone, trust, and openness from the earlier one. What are the differences and what makes it possible? For one thing, the group is not discussing Marty's wife's problems. She is not in the group. The therapy will be with Marty and his personal fears and ambivalence that interfere with intimacy in his relationships. Marty is focusing internally on his behaviors and feelings that he may change. Second, members of the group are talking about their own similarities and reactions rather than trying to provide an obvious solution to a purported problem. They are joining with him rather than directing him. Third, everyone is talking about his or her own personal feelings. Fourth, the leaders' interactions are invitations for Marty and others to explore at increasingly deeper levels. Finally, the issue is brought into the group by focusing on a here-and-now interaction between Marty and Sue: an interaction that may be understood and resolved in the present. This is the ground for quick, true, and insightful problem solving.

STAGE 17:   *Internal Focus*

During the Treatment phase, members take a more internal focus. Instead of trying to blame others for their current difficulties, they focus more directly on potential personal changes. Marty knows that his wife has some part in the marital problem, but here he is attending to the things over which he has some control—his own contribution.

Although this exploration is potentially embarrassing, he has more faith in his abilities to make changes because he has developed trust in the group. He shares "closet skeletons" with his fellow members and is willing to discuss matters that he will not talk about otherwise. More than anything else, members can begin to interact differently in this phase because they trust the leaders. The leaders have proven their abilities, they have passed the tests of leadership; and the range of issues that are appropriate for the group to deal with have been established.

STAGE 18:   *Norms Are Solidified*

Throughout the Treatment phase of the group, members become involved in the expression and interchange of feelings about their concerns. They use the theoretical language system of the leaders more consistently and focus on the here-and-now process of the group. They expose more of their deeper feelings and experiment with them—with one another and with the leaders. Increasingly, members abide by the group rules, eventually incorporating items into a common language and becoming, for the most part, unaware of the uniqueness of these forms of communication. An example of this type of communication is the following:

Janice: Bill, I sense that something is bothering you.

Bill: What makes you say that?

Janice: Well, I guess I'm picking up on your nonverbals.

Andy: Yeah, I've noticed you kind of moving around a lot and looking uncomfortable, especially when Sally was talking.

Linda (Leader 1):   What are you experiencing, Bill?

Bill: Well, it's like everyone is ganging up on me and trying to get me on the hot seat.

Linda: And you're feeling . . . ?

Bill: I'm not ready to be on the spot.

Janice: You are uncomfortable about something, but you want to bring it up at your own speed.

Bill: Yeah; is that O.K.? [*Directed to male co-leader who has not yet spoken.*]

Kevin (Leader 2):   It's O.K. with me for you to wait, but I do hope you'll feel free to share it when it's important to you.

STAGE *19: Minority Members Identified; Inclusion Revisited*

As the members grow closer, some clearly have not participated verbally in the group. They are identified by the other members or the leader and requested to take a more active role.

Most leaders allow the group members to recognize these minority members and invite their participation before the leader offers them an opportunity to become verbally involved in the group. The reasoning is that there is generally less threat in an invitation from fellow members than in a request from the leader. These heretofore nonparticipatory members are assumed to be remaining on the fringe of the group because of their fears of greater involvement. A request for participation by the leader could aggravate the fear and make it more difficult for members to enter. An important exception to this suggestion is related to the time left for the group. If the remaining time is short, the leader must recognize these less verbal members and request their thoughts and feelings.

No matter who brings up the issue of less participation, a discussion about inclusion ensues. The majority group members discuss and analyze the nonpartici-pation of these minority members and the effects of this behavior on them. A typi-cal discussion follows:

Fred: Hey, you know Rita, Gayle, and Herb haven't said anything in weeks. I wonder if you're bored or something.

Herb: I'm not bored.

Sheila: I think it's cultural, you know—I mean Rita and Gayle are Asian and I think they tend to be more reserved [*said smilingly and caringly at Rita and Gayle, who are sitting together*].

Gayle: I think that's true; nobody in my family talks much. But Rita and I talk outside. I just don't have anything to say.

Fred: Well, I think it's unfair; I unloaded all my vulnerability and you know me, but I just don't know you at all.

Kim (Leader 1):   Sounds like it's important for *you* to have them talk more.

Fred: Yeah, right. I've talked about some pretty deep stuff and I don't know if I can trust them.

M. J. (Leader 2):   Tell them!

Fred: I don't trust any of you [*looking directly at Herb*].

Kim   What would you like from Herb?

Fred: I want you [*to Herb*] to stop judging me and "dissing" me in your mind.

Herb: I don't know what "dissing" means, but I'm not judging you.

Sandra: Well, I feel judged too; it's like I say something and you just look at me and I think it's disapproval.

M. J.:   Herb, what are you feeling now?

This dialogue may continue for some time, but it's course will be altered slightly. Not only do Fred and Sandra's feelings deserve attention, but the feelings of Herb, Gayle, and Rita also need consideration. Hence, the group leaders must deal with several issues:

1. Inclusion of the three members
2. The three members' fears of participation
3. Need for approval expressed by at least two of the majority, participating members
4. Acceptance of alternative styles of communication
5. Feelings of anger from Gayle and Rita at having been lumped into an "Asians don't talk much" category instead of having their silent behavior accepted
6. Leaders' own feelings of inadequacy and desire for every member to have a positive experience in the group

During this stage, an invitation is extended to the minority members to enter or choose to participate minimally.

With guidance by the group leaders, the minority members will enter the group as verbal participants; negotiate with the group for their inclusion, albeit as quiet members; attack the other members; withdraw from the group altogether; or remain nonverbal.

A member may enter the group verbally in a variety of ways. In one example, a woman member was asked why she was so quiet. She replied, "Nobody asked me anything." Another member asked her, "Is there anything you'd like to share with us?" She replied (Example 1):

> Well, yes, I have so much to share. I don't know where to start. . . . I guess the biggest thing is that I'm deathly afraid this group will end. It's the most important thing in my life. You're the only people I've allowed myself to care for since my husband died nine months ago.

At this point her eyes became moist and she found it difficult to continue talking. With group support, she was at center stage in the group for almost two hours.

An example of negotiation occurred in the same group. Almost as soon as the previous bit of process was terminated, another "quiet" member said (Example 2):

> I also feel the group is important, but I feel very uncomfortable sharing things when they're happening. I've always been introspective. I'm not bored at all. I feel like I've been emotionally involved each minute . . . like when Joe was talking about the operation and losing his arm, I just put myself in his place and imagined the pain and fear and felt incomplete and ugly, and when Marie talked about the mess with her husband, I just knew I had to go home and talk to my husband. We had a good talk, but I don't know what's gonna happen to us. Oh, when Joanie talked about having an affair, I felt all the excitement and all the guilt. It's just hard for me to open up, but I really feel a part of this group.

Both these members found easy acceptance and felt more included.

If minority members choose to attack, several avenues are open: defensive protestations of how many things they did say; distraction techniques, such as "Well, I'd *really* like to know what's going on with Pete"; or confrontation. One extraordinary event occurred in a group of mental health professionals. A person who had a master's degree and ten years' experience with counseling and casework responded to a request for his participation like this (Example 3):

> Damn right, I haven't said anything. I thought this was a high-level group and you people have all been acting like freaks or patients. Jesus, you all have problems and share things like feelings that are best kept to oneself. You're a bunch of sickies or fugitives from the sixties. I don't want to associate with you and surely wouldn't tell you a thing about me. I mean, how could you help me? I'm much healthier than all of you.

Then addressing one of the leaders, he continued:

> I'm really surprised at you for letting this go on. A competent leader wouldn't allow a member to be attacked like I have been. I'd leave now if I didn't have to show on my time sheet that I'd been here.

Ultimately this individual withdrew from the group and from the mental health field. The group experience allowed him to feel so different from other therapists that he was able to get into a different and more appropriate profession.

Members may also simply state their belief that the request for their verbal participation is an excessive demand and indicate that they wish to withdraw; some may do so. Other members may not respond verbally to the request and may simply remain silent.

If the minority group members become verbal and do join in, as in the first example above, they are invariably accepted into full membership and receive a great deal of support from the other members. If, however, they reject the group and want to withdraw, the group may allow them to do so, or request that they stay. If the member attacks (Example 3), the group may choose to fight, allow the person entry into the group, or ostracize the attacker, disallowing his inclusion. If the member negotiates (Example 2), the group will negotiate also. Group members may allow the member to stay quiet but ask him to try to express more for the sake of other members, or make a deal that he need not talk unless asked a specific question, in which case he will try to respond verbally. When the nonverbal member is *emotionally* engaged in the group, as in Example 2, the likelihood is high that he or she will be given total acceptance. However, if the nonverbal negotiating member is emotionally as well as verbally out of touch with the other group members, he or she may well be rejected.

No matter what decisions the group makes, the leaders must respond to the range of emotions released at this time. Such feelings as insecurity, belonging, loneliness, isolation, communion, paranoia, fear, and anger all emerge. Members must recognize and work on these feelings until they reach some understanding and resolution. Revisiting this inclusion issue is the last major stumbling block to the therapeutic group process. Once these conflicts are resolved, the group can turn its attention freely to any personal or nonpersonal problem and work toward solutions.

THERAPEUTIC INTERVENTION
Levels of Intervention

During the Treatment phase of the group, the leaders encourage the continuation and deepening of the developing group norms. As group members become increasingly comfortable with the care from the group environment and learn the most effective ways to tap into those resources, the therapy expands and deepens. A major advantage of group treatment is that it allows for flexibility and multimodal pathways to the members' goals.

Normally throughout this period, the leaders intervene at three different levels of interaction: intrapsychic, dyadic/interpersonal, and group levels.

THE INTRAPSYCHIC LEVEL   At the intrapsychic level, the leader encourages members to focus more internally, to examine their unconscious motivation, personal patterns, emotions, and historical reactions. For example, the leader might say, "John, your anger right now seems familiar. What do you sense is the basis of that?" or "Where do you have this reaction outside of group?" The intrapsychic level will resemble individual treatment with an audience. Sometimes the fact that this exploration is public makes it more potent.

THE DYADIC/INTERPERSONAL LEVEL   At the dyadic/interpersonal level, the leader highlights interactions and interrelationships between members. This focus helps members focus on their impact on others and observe their reactions to other members in the group. The leader might intervene by highlighting an interaction between two members: "John, would you tell Lisa what she is doing right now that is being helpful to you?" or "Bill, it probably sounds as though Mary is reading your mail out loud." Often, this type of interaction resembles some of the work one would see in couples treatment or mediation.

THE GROUP LEVEL   At the group level, the leader asks questions of or makes suggestions to the group membership as a whole. She may, for example, check the general group mood or level of anxiety. For example, "John is saying that he's feeling upset and angry at the way the group is progressing. Where are the rest of you on that?" or "Perhaps we could take a few moments and reflect on the group's coming to an end in only three weeks."

Each level has obvious advantages and disadvantages. The intrapsychic offers the greatest depth of emotional processing and repair. However, it is limited by the relevance of one person's work to others in the group. Too much intrapsychic work in a group can lead to an atmosphere where members "take a ticket and wait for my turn."

Group level work offers the greatest amount of simultaneous group work: every member works at the same level. It is limited because at the group level, depth is circumscribed by the member who is working at the least depth. Uncovering of unconscious material is minimal.

The dyadic level allows for some members to work together at the same level, broadening the deeper work to more members, but the leader must keep the members connected, and the depth and the generalization of such interactions are both moderate.

In a maximally effective group, leaders will employ all these levels of treatment. Their choices will be determined by the existing process, the group goals, and the leaders' theoretical orientations. For example, when one member begins to outpace the group depth, it is usually helpful to limit this member's sense of isolation by encouraging the other group members to try similar, personally appropriate explorations. If two members share certain concerns, it is usually of great value to have them explore together. In psychoeducational groups, personal gains are often displayed as examples of success to encourage other members who are still struggling.

Multiple Roles of Leadership

In addition to the levels of intervention, there are different roles that leaders play to enhance group development and effectiveness in the therapy. While members are learning and using the group norms, the leader will be a resource for information dissemination; at the same time she must act as a catalyst, cajoling and igniting expressions of feelings. She must also be a major source of reinforcement and support for members as they express their here-and-now feelings. To some extent, the leader serves as a model of appropriate behaviors.

It is also the leader's job to orchestrate the group. In this role, the leader encourages and controls the relative give and take among members, attempting to bring the needs of one member into coordination with the resources of other members. The multiple roles of leadership are extensively examined in Chapter 6.

STAGE *20:   Intensity Increases*

As the group becomes more comfortable using the specialized language and topics of group discussion, its members expose more and more of the normally hidden parts of their personalities and their more important personal concerns. In return, they receive acceptance, reactions, feedback, and caring from the leader and fellow members. In this way, growing group trust and cohesion empowers members to expose progressively deeper components of themselves. In groups where the goal is rapid behavior change and symptom amelioration, the intensity appears as members experiment with alternative behaviors and reactions, with group support.

As the depth of the discussion increases, there is a contiguous increase in the frequency and intensity of expressed emotion. Members begin describing a multitude of life events and their reactions to them. Often such descriptions are heavily laden with affect. With the encouragement of the leader, and to some extent, the other members, individuals are urged to describe emotionally charged events in detail and to share their present feelings regarding these events. As members explore these feelings, the intensity of expression increases, and frequently their behavior begins to demonstrate these high levels of arousal. Anger is expressed in a loud voice or yelling, hurt is accompanied with signs of sadness such as tears, and fear can be seen in trembling lips, shaking, and "frightened" glances.

For the most part, the leader and other group members will support the expressors in displaying their affect in this way. Their support naturally engenders further similar expressions. During these emotional manifestations, the leader must employ a multitude of therapeutic skills.

Note that as levels of emotional expression intensify, other group members often become frightened. It is imperative that the group leader support these members and give them permission to express their own fear; at the same time, the leader supports the continuing display of high levels of affect by those members engaged in this action. Each group has limits for allowable levels of intensity. The group leader must be aware of these limits and keep the level of arousal within them. The leader wants enough anxiety for optimal learning, but not so much as to cause disruption of such learning. Thus, in some groups, dramatic displays of high levels of affect are acceptable whereas in other groups, a more quiet, subdued acknowledgment of shared feelings is appropriate to foster the same amounts of learning.

So far, the discussion has concerned the typical group, where levels of affect must be increased. In certain treatment groups, however, the group leader must operate in diametrically opposite ways. In groups of "acting-out" patients, teenagers adjudged delinquent, or inmates in prisons, learning frequently can occur only if the level of affect is substantially decreased. In a group of violent prison inmates, the leader customarily spends several sessions teaching group members how to respond at lower levels of aggression. In one such group (Shapiro, 1978), each time the intensity of emotional expression began to increase, a mediating response was interposed. Members were encouraged and trained to discriminate between several levels of anger and to respond to them differently. Most important, they were instructed to attend to the consequences of their actions before expressing these feelings physically, as opposed to their prior customary mode of behaving spontaneously and suffering subsequent reactions. In this group of inmates, the level of affect that was displayed was controlled, just as it is in most groups. The major difference was that encouragement was given for lower levels of expression.

The important point is for the group leader to operate within meaningful levels of arousal. Levels of intensity that allow members to be uncomfortable with their own current functioning and open to learning new behaviors must be determined by the psychological characteristics of the membership as well as the leader's style and abilities. Only within these limits can successful treatment occur.

STAGE 21: *Leader Employs Therapeutic Skills*

Each accomplished group therapist has a variety of skills and techniques designed to assist group members in changing their behaviors and attitudes. Whatever their theoretical background, psychotherapists have two aligned goals: insight and behavior change (in the order accommodated by their theories). Most therapeutic endeavors involve (1) discussion of problems and feelings, (2) reconstruction of the problems in some viable theoretical framework, (3) exploration of possible solutions, (4) attempts at new solutions or conflict resolution, (5) feedback on attempts, (6) individual reactions, (7) refinement, and (8) adjustments to back-home solutions. The therapists' tools in accomplishing these are predominantly verbal. Therapists listen, summarize, analyze, provide feedback, make commitments and contracts, offer suggestions, and provide support.

During this stage of the group, many individual therapy skills are utilized. Role playing, role reversals, psychodrama, focusing, sensory awareness exercises, systematic desensitization, guided fantasy, and myriad related techniques may be employed, depending on the individual members' receptivity and the therapist's armamentarium of interventions. Individual, depth psychotherapy techniques are also employed, suggestions are made, information or analysis is provided, hypnosis or other one-to-one work is done in front of the group, and so on.

In all these therapeutic endeavors, perhaps the most important element is *timing*. As with every professional skill, sequence and timing play a major role. Many of us have watched a baseball player with a "picture-book" swing: When he swings a bat, the motion looks ideal. However, if he cannot apply this ideal swing at the precise moment that the ball crosses the plate, he is destined to a minor league career. Similar concerns for timing must be observed by therapists; the best-planned, most elaborate intervention can be valueless unless the members are ready to receive it.

One of the most common mistakes made by novice therapists is to verbalize an analysis or understanding of the group process prematurely. Group leaders are trained in theory and are focusing on group process, but most of the members are not; therefore, the leaders are likely to comprehend process much earlier than the members. If the leaders go ahead and blurt out what they see, members will honestly not understand what the therapists are addressing and will reject it, or they will simply appear not to have heard it at all. The therapist must delay any interpretation until the group is emotionally and cognitively prepared to hear it. Those seemingly "divinely inspired" (off the wall) dramatic interpretations that seem to work so well in movies about therapy are much less likely to be effective in a real-life group.

The multiple roles and skills of group leadership and a model of requisite training for group leaders are discussed in detail in Chapters 6 and 7.

Whose Theory is #1?

Virtually every major counseling and therapy theory has been used in and adapted to groups. Each has been successful with certain client populations. Two factors are germane in determining the success of any singular therapeutic approach:

1. It must be appropriate for the group leader. Her theory must be consistent with her basic values and way of being in the world.

2. There must be a close match between the leaders' theory and the clients' "theory."[1]

STAGE 22: Problem-Solving Orientation Is Practiced

Whatever the theoretical orientation of the leader, the problem-solving stage is the prime time for members to work fruitfully on their concerns. They have resolved the issues of inclusion. They know how to belong and to whom the group belongs. They have become accustomed to each other's personal styles and the differences in the group as well as the commonalities. They have had to struggle together and face a great deal of adversity. As a result of this common struggle, they have become very close. They have shared more intimate parts of themselves than they normally do and hence have a deep sense of trust in the other members.

---

[1] Describing clients' theories is unusual, but acknowledging their existence is a crucial piece of understanding that is neglected by most writers in the psychological literature. Clients, like therapists, seem to have a definite point of view about what makes for change and how they will personally change. Clients who prefer to change behavior before analyzing it thoroughly are much more likely to get help in behavioral modes; those who believe in understanding before acting will respond far better to more analytic approaches. Creating a good match and somewhat coordinated values between therapists and patients maximizes the impact of the therapy.

Within this context, problem solving in both intrapsychic and interpersonal realms can be accomplished effectively. At this time, real, present, meaningful concerns are shared and dealt with by the group. Because the level of interpersonal trust is so high, members do not reject one another's help, as they might have done earlier in the group; rather, they seek it actively. Members frequently attempt to solve problems together and confront each other honestly and with caring. Interpersonal conflicts between members of the group are discussed with greater understanding of each person's position and concerns. Suggestions for change are encouraged and attempted with far less defensiveness than in other situations.

In the course of Stages 21 and 22, most members participate verbally in the group activity. These members will ask for and offer help and assistance. They will form close emotional ties with the other members and develop the levels of trust and cohesion that lead to a real sense of intimacy. Such intimacy enhances subsequent behavior change.

During this period, the group is truly a therapeutic milieu. If the leader has successfully negotiated the earlier tasks and stages, members are prepared to promote each others' growth. The group functions as a whole to help each member. One member may be confrontive, another supportive; yet another may offer an alternative frame of reference or share a similar experience. In this manner, group members move comfortably between helper and client roles, becoming therapeutic for one another. The leader orchestrates this process and offers occasional interpretations and guidance.

In short, this is the stage of the group that members hoped for when they entered. This is also the stage at which the leaders (in growth-type groups only) may be participants to some extent and share some of their own conflicts with less concern for their leader role. Indeed, at this point in an effective encounter (growth) group, members can comfortably contribute to the growth of the leaders. This is also the stage of therapeutic group process that is so rudely cut off by termination.

A Note About Stages 21 and 22

To discuss Stages 21 and 22 as we have the other stages may be somewhat misleading. Although they represent only two points in the entire group process, they typically last longer than all the others. In an effective long-term group, fully 40% of the entire group time will be consumed during this part of the therapeutic phase.

In shorter-term groups and managed care mandated brief groups, the work that takes place in these two stages is particularly significant. These groups are "results oriented" and centered on crisis solutions, focused behavior change, and symptom amelioration. In such a group, approximately 20% to 30% of the total time may be dedicated to these two stages. Many leaders, in an ill-advised attempt to maximize gains in a short-term group, will rush to get to these stages. Unfortunately, these stages are effective *only when the prior stages have been completed successfully.* Without surmounting the challenges of the prior stages, particularly the tests of leadership in the Transition phase, the members will not be as successful in these true problem-solving stages.

In short, there is a natural developmental process that must unfold. Without this childhood and adolescence of the group, there will not be a successful group adulthood.

STAGE 23:   *Expression of Feelings About the Process and the Group*

In the most effective groups, members actually do more than learn transferable skills. They also experience some "real-time" learning as well. In these most successful groups, the members discuss their emotions, experiences, and perceptions as they are occurring in the groups. Thus, Tim is able to learn about himself as he is in the group as well as being able to reflect on the group process after he takes his group experience home. This is an exceptionally powerful form of learning.

Tim: . . . so it just keeps on happening. As soon as I get really close to a woman and let my real self out, she finds another way of rejecting me.

Danny: Yeah. It's like they tell you they want your true feelings, and then when you give them the real feelings, they think you're a baby whose asking for a mother.

Elysa (Leader):   So the two of you can share this frustration with women.

Tim: I wish I could find just one woman who didn't play games all the time.

Elysa: There are women in here. Do you feel them playing games?

Tim: Well, in here it's different. We're all here as people to help one another. It's different from dating.

Karen: I'm not sure it's that different, Tim. I know I play some dating games, because I need to make the situation safer, but I am also reticent to tell you how I feel about you in here. I just stay quiet instead.

Elysa: Are you offering that feedback now?

Karen: If Tim wants it, I suppose I'd be willing.

Elysa: Tim?

Tim: O.K.

Karen: This may be unfair to you, but when you opened up before, you seemed so intense. It's like more than I can handle at one time. I'd like to get to know you a piece at a time, but not all at once.

Elysa: So you want Tim to share his feelings, but when he does, he's too intense? Or is it that you only want certain feelings?

Tim: It's because I get nervous. When I start feeling vulnerable, I want to back off and shut up, but I also want her to like me. So I plunge ahead, against my own best judgment. And once I get going I can't seem to shut myself off. I keep waiting for some kind of reaction and the woman just shrinks back and then withdraws completely.

Elysa: Would you be willing to tell Karen what you were feeling toward her right now?

Tim [hesitantly]:   I'm threatened by your rejection and I don't know how to get out of it. I know you haven't actually rejected me yet, but I fear it's coming. . . . To be completely truthful, I find you attractive, and that's why the rejection would be worse.

Karen [hesitantly]:   I find you attractive also, and I'm afraid of your rejecting me or your overrunning me.

Elysa: How could he "overrun" you in here?

Karen: By not giving me time to go at my speed. He seems to be either "on" or "off" full power. I am not that way. I need to go slow and in moderation.

Elysa: Tim, what do you think of that feedback?

Tim: Karen, that is really helpful. I know I do that out of group as well. I would like to go at a speed with you that is mutually satisfactory. Would you be willing to let me know if I start to go too fast? I will also try to watch it, but the more feedback in here the better. *[turning to Elysa]* I am really feeling anxious now.

Elysa then turned from the dyadic to an intrapsychic mode to help him explore the anxiety in greater depth.

During this time, the work that Tim and Karen (and other group members, vicariously) are doing with each other is on the "front lines." Any changes in Tim's feelings and behavior here are assimilated and tested in the present. The learning is quite intense and often long standing. This is the most unusual opportunity afforded by group counseling or therapy: to be able to try out novel behaviors, test limits, and get feedback in real time. The group serves as a "cultural island"—a special milieu in which each of these participants has a right to expect feedback from several individuals and an opportunity to experiment without the repercussions likely in normal environments.

This stage and these phenomena are the goal of most group leaders although a group does not have to reach this level of functioning to be successful. However, for those that do, the rewards are magnified. Even so, when the group does reach this stage, it probably will not sustain this level of interaction for long. For one thing, the anxiety that accompanies such authentic communication will grow and the group will regress to earlier stages in reaction. In addition, this stage is always truncated by termination.

SUMMARY

The Treatment phase, which occurs approximately at the halfway point in a time-limited group, should perhaps be thought of as the phase of concentrated learning. Four group norms are established during the Treatment phase: (1) a focus on here-and-now, (2) a focus on feelings, (3) an open expression of feelings and thoughts, and (4) an avoidance of judging others in the group. As the group moves to deeper levels of sharing, minority members—those who have not participated as much as other members—are identified. The decision and/or ability of these members to participate both verbally and nonverbally with feelings and cognitions often determines the level of intimacy the group is able to attain. Having learned in earlier stages the importance of sharing their own experience and feelings, members of the group serve as psychological resources for each other during this period.

During the Treatment phase, the therapist is primarily a catalyst of intrapsychic learning and an orchestrator of interpersonal learning. Theoretically informed understanding and explanation of intrapsychic, interpersonal, and group-level process is the backdrop for effectively timed interventions by the leader. In the optimally led group, members are able to learn from their own exploration and experimentation, from the experiences and perspective of other members, and from the theoretical understanding and explanation of the leader.

CHAPTER 5

GROUP PROCESS
PHASE *IV:* TERMINATION

STAGE 24   LEADER ANNOUNCES IMMINENT
            END OF GROUP TIME
STAGE 25   INVITATION TO WORK
STAGE 26   A TRUST BOOST
STAGE 27   TRANSFER OF TRAINING
STAGE 28(A) GOOD AND WELFARE
STAGE 28(B) CLOSING CEREMONIES
STAGE 29   LEADER'S CLOSING
STAGE 30   ALOHA

PREPARATION FOR TERMINATION

Termination as an Unnatural Occurrence

Prior to Phase IV, entry into each succeeding stage was prompted by completion of its predecessor. The stages of termination are determined by a different criterion. The length of the group was set before the group ever began, and the group must end at the appointed time. Very often, this timing seems intrusive, inconvenient, and clearly insensitive to the developmental stages of group process.

Termination of a group is not simply an acknowledgment that the allotted time has ended. This phase of the group is as important for group success as screening, transition, or treatment. Yet, as Gazda (1989) writes, "All too often group leaders neglect this phase of group work and termination of the group is abrupt and without much processing of termination issues" (p. 307). Toseland and Rivas (1984) note a variety of tasks associated with termination including maintaining and generalizing change effects, promoting individual functioning of members, helping members with their feelings about ending the group (and other life endings), future planning, making referrals, and evaluation. Jacobs, Harvill, and Masson (1994) include reviewing and summarizing, assessing members' growth, finishing business, implementing change, providing feedback, handling goodbyes, and planning for continuing problem resolution.

Naturally, much of this work occurs throughout the group sessions; however, termination is the time that members most poignantly confront their feelings about loss, ending of relationships, and future planning. Also during termination, the crucial process of *transfer of training* must become paramount.

Transfer of Training

Of all the skills group leaders must possess, none are more important than those that assist members to transfer the group learning to their back-home situations. Meaningful evaluation of group outcome must be based on the clients' out-of-group lives. Any group which eschews the significance of the links between in-group and out-of-group experiences will be little more than a pastime. Training excellent members, whose greatest successes are limited to the group setting, is simply not sufficient.

These situations are obviously less problematic in natural groups than in formed groups. In family counseling, couples groups, and groups formed of members from some existing work or community organization, the back-home environment is, to some extent, in the treatment group. Transfer of training occurs during group sessions and between sessions. The group goes home as a unit and continues the work that occurred in session. However, even in these natural groups, termination is a significant event and the leader must focus on skills and cognitions from the group sessions that will have an enduring impact.

Some authors recommend a "plan of action" as a part of termination (see Vander Kolk, 1985). Corey (1990) recommends a more cognitive behavioral orientation to this period, focusing on behaviors, goals, and methods of evaluation. Kottler (1982) underscores the significance of effective transfer of training to decrease dependency on the group.

Obstacles to Effective Termination

Based on years of clinical observation, we believe that termination is unquestionably the part of group therapy that leaders do most poorly. There are several obvious reasons for this:

1. The leaders' personal resistance to terminating
2. The leaders' own needs for reassurance
3. A lack of training in closing

PERSONAL RESISTANCE   "Hello" usually indicates the beginning of a relationship and of untapped potential. "Goodbye" is the end. In every goodbye there is the symbol of the inevitable final parting. No wonder many of us have developed far better social skills for greeting than departing.[1] Although the ultimate role of all counselors and therapists is obsolescence, we share the members' difficulty in terminating relationships that have been emotionally intense and meaningful.

In a termination of a group, the leaders will often experience a sense of loss and personal sadness. Sometimes they are struck with a sense of personal loneliness after a group ends. As one group therapist remarked,

> I was looking forward to this group ending. It was a chance to have Wednesday evenings free again for a while . . . a chance to care better for myself and take care of things that were hanging [yet] I felt my impending sense of loss the last three weeks and I found myself wanting more rather than less contact with a few members. Then the last night after they left and I was cleaning up the room, straightening the chairs. I heard them laughing outside the room as they walked together to the parking lot. I confess, I peeked out the window and saw them hugging. I thought of my empty apartment, and wanted to go out there and join them for their post-group beer and pizza. It really hurt that they were together and I was alone. It was all I could do to not rejoin them. I wonder if I had been avoiding closing the group for weeks.

Leaders may attempt to avoid their own fears of loss by unconsciously engaging in behaviors that prolong their role in their clients' lives. One method to avert such feelings is to ignore the impending termination of the group. Another is to create greater dependence on the group or leaders unconsciously by failing to refocus the members' attention properly to their out-of-group existence. This behavior commonly results when leaders demonstrate a lack of persistence to the members' underplaying the significance of the impending termination. Some leaders may even postpone discussion about the group's ending until the final group meeting.

NEED FOR REASSURANCE   In the business of human services, evaluation of one's personal impact is problematic. Results are neither obvious nor immediate.

When do I know I have done enough?

How can I be sure I have done the best I can for each member of the group?

When is my job really complete?

Such questions are commonly asked by group leaders.

Because long-term outcomes are rarely known by the end of a group, leaders must look for other criteria by which to judge the success of their work. Often the yardsticks they use are internal ones. Such measures are subject to all the personal doubts, concerns, and misperceptions that a counselor or therapist might have.

Unconscious needs for personal nurturance are often an important motivator for health care workers. Many of us in the helping professions are attracted to our fields because of personal experiences and needs. To the extent that we are unaware

---

[1] Some cultures see beginnings and endings more naturally as a part of existence and use the same term for hello and goodbye (i.e., the Hebrew word *shalom*, which also means "peace," and the Hawaiian term *aloha*, which also means "love").

of these personal drives, we are subject to low self-esteem. Unsure of ourselves, we seek reassurance partially by providing for others. This can make us somewhat dependent on the success of our group members. Such unconscious needs for personal reassurance that we have been successful may make group termination seem like our own personal final exam. Avoidance of this test by procrastination is understandable, if unacceptable.

LACK OF TRAINING   The third point—lack of training—requires special attention. No one would respect a plumber who could clear a clogged drain but could not reconnect the pipes, a mechanic who could take an automobile engine apart but could not put it back together, or a surgeon who could open up a patient but could not close the wound: "The operation was a success but the patient died" is simply not acceptable. Yet we tolerate an analogous situation in group therapists.

In the first place, few graduate programs provide sufficient classwork or supervised practice in group work. Training programs may offer a single class in groups, if they offer any at all. Many programs simply train students in individual and/or family therapy and expect them to learn group leadership by generalization. This may be akin to asking an orthopedic surgeon to do neural surgery.

Second, in most clinical training graduate programs, opening skills for all forms of therapy or counseling are stressed to the minimization of middle or closing stages. Students frequently complain that they finish their training before they learn how to engage in those most critical closing or transfer of training skills.[2] Of course, the quarter or semester system does not lend itself well to continuing with cases from beginning to end. Professors can much more easily demonstrate opening and treatment techniques than termination. The only way to understand thoroughly the full termination process is to follow a group (couple, family, or individual) through the entire course of treatment. Practica and internship field placements are best suited to such training, but today's caseloads often preclude sufficient individual supervision. Indeed, for many agencies, the interns provide the bulk of the service to the clients. Professional staff, cut to minimal levels, are relegated to administrative roles, fund-raising, and supervision of a large group of such interns.

PHASE IV: TERMINATION

Most therapists will argue that termination begins with the first session. Whitaker (1982), speaking about family therapy, comments that his use of a clipboard and note taking at the very first session is a way of underscoring the boundary between the therapist and the patient that will not be crossed. This, he believes, allows the patients to begin the separation process even as they begin to attach. Similarly, behavior therapists remind us that transfer of training must be a primary focus of

---

[2] Normally, students from a behaviorally oriented program, or one in which behavioral techniques are readily available, are better schooled in the transfer of training and evaluation skills.

the treatment from the earliest contact and contract. Many authors and group leaders argue about the correct timing for leadership attention to termination. However, most leaders would agree that between one-half and one-fifth of the total group time will likely be spent in this phase.

Although regard for the members' use of group experiences for their home lives should be ongoing throughout a group, termination is the phase in which such concerns become salient. In addition, during this phase the leader must bring the group to conclusion and effect an appropriate parting.

STAGE *24:*   *Leader Announces Imminent End of Group Time*

Termination officially begins when the leader verbally announces the number of hours left in the group. This initial announcement should be made when approximately 25% to 50% of the group time remains. The first announcement typically is made at the beginning of a session (or at an appropriate gap in marathon): "I think it's important for us to keep in mind that we only have three more sessions to go after tonight" or "Well, we're halfway through our group time. It may be of value to think about issues that you may want to bring up in the remaining time."

This first announcement rarely has a noticeable effect on the group members; indeed, it seems to pass by virtually unheard. The second such announcement may have only a slightly greater impact. This second notice of the imminent termination is often accompanied by a request for members to bring up any unfinished business.

Although the immediate impact of the leader's announcement is not readily visible, members may respond to it after a short period of time. Normally, one member begins to talk about a concern with, or fear of, the group's ending and not having enough time to deal with all the problems he wishes to discuss. This allows the leader to encourage members to begin focusing on the termination process and the impact of loss.

STAGE *25:*   *Invitation to Work*

Once members begin to discuss their feelings about the group's ending, the leader invites them to consider and share any unfinished business or problems. Members who have heretofore been reticent to discuss their own concerns and who have spent most of their group time helping others often accept the leaders' invitation. This is commonly accompanied by some pressure from the other members.

Two forms of unfinished business are frequently discussed at this time: problems members have in their outside-of-group lives, and problems between members of the group that are still unresolved. In a recent group, one member chose this time to talk about his homosexuality and his fears that other members would have treated him differently throughout the group had they known earlier. In the same group, two of the women worked on their seemingly interminable competition with one another.

This stage, like many of the others, can be quite time-consuming. It is imperative that the leader provide enough time for such issues to emerge and be addressed.

STAGE 26:   *A Trust Boost*

At this late stage of the group, trust among members would be expected to be high, and it usually is. However, if members are to navigate through the straits of transfer of training and departure, the highest levels of trust and cohesion are required.

This trust can be enhanced in several ways. Two of the most straightforward have worked best for us. The first is pointing out to the group that the last few hours will be hard on everyone, and each person will need a great deal of support. This statement is followed by a request that members be therapeutic for each other. In addition to reducing competition between members, this method encourages them to be altruistic and experience the ego building that accompanies helping others. Altruism is truly antithetical to low self-esteem.

A second straightforward technique asks members to share something new with the group: "Something that is important to you in your life, but which you've had no reason to bring up here as yet." The major advantages of this technique are that it allows members to present a fuller picture of themselves and helps them better coordinate their lives outside the group with their behavior inside the group.

Often a member will produce a very surprising piece of information. In addition to important clinical issues such as a history of abuse, negative personal matters, relationship problems, and so on, members also disclose aspects of their personality that have been absent in group interaction. One member in a group told that she was the local "Ronald McDonald" clown. A dour appearing fellow who worked as an engineer talked about his notable sense of humor and avocation as a stand-up comic. Another member talked of her years of service as a nun.

No matter which trust- and cohesion-building methods are employed, the members need to be prepared to bring their group learning back home.

STAGE 27:   *Transfer of Training*

The competent group leader has consistently urged members to make a connection between the group and their outside environments throughout the group sessions. Whenever members have dealt with any complex issue, the leaders have requested that they attempt any group-engendered recommendations in their back-home environment. Consistent inferences are made to how group learning can be attempted in real-life situations. During this late group stage, however, the leaders must require each member to make direct connections between the group work and the home environment.

Each group member is requested to provide answers to these four questions:

1. What have you learned that is new in this group?
2. What else? (sometimes repeated several times)
3. What will you now do with this new knowledge?
4. How will you do it specifically?

Here are some typical answers:

> Well, I guess what I've learned is how I control other people by my sickness. It's hard and . . . you know . . . scary . . . but I realize that I've been acting crazy for so long, I'm not sure I can act any other way. I guess I know that my wife likes it when I act this way—that also seems weird. What am I going to do? Well, I want to try to make it not crazy . . . me and my wife need to go into therapy. I also need to stop screwing up on the job. I know when I'm gonna act crazy . . . I can just keep off my job on those days. It's O.K. 'cause it only happens on full and new moons—so two days a month sick leave . . . ha, ha [*group joins in this joke*]. I think I can make it, especially if we see Dr. _____ .

This familiar response came from a military officer:

> You know what I've learned here? It's easy. Being right all the time isn't all it's cracked up to be. I've spent my whole life believing that if I was right, everything would be so perfect, so I did it . . . top of my class, service academy, two master's degrees . . . beautiful wife. What I learned here is how lonely I am and what I'll do is be more damn human and less a damn computer. Maybe my kids will even stop viewing me as a mountain or something. I've never felt as good as I have in here . . . it's like I've got a new lease on life. I plan to go home, get my wife, and take off to this place I know . . . no, wait . . . I'll just tell her I miss and love her and let her decide what we'll do [*group applauds*].

The therapist asks, "What else?"

> Delegate! Delegate! Delegate! I've got to let the troops in my shop do more. They all rely on me, and that's fine for me, 'cause I do the job best. But it really doesn't do much for their initiative . . . they really are good. I don't need to be the golden boy all the time.

Not all such reports are so positive, and sometimes much therapeutic work is necessary to help the members make the transfer. The following example is presented verbatim from a tape of a group of middle managers of a large engineering firm. The client, Patrick, is 42 years old and has been with the firm for almost 15 years. He is a good-looking, sturdy individual who could easily pass for a man in his middle thirties. He has a friendly smile, but during the group, many other members said that often when he smiled he looked angry.

Gary (Leader 1):   Patrick, what have you learned new in the group?

Pat: Well, I guess I finally learned how to deal with problems openly and honestly.

Gary: How do you mean?

Pat: Well, when problems come up, I'm going to be careful to pay attention to my feelings now.

Gary: How will you do that?

Pat: Well, like I really need to talk to my boss.

Gary: For example?

Pat: Well, I think the shop could really run better with a few alterations.

Joe: Like what?

Pat: Well, lots of things. I don't know, just I want to talk to him, get some things off my chest.

Carol (Leader 2):   Pat, let's role play. Who here could play your boss?

Pat: Charley.

Carol: O.K., Charley, will you?

Charley: Sure.

Gary: Pat, set the stage. Where? When? How?

Pat: Oh, I don't know.

Carol: Try!

Pat: O.K., Monday morning as soon as he comes in, I'm going to go up to his office and tell him I need to talk.

Carol: Tell your boss! [*gesturing toward Charley*]

Pat: Sam (that's his name), you know we've worked together for 12 years now and until this weekend I never admitted to myself how you've really fucked up this company. I mean I'm so pissed at you . . . you were really an asshole about that _____ matter.

This speech went on for almost four minutes. As soon as it terminated, Charley looked up and said, "Patrick, you're fired." Patrick looked as if he'd been punched in the stomach. He was speechless, hurt, and confused, but he admitted that Charley had played the boss's role accurately. He kept saying how different it was in the group.

The role playing and rehearsal that followed actually took almost 90 minutes. During this time Patrick and Charley did 11 "takes" of the role playing until Patrick had a problem solution that the members agreed would work. The final decision was for Patrick to see his boss over their regular coffee later in the week and talk about his ideas for changes without criticizing or calling Sam's parentage into question. We can add that this solution worked so well that Patrick is now

Sam's partner in their own spin-off business. Had the group leader not pressed Patrick to reveal and try out his plan, the result could have been a disaster.

So it is with all groups. Unless transfer of training is carefully and seriously administered, much of the total effectiveness of the group will be mitigated. Transfer is thus of great import in augmenting the positive effects in the group and in preventing casualties.

STAGE 28A: *Good and Welfare*

After each member has worked on the issue of his or her own personal use of the group experience, members and leaders often share their overall impressions of the group. Frequently, valuable positive feedback is shared and feelings about ending the group are explored. Often the leaders share many of their own personal feelings and observations.[3] This stage is often tearful and sensitive; it prepares the group for the leaders' final speech.

STAGE 28B: *Closing Ceremonies*

Some group leaders use a closing ritual as a symbolic way to mark termination. These ceremonies mark the process of leaving the group and reentering normal life. Ceremonies may be simple or elaborate.

One group that has used ceremonies effectively is the VetCenter. This organization, which has provided thousands of groups for Vietnam era veterans, has been responsible for many group innovations. The ceremonies used often focus on the members leaving the war behind and reentering "life in the world." Some examples include writing reactions to the past on a board or strips of paper and then burning them, leaving or destroying painful artifacts of the war such as uniforms, medals, or letters. Symbolic ways to alleviate guilt for past actions that emerge in the group have been used very successfully.

Groups with a religious or spiritual theme also commonly close with a ceremony or prayer. This can be very meaningful for members and help enhance the gains from the group. Leaders must be careful in such prayers, however, if the group contains a mix of members from different religions. In a recent group at a Jesuit university, two Jewish members had to overcome their discomfort when the leader automatically closed her prayer with the words "in the name of the Father, the Son and the Holy Spirit." There was no negative intent, and no real harm was done, but the ceremony would have been more effective if all members of the group had been Roman Catholic or if more general terms requesting God's attention and support had been used.

Some group leaders are uncomfortable with ceremonies and avoid them altogether. When ceremonial closings are held, they must be appropriate for all group

---

[3] Such explorations are dependent on the leaders' values and theories. Frequently the reason given for leaders who do become more personal at this time is to reduce the therapeutic transference and projections that have accompanied their roles during the earlier sessions. Of course, such a diminution of distance is anathema to those who espouse more classical analytic or behavioral theories.

members. Often encounter group-based ceremonies—such as mandatory group hugs or other physical contact—can make members sufficiently uncomfortable that the impact of the group experience as a whole is diminished.

STAGE 29:   *Leader's Closing*

All leaders close a group in their own characteristic way. Some prefer lengthy reviews and progress reports for each member. Others describe their own impressions of the group as a whole or possibly their personal feelings about closing.

If the leader gives a closing speech, it normally has two purposes: to give each member adequate feedback from the leader's point of view, and to provide a potential referral source for follow-up work. Some leaders keep their closing remarks short; others try to provide evaluative feedback to each member of the group regarding each one's relative strengths and weaknesses with reference to the issues discussed in the group. Here is one part of such a statement:

> Jeanie, I see you as a remarkably competent young woman with a great number of strengths to work yourself through this divorce decision you've made. I am concerned that there's a danger your fear will induce you to quickly find another man to replace Len as a way of not testing those strengths.

The leader also has the responsibility to address issues that emerged in the group only to submerge and hibernate and which are likely to come to fruition only after members have left the group setting. This does not mean that the leader does follow-up therapy with each member. It is important, however, for the leader to be available for consultation and referral, at least for issues that are group engendered. Our personal experience is that such an offer is rarely abused by group members. A follow-up offer for referral is not very time-consuming, and it is ethically essential. It can go a long way in helping to prevent group casualties. Equally important ethically is that leaders not use this as a way to create a need for their personal services and expand their own businesses.

When the consultation is offered, the group session officially terminates, occasionally with some physical contact such as hugging or holding hands.

STAGE 30:   *Aloha*

After termination, members often tend to linger and extend nostalgic alohas, often sharing phone numbers and making plans for future contact. It is not unusual for members to get together without the leader after the group terminates. Shapiro (1978) recalled a couples group he led in 1969–1970.

> We met on Tuesday nights from 7 to 10. There were four couples in the group, three of whom really wanted to stay together. The group ended in April 1970, and to this day those three couples still get together every Tuesday night. They formed a mixed doubles bowling team in a local league. They've done well, too. Last Christmas (1975), they sent me a picture of the four trophies they had won last year. They not only got their relationships together, but they developed a workable mutual support system that goes far beyond any therapy. (Shapiro, 1978, p. 112)

Annual cards from the members of that group came until 1980. At least to that time, they were still meeting on Tuesday evenings.

The entire group process is an arduous journey, but a group that makes it all the way can reap a bountiful harvest for its members (and leaders). Every group does not make the entire journey, however. Often a group will have progressed through only half the stages before termination must begin. Such a group can be of value in and of itself, and members can accrue a number of benefits. The phases discussed above make up an attainable goal, not a bare minimum. The goal pertains exclusively to *closed* groups, however. Groups with open membership progress past Phase II only when the membership is stable over an extended time. Phase II reoccurs because as each new member is added to the group, earlier phases are reinstituted to benefit them and to reestablish members' roles and inclusion.

TERMINATION IN OPEN GROUPS

Termination has heretofore been discussed with regard to closed groups in which all group members end the group experience at the same time. This text is particularly geared to such groups. Their advantage is that the whole group progresses through the termination steps together. The disadvantage is that the mutual termination does not simulate well the normal life experience of leaving important people and being left by them.

In open groups, members join and leave when doing so is personally appropriate. At any group session, some members may be dealing with issues of inclusion and others with treatment as a member will be leaving. Several issues must be considered by the group leader.

Fair Warning

A customary ground rule in open groups is for members to give notice that they intend to leave and then remain for a predetermined number of sessions before leaving the group. This policy exists (1) to ensure that other members will have the opportunity to work on any unfinished business with the departing person and not be confronted with a sudden unexplained absence, (2) to allow sufficient time for the member to prepare emotionally for the termination, (3) to allow the leaders to assist the leaving member with transfer of training, (4) to make referrals, and (5) to provide an opportunity for members who tend to avoid problems by flight to confront their discomfort.

Changes in the Group "System"

Leaders must be aware that any changes in the group membership will affect the group chemistry. Whenever a member enters or leaves the group, the group must reform into a new configuration. Alliances change; support systems are altered; power in the group may shift. At this point, the group process may regress to earlier stages of group development to reintegrate and re-form. Feelings about inclusion and exclusion commonly will emerge for many remaining members.

Perhaps the exiting member was intimidating. The group will now be able to move ahead with less fear. Perhaps she was a warm, supportive member. The absence of her support may have to be compensated for by other members. The leaders must be alert to the new integration of the group and adjust perceptions of members as well as the group process. Members will express new aspects of themselves as the group composition changes and both the quantity and quality of individuals' participation may shift.

Elicitation of Members' Feelings About the Loss

Lewis (1978) points out the differences in affect that accompany task and educational groups versus growth-oriented and treatment-oriented groups. In the former, members are primarily focused on the goal and are likely to have a far less emotional experience when someone leaves—not unlike a person completing a class. By contrast, in growth or treatment groups in which members have been more self-disclosing, members typically experience a feeling of loss when someone leaves the group. This feeling may call up other separations in members' lives. Soon after a member terminates, the first major work that occurs in the group is often on the topic of personal losses, perhaps dating back to childhood. A leader must allow for the open expression of all feelings as a member leaves. If remaining members do not have an opportunity and encouragement to discuss their reactions, they may attribute the person's departure to something they may have said or done.

Among the commonly expressed feelings after the member has gone are sadness, fear, anger, happiness, and relief. A member who feels relief when someone distasteful to them is leaving may also be struck by secondary guilt feelings. This is all grist for the group mill. Unexpressed, the remaining members' guilt about anticipating more personal time in group because of one less member may grow and diminish the benefit of the increased time and attention.

Early Terminations

Sometimes a member may decide apparently suddenly to leave the group. It is important for these members to delineate carefully their thinking and decision making in the group. Often after a particularly deep or painful session a member may miss a week with little or no reason and then decide to terminate. Yalom (1995) also identifies as early terminators patients who have difficulty expressing gratitude or positive emotions. Conversely, patients who find terminations difficult in their life may well try to truncate the painful process by ending it prematurely. It is incumbent on group leaders to encourage members to terminate at a time when both they and the other members feel somewhat comfortable with the event. Group leaders also need to encourage a member who is attempting to escape from difficult feelings or interactions to stay until these feelings have been sufficiently worked through and the termination is more natural. However, leaders must not try to hold on to patients after it is time for them to leave treatment. Kottler (1982) and others have reminded us of the ethical violation inherent in such actions.

Sudden Termination

Sometimes members leave a group without any warning. In institutions, members who are discharged or transferred simply terminate by not showing up for a meeting. This may be particularly problematic for the remaining members. They are caught between a desire to avoid talking about someone who is absent and a host of unexpressed personal feelings of rejection.

When possible, leaders are advised to invite a member who is physically able to come to a final meeting to do so. In some cases, another member of the group may know how to contact the departed member to make such an invitation. For example, members of a hospital in-patient group may prefer to come back to their ongoing group after discharge than to join a new outpatient group.

There are, of course, situations in which the departing member will not be able to attend. In military groups, sudden assignments can relocate a member thousands of miles away by the next group session. In a prison group, nobody presumes that a former inmate who was unexpectedly released would come back into the prison for a group meeting. Indeed, if he were paroled, he would be legally barred from returning and associating with convicted felons. In such cases, remaining members may wish to discuss their feelings by writing to the person who exited. It may or may not be prudent to actually mail such letters.

Finally, a group member may die while a group is ongoing. Serious attention must be paid to mourning and unrealistic fears that the group or a particular member was responsible for the death.

Ultimately, the goal of termination is to maximize the impact of the group experience for all members. Transfer of training, reminders of attention to feelings, and a final chance to practice the group skills all serve members after the group is concluded.

FOLLOW-UP

Some group leaders, especially those who work in institutional settings, schedule follow-up sessions three to six months after the group termination. Advocates of these sessions (such as Corey & Corey, 1987) believe that members will be motivated to make the changes they began in the group, knowing that the group will reconvene. A plan for future meetings also encourages members to support each other in the interim. In the follow-up session, members can discuss difficulties that have arisen since the end of the group and seek help from the group members, whom they trust. Many leaders also use these sessions to collect evaluative outcome data.

In closed groups, members may be invited back for a "graduates night." Toseland, Kabat, and Kemp (1983) use such sessions to review members' commitment to maintaining changes, to remind members of life changes since the beginning of the group, and to have members support each other regarding difficulties in implementing group learning in real-life situations. There is also the probability of general support.

There are two potential downside risks to such sessions:

1. Reconvening may be inconvenient or impossible for all members. The leaders must then decide whether to meet with only part of the original membership.

2. Knowing that there will be a follow-up meeting, some members may avoid dealing with effective termination at the end of the regular sessions. Instead of saying goodbye, they may simply say *au revoir.*

For the leaders, such postgroup sessions involve metaphorically walking a tightrope. Introducing any new material for discussion, inducing the members to regroup, or in any way creating a need for additional therapy is inappropriate; yet leaders must be available for patient needs, to make appropriate referrals, and to support continued learning and application of skills acquired in the group to the patients' independent life situation.

SUMMARY

Termination seems to be an unnatural occurrence in the group process. It requires the leader to introduce the idea and persistently focus the group's attention on the process of termination. In no other phase of the group is the leader called on as clearly to "lead" the group as in acknowledging the crisis of its own ending and symbolic death.

The leader's own personal style of termination can be the most important ingredient in the group's ability to face the end of its existence. As leaders, we have basically three styles of termination. Often leaders tend to terminate too early or too late. It is important for leaders to be able to endure the complexities and intensities of being in the moment with our feelings and personal issues germane to termination.

The process of termination begins with the first session in a closed group when the leader delineates the parameters of the group and announces the ending date. From this beginning, the leader continues to keep members apprised of the approaching termination of each individual group session as well as the remaining number of sessions. Members' heightened awareness of their thoughts and feelings about ending and loss makes the termination more poignant.

The two significant and profound goals of this phase of group are saying goodbye and redirecting members' work to their home lives. The extent of each member's satisfaction with his or her ability to apply the group learning to the real world is the measure of the group's success. Many an otherwise successful group has lost much of its therapeutic influence by ignoring or failing to face thoroughly the tasks of termination.

Three specific tasks are pertinent to the termination phase: the trust boost, transfer of training, and closing rituals. In the trust boost, the leader must make a direct request for members to support one another during the often difficult termination process. In addition, members are often asked to disclose something new about themselves, effecting an increased intimacy and reduced transference through presenting a more complete personal picture.

Transfer of training is an absolute of group work. The leader must consistently stress a connection between group learning and its application to members' lives outside the group. Members are challenged to be specific and concrete in how they will make changes in their lives.

Closing rituals need to be tailored specifically to each unique group; ideally, they grow naturally out of a particular group's themes and style. The expression of typical feelings of sadness, fear, anger, relief, and joy need to be encouraged and processed. A helpful strategy is to inform members explicitly that each new ending and loss is an opportunity to work through previous losses. Members may experience a corrective emotional experience regarding loss, separation, individuation, and the development of interdependence.

CHAPTER 6

THE GROUP LEADER

THE GROUP THERAPIST

Of the many variables operating in group therapy, leadership effectiveness is probably the most crucial. An inept leader can be harmful as well as nonproductive. Competent leadership involves mastery of a wide variety of skills and functions. This chapter investigates three major areas of leadership: leadership styles, multiple roles, and functions. Ethics, training, and leader skills are discussed in the following chapter.

Group therapists vary widely in their training, background, theoretical orientation, personality, intentions, and conceptions of their roles and goals. Most individuals who practice group therapy today were educated in disciplines such as medicine, nursing, psychology, education, public health, substance abuse, or social work. Some are very well trained in group process and techniques. Unfortunately, they are a minority. Often, group leaders are more knowledgeable of individual or family therapy than of group work. Some have had no training in group therapy. Some may have had a single graduate-level class in group process. Others may have had course work or similar training but little supervised experience in dealing with groups.

Leader Personality

Some group therapists are mild, gentle, and "low key." Others are forceful and aggressive. Some have well-defined philosophies that their group work emulates and supports; others take a pragmatic approach to their work. Some strive for improvement of personality, where as others focus on relief from symptoms or amelioration of behavior. Some see themselves primarily as teachers who have something to contribute to the relatively passive group members. Others regard themselves as clarifiers or analyzers, and still others see themselves as enablers or catalysts who help members to find themselves.[1] There are group therapists who take a very modest view of their efforts and hope only to assist people in limited ways; others take the grander view that they can reconstruct a person's entire personality. One persuasive argument claims that there are as many types of group therapy as there are group therapists (Corsini, 1957).

Qualifications

Who is a group leader? Is it anyone who is doing counseling or therapy group work? Can only people within certain professions be so labeled? From a legal point of view, most states restrict the use of the terms *psychotherapy* and *group psychotherapy* to people with specific degrees and licenses. Normally, a particular credential is required, such as an M.D., Ph.D., or Psy.D. (Clinical or Counseling Psychology), M.S.W., MFCC (Marital Family & Child Counselor), M.A. (Counseling), or M.S. (Psychiatric Nursing). However, none of the 50 states nor any of the Canadian provinces restrict the use of such terms as *training group, growth group, human relations training, T-group, encounter group,* or *sensitivity group.* There is no regulation of "educators" engaging in "group education," "psychoeducation programs," or "encounter classes." The term *counseling* has been determined to be so broad that it does not fall under the professional rubric. Thus, almost any person can engage in "counseling" whereas professional, trained counselors may be limited in their applications. Such problems frequently lead to paradoxical and ridiculous situations because of different legislative guidelines for licensed and unlicensed professionals.

For example, an individual who is trained in group therapy and holds a Ph.D. in clinical psychology but is yet unlicensed in psychology may not lead any counseling groups without supervision. However, a lay practitioner with no training or credentials, any clergyman, educator, salesman, marketer, or surgeon may lead growth, training, "motivation," or "educational" groups without fear of legal consequences.

No evidence exists to indicate that members of any particular profession are superior group therapists. Psychiatrists are not necessarily more adept than teachers, nurses more effective than public health experts, psychologists better than counselors, or social workers superior to ministers. As early as 1952, Spotnitz, a psychiatrist, said, "A gifted lay individual psychologist or social worker may do much better work with certain groups than a physician who may lack intuitive understanding of the individual in the group or of group dynamics." (p. 86)

---

[1] In the brief group treatment modalities featured in this manual, the goals are necessarily more limited than in long-term therapy groups. Leaders from any school of psychological thought must recognize the limitations of a brief focused group. Such groups may and frequently do activate members to make significant life changes, but the leaders are rarely able to be present for the full unfolding of such changes.

There are many reports of inept or unethical group leaders. Corsini (1957) recalls an elderly psychiatrist who took a position in an institution and was pressed into doing group therapy. He was observed lecturing to his semiliterate audience on brain pathology in the belief that this was group psychotherapy. Shapiro (1978) describes a psychologist whose striving to be nondirective led him to withhold a bathroom key from a group member to "help crystallize the member's resistance." In 1990, a social worker in the San Francisco Bay Area regularly took it upon herself to call and confront spouses of group members after group sessions. Similar examples may be drawn from every discipline. As recently as 1993, an MFCC was leading a generic group in which all members were encouraged to "discover the hidden memories of molestation" in their childhoods.

Not everyone is cut out to be a group therapist. Many professionals who are otherwise well trained and competent do not have the interest or the capacity to do this work whereas others take to group therapy naturally and eagerly. Handling treatment groups requires not only interest and technical knowledge but also direct experience in dealing with common, difficult interpersonal situations. Such experience can best be acquired by supervised practice.

To some practitioners, group process, with its multiple interrelationships, complex transferences, and fast-paced action, may seem chaotic. To others, those very attributes—speed, lack of protracted periods of relative inactivity, opportunities to work with several people simultaneously, patients' access to vicarious learning and general stimulation—are far less demanding than the patience and persistence required in individual psychotherapy.

For the most part, we expect marketplace factors to select out competent professionals in every field. In addition, in all mental health fields, licensees are required to practice only within the scope of their training. Normally, ethical professionals will engage in those endeavors in which they are well trained and likely to be successful. However, two factors mitigate the efficiency of this market-based selection. In many agencies, economic demands have mandated that the majority of staff do group work, regardless of prior training. Even in the private sector, many otherwise ethical practitioners, disenfranchised by closed provider panels and diminishing numbers of available patients, may find that economic necessity entices them to stretch their belief in their abilities. They may well lead groups for which their training is inadequate. In addition, the tremendous increase in popularity of encounter methodologies spawned in the late 1960s and early 1970s encouraged the appearance of thousands of untrained, self-styled group leaders. Often these self-proclaimed "gurus" led dramatic, exciting, exercise-laden, high-casualty groups (cf. Lakin, 1969; Yalom & Lieberman, 1971).

One of the most dangerous components of the encounter methodologies is that they provide any "leader" with a technology that can be used incisively to open up a group member, but they offer few corresponding closing skills. The dangers to clients of often well-meaning but naive practitioners have been well known for years. As early as 1955, Hadden argued that too many unqualified people were entering the field of group therapy. Cooper and Mangham (1971), Dreyfus and Kremenliev (1970), Grotjahn (1971), Lakin (1972), Lieberman, Yalom, and Miles

(1973), and Shapiro (1973) have all cautioned that vast numbers of group leaders may be harmful and have suggested characteristics that constitute competent leadership.

The following discussion of the roles, functions, skills, ethics, and training necessary for effective group leadership is designed to provide guidelines for readers in evaluating their own abilities and those of others.

CHARACTERISTICS OF THE GROUP THERAPIST

Are there certain characteristics or personality traits mandatory for effective group leadership? Are the skills of group therapy learned, or do they require a certain type of individual? In this section, these questions are explored from the historical, practical, and training perspectives.

Relatively early in the history of group psychotherapy, a question arose regarding the importance of the therapist's personality. In 1908, Pratt said, "Success depends on gaining the friendship and confidence of the members." (p. 1070) Pratt's (1934) theory of therapy was based on Dejerine's belief that "Psychotherapy depends wholly and exclusively upon the beneficial influence of one person on another." (p. 1) A statement by Pfeffer, Friedland, and Wortis (1949) probably fairly represented opinion on the issue at that time: "As yet undefinable aspects of the therapist's personality may be more important for his results than the technique he says he uses." (p. 214)

In the late 1960s, a series of studies by Carkhuff and Berenson (1967) and Truax and his colleagues (Truax, 1966, 1971; Truax & Carkhuff, 1967; Truax, Carkhuff, Wargo, & Kodman, 1966) identified several variables that distinguish effective from ineffective therapists in each area of endeavor. High levels of warmth, empathy, genuineness, and congruence were considered necessary conditions for success in group therapy. The authors argued that these "personality traits" were trainable skills. Demonstration of this research with regard to individual counseling therapy is impressive. Since the early 1970s, counseling psychology graduate programs have almost universally included a basic course or microcounseling curriculum to train students in these "core counseling skills" (e.g., Ivey, 1990). Such training has clearly been quite helpful in developing the students' necessary basic skills.

Although few direct applications to group therapy situations have been substantiated, a reasonable assumption is that the same skills provide a necessary core for group counselors. However, it is equally clear that mastery of such skills, while necessary, is insufficient to guarantee success. Thus, the question of some optimal personality for the group therapist has as yet not been fully answered.

To determine what characteristics are common to effective group leaders, we may explore the character structure of successful therapists. We may describe who this person appears to be. Likely, such a leader will be described as kind, firm, considerate, compassionate, personally centered, and sensitive. Another approach is to explore the role the effective leader plays in the group. Although we would expect the traits described here to be reflected in group leadership behavior, leaders may assume some roles that supersede to some extent their usual manner of social interaction. Indeed, the assumption that a person is what he does requires a total sampling of his behavior. To assume that a group leader's behavior in the group is representative of his total behavior is as spurious as to assume that his behavior in bed is equivalent to his total behavior.

Although group counselors and psychotherapists vary greatly in values and personality, there are some commonalities among effective group leaders. A number of group leader trainers believe these common traits can be learned.

THE IDEAL PERSONALITY FOR A GROUP THERAPIST

Is there a generalized personality for effective group therapists? Do certain methods call for specific personalities? According to Slavson (1951), the therapist should be friendly, generous, tolerant, accepting, and quiet. Slavson may well have been describing an ideal personality in terms of our culture. Others have presented somewhat different personality criteria for the therapist who works with groups. Grotjahn (1971), a psychoanalyst like Slavson, argues that a group therapist "must be a man of all seasons. He must be reliable; he must invite trust and confidence." Other therapist qualities suggested by Grotjahn include honesty, sincerity, spontaneity, responsibility, courage, firmness, humor, fallibility, and the ability to lead successfully.

Corey and Corey (1992) describe the following 13 personal characteristics of effective group leaders: courage, willingness to model, presence, goodwill and caring, belief in the group process, openness, ability to cope with attacks, personal power, stamina, willingness to seek new experience, self-awareness, a sense of humor, and inventiveness.

Our own formulation of the major essential characteristics of the effective group therapist is similar: honesty, integrity, patience, courage, flexibility, warmth, empathy, intelligence, timing, and self-knowledge.

Honesty

". . . and the truth will make you free" (John 8:32). Truthfulness is the sine qua non of therapy. The therapist must at all times respond to the members with honest feedback. This is not to suggest, however, that he or she needs always to be open, blunt, or brutal. There are many situations in which our first thoughts are best kept personal.

If the group members are to change their negative patterns of communication, they need accurate information about the consequences of their behavior. Similarly, because honest communication is one of the avowed goals of groups, the leader must be a model of this behavior. Honesty cannot be learned from an untruthful source.

Integrity

Integrity does not lag far behind honesty. Group members need to know that the leader will adhere to an agreed-on code of ethics. The leader must interact with members with their interests in mind. Integrity provides a solid basis from which members may experiment, confident that the leader will respond appropriately.

Patience

Another essential quality is patience. The therapist must have a high tolerance for boredom, frustration, and delay. She must have the ability to proceed doggedly in the face of disappointments and failure under conditions that induce anxiety, anger, and unrest. Patience should be the result of a deep conviction, amounting to faith in oneself, in the group, in the method, and in the theory. The patient therapist combines a feeling of assurance, security, determination, confidence, and hopefulness about herself and others. She would do well to have a generally optimistic outlook on life.

Courage

Somewhat related to patience is courage. The leader must have the capacity to act on her convictions and remain unswerved by immediate events. She needs faith to hold on to them with great tenacity, to follow with determination her line of attack, and to meet and contain opposition in an accepting manner, even when it occasionally may be forceful or explosive. Courage is needed to penetrate, sometimes blindly, into new areas or to meet crises with aplomb. The therapist must have inward qualities of fortitude.

Flexibility

Courage does not mean rigidity. Although the therapist must hold onto basic principles with tenacity, she must nevertheless be able to modify tactics without changing goals. She needs extraordinary flexibility to move rapidly from topic to topic, emotion to emotion, person to person while keeping a sense of the needs of the group as a whole. She must be sensitive to the needs of the group and of individuals, but she must also be alert to the demands of society and the desires of patients' families as well as to ethical issues.

Warmth

The ideal therapist is a warm person with a genuine liking for others, one who really wants to see others improve. She may have preferences among members, but she must value them all equally as striving individuals who are seeking change. She must be ready to give of herself fully. She must be open to members as they are.

Empathy

Closely related to warmth is empathy. An effective group therapist must be able to put herself into the shoes of her patients. She must experience their emotions as if they were her own, and must be able to communicate this shared experience accurately and articulately to members. She does not judge others; rather, she shares in members' fears, pain, anger, and joy. At the same time, she must keep in touch with other reality considerations. In a sense, the group therapist walks with one foot in the shoe of another and one foot in her own shoe.

Intelligence

It is not necessary for the therapist to be the most intelligent individual in the room, but she must be able to learn fairly rapidly, to be flexible enough to view the group from a variety of perspectives, and to make some theoretical sense of the material of the group interactions. A leader who is limited in intelligence could effectively dampen higher-level cognitive processing by the members.

Timing

There is no human endeavor that does not require timing for maximum effectiveness. The best leadership observations are worthless if the group members are not prepared to listen. To score regularly, the basketball player must fake so that his defender leaps first, then jump into the air and shoot at the apex of his own jump while his defender is coming down. The therapist must help group members relax their defenses and prepare to let him work on conflict resolution. With any variations in sequence, the effects will not be maximized. If the basketball shooter does not cause his defender to jump earlier than he does himself, the flight of the ball might be terminated in his face instead of the basket. Similarly, the group leader must time interventions carefully for best results.

Self-Knowledge

Leaders are not required to be free of all conflict or completely self-actualizing; such a requirement would eliminate all current leaders. They must, however, be aware of their personal psychological strengths and weaknesses. Unless the leader is self-aware, there is an ever-present danger that her personal conflicts, inadequacies, and needs, instead of those of the members, will guide group interventions. It is far better for a leader to acknowledge her incapacity or unwillingness to venture into certain difficult areas than to grope ignorantly in the dark with patients, perhaps compounding their fears and conflicts. In Shakespeare's *Hamlet,* Polonius gives final advice to his son:

> This above all: to thine own self be true,
> and it must follow, as the night the day,
> Thou canst not then be false to any man.

Who is this group therapist? Is this person any more than the kind of friend or mate we all cherish? Can any person who has these qualities of honesty, integrity, patience, courage, flexibility, warmth, empathy, intelligence, timing, and self-awareness be a group leader? These are all necessary conditions for effective group leadership, but they are not sufficient. In the next chapter we investigate the other characteristics—training and a code of ethics—and in effect take the reader inside the head of the group therapist during a session. Before doing so, we must examine one more consideration that is important for any therapist.

PERSONALITY AND METHOD

Earlier, we observed that the method a group therapist uses is a function of his or her own personality. To think of a really introverted therapist using psychodrama with any success is difficult, and it may be just as difficult for a truly extroverted, outgoing person to contain himself within the limits of the nondirective procedure.

The best method for any person is one that reflects his or her personal values and nature. There is no absolute hierarchy of methods. Pratt made his maximum contribution with the class method, Moreno with psychodrama, Rogers with nondirective therapy, and Dreikurs with family counseling. Even the thought of Freud attempting bioenergetics is enough to demonstrate how incongruous such a situation can be. Remember that Freud's free association method, use of the couch, and sitting behind the patient emerged from his personal preferences and introvertive personality. We have direct evidence on this point from Freud himself, who said (1924),

> I must, however, expressedly state that this technique [free association] has proved the only method suited to my individuality. I do not venture to deny that a physician quite differently constituted might feel impelled to adopt a different attitude to his patients and to the task before him. (p. 27)

Others have made similar remarks. Spotnitz (1952), for example, says "The personality of a therapist may determine whether the group has an active or passive type of therapy." (p. 87) Kline (1952) comments, "It is probable that the dynamics of different groups actually do differ radically with the personality of the therapist." (p. 113) Kline also gives a personal example:

> I have always emphasized that within limits the organization of the group and the role of the therapist should be dependent largely on the personality of the therapist himself, rather than on rigid techniques. This conviction was derived from my initial unsuccessful attempts to emulate the procedures of Dr. Paul Schilder. (p. 113)

The therapist needs some freedom to follow his own judgment. No one can tell him how to do what he must do. As early as 1953, Powdermaker and Frank tried to get therapists to operate in a uniform way. Even though the therapists wished to follow this established pattern, they managed to make subtle changes, in each case making modifications suited to their own personalities.

This book is written in the spirit of freedom for therapists to decide on their own methods. We hope that explicit examples of a variety of attitudes and methods will help therapists make a better choice among them, or will help give therapists the courage to strike out on their own. There was only one Sigmund Freud, Fritz Perls, Virginia Satir, and Carl Rogers. Saul Scheidlinger (1994), reflecting on his six decades as a group therapist, commented: "For many years I believed in the classic one true way—that of Father Freud. Then as I grew older, I began to realize that as the world was different and I was different, the group approaches were also best different." When therapists learn from their predecessors and apply this learning in their own unique ways, it is a bonus. However, when they try to be Freud, Perls, Satir, Rogers, or take as gospel the perspective favored in this text for that matter, they are not only doomed to failure, but they will appear stressed, phony, and foolish in the endeavor.

TYPES OF LEADERSHIP

Methods of group treatment and styles of leaders vary widely. Each leader brings unique skills, personality, beliefs, and values to the group. Similarly, each co-leader team is unique in its approach to any constellation of group members. For this reason, any formal classification system may do injustice to individual group leaders. However, to investigate and compare the types of leadership, it is necessary to cluster leaders in some way. We have chosen two dimensions: theories of group psychotherapy and leadership focus.

Theories of Group Psychotherapy

The predominant theories of group psychotherapy are well represented in several texts. For comparative investigations of group leadership, readers are encouraged to explore Corey (1990), Kaplan and Sadock (1983), Schaffer and Galinsky (1989), and Vander Kolk (1985). Most group leaders claim to be representatives of one of the following psychotherapeutic approaches: Adlerian, behavioral, cognitive, dynamic (general), eclectic, encounter, existential, Gestalt, nondirective–Rogerian, object relations, psychoanalytic, psychodrama, psychoeducational, rational–emotive, self-help, Sullivanian, transactional analysis, or twelve-step. Each of these approaches provides a template with which to focus and highlight leaders' attention on specific member behavior and interactions, methods for understanding and interpreting members' communication and needs, and guidelines for interventions. Each theory considers specific elements to be critical, so leadership behavior will be substantially different among these theories depending on the leader's particular allegiance.

In addition to the substantive differences based on theoretical orientation, individual variations within methods can be significant. Thus, simply knowing that someone is "a Gestalt therapist" does not mean that person's approach is identical with those of the late Fritz Perls or James Simkins. In their classic study of encounter groups, Yalom and Lieberman (1971) concluded that Gestalt leaders produced the most and least casualties.

Students in the process of developing their own preferences among theories should be warned that being a "Rogerian" does not make them the therapeutic equivalent of Carl Rogers. Individual differences are still the core of psychological practice, and ultimately each group member must be approached uniquely. In a sense, therapist's theory provides eyeglasses or filters through which an apparently chaotic group process can be viewed systematically, understood, and acted on strategically.

These glasses do not remain constant throughout a therapeutic career. At different stages of life and experience, therapists often find themselves more attracted to one theory than another. Frequently, one's preferred mode of working is influenced by life events, maturation, and changes in values. Often, best group counseling or therapy is influenced by recent fluctuations as well as basic enduring positions. For present purposes, we first examine differences, then commonalties among leadership styles.

Leadership Focus: A Continuum for Comparison

Leadership orientation is one dimension that can be used to highlight dissimilarities between group leaders. The two poles of this dimension are the *interpersonal* and *intrapsychic* (Figure 6.1). As with any continuum, the two ends represent extreme, low-frequency values whereas the middle positions are more common. Individual

Figure 6.1   **The Leadership Continuum**

| Extreme Intrapsychic | Moderate Use of Both | Extreme Interpersonal |

Intrapsychic Intrapersonal	**Interpersonal**
Leaders dealing with individual members	Leaders dealing with interactions between members
Group as stimulus situation to investigate individual	Group as situation to investigate interactions
Techniques that isolate individual	Techniques that isolate interactions
Therapist as source of therapeutic goals	Members as source of therapeutic goals
Historical focus	Here-and-now focus
Within-individual focus	Between-people focus
Leader ⟶ Therapist	Leader ⟶ Members
Unconscious determinants of behavior	Conscious determinants of behavior
Success = Individual's relationship with self	Success = Individual's relationship with other people

leaders can be compared with regard to their relative positions on the continuum. Treatment effectiveness for specific groups may be explored with this orientation in mind.

Dissimilarities between intrapsychic and interpersonal leaders can be viewed most easily by looking first at the extremes. The *strict intrapsychic leader,* for example, works with individual members of the group in a *one-to-one* fashion. Techniques are designed to *isolate the individual.* The group itself is seen as a stimulus situation within which *the individual* can be treated. Success in such a group is measured by the *relationship of each member to himself* (i.e., the balance of cognitive, sensory, and perceptual systems; id, ego, and superego coordination; Parent, Adult, and Child working interdependently, etc.).

A major *focus* of the group is on the barriers or *defenses* of an individual that prevent his or her full cognitive and emotional expression. Techniques are designed primarily to work directly with these barriers. The leader's role approaches that of an individual therapist. It is active, directive, and frequently centered on *unconscious determinants* of behavior. This leader regularly employs a historical orientation. Such terms as *catharsis* and *working through* a transference relationship with the leader appropriately apply to this style of leadership. Classic analytic, Adlerian, and Gestalt-oriented leaders can most often be described by this side of the continuum.

The *strict interpersonal leader* addresses relationships between members. Dyadic interactions, communication between members and the group as a whole, and the interpersonal consequences of behavior are highlighted. Techniques are designed to *isolate interactions* between members. The group provides a unique stimulus situation within which interactions between members can be explored. Success is measured by the *relationship of members* to one another. A primary focus in the group is on the *between-people barriers* that prevent full interpersonal interaction. Treatment approaches utilize the simulation of real-life interactions possible in a group. Opportunities then exist for members to try out novel strategies and resolve interpersonal problems.

The leader's role is more orchestrative, commonly active but generally nondirective. This focus is here-and-now or future rather than historical. In general, between-member rather than within-member concerns are customarily stressed. Success might be measured by the ability of the group to function "without a leader." The group, not the individual is the center of attention.

Each extreme of this continuum offers valuable ways to help members face and resolve dilemmas in their lives. However, adhering to either extreme will limit a leader's use of the opposite skills and fail to maximize the impact of the group treatment, particularly in a brief format.

For this reason, most successful leaders use a combination of interpersonal and intrapsychic interventions. Different stages of a group call for shifting foci. In a typical group, an intrapsychic orientation predominates in the Treatment phase whereas an interpersonal mode is more evident during the Transition phase. Of course, group goals and population will affect the relative use of each orientation.

Leaders proficient in both intrapsychic and interpersonal skills seem to have definite advantages. Frequently these abilities are consistent with greater training in group therapy.

What People Learn in Groups

Before comparing the interpersonal and intrapsychic styles, we should examine exactly what people learn in groups. What behaviors do change? What are the expectations for a "successful" graduate of group training?

LEARNING TO LEARN   At first, members must learn how to be available for what the group has to offer. They are confronted with

- a new language system
- a new way of looking at themselves and others
- a new set of rules, mores, or group ethics

NEW BEHAVIORS   Behaviors that make for good group membership are frequently quite different from those that provide back-home success.

- Members learn how to cope differentially with stress situations.
- They become more able to cope effectively with ambiguity and the elimination of status or roles that typically govern social interactions.
- They give and receive honest feedback.

The group in general, and the leader specifically, create an environment where all this learning can take place.

In the process, each member experiences anxiety, responds to it in his characteristic manner, and receives feedback from others about the impact and effectiveness of his particular anxiety-reducing strategies. Through such interactions, members learn how to separate their anxiety about the unknown from their fear of anxiety itself. This allows them to reduce their neurotic anxiety (fear of fear) and make informed decisions about how to experiment with their lives safely (cf. Frankl, 1963; Yalom, 1980).

NEW SKILLS   In the process of exploring their anxiety and characteristic behaviors and experimenting with new behaviors, members acquire some new skills that transfer well to their lives outside of group.

- They learn how to reduce anxiety through self-expression.
- They may learn how to be less fearful when not in control.
- They learn to cope with and be less fearful of rejection.
- They may become more skilled in assertiveness when dealing with authority figures.
- They increase their ability to be empathic.
- They learn how to be more trusting and trustworthy.
- They learn to be more responsible for their own thoughts and behavior.
- They become increasingly comfortable living more in the present.
- They experience a greater sense of community with others.
- They become more adept and open to helping others (altruism) and of being helped.
- They become much better problem solvers.

Each of these skills has been well documented in the short-term group literature (see Coche, 1983; Diamond & Shapiro, 1973; Dies, 1979; Dies & MacKenzie,
1983; Erickson, 1975; McCallum & Piper, 1990; Nicholas, 1984; Parloff & Dies,
1977; Shapiro, 1978; Shapiro & Diamond, 1972).

Comparing Leaders' Roles and Skills

Leaders normally employ a variety of roles and skills. Two of the most critical components in generating the various types of group learning are the leader's capabilities as a *model* for appropriate group behavior, and her enhanced power as a
dispenser of reinforcements.

Despite protestations to the contrary by many group facilitators, trainers, and
leaders, the group leader does lead. He or she plays several roles during the course
of a group: catalyst, orchestrator, information disseminator, a model for sharing
and communicating, reinforcer, and (sometimes) participant. Because of the nature
of groups, creation of ambiguity, elimination of typical roles, anxiety, and so on, the
therapist's behavior stands out as a beacon and a model of appropriateness in a
unique environment. In addition, because the therapist is usually the only person in
the room who knows what is expected in this ambiguous situation, her power and
influence as a model and reinforcer are greatly enhanced.

In examining leadership orientation with reference to these abilities, keep in
mind that the therapists' orientations we are describing here are on the extremes of
the continuum. Most individual leaders' orientations will fall somewhere between
the two poles.

In the role of therapist, the intrapsychic leader models behaviors such as getting clients to confront and work with the divergent aspects of their own personalities, probing, questioning, and interpreting past events, dreams, or unconscious
determinants of behavior. These roles are hardly appropriate for members to adopt.
Even if such behavior were acceptable for members in a group, it would be very
inappropriate in their day-to-day lives. In fact, members exhibiting these types of
behaviors in group are confronted with that most feared expletive: "You're acting
like a THERAPIST!"

Furthermore, members in a group with strict intrapsychic or highly charismatic leaders can learn to maximize rather than minimize problems. This is because
problem solving occurs for the individual only in the presence of a very potent,
apparently "omniscient" professional group therapist. This condition promotes a
belief among the members that they must have been quite psychologically disturbed
because of the level of professional assistance they needed to change. Indeed, strict
intrapsychic leaders tend to make no distinction between therapy and growth
groups; they may see the clientele of the latter groups as suffering from some relatively less severe level of neurotic conflicts. By contrast, help received from a fellow
member in the group setting tends to minimize the scope of the problem and helps
a person perceive himself as less sick and his or her problem as more workable.

When the intrapsychic leader works individually with members, others tend
to "wait for their turn" to expose "their problem." At times, waiting may be difficult, nonspontaneous, unfruitful, or boring. When members are encouraged to

interact with one another, however, issues emerge spontaneously, without dependence on the leader, and with the full ownership of feelings by members. They have not been pushed into anything they can subsequently dismiss as "the therapist's agenda." An additional danger from a leader with a strict intrapsychic approach is the ability to project his own intrapsychic conflicts onto the group members and (assuming similarity) help them resolve their conflicts.

If the leader is the sole therapeutic agent, the members do not have the altruistic experience of serving as therapeutic agents themselves. Thus they lose an experience that can be ego building and self-satisfying, and can have great potential for emotional growth. The total amount of sharing among members is also reduced, diminishing their value as reinforcers for one another.

Finally, studies on encounter group casualties (Lieberman, Yalom, & Miles, 1973) have demonstrated that the intrapsychically oriented, highly charismatic leader is the most likely to produce casualties. The "guru" is impressive and develops many "groupies," proselytizers, and converts to his personal religion, but an approach that combines the in-depth intrapsychic approach with an interpersonal focus is more successful and potentially less dangerous for group members.

Like the extreme intrapsychic therapist, the strict interpersonal group therapist also has failings. A leader who functions primarily as an interpersonal process commentator, bringing people together, then fading into the background is a poor model for problem solving, interpersonal interaction, and spontaneity. The group essentially is denied the special distance and expertise of a professional counselor. The pure interpersonal leader also has low value as a dispenser of reinforcement.

The accomplished leader is able to be both interpersonal and intrapsychic to varying degrees at different times with different members and must be able to distinguish among these times. Some groups call for a more intrapsychic or interpersonal style throughout. Leaders best serve a group when they allow members to test their ability to develop both freedom and control, encourage their interaction and mutual help, and yet protect them from going too far astray in their experimentation. In this realm, successful leadership is similar to effective parenting. One needs to let children explore their world freely while assuring that the child is safe during the exploration.

The accomplished leader will have an orientation to groups that fits his own personality, beliefs, and values. Whether it leans more toward the interpersonal or intrapsychic is of less import than the congruity with the leader's personal values and ethics. For the novice group therapist, however, an interpersonal orientation is less dangerous than an intrapsychic one: The positive strengths of group members are more easily elicited by interpersonal group leaders; power and influence in the group are more widely dispersed.

Group therapists can be compared to one another by reference to their leadership orientation, but this is not an absolute scale by any means. It is presented as a way to cluster therapists and make generalizations about their "fit" with a particular patient group. Each style is appropriate with different populations of patients. With young children, severely disturbed individuals, and many institutionalized populations for example, a more intrapsychic, leader-to-member orientation may be necessary. In higher-functioning groups, a more interpersonal, member-to-member style may be the more productive orientation.

Depending on the extent to which the leader is oriented toward depth and personality restructuring or interpersonal skill development, each leader will fulfill the variety of leadership roles to varying degrees. The intrapsychic leader may put more effort and group time into the catalyst function than into orchestration. An interpersonal leader in an encounter group may actually participate in the group, not unlike a member might, whereas a more intrapsychic leader would not approach memberlike behaviors except in the rarest circumstances.

THE MULTIPLE ROLES OF GROUP LEADERSHIP

Group leaders generally play five major roles in the course of the group process:

- Information disseminator
- Catalyst
- Orchestrator
- Model-participant
- Dispenser of reinforcement/environment manipulator

Each role continues throughout the process, but at certain times, a single role has primacy. The *timing* for heightened employment of a given role is often a major determinant of group outcomes.

The Group Leader as a Disseminator of Information

In the most traditional role for leaders of all groups, the leader provides information. The counselor, therapist, or mental health worker is an expert who shares his or her expertise with group members. In this sense, the group is similar to most physician-patient interactions or educational experiences, in which the leader is the teacher or expert and the members are students or supplicants. The leader presents a curriculum that he or she hopes will be acquired by the members. To be effective, this information must be individualized to the recipients' needs and motivational levels. The group leader must be aware of resources and content that relate to the group experience.

The information dissemination role attains primacy during two group phases. The first occurs early in the group process. During Phase 1, Preparation, the leader presents members with a considerable amount of specific information about the group. This role carries over into the first few stages of the Transition phase (i.e., ground rules, beginning exercise.) The second time for heightened use of this role is in the Termination phase of the group process. At this time, leaders may suggest follow-up work or provide specific suggestions for members.

Information dissemination must be done moderately. Overuse of this role can become a simulated lecture, hardly useful for the kinds of learning expected in a group. Underuse may also lead to wasteful nondirectiveness. In some cases, a single piece of information can save large quantities of time and effort. The following "comical" event is presented verbatim:

Bob: Lew, where's the bathroom?

Lew (Leader): You'd like to know where the bathroom is.

Bob: Yeah, that's what I asked.

Lew: You seem irritated.

Bob [*patronizingly*]: Lewis, where's the bathroom?

Lew: You're upset with me, because I haven't told you where the bathroom is.

Bob [*angrily*]: WHERE'S THE BATHROOM?

Lew: Now you sound angry.

Bob [*with cold anger*]: If you don't tell me where the bathroom is right now I'm going to use your pants leg as a urinal.

At this point the "leader" produced a door key and instructions. Bob took the key and left. He did not return for four sessions.

Such evasive refusal to give information is atypical, but many leaders, trained to be wary of personal disclosure that will inhibit the development of appropriate transference, do balk at providing facts for members. It is important for a group therapist to know when to give information, how much to give, and what the implications are of giving or withholding specific information.

In addition to information regarding group procedures and helpful hints to members of how to use the group more effectively, leaders are sometimes asked for personal information by members. As a rule of thumb, it is more facilitative for leaders to attend to the process extant in the group than to disclose specific details about their lives. When leaders do share their personal reactions, it is generally more important for them to disclose their momentary in-group experience than particulars of their back-home life. For example, it is more appropriate for a leader to share a feeling of sadness in the group than to detail a recent personal romantic failure.

The Group Leader as Catalyst

In the role of a catalyst, the group therapist serves two functions: As a generator of excitement or spark plug for the group, and as a mover of the group to its critical point, leaders highlight and channel patterns of verbal and nonverbal communication within the group, acknowledge less obvious or nonverbal expressions of affect, ask about members' feelings, and aim the group in the direction of a present, here-and-now focus. The leader uses a cooperative rather than competitive mode of communication and urges participants to risk revealing their personal beliefs and feelings rather than challenging those of others. She is most responsive to group levels of arousal and group feelings that reflect members' concerns. Fiebert (1968), to whom credit is given for naming both the catalyst and orchestrator roles, says that the catalyst "holds up a mirror to the group so that they can view their behavior, chides members for their superficiality, and urges them towards bonds of intimacy" (p. 935).

The catalyst role reaches its apex during Phases II and III of the group process, while members are learning how to be group members, and are going through the therapeutic intervention stages. The more intrapsychic a leader, the more he or she will use the catalyst role. Most intrapsychic interventions use catalyst skills.

Overemployment of this role can create a group dependency. The members will consistently look to the leader to entertain and provide therapy for them; they will not learn to become catalysts for one another.

Underuse can also have negative effects. In a group where the leader shies away from the catalyst role, members may become confused, directionless, bored or apathetic. They may also never learn the major focuses of the group process and will not know what parts of their experience to discuss; they may therefore wander aimlessly through the time allotted for group meetings. The level of arousal may be so low as to be nonfacilitative as a motivating factor.

The following is a vignette from a group experience during the therapeutic phase, showing a leader acting as a catalyst. One member had just finished talking about her lack of interest in sex with her husband as a result of her ongoing affair with one of his friends. As the group was working with this problem, one of the leaders noticed that another woman member's face was pale and she was showing general signs of anxiety.

Jerry (Leader 1):   Betsy, could you verbalize that?

Betsy: Huh . . . what . . . well . . .

Jerry [supporting]:   What Joan was talking about seems to be affecting you a great deal.

Betsy: I feel scared.

Jerry: About what?

Betsy: My husband seems disinterested in me lately, and I'm really scared.

Susan (Leader 2):   What Joan said makes you wonder whether he's having an affair and that's why he's not interested in sex with you.

Betsy [tearfully]:   Yes!

Susan [after Betsy was somewhat consoled]:   Can you verbalize your feelings now?

Betsy: I'm really scared that he found someone better, and I've been ignoring his coming home late at night.

Jerry: You sound scared . . . and angry.

Betsy: Yes, I think I am angry, I was a virgin when we got married and never had the chance to explore like Joan.

At this point the leaders orchestrated the process and had Joan and Betsy talk together. Subsequently, they came back to Betsy more intrapsychically and allowed her to explore the relative reality of her fear and a long-term suspiciousness and jealousy. She was then able to probe her own desire for distance from her husband, ultimately concluding that her husband was more likely to be working late at the office and wanting more contact with her than he was to be involved with another woman. She did resolve to talk more openly with him.

The Group Leader as Orchestrator

The role of orchestrator shares precedence with the catalyst role during the two middle group phases. The leader serves as a conveyor of issues, feelings, and information. In a sense, she mediates the communication between members of the group. The members begin to learn that they have the ability to help one another.

Orchestration involves connecting one member's needs with other members' resources. Leaders put members with problems in touch with members who share their difficulties and can assist in resolution. Rather than leading the discussion, the group leader assists it by asking questions, reflecting individuals' feelings, underlining considerations that are growth producing, and highlighting and interpreting communication patterns. The leader is particularly sensitive to nonverbal aspects of communication such as tones of voice, body language, kinetics, and discrepancies between verbal and nonverbal components of messages. However, as an orchestrator, she does not interpret these directly, as she did in the catalyst role. Instead, she observes patterns that indicate resources and alignments within the group, and connects members, based in part on these observations and in part on their expression of similar content.

Effective orchestration requires an ongoing understanding of group process. Appropriately administered, it will maximize group learning as it increases members' participation in problem solving. It is thus a most powerful mode of learning. Orchestration skills are quite often used by leaders with interpersonal orientations.

Perhaps the most crucial aspect of this role is that it is ultimately expendable. A major index of its success is obsolescence. When group members learn to communicate spontaneously, freely, and openly they eliminate the need for the leader to manage their interactions.

An example of orchestration occurred in a couples group at the onset of the therapeutic phase. Sherry and Michael are a young married couple.

John [*addressing the leaders*]:   You know, I think Michael and Sherry really are in a bad way.

Gail (Leader 1):   Tell them that. [*orchestrating*]

John: You guys seem angry at each other every single session.

Paul (Leader 2):   You're concerned about them? [*catalyst*]

John: Yeah, I'd like them to get it together more.

Sherry: I feel O.K.

Michael: That's the problem: whenever I confront her she says, "Hey man, it's cool."

Peggy: Sherry, it doesn't look O.K. to me.

Paul: Sherry, what do you hear John saying? [*orchestrating*]

Sherry: That he's uptight.

Paul: What was he saying?

Sherry: Well, he says he's concerned, but it's more like a put down.

Gail: So you feel . . . [*catalyst*]

Sherry: Angry and unwilling.

Paul: John, is that what you wanted? [*catalyst*]

John: She just doesn't listen.

Paul: What message did you want to give her? [*orchestrating*]

John: That I do care and that I think she's denying and repressing.

Paul: How could you say that so Sherry would hear it? [*orchestrating*]

John: I could say, "Hey, I feel uptight when you look angry."

Gail: Try that. [*orchestrating*]

John: Sherry, I get scared to talk to you when you and Michael are fighting and you seem so angry.

Gail: Sherry, what do you hear him saying? [*orchestrating*]

Sherry: When I'm angry it scares him.

Gail: But when you're angry you're also scared.

Sherry: [*Nods and looks down.*]

Gail: Who in here would you like to know that you're scared, without having to tell them? [*orchestrating*]

Sherry: Michael.

Gail: How could you let him know? [*orchestrating*]

Sherry: I don't know.

Paul: Michael, what is your reaction to what Sherry is saying? [*orchestrating*]

The orchestration done by both leaders was facilitative in allowing Michael and Sherry to become more empathic with each other and to improve their own communication. The leaders did not return until later to the other issue: John's role and motivation. At this point, the key issue was the couple's interaction.

Overutilization of the orchestration role at the expense of other roles can eliminate the leader's special therapeutic expertise. In this case, the leader serves only as a conveyor/facilitator and not as a catalyst, information disseminator, model, or reinforcer. In such a situation, the highest level of functioning for the group is determined by group members rather than the leader. Because the group cannot surpass the functioning level of its participants, overuse of orchestration severely limits its effectiveness. Characteristically, this deficit occurs with an extreme interpersonal style or novice leader.

Underemployment of the orchestration role also limits group effectiveness. Lack of orchestration reduces the impact members can have on one another, ameliorates altruism on the part of the members, and limits between-member learning. In a group with minimal orchestration, what is going on may resemble individual psychotherapy with an audience. This type of deficit is most likely to occur with a leader who has a strict intrapsychic orientation or with an individual psychotherapist untrained in group dynamics.

The Group Leader as Model-Participant

A major component of most complex learning is imitation. In their role as models, leaders demonstrate how to share information and feelings and demonstrate authentic, honest communication. The group leader needs to be flexible in applying values, open to new learning about himself, and able to show, by example, the process of learning how to learn. Leaders may also model spontaneity, genuine caring for others, sincerity, assertiveness, ability to contain anxiety, and conflict resolution skills.

In an unstructured situation, participants will naturally attempt to reduce their anxiety by providing structure. A common tactic by which members accomplish this is to look to the authority figure for clues of appropriate (tension-reducing) behavior. It is here that most members begin to imitate leadership behaviors. Some obvious forms of this imitation are the adoption of the leader's language by members and the seemingly unconscious appropriation of the leader's nonverbal communication cues. One example of this occurred in a group led by a colleague who had a habit of rhythmically stroking her long hair during periods of silence and high tension. By the fourth week of the group all six female group members were occasionally stroking their own hair the same way. This was even true for one woman who had short hair and who in effect was stroking hair that would not be long for years!

These examples are an indication of external modeling. Although interesting, they are relatively impermanent and not meaningful as changes; they simply illustrate how rapidly and insidiously modeling occurs. An example of a more psychological form of modeling was seen in a therapy group in which a member was describing relatively dispassionately the recent death of his father.

Harvey: So I had to go to the funeral . . . that was a bummer . . . missed all my friends here.

Michael (Leader 1):   You know, I hear a very sad-sounding message, but I don't see any emotion. [*catalyst*]

Marion: Yeah, I can't even feel any sympathy for you.

Harvey [*coldly*]:   I wasn't asking for any.

Larry (Leader 2):   Harvey, what was your dad like?

Harvey: He was O.K., pretty cold, never really paid much attention to any of us. I don't really miss him . . . but I feel like I should.

Larry: When someone is cold to me and I love him, it hurts a lot. [*modeling-participating*]

Marion: I don't know; sometimes when someone is cold to me, I just understand it's the way he is.

Larry: Like Harvey was to you just now. [*orchestrating*]

Marion: Yeah. [*Then smiling, almost embarrassed*] I do care for you Harv, and I don't like being shut out.

Harvey: It's just hard to get into those feelings.

Sarah: Do you want to?

Harvey: Yes, but I'm not sure.

Michael [*with moist eyes*]: My father died seven years ago and it still makes me very sad when I think of how I miss him. [*model-participant, catalyst*]

Harvey [*looking at Michael*]: It's just so frustrating. There's so much I wanted to say and some of it is not nice at all . . . [*Here he began crying and opening himself to his grief.*]

Without question, the leader's empathy and willingness to share his own sadness played a huge role in helping this patient experience some of his necessary grief.

If the group leader can be accepting, spontaneous, self-disclosing, encouraging of others to examine themselves, cooperative, intimate, expressive of feelings in a here-and-now context, and nondefensive, group members can imitate these behaviors. Bandura and Walters (1963) have shown that imitation learning is maximized when the model has high status and receives positive reinforcements for behavior. The group leader comfortably fits these criteria.

Overuse of the model-participant role can not only diminish its effectiveness but also reduce the value of all the other leadership roles. A leader who becomes, for all intents and purposes, a member of the group can cause it to follow his own personal agenda. In this way, the group members are used as therapists or sounding boards for the leader's own growth, instead of the reverse. In addition, the level of self-disclosure by the leader can be either more superficial or deeper than that of members. Thus, members may hasten to conform to the leader's level of self-disclosure and in the process, lose their own. When this happens, and one individual is more responsible than others for setting a level, a greater artificiality results.

An example of overusing the model-participant role occurred in a growth group.

Bob [*to leader*]: You know, I'm not sure I feel comfortable enough here to really talk about some things.

Brian (Leader): That really pisses me off. You've just got to take more responsibility for yourself.

Bob: I'm trying to; I just feel punished and untrusting.

Brian: Bullshit; you're trying to suck me in to begging you to "tell us" and then [*in a mocking voice*], "I've got something to tell you but I won't tell you what it is, nyah, nyah."

Bob [*angrily*]: Sounds like that's your problem, not mine.

Brian: *That* puts *me* down, like I'm not listening, or not following your expectation of me as a leader.

Pat: I think you're being a bit hard on Bob. Is this pushing one of your buttons?

Brian: You may be right. I guess it's my struggle with authority and being a good leader.

He then proceeded to analyze his own behavior in detail. Brian may have provided an example of self-disclosure to the group, but very much at Bob's expense. His solipsistic approach to the group will encourage members either toward being the leader's caretaker or imitating his "me first" self-centered approach.

Underparticipation may also be detrimental to group process. When members see the leader engaging only in nonparticipatory roles, they are apt to imitate his or her behaviors. Such behavior on the part of members is inappropriate. Members are not encouraged to orchestrate and catalyze without self-disclosure. Indeed, they are often criticized by other members for doing so. If the leader does not model appropriate behaviors for members, his potency as a model will be diminished, and members may simply imitate the inappropriate behaviors.

The Group Leader as Dispenser of Reinforcement and Environment Manipulator

Because the group is an ambiguous situation, it is anxiety producing. Some therapists believe that moderate levels of anxiety must be present for optimal amounts of learning to be produced. Given these two parameters, the group leader is in a position to create a group environment that maximizes growth and learning by controlling the level of anxiety. The most efficient way for the group leader to control the level of anxiety is to regulate the level of ambiguity. In much of Western culture, ambiguity and anxiety are related approximately linearly. The therapist can lower levels of anxiety by adding structure or add anxiety by reducing structure.

One manner of adding structure is through judicious selective reinforcement. In a group setting, this can include such behaviors as head nodding, verbal acknowledgment, attention, or smiling. In providing this kind of acknowledgment, the leader lets members know that they are on the right track, that this is approved behavior, and that they should continue on this path. Such reinforcement has double value. It helps members feel positive, and it helps reduce anxiety by structuring the situation. Conversely, the ambiguity anxiety can be increased by nonreinforcement from the leaders.

Leaders can cause group anxiety to fluctuate by other techniques. They can raise anxiety by calling attention to a specific group member's behavior or making expectant eye contact with one member. Conversely, by making group-level interpretations (e.g., "Seems like we're all feeling uncomfortable now, but it's hard for anyone to change the situation"), leaders can lower anxiety. In one sense, much of the learning in a group setting can be viewed as a function of motivation produced by the leader's control of group anxiety.

In dispensing reinforcement, the group leader does more than simply provide structure. She is a powerful model and respected authority figure in the group, whose approval is valued tremendously. Members quickly learn how to please the therapist by acting in accordance with her apparent desires. In the group setting, members are reinforced for openness, genuineness, honesty, hard work, self-disclosure, motivation to change, listening and responding to others, flexibility in application of values, acceptance of others, and so on. These abilities stand members in good stead outside the group setting as well.

Overmanipulation by the group leader will cause group members to mistrust her. If they perceive her as a somewhat inhuman dispenser of reinforcement, members will curry favor by producing reenforceable behaviors without any commitment. This is similar to students "psyching out" what a teacher wants to hear or see on an exam and producing those bits of information on paper while forgetting their content and meaning almost simultaneously. They may get the reinforcement of high grades, but understanding the material requires a different type of incorporation.

By contrast, underutilization of this role may produce a rather laissez-faire chaos. In this situation, the group can remain over- or understructured, and hence over- or underaroused for long periods of time. In such an environment, learning takes place only minimally and by chance.

There is more to group leadership than multiple roles. Stylistic and personality characteristics distinguish leaders, but there is not yet consensus on the characteristics mandatory for effective group leadership.

INFORMATION SYSTEMS OF GROUP LEADERS

To conduct a group successfully, leaders must play the several roles described earlier in the chapter: information disseminator, catalyst, orchestrator, model-participant, and dispenser of reinforcement. To do this, they rely on basic skills to take in the information they need to intervene effectively. Above all, the leader must be perceptive and open to the data available in a group setting.

If individuals are to function effectively in multiple leadership roles, they must be able to incorporate and evaluate simultaneously several major sets of data. In a sense, the leader must operate like a multitrack tape recorder, receiving messages from five overlapping yet distinct sources, mixing these inputs, and then producing a single response. The leader must be sensitive to

1. The verbal content of members' messages
2. Nonverbal messages of members
3. The context in which the message occurs
4. His or her own feelings
5. His or her theoretical understanding or interpretation of the group process

To respond to the group members effectively, the leader must be able to incorporate all five inputs and decode them. With all these data, however, the leader can respond to only a fraction of the information received. What distinguishes the most effective leaders is related to *which fraction* the leader responds to and the *timing* of the intervention. This is a complex task involving each of the five data sources.

Content of Members' Messages

The most obvious source of data is what is being said by the members at a given time. The content of a message is simply the verbal component—the words—as they would appear in written form. The content of a message is the precise statement made by the sender.

Two examples help clarify this data source. Here is the first:

Jim: I really feel happy today.

The content of this message, "I really feel happy today," may not be very believable if it is said in a loud tone of voice, through clenched teeth, or as the person is banging the door of the room as he exits. Even though the message is not believable, the content remains the same.

The content is the same in the following example, even though the total message may be interpreted otherwise:

Sam: Jim, you'd better sit down; I've got some really bad news.

Jim: I really feel happy today.

Here the content "I really feel happy today" is the same as it was above, but the context alters the message considerably.

These examples show that the verbal content is only one component of the message received by a group leader. It is an important component, however, and leaders need to be aware of what is being said.

Nonverbal Messages of Members

Communication is not entirely verbal. Tones of voice, body positions, body movement, relative distance between people, and eye contact all serve to qualify verbal messages, and they communicate in and of themselves. Normally, verbal and nonverbal components convey the same message. When they do, we hardly notice the nonverbal message. However, when the verbal and nonverbal components are discrepant, the receiver must realize that the message is complex. What part of Jim's communication will we believe? He says, "I really feel happy today" in a loud tone of voice, through clenched teeth, banging the door. Choosing either the verbal "happiness" or the nonverbal "anger" will give us only a partial picture.

Similarly, in our culture, if one person says, "Have a taste of this pie, it's really delicious" to another, and winks one eye in the direction of a third person, an observer would expect collusion between the speaker and the third person and an unpleasant surprise for the pie taster. The verbal message is qualified by the nonverbal wink.

Most people in mental health fields, trained in nonverbal communication, have a tendency to give primacy to nonverbal meanings. Such cues as eye contact or lack of eye contact are taken to reflect emotional states or veracity. Movement toward an individual while conversing with him or her is interpreted as a desire to communicate; and movement away is seen as the reverse. Keeping one's arms folded across the chest and sitting behind a barrier are generally interpreted as signs of defensiveness. Nonverbal data are collected and analyzed even with reference to a person's location in the group; members tend to sit close to people they believe are supporting them, across from people who attract them, and at right angles to people with whom they are not comfortable.

In receiving such nonverbal data, leaders must be cautious in their interpretations. If two distinctly different messages are received, assuming that one is correct and the other incorrect is generally a mistake. The fact that there are two conflicting messages is the critical piece of information. This observation may be presented as feedback to the member or filed away by the leader for later use. Here is an example of feedback.

Kathy: This group has helped me so much I feel like a new person.

Norman (Leader 1):   You're saying something that would seem to indicate that you're happy, yet you look sad when you say it.

Kathy: Well, the group *has* helped me.

Norman: But there's more that you need.

Kathy: Yes.

Norman: Would you like to share that?

Kathy [*smiling at Norman and leaning forward*]:   I'm not sure.

Harriet (Leader 2):   You'd like to share, but you want Norman to ask you.

Kathy [*angrily*]:   Why do you always have to psychologize with us?

Harriet: This is between you and Norm and you resent my joining in.

Kathy [*to Norman*]:   When I saw you on the bus yesterday, you didn't even notice me. I felt put down.

Norman: I never saw you. Did you say hello?

Kathy: I was embarrassed.

Both leaders in this example confronted Kathy with her "double messages" in the context of several other leadership interventions. This type of feedback, properly timed, can be remarkably effective. For the most part, however, leaders will confront a member like this only after they have seen similar behaviors or have developed enough understanding of the individual that their confrontation occurs *with a particular goal in mind*. In this case, both leaders were willing to work with Kathy on her transference feelings with them.

Nonverbal behaviors are an important source of input with reference to other aspects of group process, especially when they contradict verbal content.

Contextual Cues

No communication is delivered in a void. As Haley (1963) so clearly indicates, each message contains two components: information, and a redefinition of the current relationship between the communicators. In a two-way communication, each message given by either party confirms the current definition of the relationship as symmetrical or complementary, or it is an attempt to redefine the relationship.

Understanding the nature of such communication in a two-person situation is difficult; understanding such communication in a multiperson (group) setting is a mammoth undertaking. If we follow this assumption, each time a group member communicates with any other member or leader, he or she is in effect simultaneously defining his or her relationships with each other member and the leader as well.

Whenever a person instigates a communication, the context in which this message is sent plays an important function. For example, it may be appropriate to say something at a baseball game that would be very inappropriate in a church. Whenever a member sends a message in a group, he or she does so with some awareness of the total context; frequently the statement is made strategically. Thus, a member may say something to the leader as a way of presenting himself to another member. In the following example, the member was talking directly to the leader but was much more interested in communicating to another member.

Peter: I just think that if people dig each other, whatever they do is cool.

Betty [*looking at Doris, a leader*]:   You know, I think my husband's really uptight. He's old fashioned . . . it's like he thinks that if I ever get it on with another guy I'd be ruined forever.

Harold: Does he feel that he can screw around?

Betty: You mean double standard? No . . . he's not interested. [*Then, turning to leader*] Doris, what should I do if I feel turned on to someone and want to go with those feelings, but Herb [husband] would really flip out?

Doris (Leader 1):   Is there someone here you're turned onto now?

Betty [*embarrassed*]:   That's not the issue. The issue is that he set the rule and he doesn't want to break it, but what if I do . . . ?

Doris: Are you concerned about who make the rules, or the consequences of violating them?

Len: Why don't you do it and not tell him?

Betty: But then if he found out . . .

Richie (Leader 2):   Which is your concern?

Betty: I don't think it's fair.

Richie: Is there someone here you'd like to explore this with?

Betty [*looking down, and in a soft voice*]:   Claude. [*At this point Peter looked very disappointed.*]

Claude: Uh, oh, . . . um . . . I mean.

Richie: That surprises you?

Claude: Yes.

Doris: What about Peter?

Here both Betty and Peter blushed and proceeded to share some elaborate fantasies they harbored for one another. Peter's general comment to the group was accurately perceived by Betty as an invitation, and Betty's comments to Doris were as much an acknowledgment of Peter's invitation as they were a comment about her husband.

The leaders were cognizant of this, and they acted as catalysts and orchestrators to bring the issue to the fore and deal with it. In this situation, Betty and Peter both felt tremendous relief in sharing their fantasies, and they did not act them out. Once the feelings were exposed, the excitement was experienced, and the need for action was reduced.

In this case, the content and nonverbal messages were secondary to the implied relationship between members. The leaders' understanding and acknowledgment of the interactions between the members allowed them to deal effectively with the issue.

Leaders' Own Feelings

Of all the sources of input, the most predominant spur to direct action is the leaders' emotions. Most individuals generally act from what they feel rather than what they think. Group leaders are no exception. If a group leader feels angry or happy or sad in a group setting, his interactions with members will reflect this. Consequently, leaders must know themselves well. If emotions are generated from group process, leaders can use their own emotions as a highly tuned pickup system. If, during the group session, a leader suddenly starts feeling anxious, he must search around the group to discover the source of this anxiety. Is it something a member is saying? Is it a feeling in the room because of what members are not saying? Is it that the topic has much unresolved conflict for the leader?

Two Crazy Yet Utilitarian Assumptions

Each leader makes two heuristic assumptions in a group setting that reflect otherwise indefensible beliefs.

1. My feelings are an accurate and in-depth index of the group process.
2. Whatever I feel is a result of something that is going on in the group.

If leaders are to be guided by these assumptions, they must be aware of their own needs, expectancies, weaknesses, and reactions, and they must have a clear understanding of any nongroup-related pressures. If the leader had a fight with his wife before coming to the group session, his reactions to members may be more a reflection of those feelings than of anything actually occurring in the group.

One example of such nongroup-related emotion took place in a group in which one of the co-leaders had an important romantic relationship painfully end at 3 A.M. prior to a 9 A.M. marathon session. By the time the group began he was feeling hurt, sad, lonely, and frightened. In this position, his sense receptors for such feelings in others were hypersensitive. As is so frequently the case in such situations, a member of the group had similar problems, and the leader was extraperceptive and effective in helping her through a five-year emotional block. Because the situations were so similar—rejection, feelings of loss and helplessness—he was almost brilliant in this intervention and helped the member substantially.

When the co-leader, who was aware of the entire situation, invited the troubled leader to share his own grief, the latter appropriately declined but was unable to continue effectively in a leadership role for several hours. Fortunately, the group could treat him as a member, and the co-leader could take charge. Had the co-leader not been fully aware of the situation, and had the outside problem not been the clear generator of all these feelings, misunderstanding and confusion could have resulted.

Leaders frequently rely on their feelings. They assume that if they are responding in a certain way to an individual, significant others may be responding similarly, and this may be a clue or manifestation of an individual client's problems. To keep this sensory channel clear, leaders must be self-aware and understand their own sensitivities.

Theoretical Understanding

From our perspective, a theory provides a leader with several essential qualities necessary to make sense out of the apparent chaos of group interactions. Theories operate as filters, letting in relevant (understandable) data and blocking out irrelevant stimuli. They increase the amplitude of the primary signal and reduce others as noise. In addition to pointing out where the leader should look, theories provide sets of constructs that explain what the data mean when the leader finds it. They also provide a manner of response so that the therapist, having discovered and interpreted the data, has clear options for reactions to the data.

Thus, leaders use their theories to tell them what is important, why it is important, and what to do about it. Without a theoretical or interpretive understanding of group behavior, a leader is confronted with a wide array of uncoordinated information, no consistent way to understand it, and no step-by-step plan of action. In short, without a theory, a group leader will respond spontaneously, inconsistently, and ineffectively.

The particular theory a group therapist holds seems relatively unimportant. The essential point is that the leader must apply it consistently and be aware of its limitations in helping him or her identify, classify, and act on diverse data.

ONE PIECE OF GROUP PROCESS

The way a group therapist uses these five systems (verbal content, nonverbal messages, the context in which the message occurs, leaders' personal feelings, and theory) and applies them to the leadership roles is shown in the following example and process analysis. The 10 group members are briefly described as follows:

Agnes   39 years old, divorcee. Very angry outwardly, seems to direct anger at men in general. When not speaking, seems depressed.

Barbara   30 years old, married, two children. Describes herself as happy but unfulfilled. Husband reportedly treats her as object of his own gratification rather than understanding her needs.

Betty   29 years old, military wife, husband away for nine months. Working on B.A. at university; regularly has affairs while husband is away.

Charles   48 years old, psychiatrist. Has been an effective private practitioner for several years. Divorced and living alone. Tends to be more "therapeutic" than involved in relationships with others.

Karl   41 years old, minister, married, five children; has been sexually involved with several women in congregation. Very concerned that wife or church authorities will find out. Reportedly anxious to end this "addiction."

Ray   26 years old, married. Very athletic, engages in various sports at least three nights a week. Presents a strong machismo image but appears very sensitive underneath it. Currently his wife is very angry with him, threatening to leave him; he is confused about this.

Sandy   28, nurse, has lived with 49-year-old lover for five years. Not happy with relationship but frightened of moving.

Susan   29, successful, high-paid model. Unsure of life goals, very unsure of relationships with men. Aware that she presents herself sexually but resents it when men relate "only to my body." Looking for permanent relationship. Divorced twice, had an eating disorder in her teens.

Toshio   34, immigrated to United States at age of five. Very quiet and polite, seems accepting of others. Painfully unable to request anything for himself.

Willie   32, Single. Describes himself as a swinger and has been in an untold number of relationships. Proudly revealed that he doesn't use "safe sex," and that he had slept with 100 women in one year. Groupwise, he says all the right-sounding things, but they seem somehow disconnected from him. Has been in every "growth" experience to hit town in past five years.

This event occurs during the early stages of the therapeutic phase of the group. The scenario is first presented in its entirety; then a process analysis is provided in tabular form. Note that the analysis sequence is described as if we were inside the leaders' heads.

Susan: There's something that is bothering me that I'd like to talk about.

Fay (Leader 1):   Go ahead.

Susan: I just ended another relationship with this weekend. He's a good guy, too.

Fay [*expectantly*]:   But . . .

Susan: It's like all he's ever interested in is sex. I like sex too, but it's like my body is all he wants.

Ray: Well, you do have a really nice bod.

Susan: Yeah, I know, and I feel good about that, but I'm more than just big boobs and a piece of ass.

Fay: You'd like him or anyone to appreciate your body, but also to appreciate the inner parts of yourself.

Susan [*weeping*]:   Yeah, I need to know if he loves me.

Agnes: Your body won't last forever and as soon as you start to sag, he'll take off and find some other honey who's younger. You know, Susie, most men are bastards like that.

[*30-second silence*]

Karl: I don't think that's fair. There's so much more important than a woman's figure.

Sandy: Sue, I know what you're talking about. I think a guy like that is better off gone.

Susan: Yeah, but what if they're all like that?

Willie [*smiling and looking at Susan*]:   You just need to find another kind of man.

Sandy: Easier said than done.

Ray: Like Willie?

Charles: I wonder, Susan, if you attract only those kinds of men.

Agnes [*sarcastically*]:   Right, it's always the woman's fault. "She didn't get raped, she led him on."

Charles: Your anger is really getting in the way. I feel that perhaps Susan is attracting these kinds of guys because of where she looks, because of what she does with them, or maybe as a subconscious way of proving that all men are no good.

Betty: Do you think that's possible?

Susan: Yeah. I've screwed up two marriages, and sometimes think I married bastards as a defense against letting myself be intimate.

Larry (Leader 2):   Sandy, can you verbalize that?

Sandy [*tearfully*]:   That just hits home.

Larry: You're in a similar situation?

Sandy: [*nods*]

Larry: Can you tell Susan?

Sandy: You know Bob, the guy I live with? Well, he's a good man, but he's just insensitive to my needs. Maybe I won't let him try, but it's just that he won't listen to any really deep feelings.

Fay: That really hurts.

Sandy: God, it's like there's a part of me that's too ugly for anyone to live with.

[*During the silence, both women are crying now, and Larry moves over to where Barbara is sitting and puts his arm around her shoulders. She also begins to cry.*]

Ray [*with trembling lips*]:   That's not only true for women.

Larry: You've felt that also.

Ray: [*nods*]

Larry: I've experienced a feeling of not being understood also. It really hurts when you pay attention to it.

Charles: You've got to pay attention to it. If you understand it, you can come to grips with your humanity.

Willie: That's the asshole way. You just experience it as that's the way it is, and it's O.K.

Karl: What does that mean?

Willie [*condescendingly*]:   It's all the same. It's what *is*. You can't take responsibility for anyone else.

Fay: Susan, where are you now?

Susan: Feeling hurt and scared.

Fay: Talk about the fear.

Susan: I'm scared I just drive all men away because I'm not open. But if I open up I get clobbered. It's like if you're a model, only one kind of man approaches.

Larry: Barbara, can you share your feelings with Susan?

Barbara [*very tearfully*]: It's not [related to] being a model. Bill and I have been married eight years and I really love the guy, but I use sex to avoid sharing really intimate parts of me. I started to get involved with Charlie, just to have someone I could tell those things to, but it started to get sexual and I pulled out.

Fay: If you got involved that way with Bill, you'd be vulnerable to hurt, but if you don't open up with your husband, you need a relationship on the side, which has even greater problems.

Barbara: Really!

Fay: That hooks into Susan's feelings of frustration also.

Larry: Karl, you look like someone kicked you in the stomach. What are you feeling?

Karl: It's like something really important is being said and I've got to face some stuff too.

Larry: You've gone the route of an affair also.

Karl: Several.

LEADERSHIP AND GROUP PROCESS

As shown in the process analysis (Table 6.1), the leaders respond verbally to only a fraction of the data they take in. For each comment they make, they must process their observations and feelings and incorporate them within their theoretical framework. The resulting interventions will be most potent when they are delivered with proper timing. Such skills take training and extensive supervised practice. Groups do not always move smoothly or in a linear fashion. The process ebbs and flows, and leaders must be prepared for untold variability.

Note that the leaders frequently respond verbally to nonverbal messages, interactions between members, and their own feelings. Both leaders choose the content of their interventions carefully and employ one of the leadership roles for delivery. Their goal is to help the group members move consistently to deeper levels of interactional involvement and to be more nurturing for each other. They participate, model, reinforce, catalyze, and orchestrate in such a way that the group becomes increasingly therapeutic. Realize, however, that not every intervention by the group leader has an immediate (or any) therapeutic impact. Often, apparently well-timed, accurate, and meaning-laden leader statements have little to no noticeable corresponding response by the group members. Learning and behavior change in group therapy occurs as it does in other settings; it requires time, practice, and repetition.

SUMMARY

An effective group leader plays many roles and performs many functions concurrently and sequentially. A continuum of leadership orientation from intrapsychic to interpersonal is presented as a backdrop for five major leadership roles. Strategic and tactful employment of orientation and role provides a fertile ground for group members' growth and learning. In addition, a number of personality characteristics enhance therapeutic success when they are present.

A leader's ability to use both an intrapsychic and an interpersonal orientation increases flexibility and effectiveness within a group. The intrapsychic orientation provides depth of individual learning as well as integration of historical with present interaction. The therapist is largely active and is a catalyzer and interpreter of intrapsychic processing. The strengths of this approach are that it models effective problem solving and can move the group to greater depth more quickly. The

(text continues on page 157)

Table 6.1 Process Analysis

Content	Nonverbal Messages	Interactions Between Members	Leader's Feelings	Leader's Thoughts/Theory	Leader's Role
Susan: There's something that is bothering me.	Susan's lips trembling. No large affect in others.		Comfortable, anticipatory.		
Fay: Go ahead.	Eye contact between Fay and Susan.	Everyone tuned in to Susan.	Anticipatory.	Probably something to do with men.	Catalyst
Susan: I just ended another relationship this weekend. He's a good guy, too.	Looking down, sad. Sandy avoids eye contact.	Sandy leans toward Susan. Willie tries to make eye contact.	Sadness about end of relationships in personal life. Caring for Susan.	Wonder what she does to pull men close and then push them away.	Model-participant (listening)
Fay: But . . .	Fay leans forward.	Everyone looks expectantly at Susan.	Caring for Susan.	I'd like to get her to share this openly.	Catalyst
Susan: It's like all he's ever interested in is sex. I like sex too, but it's like my body is all he wants.	Susan close to tears. Fay/Larry very tuned in. Sandy looking down.	Agnes seems to be sitting above Susan. Ray, Karl, Charles all seem close and open to her.	Caring for Susan. Fear that she will stop halfway. Confidence that group can deal with problem.	Want to keep her talking and avoid interruptions of other members.	
Ray: Well, you do have a really nice bod.	Ray looking at Susan's breasts. Susan turns red, smiles.	Willie, Ray, Karl looking at Susan's body. Agnes glaring at the men.	Fear this will sidetrack. Slight initial anger at Ray for his lack of sensitivity.	Ray broke the tension. He probably tried to do something nice. It should backfire. Susan is embarrassed. Wonder if she'll be angry or seductive.	Model-Participant

Table 6.1 **Process Analysis** (*continued*)

Content	Nonverbal Messages	Interactions Between Members	Leader's Feelings	Leader's Thoughts/Theory	Leader's Role
Susan: Yeah, I know, and I feel good about that, but I'm more than just big boobs and a piece of ass.	Susan looks embarrassed; sticks out breasts while she talks about them.	Seduction, competretion.	Attraction to Susan's body; competition.	She's being seductive. Could be an example of what she's describing—men treat her as sex object because she presents that part when she's emotional.	
Fay: You'd like him or anyone to appreciate your body but also to appreciate the inner parts of yourself.	Fay looks empathic. Susan about to cry. Agnes looks angry.	High anxiety. Each member seems to be focusing inward.	Tenderness toward Susan. Understanding of both needs.	See the fear reaction—seduction. See how she needs both caring for inner self and attractiveness to physical self. Wonder about confronting. Want to see group reaction.	Catalyst Reinforcer
Susan: Yeah. I need to know if he loves me.	Susan crying. Sandy near tears. Barbara pale. Agnes moving around a great deal.	Most seem to be focusing inward: little contact. Willie looking at Susan.	Tenderness toward Susan. Recalling personal hurt feelings.	Susan is at point of crying and feeling better temporarily versus going fully into the pattern. Decision to push her into greater awareness. Still waiting for group reaction.	Model-Participant (listening; nonverbal encouragement to continue).

Table 6.1 Process Analysis (*continued*)

Content	Nonverbal Messages	Interactions Between Members	Leader's Feelings	Leader's Thoughts/Theory	Leader's Role
Agnes: Your body won't last forever and as soon as you start to sag, he'll take off and find some other honey who's younger. You know, Susie, most men are bastards like that.	Agnes talking through clenched teeth, pressured speech, loud tone. Others pull back.	Attention focus shifts from Susan to Agnes.	Anger, disappointment, anxiety at this turn of events.	Agnes is anxious, expressing it as anger toward herself—interesting form of seductiveness. Wonder if anyone will fall for it and make political feminist response. Wonder if I/my co-leader should intervene or let group do it.	Model-Participant (nonverbally looking at Susan; away from Agnes). Environment Manipulator
[30 second silence]	Agnes glaring. Karl staring at Agnes. Susan weeping.	Karl staring at Agnes. Barbara looking at Susan. Others looking down.	Tense.		
Karl: I don't think that's fair. There's so much more important than a woman's figure.	Karl looks like he's holding back anger with "calm." Barbara looks anxious.	Lot of head nodding. Barbara looking at Susan with caring.	Disappointed that Karl opened door to Agnes.	Resolve to get focus back to Susan. Avoid Agnes's anger until more appropriate time.	Environment Manipulator

Table 6.1   **Process Analysis** *(continued)*

Content	Nonverbal Messages	Interactions Between Members	Leader's Feelings	Leader's Thoughts/Theory	Leader's Role
Sandy: Sue, I know what you're talking about. I think a guy like that is better off gone.	Turned toward Susan—back toward Karl who is staring at Sandy. Agnes taking a prone position.	Sandy obviously not reacting to Karl.	Confused; a bit uncomfortable. Interest in process.	Wonder about Sandy's cutting off Karl. Desire to refocus on Susan or unhappy with what he said? Could she have some feelings or history with Karl?	
Susan: Yeah, but what if they're all like that?	Agnes sits up. Sandy shakes head.			Sounds a bit facile. Will wait it out— too easy a response.	
Willie: You just need to find another kind of man.	Willie smiling, looking directly at Susan. Agnes turning red.	With Willie's seductive approach, Charles, Sandy, Karl, Agnes all pull back.	Angry at Willie's seductiveness. Jealousy.	Unhappy with Willie's seductiveness. Okay, here's a chance for enactment. Susan can deal with problem here and now.	Participant
Sandy: Easier said than done.	Ray grinning. Susan showing little affect.	General negative reaction to Willie.		Waiting to see how group reacts.	
Charles: I wonder, Susan if you attract only those kinds of men.	Speaking quietly.	Group attention turning to Charles.		Charls is in his familiar junior therapist mode. Wonder if he should be confronted or will he offer Susan/group something?	

Table 6.1 Process Analysis *(continued)*

Content	Nonverbal Messages	Interactions Between Members	Leader's Feelings	Leader's Thoughts/Theory	Leader's Role
Agnes: Right! It's always the woman's fault. "She didn't get raped, she led him on."	Sarcastic tone.	Group almost audibly groans.	Sad she's maintaining that stance. Wonder about source of her anxiety.	Mental note to get back to Agnes's anxiety. Have to keep it out now—bad time to deal with it.	
Charles: Your anger is really getting in the way. I feel that perhaps Susan is attracting these kinds of guys because of where she looks, because of what she does with them, or maybe as a subconscious way of proving that all men are no good.	Charles leaning forward. Looks confident.	Group looking at Charles and Susan.	Glad he's doing it. Wondering if there'll be a leadership challenge.	He sounds like he's on to something for Susan to consider. Hope it's concern for her and not defensiveness or self-aggrandizement.	
Betty: Do you think that's possible?	Looking at Susan, who seems sad.	Many members focusing inward.	Concern for Susan and Sandy.	See if Susan will respond or pass it off.	
Susan: Yeah. I've screwed up two marriages and sometimes I think I married bastards as a defense against letting myself be intimate.	Susan has tears in eyes. Sandy very pale.	Group moving toward Sandy.	Concern for Susan and Sandy.	Want to connect Susan and Sandy.	

Table 6.1 Process Analysis *(continued)*

Content	Nonverbal Messages	Interactions Between Members	Leader's Feelings	Leader's Thoughts/Theory	Leader's Role
Larry: Sandy, can you verbalize that?	Sandy apparently in pain.		Concern for Sandy.		Catalyst
Sandy: That just hits home.	Begins to cry. Susan looks at Sandy.	Group moves toward Sandy.	Comfort in process.	Want to connect Susan and Sandy and work on fear of intimacy for them and in this group.	
Larry: You're in a similar situation.	Sandy nods. Susan gets teary.	Group looks at Susan and Sandy.		Now need to connect them.	Catalyst
Larry: Can you tell Susan?	Sandy nods. Susan looks expectantly.		Comfortable.	Need to get her to explain content.	Orchestrator
Sandy: You know Bob, the guy I live with? Well, he's a good man, but he's just insensitive to my needs. Maybe I won't let him try, but it's just that he won't listen to any really deep feelings.	Sandy's eyes are clear. Susan crying. Barbara looks sad. Ray avoiding eye contact.	Cohesiveness developing. Focus on Sandy.	Bit anxious to bring out more feelings, but believe it's necessary.	Want to bring feelings to a head now and facilitate their going deeper.	
Fay: That really hurts.	Said with caring and understanding.		Relief for saying it Caring for them.	Bring arousal to optimal levels. Will have to support members.	Catalyst Model-Participant

Table 6.1 Process Analysis (continued)

Content	Nonverbal Messages	Interactions Between Members	Leader's Feelings	Leader's Thoughts/Theory	Leader's Role
Sandy: God, it's like there's a part of me that's too ugly for anyone to live with.	Looks very hurt and angry. Susan crying. Barbara looking very sad.	Barbara, Charles, Ray, Susan all moving closer.	Empathy, hurt. Concern for Susan and Sandy.	Desire to make supportive physical Better if Susan does it. Barbara also needs help.	
[Silence]	Susan and Sandy embracing and crying. Larry puts arm around Barbara's shoulders and she cries. Ray's lips trembling.	Susan and Sandy holding each other. Larry supporting Barbara.	Sadness, concern, anxiety about boundaries.	Have to ascertain members' reactions.	Participant, Reinforcer, Catalyst, Orchestrator
Ray: That's not only true for women.	Lips trembling.	Women look to Ray with support.	Concern for Ray, personal sadness.	Ray's sensitivity coming through.	
Larry: You've felt that also.	Ray nods.		Sadness about rejection.	Important to support Ray.	Reinforcer, Catalyst. Participant
Larry: I've experienced a feeling of not being understood also. It really hurts when you pay attention to it.	Larry's eyes are moist. Susan, Sandy, Barbara weeping.		Sadness, concern, anxiety.	Reaching out to Ray. Good contact.	Model-Participant

Table 6.1 **Process Analysis** *(continued)*

Content	Nonverbal Messages	Interactions Between Members	Leader's Feelings	Leader's Thoughts/Theory	Leader's Role
Charles: You've got to pay attention to it. If you understand it, you can come to grips with your humanity.	Crying stops.	Members pull back, look to Charles quizzically/skeptically.	Negative about Charles's interruption.	Assume Charles is uncomfortable with the intimacy being expressed. Changed tone to be safe in "expert" mode.	
Willie: That's the asshole way. You just experience it as that's the way it is, and it's O.K.	Willie smiling, but looks pressured. Interpersonal group distance increases.	Members pull back further. Willie is somewhat isolated.	Fear of loss of control.	Charles reduced anxiety enough for Willie to issue challenge. Expect a strong reaction from group.	Participant
Karl: What does that mean?	Question posed in challenging tone. Susan withdrawing.	Most of sadness changed to detachment. Little closeness.	Glad for Karl's challenge. Sad to lose Susan and Barbara.	Karl is challenging Willie. Need to get back to Susan, who seems to be withdrawing.	
Willie: It's all the same. It's what *is*. You can't take responsibility for anyone else.	Almost detached. Speech seems like recitation. Susan staring at ground.	Group becoming more distanced.	Anger at Willie. Impatience with his "est" speech and detached language.	Need to return to main process and get away from this.	
Fay: Susan, where are you?	Relief from group to focus on Susan. Agnes looks hurt.	Focus on Susan. Charles looks approvingly at Fay.	Comfort with intervention. Anxious to get Susan back to her feelings.	Susan could pull out now. If we don't get her to focus on her feelings of hurt and fear, it could be another rejection/failure experience.	Catalyst Model-Participant Environment Manipulator

Table 6.1 Process Analysis (*continued*)

Content	Nonverbal Messages	Interactions Between Members	Leader's Feelings	Leader's Thoughts/Theory	Leader's Role
Susan: Feeling hurt and scared.	Group focus on Susan. All look calm and involved except Agnes—still appears angry, and Willie smiling almost condescendingly.	Barbara and Sandy very tuned in to Susan.	Comfortable. Anxious to get Susan working with her feelings.	Pressing in on Susan. This is the time for her to open with Sandy and Barbara's support.	
Fay: Talk about the fear.	Susan fidgeting.	Attention on Susan.		Encourage Susan. Be aware of effect on other members.	Catalyst
Susan: I'm scared I just drive all the men away because I'm not open. But if I open up I get clobbered. It's like if you're a model, only one kind of man approaches.	Susan fidgeting, Barbara shaking her head negatively.		Glad she's beginning.	Keep her focused on this. Key is her fear of involvement-commitment and possibly that this fear manifests itself in behaviors that are contrary to her desires.	
Larry: Barbara, can you share your feelings with Susan?	Susan looking to Barbara who is tearful. Almost detached. Speech seems like recitation. Susan staring at ground.	Attention shifting to Barbara.		Trying to get Barbara to share obvious feelings with Susan. Provide/get support for Barbara and Susan.	Orchestrator

Table 6.1 **Process Analysis** *(continued)*

Content	Nonverbal Messages	Interactions Between Members	Leader's Feelings	Leader's Thoughts/Theory	Leader's Role
Barbara: It's not being a model. Bill and I have been married eight years and I really love the guy, but I use sex to avoid sharing really intimate parts of me. I started to get involved with Charlie just to have someone I could tell those things to, but it started to get sexual and I pulled out.	Barbara and Susan talking and looking at one another. Others looking at Barbara Willie still smiling.	Barbara talking directly to Susan.	Comfort with intervention. Anxious to get Susan back to her feelings.	Interesting. Barbara is sharing her own identical fear— covered other fears of intimacy by increasing sexual activity.	Catalyst Model-Participant Environment Manipulator
Fay: If you got involved that way with Bill, you'd be vulnerable to hurt, but if you don't open up with your husband, you need a relationship on the side, which has even greater problems.	Barbara looks scared. Susan nodding her head. Karl becoming pale.		Anxiety that they could lose Susan, but wanting to support Barbara.	Try to tie Barbara's problem with husband to Susan's problem with men. Concern for Sandy and Karl.	Catalyst
Fay: That hooks into Susan's feelings of frustration also.	Barbara and Susan looking at each other. Karl more pale.	Barbara and Susan mutually supportive.	A bit confused, generally comfortable.	A lot of things going on simultaneously. Need to pick up most critical. Worried about non-verbals from Karl.	Orchestrator

Table 6.1 Process Analysis (continued)

Content	Nonverbal Messages	Interactions Between Members	Leader's Feelings	Leader's Thoughts/Theory	Leader's Role
[15-second silence]	Willie smiling. Karl very pale.	Leaders making eye contact for support.	Anxious about introducing Karl into this mix.	Decide to include Karl.	
Larry: Karl, you look like someone kicked you in the stomach. What are you feeling?	Karl exhales loudly.	Focus on Karl.		Hope Karl is in with Susan and Barbara. Want to keep this together and on topic of intimacy.	Catalyst
Karl: It's like something really important is being said and I've got to face some stuff too.	Karl agitated. Others focused on him.	Focus on Karl.	Anxiety about Karl's "secret."	He's probably had an affair also—related to Barbara's earlier statement.	Catalyst Participant (listening)
Larry: You've gone the route of an affair also.	Karl exhales noticeably.	Others look nervously at Karl, admiringly at Larry.	Fear of being wrong.	What if I'm wrong? Either way, have to keep the topic on fear of intimacy.	Catalyst
Karl: Several.	Karl exhibiting several emotions: fear, pride, relief, etc.	Focus on Karl.	Interest.	Want to be careful about curiosity. Is he being seductive? What's his affect?	

(continued from page 145)

interpersonal orientation focuses on relationships within the group. The focus is on the here-and-now of group interactions, which is often more anxiety provoking than exploring more serious personal problems outside the group. The therapist with primarily an interpersonal orientation is more of an orchestrator, with less direct involvement in providing answers for members. The strength of this orientation is the increase in self-esteem afforded members through their altruistic and successful attempts to help each other.

Five major roles of the leader are identified and paired with specific stages of group process. The role of information disseminator is largely employed during the preparation and termination stage. During these two stages the leader needs to disseminate expert knowledge that helps members prepare for therapy as well as later integration of specific insights and skills. Another role associated with the preparation stage and also with the transition stage is the role of reinforcer and environmental manipulator. The leader must maintain an awareness of the level of anxiety within the group and be responsible for intervening to optimize the members' learning and growth. In a group setting, there is an inverse relationship between anxiety and structure and a curvilinear relationship between anxiety and learning. The leader modulates anxiety and optimizes learning through the judicious application of structure.

Acting as orchestrator, the group leader connects needs with resources within the group. During the therapy phase, the leader encourages members to share similar experiences; this provides an awareness of universality, cohesion, and altruism between members. The role of catalyst is used to focus the energy of the transition stage in order to address directly any challenges to the leadership. In the therapy phase, the role of catalyst is used to deepen interpersonal and intrapsychic work. However, it is during the termination stage that the role of the catalyst is most important. The therapist is responsible for initiating and completing the termination process. Termination is often avoided by the group as a whole and must be actively structured by the group leader. The role of model is used throughout the group and perhaps provides the most subtle and sophisticated learning for members.

The personality traits that a leader might aspire to model would include honesty, integrity, patience, courage, flexibility, warmth, empathy, intelligence, timing, and self-knowledge. The optimal group leader would have the maturity of an integrated self. In other words, honesty is tempered by warmth and empathy. Patience is balanced with courage, and both are guided by an intelligent use of timing. Self-knowledge allows the leader to be true to his or her own values while being accepting and flexible in his or her approach to others.

ETHICS

PROFESSIONAL ISSUES IN GROUP LEADERSHIP

The therapist should operate in a way that is comfortable and natural. Nevertheless, there is an etiquette of group leader behavior that should be considered. In life, we must follow many conventions. We do so, maintaining our uniqueness while adjusting to various situations and environmental demands.

We play different roles on the street, on the beach, at a party, and in the office. If we were to act in precisely the same manner, regardless of the occasion, we would demonstrate an unacceptable rigidity or inflexibility. The same is true for the group therapist. In this chapter, we describe appropriate leader behaviors. These are presented as guidelines to be fitted to the leaders' values and professional standards and to the rights of group members.

ETHICS

Never have ethical standards been so demanding or so fluid for mental health practitioners. Standards that recently seemed clear, safe, and fixed have been called into question and altered by forces and institutions that are outside professional or practitioner organizations. A litigious society, changes in professional ethical guidelines forced by the Federal Trade Commission, previously unknown dangers of certain therapeutic procedures, potentially conflicting demands of "best practice" and managed care constraints, and the general influence of economics on therapeutic practice all combine to make ethical mental health practice far more challenging and complex than ever before.

Many ethical issues can arise in therapeutic groups, and whereas a well-intentioned person of any background may deal with them adequately, a leader who has had professional training in proper behavior with patients and current standards in the field will probably be able to address them more satisfactorily.

A core precept of the Hippocratic Oath taken by physicians is the duty to do no harm. So it is for group leaders. We are there to assist and enhance processes that promote the members' health. To be most effective, leaders enlist members' cooperation and confidence. We must be scrupulously careful not to misinform clients or to misrepresent or exaggerate the benefits to be derived from the group sessions.

Group leaders are there to help members, but at what cost? It is not unusual for group members to want to discuss matters that the therapist feels are unsuitable for group discussion. For example, they may wish to criticize the therapist's supervisor or other staff members. Leaders also may be asked personal questions about themselves, other patients, or other people. These are questions the leaders could answer but feel they shouldn't. What is a leader to do if one member makes sexual overtures to another? What are the ethical requirements when the problem goes beyond the active group participant, when it also involves the leader, the group, the other members, the institution, even the psychotherapy profession? When does the member's need supersede the leader's?

Is it appropriate to refuse to answer any particular query? Such a refusal may affect the group. Is it more beneficial for members to have more complete openness or limits that will offer security? What if a member requests something unprofessional or illegal?

We take the position that therapists' ethical responsibility is to establish clear limits in the group interactions. Leaders must act in conformance with their conscience, their capabilities, the ethics of the profession, and the laws of society. Normally, this will not inhibit or interfere with effective group progress. However, such limits must come from adequate self-knowledge. Every leader has personal limitations. Leaders who are unaware of their personal "blind spots" may not set appropriate limits.

Leader Training

The prime directive of all professional therapy is never to practice beyond the scope of one's training. The dictum "A little knowledge is a dangerous thing" is particularly germane to group leadership. A very strong argument for requiring graduate school training for professionals is that graduate school is the setting in which the ethics and mores of functioning professionals are learned. Untrained leaders often get into ethical binds or never see the ethical side of the issue at all. They may be well meaning as leaders, but they may still do grievous harm to group participants.

An untrained leader who does not understand the full scope of ethical responsibility can naively apply a few simplistic guidelines to all group situations. One common example of this concerns the locus of responsibility, an issue that many encounter group leaders give primary emphasis. Schutz (1973), for example, argues that health and success for members are contingent on the extent to which they take responsibility for their actions. In this view, the following are all examples of unacceptable behaviors: "The devil made me do it," "I just can't do this," "You make me feel so sad," "If only my karma was better," "My Enneagram or Myers-Briggs is opposite his. There's no chance of understanding," or "I'm a Gemini; that's why the Pisces guy hates me." Schutz's belief is that if individuals will own their feelings and actions, they will be able to be more assertive and more effective in their day-to-day interactions.

Employing this belief ethically and responsibly within a well-delineated theory of personality can be extremely valuable. Within such parameters, responsibility taking is defined clearly, modeled by the leader, and developed in concert with other skills. However, an unprofessional therapist may employ this construct by itself, as a stand-alone "mandate" without placing it into a network of related constructs. Such misuse is characterized by much of "pop psychology." These leaders characteristically have mastered reasonably effective skills for opening up an individual emotionally, without the necessary capabilities to help the individual integrate or close.

In the next example, the leader led the group on a guided fantasy and hypnotic regression to open the third group session. As this regression approached its end, he gave the following suggestions:

> Now you're feeling totally relaxed . . . totally open to your experience . . . and now as I count backward from 10 to 1, you'll get younger and younger. You'll actually be 10 years old and you'll feel all the 10-year old feelings. 10 . . . 9 . . . 8 . . . you're getting sleepy and open; 7 . . . 6 . . . 5 . . . you know what it's like to be 10 years old; 4 . . . 3 . . . 2 . . . 1 . . . now be 10, act 10, feel 10. Now you see your parents. Look at them . . . feel the helplessness you feel with them . . . how much you need their love and how they never give you enough . . .

At this point, one member burst into tears and began mournfully crying out, "Don't leave me, please don't leave me."

Rama (Leader):   OK . . . let's hold this exercise. [*Turning to the crying member*] What are you experiencing, Ben?

Ben: I don't want to lose her.

Rama: Your mother?

Ben: She died when I was 10. She had no right to leave me alone like that.

Rama: *You* didn't believe *she* had a right to die.

Ben: She made me so lonely.

Rama: You mean you felt lonely when your mother died.

Ben: I can't help feeling so scared now and sad.

Rama: You mean you're choosing to feel sad and scared.

Ben: I'm *not* choosing; you're setting me up to experience these things and I do.

Rama: I'm not willing to take responsibility for your feelings.

Not only does this leader fail to confront the emerging clinical material, but he is also a poor model. In instructing Ben to take responsibility, the leader is himself being irresponsible. Furthermore, instead of empathizing with Ben, he constantly restructures Ben's words to fit into the leader's own nascent theoretical language. In this case, a single dictum regarding the concept of "responsibility" is guiding the leader's total interaction to the detriment of all group members. As a Charles Schultz *Peanuts* cartoon character has observed, "There's a difference between a bumper sticker and a philosophy of life."

A professional training program is a hedge against a "bumper sticker" approach. If students learn anything, they must learn the ethical guidelines of their profession.

The American Psychological Association has separate but related sets of guidelines for group therapists and growth-group leaders. The American Group Psychotherapy Association (1978), the Association for Specialists in Group Work (1983), and the American Psychiatric Association (1981) have issued single sets of guidelines for all group leaders. Relevant portions of all these professional standards are summarized below. Similar guidelines are observed by members of the medical, nursing, family therapy (American Association of Family Therapists, 1988) and social work (National Association of Social Workers, 1979) professions and by the National Training Laboratories (1970).

1. Group therapists are committed to acting objectively and with integrity, maintaining the highest standards in professional practice. They must not violate accepted moral and legal codes of the community or misrepresent their qualifications.
2. With regard to client contracts, therapists are mandated to preserving confidentiality and protecting the integrity and welfare of the individuals. In cases of conflict between professionals, the group leader's primary concern must be for the members' welfare. This includes the situation in which the leader believes there is no reasonable expectation that a certain individual will benefit from the group. In such a case, termination of this member from the group is required.
3. In every group, leaders must receive *informed* consent from members regarding any and all group endeavors.
4. Administration of services, treatment diagnosis, or personalized advice can occur only within the context of a professional relationship. It is appropriate to offer only those services that may reasonably be expected to benefit members in the group. Creating exaggerated expectations of success in clients is improper.

5. Financial and interprofessional matters must be in accord with community standards, and respect for other professionals and clients is expected. Clients' right to privacy and nonparticipation are to be protected.

Several similar guidelines have been written for growth-group leaders. Participation in a growth group should be voluntary. Explicit information regarding group purposes, procedures, goals, fees, availability of follow-up training, educational qualifications of leaders, issues of confidentiality, and any restrictions on members' freedom of choice must be available. Screening is necessary for both inclusion and exclusion of members and for exploration of terms of the contract. Client welfare must be considered more important than research or experimental concerns. Experimental procedures should be fully disclosed and evaluated publicly, and the relative responsibility of group leaders and members specified. Leaders are expected to respond ethically as both therapists and educators.

These ethical concerns are primary regardless of the leader's professional discipline. Members of groups must be informed of the group goals, procedures, purposes, and costs. They must give their consent to participate, and they have the right to refuse to participate in any specific group activity. They must be honestly assured that client welfare will be safeguarded and that the leader will not exploit clients for political, special interest, or personal reasons (cf. Pinney, 1983). Furthermore, leaders must treat members' activity within the group as privileged communication.

Certain qualifications apply to privileged communication. When a patient is likely to be dangerous to himself/or herself or to others and the therapist would violate other ethical responsibilities by concealing this knowledge in the name of preserving confidentiality, the therapist must reveal this information to the appropriate professional or public authorities. With respect to sensitive material, however, the therapist must consider the possibility that the information may harm the patient if it is made public to others. For this reason, he or she will do well to warn group members that individual members may be fallible and can leak information to outsiders. To attempt to handle this problem by forcing a compact of silence is probably foolish. However, it is our experience that confidentiality is regularly maintained by group members. Corsini (1957) concurs, citing his 10-year experience with groups in prisons: "Only one case of revealing of information came out—and it was reported by the guilty one himself!"

In a related concern, Yalom (1990) cautions that in his experience, members of the group will almost always discuss group matters out of group sessions. Instead of trying to prohibit "the inevitable," his solution is to request that these members report to the group what was discussed outside.

Without such guarantees of safety, group members are left unprotected and can be seriously hurt by the machinations of an unprofessional group leader. Martin Lakin of Duke University has been one of the strongest proponents of ethical standards in growth groups. In a series of articles and texts, Lakin (1969, 1972) elucidates critical concerns for leadership. He contrasts the psychotherapeutic intent in groups and the growth motive in groups: "The therapists' mandate is relatively clear—to provide a corrective experience for someone who presents himself as psychologically impaired" (1969, p. 924). On the other hand, in a training group, "There is no way for a participant to know in advance, much less to appraise intentions of trainers, processes of groups or their consequences for him" (p. 924).

Lakin also made a distinction between participants of early and more recent groups. Early participants were mostly psychologically sophisticated and mainly professional; in general, they had intellectual understanding as their goal. In contrast, in the late 1960s and early 1970s, vast segments of the general public became participants. Since those early years, members have been generally less sophisticated and more psychologically disturbed; they are most often seeking a cathartic rather than an intellectual experience. Furthermore, there are a great number of inadequately prepared group leaders.

Lakin also decries the lack of adequate screening and group preparation for both members and leaders and a corresponding lack of follow-up or posttraining. Coulson (1972), Beymer (1969), Shostrom (1969), and Dreyfus and Kremenliev (1970), as well as Lakin, have all warned against the ethic of drama in growth groups. The tendency to view the value of an interaction as linearly related to the amount of affect expressed is common among growth group leaders. Techniques and exercises designed to bring members to high levels of emotional arousal are easily acquired and frequently used. Leader and peer pressure in a group can push members to levels of emotion and affect-induced behaviors that are not easily reincorporated into their lives. It is inappropriate for any group leader to create such drama and subsequently absolve himself of responsibility by rationalizing that patients who are harmed are "choosing" to lose control.

These rationalizations are simply not defensible with unscreened, unsophisticated clients. Lakin (1969) and Shapiro (1975) point out that the principle of caveat emptor is professionally indefensible. The "consumer" may in fact agree to a contract that he really does not understand. Lakin says, "It cannot be assumed that the participant really knows what he is letting himself in for" (1969, p. 926). At the request of a very powerful leader, or with group pressure, members may engage in affectionate, aggressive, personally revealing, or sexual behavior in the group that they will regret later and that may have subsequent negative repercussions.

A leader who is unaware of the power she wields or of the nature of transferences formed in a group setting can tread on sensitive ground and create a vulnerability in members that she then cannot or will not handle effectively. Even more dangerous is the leader who accepts this position of power as a means of self-enhancement. Instant "gurus," people with a mission or point of view to sell, and those who are insecure may comfortably bask in the facile glory of group leadership. Such self-aggrandizement may come at a high cost to members.

Such an individual was operating in Hawaii during the 1970s. He falsely claimed to be a clinical psychologist. In the course of his group meetings, which consisted of approximately 10 to 12 regulars and 2 to 3 new members, each member was to take the "hot seat" and tell what was most upsetting to him or her. In one case, a psychology graduate student was accused of "not owning" his latent homosexual fears. The student in question seriously examined himself and after a time denied any homosexual leanings. The leader, with support from the group, then "worked" with this student *for six consecutive hours* to get him to accept his homosexual feelings. The student fled the room when the leader suggested that he remove his clothes and let other men in the group touch him. In a state of panic and questioning whether he did the right thing to leave, he called his professor-adviser to ascertain whether this procedure was acceptable "therapy." He was advised not to return to that group and to explore in personal psychotherapy the feelings that had resulted from the marathon session. This particular student had considerable ego strength to sit through six hours of such treatment and to leave the room to make a phone call. A group member with less strength could have suffered much more serious harm. The group leader was himself subsequently hospitalized after several similar incidents, and a check of his credentials led to his investigation by the authorities (Shapiro, 1978).

By modern-day standards, it would also be appropriate to inform members of proper standards for group leader behavior, to inform them of their rights for redress, and to provide them with information about appropriate state consumer protection and professional boards.

SAFETY PRECAUTIONS ON ENTERING GROUPS

The public should be protected from excesses such as those described here and fore-warned of the possible dangers of participation in certain types of groups. Leaders should take care to provide answers to all the concerns a reasonable consumer may have. The guidelines for potential group members, delineated below, is a bare minimum, designed to increase the probability that ethical, responsible group principles will be applied. There is, of course, no guarantee that any group will be effective. These criteria are intended to function as warning signals. To the extent that groups fail to conform to these indices, the probability of unethical, irresponsible, and dangerous leadership is increased.

A Basic Consumers' Guide to Group Counseling and Psychotherapy

LEADERS' CREDENTIALS   A degree from an accredited graduate training program in one of the mental health fields is no guarantee of ethical leadership, but lack of such credentials is considered a negative indicator. There is a greater probability that a nonprofessional leader will fail to be aware of, or to conform to, ethical standards than will a professionally trained leader. If the leaders themselves are not professionals, they should be supervised by a recognized professional expert.

ADVERTISING   Although recent rulings by the Federal Trade Commission have eliminated the former professional restrictions on advertising, the wise consumer and professional are advised to be wary of immodest claims of success, promises of dramatic life changes, or erotic inducements in newspapers, bulletin boards, or public magazines. Professionals normally advertise groups by referrals, modest brochures to other professionals, mailings to a self-selected list, word of mouth, and reputation.

SCREENING   If a group does not provide screening, there can be no control over membership. Members can be placed in thoroughly inappropriate groups. The profit motive seems the only explainable justification for failure to screen potential members. This may be a special problem in the current managed care mental health environment. Patients are more likely to be assigned to a group by time, location, or cost criteria rather than clinical suitability. Often a Preferred Provider Organization or health maintenance organization (HMO) offers a single group or a small selection of groups to anyone needing group treatment in their catchment area or system. In addition, practitioners, faced with decreasing availability of clients, are increasingly prone to stretch the range of clients screened into a particular group. When dealing with one's personal beliefs, values, or behaviors, profit is a uniquely inappropriate screening criterion.

GROUP SIZE   Groups of fewer than 6 or more than 14 members are inappropriate except when the group is made up of certain specific patient populations. In a too-small group, cliques can form and scapegoating can occur. Each member may be pressured to produce an uncomfortable level of verbalization, often at a faster rate than is desirable. In a too-large group, process cannot be effectively monitored, trust is difficult to develop, cohesion is limited, and often members who are shyest and most in need of attention can get lost in the shuffle. As a general rule, as pathology increases, the group size decreases. Thus a group of 12 "normal-neurotic" outpatients is quite appropriate as is a group of 6 or 7 schizophrenic inpatients. Similarly, groups for young children tend to be quite a bit smaller than groups for older individuals. It would be unusual for example, to have a therapy group of more than eight preschoolers.

COSTS   The average rates for group work vary little in most settings, usually being set by professional consensus, insurance or agency coverage, and population served. Groups that are offered for token low payments or excessively high costs should be carefully investigated. Sometimes groups are offered at very low cost because they are subsidized by other funds, or competent professional leaders are trying to build practices and therefore offer services at a reduced rate. Sometimes professionals charge very low fees as part of their pro bono (charity) work. By contrast, other leaders charge low rates because that is all they are worth. That is not a true bargain. Group leadership is difficult work, and when professionals put in time and effort, they have a right to adequate remuneration.

Some group leaders charge excessively high rates for their work. They rationalize that the more people pay, the more they will get out of the experience. This attitude seems irresponsible to most professionals. Often, members pay for elaborate settings, resort costs, catered meals, and so on; these amenities may be desirable but they are certainly unnecessary to successful group therapy. Sometimes these high-priced group leaders are on a workshop circuit; they come into town for a session and leave promptly afterward—taking the money and leaving no provisions for follow up.

FOLLOW-UP SERVICES   If a group leader does not provide some level of follow-up services, group members can miss the opportunity to maximize important group learning. Even worse, they can be left in a new wilderness, opened by the group, without adequate survival skills. If the leaders are not available for referral or therapy services after the group is over, a major safeguard against casualties is neglected.

GROUP GOALS AND PROCEDURES   Each group has methods and value systems that are tied to its goals. Members need to be made fully aware of the intent of the group before they can make an educated decision to join. Hidden agendas of group leaders often lead groups into directions they would not have chosen had they been better informed. An example of this occurred recently with a group leader who believed very strongly that members had to reject all aspects of their childhood, including their parents and relatives, before they could be totally functioning adults. However, he advertised his group as a place where members would "come to know themselves more fully, become freed of blocked energy, and gain a fuller connection with their past." Needless to say, his way of accomplishing this aim involves a series of procedures that many potential members would reject if they were informed of them in advance. Once participants are in the situation, group pressure may be brought to bear on them to force their compliance.

CONFIDENTIALITY AND SECRECY   To safeguard members' privacy, confidentiality must be a group norm. For members to disclose very personal information without some sort of guarantee that their secrets will not be reported to significant others is absolutely essential. There is no justifiable rationalization for violating this precept except those required by law (potential danger to self or others, child or elder abuse, etc.). Any breach of confidentiality can cause much damage to members' lives. Potential members need to be forewarned about any possibility that confidentiality, might not be honored. If the issue is not specifically discussed in the group, the probability of such a violation is high.

Although confidentiality is necessary, secrecy is severely discouraged. Group procedures and processes must be able to stand the test of scientific research. If a group leader does not wish to allow his methods to be open for public or professional scrutiny, the reasons for such secrecy should be seriously questioned. Such secrecy may enhance cohesion by supporting a dichotomy between group members and those who are not in the group. Strong exclusive allegiances to group members and a corresponding sense of elitism however, make transfer of training extremely difficult and reinforces alienation from any people in their lives who are "uninitiated." The result of secrecy thus is the precise opposite of the group goal.

GROUPS AS PARTS OF A MOVEMENT   Whenever the leader has a particular philosophy to sell or an "axe to grind," group members can get lost in the process. Groups are designed for individual growth in directions determined by the individuals themselves. When individual needs become subjugated to other, often hidden, designs, the individual may suffer. A member of a group led by a self-appointed "guru" leader can find acceptance only within a certain framework. He must conform to role expectations of a larger body, and his development is limited to the lines sanctified by the movement. In such a situation, individual freedoms frequently get set aside. This is not to suggest that belonging to an organization larger than oneself cannot be a rewarding experience. However, group therapy or growth work are not the appropriate places for this. One man's mission can be another man's destruction. A men's or women's group leader who is sexist and promotes the "war between the sexes" as a way of supporting a personal angry agenda may be a poor guide for members who wish to comprehend differences, honor their own gender, and connect with the other sex.

Psychological movements may be as influential and dangerous as political ones. Frequently, diagnoses and treatments, particularly in the pop psych culture have a "du jour" quality. In the mid 1990s, for example, some leaders seemingly held beliefs that the vast majority of their clients have undiscovered multiple personalities, were sexually abused as children, or have adult Attention Deficit Disorders. When they promote these beliefs as group leaders, members may be at risk. Unless members are aware of such prejudices, they may be influenced to perceive all their life difficulties as the result of some unique cause, or they may develop symptoms that will fit with the leader's proselytizing.

MEMBERS' RIGHTS   Entrance to a group does *not* constitute a carte blanche acquiescence to anything that might follow. Members must be informed of their rights to participate or not and the ramifications of refusal to engage in any particular group activity. For example, if the group leader decides that breaking a couples group into temporarily separate male and female subgroups would enhance group communication, does a member have a right to decline? What if the leader believes that a prayer at the end of each session is proper? What about a leader's belief that nudity in a group enhances self-acceptance? What pressures will be brought to bear? Does anyone have veto power over such a recommendation? Entering a group without having these issues specified is dangerous.

JARGON   Each group, of necessity, has its own language system to describe the group process. However, language systems can be used to mask differences as well as to delineate issues. If a member finds people speaking in a manner he does not comprehend, he is in a high-risk situation. This situation is compounded when a group employs commonly understood words but in a way that has special meaning. One example of this is the word *experience*. In some groups, this word describes the sum of all input for an individual. In another group, it refers only to emotion or feelings, and in a third, experience means compliance. Thus, if a leader is not easily understood, or if the group employs an unfamiliar or confusing language system, the group should be avoided.

CHOOSING GROUPS CAREFULLY   A group experience can be very powerful, and entering such a situation should not be done impulsively. The decision to enter a group should be weighed; each individual should be aware of what goals he or she has for participation. Several group approaches can be examined and a choice made that agrees with the individual's goals and abilities, if possible after consultation with others the person trusts.

To help the individual evaluate various groups, the ethics and standards of the group leaders must be clearly specified. These ethics are inextricably woven with the extent and quality of their training.

SUMMARY

General principles of ethics for psychotherapists are applicable to the group setting with certain specific considerations and adaptations. The principle of competence is perhaps most directly addressed as the authors propose a model educational program for group leaders. The importance of awareness, knowledge, and skills specific to the group modality are stressed. The group therapist needs to model integrity, respect, concern for others, and social and professional responsibility.

Ethical considerations specific to group psychotherapy include competence of the leader, screening, informed consent/rights of group members, and confidentiality. Leaders need to have specific training in group therapy. Competence in group psychotherapy includes an understanding of group process, skill as a leader, and knowledge of the specific population of group members.

Screening for a therapeutic group involves matching an individual with a group compatible in composition and goals. One advantage of HMOs and other large mental health contract providers is a large patient pool from which to form appropriate groups. Group members ideally would be homogeneous in ego strength, developmental level, and goals; the group would also have a short-term focus on the presenting problem.

Informed consent involves a two-way communication with the leader responsible for determining the prospective group members' understanding and agreement regarding group goals, procedures, and leader qualifications. Members' rights and agreements should be communicated verbally and in writing. An initial and intermittent discussion of the limits and importance of confidentiality is another ethical responsibility of group leadership.

CHAPTER 8

GROUP LEADER TRAINING

Two statements can be made without qualification regarding the availability of qualified group leaders:

1. With the tremendous increase in the use of groups in a wide variety of settings, there is a great need for qualified group leaders.
2. Group leadership skills are complex and varied.

Given these two conditions, the training programs for group therapists must address a wide variety of needs. Effective group leaders must understand and work with the group process. They need to be aware of individual intrapsychic phenomena and interactions between people. They need to have a working theory of psychotherapy, an understanding of normal and abnormal behavior, and respect for individual differences. They must have a clear understanding of their own personal dynamics and their strengths and weaknesses.

TRAINING

Training programs for the most part have been fairly inadequate. In most graduate mental health programs, trainees have received instruction in individual psychotherapy and only informal instruction in groups, usually in a practicum setting. Although Hollis and Wantz (1990) describe a steady, consistent growth of university courses and practicum offerings, it has occurred primarily at the undergraduate and master's level. A 1996 review (Shapiro, 1996) of curricula for dozens of graduate programs nationwide indicate that in both psychiatry and clinical psychology doctoral programs, no courses in group therapy are required. Most master's programs have a single term course required for students who will be practitioners.

More complete training is scattered and somewhat rare, reflecting the generally held view that expertise in group therapy arises naturally from expertise in individual therapy or family therapy. Because of this opinion, many practitioners have a negative view of group therapy. Many individuals, without training in group dynamics, have been thrust into leadership roles only to find their individual counseling skills less than fully effective in such settings. After one such experience, a psychiatric resident commented, "This isn't therapy. . . . it's chaos."

A psychologist with many years of expertise in individual therapy was struck by the "interruptions at the most inopportune moments, and the inability of people to wait their turn." Similarly, family therapists may have difficulty adapting to the group's unwillingness to act as a unit.

Although some individual and family therapy skills are common also to group therapy, the reality is that group counseling and therapy is different from other forms of mental health delivery. That is its strength. Because of such differences, specific training in group therapy is *essential*. Although practitioners have known this for decades, change in training has been slow to come (cf. Kaplan & Sadock, 1971).

The group leader programs that do exist seem to have certain core elements (cf. Dies, 1980; Alonso, 1993):

1. Supervised practice as a group leader, with extensive feedback
2. Observation of professional group leaders
3. Personal group experience as a member
4. Theory and skill learning

In addition, personal individual or group psychotherapy and continuing education in group methods are frequently recommended (Glass, 1997).

Supervised Practice

In any profession, the learning-by-doing approach seems central to mastery. The group therapy situation is so variable and the interactions between unique combinations of participants so unpredictable that preparing a novice group leader adequately for all contingencies is not possible. The leader must learn, in part, through on-the-job training. However, trial and error learning without immediate and accurate feedback commonly leads only to repetitive errors. *Supervision* of the practice is the element that makes the difference. Supervisors must be able to observe the interactions between group members. They must also be able to offer suggestions and alternatives in such a way that trainees can listen non-defensively rather than simply mimicking the supervisors' words or actions in the next session. Supervisory suggestions need to be integrated into the leader's repertoire and applied as they fit the situation. Feedback from several sources is helpful—from co-leaders as well as from supervisors. Another important source of input is less-trained observers (videotape operators, students in training, group members, etc.); their observations can often be remarkably helpful. The most effective way to provide accurate and sensitive feedback that we have employed over the past 30 years is delivered when the supervisor observes the group through a one-way mirror or by videotape playback. In supervisory periods, the interactions that occur between the leaders and supervisors are often the major topic of discussion. Frequently, the blocks that inhibited interactions in the group sessions are reproduced in the supervisory hour. Competent supervision thus involves both the sharing of knowledge and a form of individual or group psychotherapy. The competent supervisor can use his or her own group leadership skills in the supervisory hour and almost simultaneously serve as a teacher, a therapist, and a model of effective therapy. Alonso (1993) strongly suggests that supervision of group leaders be done in supervisory groups—a method that certainly reinforces the supervisors' faith in the group method. She underscores the importance in such group supervision of mitigating shame for errors and faults, providing peer and supervisory support, affording opportunities for vicarious learning from peers and experts, encouraging healthy intellectual experimentation and competition, expanding the capacity for empathy, and relieving problems of projective identification common in trainee groups.

Observation of Professional Leaders

Learning by imitation is exceptionally powerful when the model has attained a desired level of achievement. In most trades, the rewards of apprenticeship have included the opportunity to practice developing skills under the supervision of a master craftsman and the experience of being in the presence of that craftsman in action. Watching a professional group leader is a similar opportunity for a trainee to obtain a realistic view of the true nature of group leadership. Observing such a therapist, trainees can view successes and failures, begin to discover weaknesses in their own developing skills, and see the results of specific therapeutic interventions in specific situations without being in a personally threatening situation. Hence, they can maximize personal time spent in trial-and-error learning and can get a feel for the scope of a therapists' duties.

For optimal learning, the observation may be paired with feedback sessions in which observers can discuss with the professional leader the events and choices from the group meeting. During these sessions, questions can be asked, various solutions can be discussed and evaluated, and a great deal of mutual learning can take place. Professionals also benefit from such feedback. Yalom (1975), for example, states, "I have always found the reflections and feedback of observers, regardless of their level of experience, to be personally helpful to me and thus to the functioning of the group" (p. 504).

The National Training Laboratories groups that have provided such a spur to the use of groups in business and clinical settings date much success to feedback sessions in which group participants observed the process and commented on the group leadership team's evening meeting (Bradford, Gibb, & Benne, 1964). In the group training programs we have led, students are able to view videotapes or live group therapy through two-way mirrors and then to ask the therapists what they were thinking when they made a certain intervention or declined to respond to something in the group. Graduate students report that such interactions are a highlight of their training careers.

Not every professional will be comfortable with observation. It is important, for training purposes, to find group leaders who do not become overly defensive in discussing aspects of their groups and who are open to a variety of solutions to problems, not necessarily their own singular method.

Personal Group Experience as a Member

For trainees to learn about the effects of a group in nonacademic, nonintellectual ways, they must experience a group as a member. The group experience is emotionally powerful. Unless a leader can empathize with the intense pressures and fears of membership, his understanding of members will be subsequently diminished. Group leaders must understand group phenomena affectively and sensorially as well as intellectually. They must fully comprehend what it is like to be vulnerable in a group. Before requesting self-disclosure by members, leaders should realize the level of fear and courage this action entails. They must know in a firsthand way what the fears of nonacceptance and peer pressure can be like. In this way, leaders learn how to make informed and timely requests for members' participation.

Empathy is only one component of this aspect of training. As members, trainees also have another opportunity to see an experienced leader in action concurrent with their own high levels of affect. This is different from pure observation, in which trainees can view the group action more dispassionately. Trainee members in such a group can also observe the coordination between co-therapists and the maximum use of each co-leader's special strengths.

Finally, these training groups are therapeutic for members. Trainees can discover their personal strengths and weaknesses in such a group and take corrective steps. Typically, training groups are not designed for deep therapeutic intervention, and members with deep-rooted or pervasive psychological problems are encouraged to resolve them in separate individual or group psychotherapy. Less severe problems can be effectively treated in training groups once competitive defensiveness is reduced.

In developing a training group, three cautions are mandatory. These involve (1) political, (2) personnel, and (3) competitive considerations.

POLITICAL CONSIDERATIONS   Even in an era of "enlightened" acceptance of alternative paths and solutions to problems, administrators, practitioners, and faculty members are likely to be threatened by the use of groups. Often these individuals are very persuasive in developing support against any such nontraditional or popular innovations. In developing training programs in several locations, founders of group training programs are regularly accused of "forcing psychotherapy onto students," "having personal needs for intimacy met in group settings," "forcing students into nervous breakdowns," "playing with fire," "creating unemployable trainees," and even "introducing students to communism (or God-lessness)." Despite a lack of information and the absence of truth in any of these statements, the harassment, threats, and pressures to terminate group training programs continue. This sort of difficulty seems relatively universal and must be confronted in almost any setting in which a group training program is instituted.

PERSONNEL CONSIDERATIONS   The best paper program or plan of action in the world cannot withstand the effects of inappropriate personnel. In this age of technical expertise, the critical component in virtually every personal equation remains the human one. In a group leadership training program, proper staff is the *sine qua non*. Because the trainees will imitate their trainers, these leaders must have high levels of technical skill and integrity, follow the ethical standards of the profession, and be personally well adjusted and nondefensive. Despite their own professional orientation, these group leaders should also be eclectic with regard to their expectations of member behavior. Yalom (1975) believes "that the trainee's first group experience should not be one of a highly specialized format (for example TA or Gestalt)" (p. 511).

The particular profession of the leaders is less important than their skills in conducting these very difficult groups. In fact, having group leaders from a profession different from the one for which the students are training is often valuable. This mix helps build necessary interdisciplinary respect.

COMPETITIVENESS CONSIDERATIONS   Training groups are difficult to lead. Members are sometimes highly competitive with one another and the leaders. After co-leading psychology intern training groups for a number of years, we believe that we have seen every possible manner of challenge. Because of the competitiveness and desire to practice the therapy role, training group members sometimes open up cautiously and slowly by comparison to members in other groups. They take fewer personal risks, and a large part of the leaders' job is to enhance interpersonal trust, cohesion, and cooperation among members. The earlier in the training these groups are instituted, the easier it is to develop a cooperative, rather than competitive, spirit. By the time trainees are clinical psychology interns, psychiatric residents, or last-semester master's students, the task is massive because of their ego-threatening fears of professional incompetence. Normally, once students know what is expected of them in the field and in the group, they are ready for a meaningful personal group experience.

One additional strategy can help to diminish the anticipated competitiveness and suspiciousness regarding the use of material that emerges in the group. This involves the employment of nonfaculty members from the professional community as group leaders. Using such clinicians has several additional positive effects: greater confidentiality; exposure to working clinicians whom students may emulate; and enhanced connection between the professional community and the training institutions.

Theory and Skill Learning

The emphasis on the psychological needs of group leaders should not in any way lessen the importance of academic competencies. Several skills are mandatory. Group leaders must be able to perceive, understand, and articulate group process and content. They must have an active knowledge of normal and abnormal behavior patterns, including principles and theories of learning and motivation. They must also have a working theory of behavior and a solid understanding of the ethics of their profession. In addition to exemplary individual psychotherapy skills, group leaders must have an understanding of the effects of groups on individuals and the power of interaction matrices.

The model group leaders training program presented in the next section, emphasizes the relevance of courses in personality and counseling theories, abnormal psychology, and psychopathology; individual training in counseling and psychotherapy as well as family therapy; and a variety of listening and research skills.

A MODEL TRAINING PROGRAM

In describing a model National Training Laboratory (NTL) progrm, Appley and Winder (1973) delineated five developmental stages: *participant* (no experience necessary), *beginning trainer* (two labs of experience), *intermediate trainer* (20-25 labs required), *trainer of trainers* (lab experience, senior trainers, and current practice), and *consultant*. This program is quite similar to the group leadership training program Shapiro created and headed at the University of Hawaii in the 1970s and at Santa Clara University in California in the 1980s and 1990s. Similar progressions have been described by Foulds and Hannigan at Bowling Green State University in Ohio, Gerald Corey and his associates at California State University at Fullerton, and Irvin Yalom at Stanford University Medical School. The Shapiro (1993) model is a four-term, two-year program during which group leader trainees experience a variety of roles associated with group leadership. The curriculum for the four terms, outlined in Table 8.1, is described in the next sections.

Stage I: First Term

Potential group leaders are enrolled in an interpersonally oriented personal growth group (Group 1) provided by the training institution. The groups are led by a professional, licensed practitioner from the community and co-led by an advanced (fourth-term) student in the training program. All group leaders are supervised by another experienced community group leader.

Group sessions—which run for two hours weekly, with one, 8-hour marathon session approximately midway—are videotaped in their entirety. Members are encouraged to view the tapes after each session. The tapes are held for the week between sessions and are available only to members of the group and the co-leaders. In addition to their membership in the encounter group, trainees learn basic communication, listening, and counseling skills and engage in a supervised individual psychotherapy practicum. During this first term, trainees are expected to consolidate their knowledge in two adjunct areas: psychopathology and theories of counseling and personality.

Table 8.1   **Stages of Model Group Leadership Training Program**

Stage I	*Stage II*	*Stage III*	*Stage IV*
Group Work Membership in interpersonally oriented encounter group, led by licensed professionals and advanced students in program.	*Group Work* Membership in second encounter group. This group is more specialized, more intra-psychically oriented.	*Group Work* Co-lead Stage I groups under direct supervision of former group leaders.	*Group Work* Supervise Stage III co-leaders of Stage I group.
	Serve as apprentice co-leader in psychotherapy group with real patients and a professional co-leader.	Attend class sessions with other group leaders, supervisors, and training director.	Attend class sessions with other group leaders, supervisors, and training director.
	Videotape and observe Stage I groups and sit in on supervision.	Co-lead a mental health group in a community setting.	Provide running audiotape supervision while group is in session.
	Take course in theories, practices, procedures of group leadership.		
	Complete individual practicum counseling or psychotherapy work in community.		
Adjunct Work Training in basic communication skills. Supervised individual psychotherapy practice.		*Adjunct Work* Supervise individual therapy interviews of Stage I trainees.	*Adjunct Work* Complete internship or equivalent in supervised professional setting, including consultation, individual, and group in-service staff training.

(continued)

Table 8.1 Stages of Model Group Leadership Training Program *(continued)*

Stage I	Stage II	Stage III	Stave IV
Adjunct Work		*Adjunct Work* Videotape replays. Audiotape replay with supervisors' comments. Attend class sessions with other leaders, supervisors, and training director. Review videotapes and problem areas. Complete practicum or internship	
Remedial Work Consolidation of knowledge in theories or personality and counseling and abnormal psychology and psychopathology.	*Remedial Work* Engage in individual or group psychotherapy as needed.	*Remedial Work* Engage in individual or group psychotherapy as needed.	*Remedial Work* Engage in individual or group psychotherapy as needed.

Stage II: Second Term

Potential group leaders take an extensive course in the practice and procedures of group leadership containing the curriculum presented in this text. In addition, trainees are required to be members of a second growth group in which the leader has a different orientation (i.e., more intrapsychic) and are encouraged to volunteer at an agency to observe or assist in a counseling or psychotherapy group led by a professional group leader in the community.

In addition, trainees also serve as videotape camera operators in the Group 1 for the next group of first-term trainees. In this role they have the opportunity to observe a group without being personally vulnerable or responsible. They are also included in the supervision sessions that follow each group session. During this term, trainees are expected to be enrolled in individual counseling, family therapy, and assessment classes.

Stage III: Third Term

Trainees are enrolled in an advanced group leadership seminar and in praticum in the community. In the latter, they are encouraged to participate and to lead under supervision any groups in their placement that are appropriate.

In the advanced group seminar, students are again members of a group with professional co-leaders. The group sessions are videotaped and the leadership is explored in weekly class sessions. Member behavior is not open for discussion, but the leaders are available to describe their interventions, timing, rationales, and theory in a give-and-take format. The videotapes are explored in depth as are alternative interventions. The essential component in this stage is the leaders' willingness to be open and vulnerable. The effective seminar leader is willing to respond to student questions with theories, rationales, and concerns and is willing to admit to a lack of ideas, missed opportunities, and openness to alternatives.

Stage IV: Fourth Term

Trainees co-lead a Group 1 with an accomplished, licensed, community group leader under direct supervision by that leader and also by the group leader's supervisor. They meet the group for weekly 2-hour sessions and one 8-hour marathon session. Each session is videotaped and audiotaped. Prior to and immediately after each session, the leader and co-leader meet for debriefing and supervision. In a supervisory session of all the group leaders and the professional supervisor, leaders are required to view the videotapes and to present the parts they found most difficult to handle. During these weekly class meetings, issues and problems in leadership and specific incidents in the groups are discussed. Trainees are given a copy of the audiotape to review and study during the week. They are also expected to review the videotapes at least once during the week.

Alternative Supervisory Procedure

When trainees are advanced in a doctoral program or are already licensed at the master's level, two trainees may lead the Group 1. The professional leader from the community becomes a supervisor and observes the group from behind a one-way mirror. All sessions are videotaped as above, but here the audiotape is made differently.

During the session, an audiotape is also made on a stereo cassette. Track 1 contains the conversation in the group meeting and track 2 contains simultaneous process comments made by the trainees' supervisor while he or she is observing the group. As soon as the session is over, trainee leaders meet with the supervisor for feedback and analysis of the session, consulting the videotapes as appropriate. They also review the audiotape with the real-time commentary during the week between sessions. In this model, both trainee leaders and the supervisor attend the master supervisory sessions in which trainee leaders and supervisors from all concurrent groups meet with a faculty expert. During this term, trainees are also expected to do practicum or intern-level work under supervision at a mental health or counseling center and to co-lead a community group with a mental health population.

Throughout this training, extra care must be given to maintaining the highest possible standard of confidentiality. Group members' identities must be protected, and except for extraordinary circumstances normally governed by law, their names should not be part of supervisory discussions. It is the leadership concerns, dilemmas, and strategies that serve as the focus of discussion. At no time is the content of group performance to be graded.

Beyond the Model: Fifth Term

After trainees complete their degrees and become licensed, they are invited to be professional group leaders and supervisors for subsequent populations of students. This builds in a continuity and ongoing connection between alumni and the training program. It also provides the program with relevant expertise. To avoid inbreeding and a lack of critical discussion, a good strategy is always to have a mix of people from various backgrounds as leaders.

The Group Training Sequence

During the entire model group leadership training program, appropriate reading is assigned, and trainees take adjunct courses to fill in related deficiencies. Trainees are also encouraged to undertake individual and group therapy as clients, for both training and personal concerns.

Review Table 8.1 and observe how trainees move through this group training sequence from member, to observer, to leader, to supervisor. Each succeeding stage is built on successful completion of the previous one, and each represents a building block for the next. Success in each stage requires a major effort and increasing responsibility. By the conclusion of the sequence, trainees must demonstrate competence in the identification and use of the group process. They must be effective group leaders capable of using and transmitting the ethical values of professional leaders, and they must be aware of their own personal dynamics and limitations. Each trainee must also be able to work independently as well as part of a co-therapist team.

We believe that a two-year intensive program is necessary to accomplish all these goals. Individuals with a broad background in mental health may not need to go through as extensive a group therapist traineeship as described here, but the total amount of training in this program is not excessive for a novice in a mental health discipline.

SUMMARY

In this chapter, four universal components of group leadership training were identified. Training begins with the individual's personal experience as a group member. This experience provides emotional learning as well as a foundation for empathy with future clients. Training groups are often a student's first experience with formal "therapy" and ideally are the beginning of increased self-knowledge and continued growth—both vital to effective leadership.

Although theory and skill development can be accomplished within a didactic setting, observation of professional group leaders is necessary for modeling of the complex behaviors and attitudes necessary for therapeutic groups. Ideally, at least one term would be devoted to group process and another to group leadership. Finally, supervised practice as a group leader, with individual feedback, integrates theory with practice.

CO-THERAPY

CO-THERAPY

In most examples presented in this text and in the model training program, the groups are led by two leaders. We believe that every group can be conducted best by more than one therapist. For the most part, clinical practice and some recent research also support the use of co-therapists for both training and therapy functions. Rosenbaum (1971) suggests that the presence of a co-therapist increases the validity and intensity of specific interpretations, helps root out and break through therapeutic impasses, helps neutralize or clarify neurotic problems of the therapist, increases the depth and movement in therapy, allows for simultaneous probing and support, and aids transference. Corey (1990) includes the advantages of the different perspectives of life experiences and insights of two therapists, the combined strengths of a complementary leadership team, and re-creation of early family experiences with a male and female co-leader. The leaders may also gain in knowledge by observing and working with another professional and by splitting the work load in the group. Thus, while one leader focuses on an individual intrapsychically, the other may process other members' reactions.

In times of economic cutbacks and restriction of mental health services, such thinking is almost anathema to cost-cutting health management. However, we believe that co-therapy is sufficiently more effective that it actually will result in long-term cost saving.

Economic reasons are not the sole arguments against co-therapy. For many years, the notion of using more than one therapist was directly discouraged on theoretical grounds. Classic psychoanalytic theorists were particularly averse to the addition of a co-therapist on the grounds that it would severely and negatively complicate the transference relationship. General cautions about co-therapy have consistently been issued by Slavson (1964) and others.

Many have also argued that personal factors between the leaders will complicate group progress. For example, Cooper (1976), Corey (1990), and Shapiro (1978) have warned of dangers when the leaders fail to maintain an effective working relationship or have conflicting theories.

By contrast, many group theorists have long been proponents of co-therapy groups. Early proponents of co-therapy were Hadden (1947) and Whitaker (1949), who used co-therapy as a training device; Dreikurs (1950), Grotjahn (1951), and Hulse (1950; Hulse, Ladlow, Rindsberg, & Epstein, 1956), who investigated the use and implications of multiple therapists in a group setting; and Lundin and Aranov (1952), who have provided a lengthy description of their use of two therapists in groups of schizophrenics receiving insulin treatment at Chicago State Hospital. Later work (e.g., Dick, Lessier, & Whiteside, 1980; Diamond & Shapiro, 1973; Harari & Harari, 1971; Levine, 1980; Napier & Gershenfeld, 1983; Rosenbaum, 1971; Shapiro & Diamond, 1972; Shapiro, Marano, & Diamond, 1973; Yalom, 1995) supports the use of co-therapists in a variety of group settings.

Two predominant reasons were given for the use of co-therapists in the early work. Dreikurs (1950) and Hulse (1950) and his associates (Hulse et al., 1956) favored co-therapists for their value in reproducing a "family setting" within the group therapy context. Hulse et al. also recommended the use of male and female co-therapists to stimulate this "family" reaction. Several articles have reported on investigations of the transference phenomena in such a setting for husband-and-wife co-therapy teams (Harari & Harari, 1971; Low & Low, 1975), father-and-son teams (Solomon & Solomon, 1963), and interracial leader teams (Shapiro, 1976). The conclusion is that the generated transference provides a great deal for group members to explore.

In addition to the family simulation, the early use of co-therapists for training was frequently reported. Whitaker's (1949) early work training physicians and Hadden's (1947) training with interns and residents are excellent examples. Anderson, Pine, and Mae-Lee (1972), Gans (1957), Rosenbaum (1971), and Yalom (1995) have also indicated the value of a co-therapy model for training. Two forms of co-therapy can be used in training: an egalitarian model (Getty & Shannon, 1969; McGhee & Schuman, 1970) and an apprentice model. Most authors seem to feel that for greatest impact, group co-leaders need to be equal. Yalom, for example, states that "a co-therapy arrangement of anything other than two therapists of completely equal status is, in my experience, inadvisable" (1975, p. 420).

In the egalitarian model, the leaders are generally equal in ability and are held out to the group as equals. In the apprentice model, there is a clear leader and a co-leader. Each model has obvious advantages and disadvantages. The co-leadership relationship is a powerful, intimate liaison. Shapiro (1993) has suggested that the same level of scrutiny be put into finding a co-leader as one gives to finding a close friend, personal therapist, or spouse. Issues of power and status must be worked out as well as stylistic and theoretical differences. Such adjustments take patience and flexibility. Because we are dealing with group leaders, however, we expect such patience and flexibility. Usually, problems of co-leadership can be resolved. Generally, therapists whose personal styles mesh and whose theories coordinate will be most effective as co-leaders. Thus, it is not surprising to find co-leader teams in which one leader has an existential orientation and another object-relations. However, a less likely match would be a behaviorist and an object relations-oriented leader as effective partners.

Advantages of Co-Leadership

Although training and transference-family simulation issues were the early reasons for co-therapy, several other excellent reasons have been advanced as co-therapists have worked together. These include better coverage for the group, mutual support for the leaders, feedback mechanisms, opportunities for better interactional fit, self-therapy, on-the-job learning, greater opportunities for role flexibility, modeling, and greater effectiveness.

BETTER GROUP COVERAGE AND GREATER EFFECTIVENESS   Even the seemingly omniscient group therapist is not infallible. In every group, an individual leader's attention will be focused on some members and not on others. Whether because of theory, personality, or the interaction between leader and members, each leader will tune in to some members and some processes in a group while missing others. Every individual therapist has blind spots. The addition of a second leader with unique perceptions, theoretical orientation, and personal reactivity to members helps reduce the number and size of these blind spots. When one leader cannot empathize with a particular member, the second leader may; the reverse is also true. In this way, co-leaders provide greater coverage.

Similarly, each therapist has preferences in terms of the members with whom he or she works most effectively. With two leaders, the negative effects of such a preference can be minimized. Thus, more voluntary and effective treatment can be offered to each individual.

MUTUAL SUPPORT AND SELF-THERAPY   In addition to being able to fill in for each other, co-therapists also work together. When co-leaders support the same perception, it is more difficult for members to resist. Rosenbaum notes that "patients are more prone to accept two interpretations that are constant than one solitary interpretation" (1971, p. 501). Similarly, when one leader makes a tentative response and finds support from the co-leader, he or she can then follow up with less fear of being totally off the track. If co-leaders disagree, they can negotiate and find an adequate alternate path, with less tentativeness by either. In this way, co-leaders check and balance one another.

There is also tremendous personal value in a co-therapy situation. When people are consistently in a highly charged emotional climate like that of group therapy, they need someone to talk to about their own feelings and reactions to group members and process. Group members regularly deal with basic human conflicts. Group leaders share these life strifes and are not immune to personal response. The perfect partner to discuss these problems with is another person who was subject to identical stimuli—the co-therapist. Each co-therapist serves as a reality-based sounding board and therapist for the other partner. There is also the advantage of being able to discuss the group without inadvertently violating confidentiality.

For these and other reasons, the choice of a co-leader is a major decision not to be taken lightly. Co-leaders who have a personal as well as a professional relationship may be mutually therapeutic, a connection that is especially important immediately following the group session. The co-leaders also serve as peer diagnosticians for each other. Often a co-leader's responses in the group meetings will be an indication of certain psychological blocks or problems. It is the other leader's job to observe and relay such information back to the partner.

INTERACTIONAL FIT, ON-THE-JOB LEARNING, ROLE FLEXIBILITY, AND MODELING   Frequently in a group setting, a member will need to confront personal issues and to feel support at the same time. Co-therapists are ideally positioned to do this. Instead of having a single therapist engaging in both challenging and supporting behaviors, a very complex therapeutic task, each of the therapists can choose a single role. One of the leaders can provide sufficient support that the members feel safe enough to drop some of their psychological defenses and hence be more receptive to otherwise threatening feedback. In this way, members can attempt new behaviors in a supportive environment.

Often these co-therapist roles switch, depending on the interactional makeup of the group. Thus, one leader will be the supportive therapist with some members and the confronting therapist with others.

When groups are co-led by a male and a female therapist, members often see the female as warm and loving and the male as authoritarian. In the breaking down of such sterotyped projections, many members revisit experiences with their parents and experience major therapeutic breakthroughs.

In the course of a group, co-leaders will, of necessity, disagree. If they can express this disagreement openly in the group and negotiate a settlement, they serve as powerful role models in effective conflict resolution. Harari and Harari (1971) discuss the value of a husband and wife co-therapist team fighting fairly to resolution as a valuable component of the co-therapy approach. Naturally, co-therapist problem sharing should be kept to a minimum and dealt with only once the group has evolved far enough to deal with such conflicts. In terms of our group process model, Phase III should be well underway before such leadership problems are exposed. If too many co-therapy conflicts are publicly resolved in the group, members can become wary, lose their faith in the leadership, and develop feelings that the group is not equipped to deal with their own problems.

OTHER VALUES OF CO-THERAPY   Co-therapy provides for personal growth (Benjamin, 1972) of the leaders. It is also convenient when one therapist is sick or on vacation (Rosenbaum, 1971), and it is economical in terms of providing better coverage, more therapeutic resources per hour, and so on.

Dangers of Co-Therapy

All the dangers in a co-therapy situation seem to be a function of inappropriate selection and/or competitiveness. Heilfron (1969), MacLennan (1965), and Yalom (1995) have all addressed the problems inherent in a co-therapy relationship.

Competitiveness in the co-therapist situation is devastating. In no case can one co-leader work to further himself at the expense of his partner and still have an effective group. A crucial test of their cooperativeness comes in each group when a challenge is issued to one of the leaders. If the co-leader comes to the support of the challenging member(s) at the expense of the co-leader, an almost unclosable gap can ensue. Actually, the non-challenged leader's role in this situation is to support both and focus on process. In any case, vying for the members' affection can be as destructive in a group as it is in a family when parents fight for children's affection.

Competitiveness seems especially prevalent in groups of advanced students where the status dissimilarity between the leaders and members is not apparently great, such as groups of psychology or social work interns or psychiatric residents. Having the co-leaders simultaneously be members of another training group usually reduces such competition.

Selection of a co-leader is an important decision; one leader should never feel that he or she is "stuck" with the partner's judgment. They should have complementary skills and styles rather than identical ones. Most therapists agree that a male-female team is good, but physical characteristics are outweighed by skill and mutual sensitivity. It is also important that co-therapists be clear about their own relationship. If co-leaders have a dual relationship (professional and personal), it is essential for them to be explicit with regard to these roles and in agreement as to the relative place of each. Co-leaders must also be able to work at relatively equivalent speeds to keep the group process moving consistently.

When Co-Leaders Are "Too Expensive"

Despite all the compelling arguments favoring co-leadership, a practitioner may well be in a situation in which immediate cost is paramount and/or the third party payer or its agent simply refuses the extra cost of another professional. Even though we might prefer an equal partner, there is much to be gained from an apprentice co-leader who has less training or experience. We strongly recommend that practitioners regularly contact graduate mental health programs and give advanced students opportunities to be co-leaders in any group. This certainly serves the profession as well as clients. There is also the benefit of having one's work viewed through a novice's eyes. Not atypically, a student's perception will often be novel and on the mark, uncovering surprises that trained eyes miss. We can learn from their perceptions and from the questions we professionals are forced to answer when working with trainees.

SUMMARY

The co-therapy model for group leadership offers many benefits. It allows training and modeling to occur within the leadership dyad. In both an equity and an apprentice co-therapy model, mutual feedback, support, and personal growth are available.

Although a co-therapy arrangement offers emotional support and supervision to each therapist, it is the group that benefits most from the presence of two therapists. A co-therapy team is a more effective therapeutic agent within a group setting. Two therapists working together can provide better coverage of the three levels of group process: group, interpersonal, and intrapsychic. The therapists can provide mother and father transference figures and contribute a greater repertoire of therapeutic resources to the group.

Despite the benefits of a healthy co-therapy relationship, there are dangers inherent in having two therapists share the leadership role in a group. Similar to a marriage, problems of inappropriate selection and/or competitiveness within the co-therapy relationship can result in more harm than good for the group. Leaders need to pay as much attention to the foundation of their co-therapy relationship within the group as they do to the emerging group process.

GROUPS FOR SPECIFIC POPULATIONS

NOMINALLY HOMOGENEOUS GROUPS

In this section of the text, we explore theme-oriented groups within the context of the group model. Although heterogeneous and nominally homogeneous populations advance through identical phases of the group process, we can benefit from observing certain specific needs of both types of groups that add to and diverge from the generic process.

We have not tried to present a comprehensive review of the extensive research or clinical observations for each population. That is beyond the scope of this text. Our purpose is to provide a sense of the ways that the Brief Treatment Model may be adapted to several specific populations who commonly utilize group treatment. Whenever possible, major references are provided for further study.

Advantages of Homogeneous Group Membership

One of the predominant advantages of a relatively homogeneous group is that members often initially feel more connected to the group by virtue of their common need. Because of the obvious commonalities (of symptoms, age group, life stage, etc.) among members, early inclusion stages in the group are often accomplished quickly. In addition to enhancing group members' feeling of belonging, the commonality of a presenting problem allows for greater understanding during the there-and-then discussions, and encourages early self-disclosure.

In the treatment phase, the perceived similarity shared by members significantly promotes vicarious learning. For example, in a group of breast cancer patients, when one member finds some answers for herself, others in the group can find similar or contrasting answers by modeling, imitating, and comparing.

In the brief treatment groups mandated by managed care, any time-saver that does not significantly detract from the effectiveness of the therapy is to be embraced. The obvious caution is that the level of treatment must also be adjusted to the allotted time and demands of nontherapeutic factors such as cost containment and limits of care. Thus, many brief treatment groups are focused on ameliorating symptoms and learning specific coping strategies.

Disadvantages of Homogeneous Group Membership

The two biggest disadvantages associated with theme groups are the reduced diversity and "assumed similarity." The former is obvious. If all the members are drawn from a similar population, there is less room for alternative approaches to the problems or for perspectives that are not customary for people who are suffering from that disorder. Thus, if all the group members are depressed, coping skills common to nondepressed persons, which might otherwise be adopted, may not be available as there may not be a group member who can model them.

The problem of assumed similarity is more insidious. Many counselors and therapists describe their most telling failures as not recognizing the unique characteristics of their clients because they assumed that the clients were similar to some expected norm. It is easy in a homogeneous group to mistakenly generalize from a few shared characteristics and to assume that members are in fact similar, or have identical needs, in all ways. All group leaders know that any two individuals in a group are likely to be quite different. Thus, in a group of adolescents, leaders cannot treat the acting-out, threatening youngster the same way as an "acting-in," withdrawn member. Similarly, as Vanicelli (1989) reminds us, there is greater diversity than similarity among clients who are identified as adult children of alcoholics.

The trap for practitioners in theme-centered brief treatment groups is that they sometimes tend to diagnose and treat a "disembodied" symptom. Thus, instead of perceiving Joseph as a complex individual with a presenting problem of depression, we might see Joseph only as a *depression*.

HOW TO USE THIS SECTION

The next short chapters, describing six different theme-centered groups, are all predicated on an understanding of the basic model presented in Part I. The information contained in these chapters represents additional resources germane to specific needs along with treatment recommendations. Every chapter provides this information:

1. A brief history about the use of group treatment for the population
2. Advantages of group treatment for this population
3. Deviations from the basic model in each of the four group phases
4. Specific treatment recommendations

The six special populations are these:

1. Adult children of alcoholics
2. Adolescents
3. Individuals with eating disorders
4. Couples
5. Those involved in domestic violence (perpetrators, victims)
6. Single-gender groups (women's groups, men's groups)

This particular set was chosen for several reasons: their treatment needs in some way uniquely require modification of the basic model, the groups are popular in clinical practice, and each has generated a wide research literature.

CHAPTER 10

ADULT CHILDREN
OF ALCOHOLICS

In the past two decades, the long-term effects of alcohol and other addictions have been researched far more than any other area of mental health. In part, this trend reflects the available funding for study and treatment. In part, it reflects a growing national understanding of how severely alcohol and drug addictions affect the population and the business bottom line. Indeed, studies in the military in the early 1970s clearly indicated the cost effectiveness of alcohol treatment. The value of regained work and reduction of losses from absenteeism and military police "domestic" action among the service personnel who were treated represented 6 to 15 times the cost of treatment. Since that time, studies have repeatedly shown the treatment of addictions to be cost efficient.

As the study of addiction has progressed, researchers and clinicians have become increasingly aware of the therapeutic needs of the family members and others who are close to substance abusers. Family therapy has been suggested for treatment of both populations.

The impact of unresolved conflicts for family members seems to be long term (cf. Brown, 1988; Cermak, 1985). Thus, children who grow up in substance abusing families (adult children of alcoholics, or ACoAs) appear to develop a constellation of developmental symptoms that they carry into adult life. These developmentally based concerns tend to define the ACoA experience.

THE (INVISIBLE) ELEPHANT
IN THE LIVING ROOM

The alcoholic[1] family system requires a significant level of denial, involving a restriction of thought, feeling, and acknowledgment of such addictions. The denial is designed to keep the *secret* of alcoholism: a crucial component in a dysfunctional family system. Theoretically, alcoholics fear that if they must give up drinking, their survival will be impossible. The likely result of this unconsciously held belief is the execution of "the addicts' bargain"—an attempt to continue drinking within acceptable limits and simultaneously maintain relationships and responsibilities.

As the alcoholic struggles to maintain this balance, family members are lured into a comparable denial required to support the effort. They normally share a semiconscious fear that the family will self-destruct if the alcoholic is forced to give up drinking. As each family member adapts to survive in this atmosphere, inevitable conflicts arise. Many describe a tension between the need to support the family and an equivalent need to separate from the family dysfunction. Such struggles provide fertile ground for intense ongoing internal conflict and the resultant emotional toll.

Cermak (1985) identified some of the feelings and behaviors commonly associated with the ACoA experience. Among these are specific fears of loss of control, conflict, abandonment, and intense feelings in general. Adult children of alcoholics commonly experience intense negative self-judgment, guilt when attempting to assert themselves, hypervigilance, and a corresponding difficulty relaxing.

Combined with the denial of the alcoholism, these difficulties produce problems with intimate relationships; a "victim's life stance"; compulsive behavior; comfort with and thus production of chaos; confusion regarding the difference between love and need; a tendency to split (hold a "black or white" perspective) under pressure; increased somatic complaints; reactive versus proactive behavior; and the burden of long unexpressed grief.

The concept of "adult child" is rooted in traditional psychoanalytic and object relations theories. Until recently, treatment for these survivors of alcoholic family systems was offered primarily as an adjunct to the essential treatment of the practicing alcoholic. An increasing interest in the other members of the family has correlated with a dramatic increase in participation in Al-Anon, Al-Ateen, and ACoA self-help meetings for family members and adults who were living with alcoholics or who as children grew up in an alcoholic family. Probably because of the long-term success of the AA meeting approach and effective treatment of addictions in Veterans Administration, hospital, military, and private groups, group treatment for family members has found ready acceptance.

UNIQUE CHARACTERISTICS OF THIS POPULATION

The themes and problems that emerge in ACoA groups occur in all dynamically oriented therapy groups. Moreover, an ACoA who is placed in a group that is not specifically designed for ACoAs (e.g., a group of substance abusers or a group for family members—or even in a generic outpatient group) is still likely to enact many of these same themes. What differentiates the ACoA group is not the presence of these themes,

---

[1] *Alcoholic* here is used somewhat generically to indicate all addictions. Not only is the predominance of research with alcohol abuse, but most addictions follow a similar psychological pattern. When appropriate, distinctions will be made between substances of choice.

but, rather, the frequency with which they occur, the enthusiasm with which they may be embraced, and the group's tenacity in holding onto them. (Vanicelli, 1989, p. 41)

The ACoA Constellation

Although there seems to be some consensus of "typical" dysfunctional characteristics common to ACoAs, the lists are broad and empirical, and validity is still minimal. However, there is agreement among clinicians on certain commonly cited problems. These include (1) difficulty with intimate relationships (Ackerman, 1987; Gravitz & Bowden, 1984; Wegscheider-Cruse, 1985; Woltiz, 1983); (2) lack of trust in others (Seixas, 1982; Vanicelli, 1989); (3) fear of loss of control (Black, 1981; Cermak & Brown, 1982); (4) irresponsible or hyperresponsible behavior (Ackerman, 1987; Cermak & Brown, 1982; Greenleaf, 1981; Wegscheider-Cruse, 1985); (5) denial of feelings and of reality (Gravitz & Bowden, 1984; Greenleaf, 1981); (6) inordinate and relentless self-criticism (Cermak, 1985; Woltitz, 1983); (7) low self-esteem (Gravitz & Bowden, 1984; Vannicelli, 1989; Wegscheider-Cruse, 1985); (8) a higher than average risk of becoming or marrying an alcoholic (Black, 1981); and a higher risk of suicide (Bogdaniak & Piercy, 1987).

THE CHILD IN THE DYSFUNCTIONAL FAMILY   As a way to cope with the continuing stressors common to alcoholic families, children develop certain mechanisms that allow them to adapt to an unpredictable and often chaotic home life. Certain family roles have been reported that represent such adjustments. Wegscheider-Cruse (1985), for example, names the family roles of *hero, scapegoat, lost child,* and *mascot.* Similarly, Black (1981) employed the terms, *the responsible one, the acting-out child,* and *the adjuster.* In families with several children, it is possible to find one child in each of these roles. Such stereotyped roles and role expectations are normally considered adaptive strategies and defenses against the terror of chaos, disappointment, and unpredictability.

ADULT RELATIONSHIPS   The patterns they develop in childhood may lead to certain intrapsychic and interpersonal difficulties when these individuals become adults. Thus, the survival skills of childhood become anachronistic, deleterious, and "addictive" when employed in adult relationships. The following difficulties are thought to emerge through the addictive use of relationships to ameliorate intolerable feelings. These difficulties routinely emerge in ACoA group treatment as major themes:

1. Difficulty with self-esteem
2. Difficulty setting and understanding functional personal boundaries
3. Difficulty with personal reality
4. Difficulty identifying between and meeting needs and wants
5. Difficulty with internal experience of reality and with expression of that internal reality
6. Difficulty with dependency issues and feelings of shame

7. Difficulty expressing or being around anger or other strong emotions
8. Difficulty holding appropriate levels of personal responsibility

The ACoA Constellation and Group Treatment

Black (1981) defines the operative rules in addictive family systems: *don't think about the problem; don't have feelings about the problem; and don't talk about the problem.* People who grew up with these guidelines commonly have little experience or support in coping with or expressing feelings in healthy ways. They have little experience with honest and impartial feedback about their behavior. Self-esteem, particularly in interpersonal situations, is frequently inadequately developed.

The group therapy environment provides an alternative. It is designed to elicit the same kinds of dilemmas, yet does not allow collusion with denial by other members. In the group, ACoAs are confronted with a new set of "rules" that contradict those historically operative in their families of origin. They enter an environment in which the acknowledgment and expression of a wide range of emotions is acceptable and desirable. Furthermore, the group culture underscores each individual's self-respect and the respect of others. In the group "lab," members are encouraged to give and receive feedback as they develop a more accurate sense of themselves in relation to others. Ego-protective distortions of self-perception and personal value based on a co-dependent culture may begin to shift toward accurate self-perception and acceptance in response to healthy, supportive leaders and motivated group members. A group climate of acceptance helps members incorporate new reference norms vis-à-vis self and others.

By providing opportunities and encouragement for honest and direct feedback, the group helps the participants acknowledge and develop emotional boundaries, which in turn help them balance self-protection and vulnerability. Internal boundaries or limits refer to thoughts, feelings, and behavior and to the ability to assert them appropriately in relation to others. Effective use of internal boundaries implies a developed ability to separate one's own thoughts, feelings, and behavior from those of another and to take responsibility for what one thinks, feels, and does. External boundaries involve the physical self and its protection and vulnerability. They are evidenced by one's ability to value and protect the physical self in relation to others and to respect the external limits of others (Mellody, 1989).

The types of porous boundaries that are effective and rewarded in group and subsequently in healthier adult relationships are quite different from the rigid boundaries that are formed to maintain survival in an addictive family. Denial and the "don'ts" identified by Black (1981) meet with negative consequences in the group environment. In short, if members engage in symptomatic and anachronistic behavior, it yields a very different result from its response in their families of origin or in most other current relationships. Although the group setting may seem to represent a personal risk to members, it offers the potential to help them develop valuable adaptive interpersonal skills. Among these are opportunities for members to learn and practice healthy limit setting and to identify and respect others' boundaries as well. The articulation and enforcement of the group rules by the leaders, their responses to leadership challenges, and their abilities to meet their own needs in healthy ways as the group unfolds provides invaluable modeling for participants.

If the group therapy experience is to help participants learn to meet their needs and wants more effectively, the group must confront any member's hyperdependency and seduction and demand that all members take a proactive stance to meet their own needs and wants. They must not hold back with the expectation that others will volunteer to be their caretakers. At the other extreme, members who will not allow themselves to depend on others have the opportunity to experiment with vulnerability in a relatively safe environment. Those who confuse needs and wants (e.g., needing comfort from caring intimates but wanting and seeking a vanilla milkshake instead) have the opportunity to experience the underlying emotions motivating their behavior as well.

Leaders, representing authority and parental models, may come to be seen as moderate and different from the extreme models of behavior common in members' families of origin. This moderation encourages members to express their own reality in reasonable terms. When members are heard accurately, they may begin to see themselves as having enhanced value in the group. This may lead to a dramatic increase in their ability to hear accurately what group leaders, other members, and significant others outside the group have to say.

Finally, the customary approach of separating "self" from the "disease" and family of origin trauma can lead to a reversal of the process of dependency and of negative self-evaluation and shame.

In summary, group psychotherapy first affords ACoAs the opportunity to observe and identify the rules and patterns that operated in their families of origin. The group then provides an arena in which members can experiment with behavior patterns that serve them well, those they need to modify, and some they need to discard as dysfunctional.

The group process and environment are particularly conducive to the exploration of commonalities that emerge from alcoholic family systems. The simple fact of a member's identification as an ACoA may well provide hope that he or she can identify, address, and resolve the problems that arose from unpredictable, insufficient, inappropriate, and/or erratic parenting. For many, the confession "I'm an ACoA" delivered to a sympathetic group is the ticket into treatment that might otherwise be unconsidered or unavailable.

Steinglas (1989) and Vanicelli (1989) recommend dynamic interactional group therapy as the approach of choice to maximize these treatment goals.

PREPARATION
Screening

ACoAs are three to four times as likely to develop alcoholism than members of the general population (Bohman, Sigvardsson, & Cloninger, 1981; Goodwin, Shulsinger, Hermansen, Guze, & Winokur, 1973; Schuckit, Li, Cloninger, &

Dietrich, 1985). As part of the screening, extra attention must therefore be paid to the client's personal alcohol and drug history. Asking general questions about use or abuse is insufficient. Such questions are likely to be met with minimizing and resistance. In addition to asking about the potential client's use, the alcohol and drug history questionnaire should ask for details regarding the histories of all family of origin members and extended family members as well.

A major reason for such a detailed questionnaire is that these groups are specifically designed for non-substance-abusing members. It is clear that treatment of substance abuse must precede any possible treatment of ancillary or subsequent problems.[2] A single substance-abusing member in an ACoA group might serve as a lightening rod for all other members' histories, but the nature and intensity of the ubiquitous denial will also tend to shut down such members and inhibit their ability to participate in the group. A general rule of thumb is that individuals should be at least a year into their own recovery to be screened into the typical ACoA group.

When leaders suspect that an alcohol problem exists, they may employ an alcohol screening inventory such as the Michigan Alcoholism Screening Test (MAST) (Hedlund & Vieweg, 1984). The MAST is a 25-item inventory concerned with social consequences of drinking, addictive symptoms, and the relationship and health problems associated with drinking. The MAST is the most widely used alcoholism screening inventory and is a reliable and valid measure (Selzer & Vinokur, 1975).

For those currently living in a situation where others' substance abuse is evident, the treatments of choice might be family group therapy with a specific focus on the substance abuse and participation in the Al-Anon 12-step program rather than in a group. On resolving the immediate concerns regarding substance abuse, the potential group member may become ready for eventual inclusion in ACoA group therapy. Occasionally, difficulties with substance abuse surface only after a member becomes sufficiently comfortable in an ACoA therapy group to talk about them. When that does occur, it is the group leader's responsibility to direct the group member to services through which he or she can work with the substance abuse problem directly.

As part of acceptance into a group, the leaders may require some level of participation in a concurrent Al-Anon or similar 12-step program. Often members have a long history of attending such programs before entering a group. The group leader must be prepared for some inevitable conflicts in the rules of the two modalities.

HOMOGENEOUS VERSUS HETEROGENEOUS MEMBERSHIP   Some leaders, as well as many members, favor homogeneous membership. However, as we consider the basic set of dynamics that constitute the ACoA experience, we see a tremendous variability within the ACoA population. What may appear on the surface to be a homogeneous group because of the commonality of members' ACoA history may in fact have maximum heterogeneity.

---

[2] See also Chapter 14, which deals with violence.

Vanicelli (1989) considered the clinical implications of group members' tendency to identify themselves as ACoAs in addition to addressing the many issues of concern for therapists working with this population. Her text, *Group Psychotherapy with Adult Children of Alcoholics,* stands as a solid basis for group leaders working with ACoAs. According to Vannicelli, variability within the ACoA population seems to be the norm. However, just as important as recognition of variability among members is the common bond that enables them to begin the exploration of their personal concerns on "safe ground." The safety of this common bond in the context of effective leadership may provide the base from which to discover, value, and trust the individual differences that become apparent to members as their self-esteem begins to increase.

GROUPS ARE NOT MEETINGS   Some of the major differences that must be clearly explained and impressed on members during screening include the importance of a consistent group membership. Specifically, therapy groups require timely attendance and notification of rare absences. In addition, the stipulation that members notify the group before discontinuing treatment must be made and emphasized. Because members of ACoA groups are frequently concurrently in, or recently from, 12-step programs, the different rules need to be underscored early and often. Thus, for example, in 12-step meetings, there is a rule of "no crosstalk." Yet in a therapy group, such spontaneous simultaneous conversations may well be the most important grist for the group mill.

The therapy group's focus on unfolding group process, attention to feelings, and emphasis on exploring past as well as present behavior all contrast with traditional 12-step group participation. It is important for leaders to help members acclimate to a novel group situation by addressing these differences in pregroup interviews.

TRANSITION

Because of homogeneity around the presenting issue, the level of cognitive, emotional, and behavioral intensity for ACoA psychotherapy group members is greater than in generic groups. Their group silences are shorter, emotion runs higher early in the group, there is a more intrapsychic than interpersonal focus, and much more of the early content centers on family of origin than in a generic group. The tests of leadership may also be more intense. Normally in such groups the unsolvable problem is focused around the desire of a member to change the past—his or her childhood or prior relationships.

Because each member enters the group with the recognition that the major task is to come to terms with the family circumstances in which he or she developed, there is an early and dominant focus on how those circumstances affect current relationships. In essence, the family is a more immediate and available focus for the content of therapy, and the family transference is more readily enacted.

Tests of leadership may well develop out of the differences between the 12-step and group environment and rules. Leaders must be well versed in and respectful of Al-Anon and AA methodology and distinguish the group process and modes as different. Attempts to turn the group into a 12-step meeting are normally seen as a test of the leaders' abilities to cope with conflict.

TREATMENT

The tests and themes may differ, but the process of ACoA groups is remarkably similar to that of general population groups. Even though the members have identified around a common issue, the themes that routinely emerge in group therapy with ACoA's may be addressed effectively by a competent group leader with any consistent psychodynamic orientation.[3]

One difference in an ACoA group is the enhanced feeling of universality. When certain themes inevitably appear, several members relate more personally to them. This happens at both a personal level and in a parallel process in the group. Thus, when one member begins to reflect on the events from her childhood in an emotional manner, more members are likely to focus simultaneously on their own feelings and past events than in a more heterogeneous group. In addition, projection of these feelings from the past onto other participants and leaders in the group may be more concentrated. In short, family transference in such groups is potentially greater than in other groups. Leaders must therefore rely less on the members' "observing ego" and thus have to be more active and interpretive in such groups.

One major issue that distinguishes work with this population is the emergence of a core unconscious existential concern: The Addicts' Bargain. This myth that stopping the addiction will be fatal provides the child in an alcoholic family with a special dilemma. Such a child must simultaneously attend to personal survival and help to maintain the stability of an obviously unstable situation. This task is often accomplished in ways that are extremely costly to the child, including keeping secrets about the existence and extent of dysfunctionality present in the family. The child is taught to fear abandonment because of the possibility that the family will cease to exist at all if the secrets are told (Black, 1981; Beletsis & Brown, 1981).

The ongoing dynamic emerges in group psychotherapy when members begin to open up the events of their pasts and come face to face with the concern that talking about family secrets is emotionally tantamount to family betrayal. It is the therapist's task to help the client understand the historical necessity for such rigid loyalty and to determine how loyalty may be manifested more appropriately in the present.

As group therapy progresses, it is common for the conflict-laden theme of wishing for emotional separation from the family of origin to emerge. The dance between the seemingly paradoxical needs for separation and affiliation plays itself

---

[3] The dynamic orientation is especially geared to family of origin issues that are generally at the core of the ACoA experience. Any theory that pays attention to historical roots of behavior will usually suffice. Therefore, we use the rubric *psychodynamic* in its broadest possible manner, encompassing such divergent approaches as psychoanalytically oriented, object relations, Gestalt, transactional analysis, neoanalytic, existential, structural family therapy, and so on. Behavior therapists, by contrast, might work with similar patients and problems, but not focus on the Adult Child aspects.

out, frequently with great intensity, as members struggle to assert themselves and continue to be nurtured by the group and its leaders. Vanicelli (1989) warns about the intense transference relationships that play out in the group, especially as reflected in certain themes:

> Flight from the group; finding (and removing) the identified family problem; the search for a rescuer; rigid role assignments, hanging on; negative self-view to preserve parental goodness, the ACoA label; the myth of equality; resistance to "taking a look" at what's going on; fear of losing control or "becoming unglued" (riskiness of opening up in the group); the problem is outside of me; will the leader understand (therapist transparency about her own past); and "concerns about early problem drinking." (Vanicelli, 1989, pp. 41–59)

Because the transference issue is especially intense in group psychotherapy with ACoAs, the countertransference issues are equally powerful. Just as the group members tend to play out their unresolved issues with each other much as siblings would in a family, the group therapist is the focus of the child's expectations of "parent" and is the focus of much positive and negative reaction. In many ways the therapist fills the role of the parent and faces his or her own idiosyncratic reactions to group members just as they do to the leader. These reactions may or may not be within the immediate awareness of the group leader. Therapists working with ACoAs often report the same kinds of intense countertransference as what they experience when working with Axis II type clients, especially those with borderline characteristics.

Although it is inappropriate to treat ACoA's as "borderlines" or to assume comordibity, some of the same kinds of interventions around the transference-countertransference issue are appropriate. We cannot stress enough that maintaining clear boundaries, seeking consultation when necessary, and highlighting and interpreting interactions between therapist and group members are all necessary to move the group through seemingly impassable terrain. The group has the potential to help members toward knowledge and trust of self as well as toward growth marked by increased levels of self-regard; and to actualize that regard in the world so that each member's beliefs, goals, values, and resources are available and experienced consistently and effectively.

TERMINATION

Regardless of whether ACoAs entered treatment to face the denied realities of their families of origin, to break the identification and emotional ties with the addicted parents and families, or to face their fear of the emergence of their own alcoholism (Cermak & Brown, 1982), the process of empowerment to cope with the consquences of the alcoholic family syndrome is what group treatment provides.

If the group environment provides a familylike atmosphere in general, the ACoA group environment is especially powerful in this regard. During termination is when difficult transference/countertransference issues are very likely to be worked through. Leaders who have maintained therapeutic boundaries throughout treatment will have less difficulty helping clients negotiate their way through this phase than leaders who have allowed social convention or inattention to their own process to influence the ongoing group process negatively.

It is natural for members in any closed group to be reluctant to leave treatment. In closed ACoA groups, the simultaneous needs for autonomy and contact continue to unfold during termination as members struggle to "leave the nest" and to test whether the leaders will consistently support and encourage the process. The importance of leader abilities to enforce clear personal and group boundaries is especially important during termination to ensure that termination does occur on both process and pragmatic levels. It is tempting to contemplate extending group meetings or to change the group from a closed to an open format. When a leader is seduced into taking such action or succumbs to his or her own unaddressed needs to continue, the group members will likely suffer. Members may be faced with insurmountable trust and control issues should boundaries regarding termination not be maintained. The leaders are responsible for ensuring that termination occurs on a process level. All members are invited to address issues of termination such as loss, grief, and separation together as a group and to relate current feelings to those revisited in their families of origin. Members may further separate and individuate intrapsychically by exploring specifics of their personal development relative to the group context. In this way, termination occurs on three levels: group, interpersonal, and intrapsychic.

Because many ACoA members will have worked through issues that may have been impeding or arresting their psychological and emotional development for many years, the group experience will have likely become an extremely important "home base" for support and development. It is therefore important for members to be further supported as they transfer training to their lives outside the group and for leaders to remember that a major goal of treatment is its obsolescence.

For members requiring additional treatment, the options include referral to appropriate follow-up resources or inclusion in future treatment with the leaders as such options become available (e.g., an invitation to be included in a future group that will be forming).

SUMMARY

The many symptoms and themes that are commonly encountered in group treatment with an ACoA population may be seen as emerging under the umbrella of the issue of control (Cermak & Brown, 1982) or codependence (Mellody, 1989). The latter may be viewed as a base on which lie both active substance abuse and the ACoA syndrome. These symptoms may also be regarded as the result of attempts to cope with stresses of living in abusive situations. Whereas the alcoholic may be attempting to resolve the basic symptoms of co-dependence through the abuse of alcohol, ACoAs may use relationships for the same purpose. Working through co-dependency occurs in a context where control is always an overriding issue.

Despite the likely discomfort involved for members, the presented group model supports efforts to struggle toward the attainment of the above stated goals. This is accomplished through leaders' adherence to firm, fair limits, their personal expression and modeling of feelings, and encouragement for members to work out their conflicts between their needs and their family of origin loyalties and resultant ego-syntonic defenses.

The potential benefits for members successfully addressing the issues of addiction and codependence are enormous on a personal and business productivity basis. It is our view that business relationships replicate unresolved issues emanating from families of origin. Just as dysfunction exists in families of origin, so does the potential for that dysfunction to intrude destructively into the work setting. Resolving these unresolved systemic and personal issues helps members to fit in and function more productively.

The potential benefits in the social, family, and spiritual arenas are evident as well. Not least among these is the exponential possibility of providing, through effective group treatment, a way to address prior, present, and future generations. The possibility exists to greatly reduce the negative effects and costs of addiction and codependency for the generations that will follow.

A Note About Training and Preparation

Leaders must be familiar with the complex territory that alcoholism encompasses. They need a working knowledge of the multiple definitions of alcoholism as well as an understanding that no one concept of the phenomenon applies in all cases. Knowing the course the illness might take, its variable progression, and the numerous ways its effects may become manifest in family systems is prerequisite to leading an ACoA therapy group.

As echoed elsewhere in this book, there is no substitute for formal training in group psychotherapy. Without this training and experience with more generic populations, the ACoA group leader may become mired in unfathomable material or overwhelmed with the intense interaction and complicated transference he or she encounters. Even experienced group leaders are usually especially vigilant in working with an ACoA population and have their support resources such as consultants and their own therapists at the ready.

ADOLESCENTS

CHARACTERISTICS OF ADOLESCENTS

Adolescence, roughly spanning the ages 11 to 22, is a period of intense development requiring the accomplishment of important, specific tasks, each leading toward independence. In healthy development, the adolescent will emerge as a self-sufficient adult. While the developmental process unfolds, parents and other adults allow increasing freedom, corresponding to their children's demonstrated ability to shoulder the responsibilities that such freedom requires. This adolescent period is a time for gradual emancipation from parental attachment (Gallatin, 1975; Adelson & Doehrman, 1980; Adam, 1982).

For adolescents, there is a general shift in attachment from the family of origin to peer relationships. Focusing on the formation and maintenance of satisfying, self-realizing peer relationships is characteristic of this period of human development (Berkovitz, 1975; Coleman, 1980; Conger & Petersen, 1984; Adams, 1982). Often however, the attainment and maintenance of such relationships are chaotic, shifting, and confusing. Most adolescents are faced with forming a new sense of identity while they are also training for their life's work and careers. Many also make commitments to families of procreation at this time. Yalom (1980) defines the period as a time to develop flexible hopes and goals for the future.

Although the adolescent years are commonly viewed as particularly problematic, recent research suggests that adolescence may not be any more difficult than other stages of life (cf. Dacey & Kenny, 1994). However, the adolescent transition is at times hard on both the adolescents and the adults nearest to them. The difficulties of adolescence tend to be generated by conflicting demands and sometimes minimal resources for meeting such demands. In Elkind's (1989) words,

Young teenagers today are being forced to make decisions that earlier generations didn't have to make until they were older and more mature and today's teenagers are not getting much support and guidance. This pressure for early decision making is coming from peer groups, parents, advertisers, merchandisers and even the legal system. (p.13)

Rapidly increasing demands to grow up, to experiment, and to test parental standards are commonplace. In addition, adolescents experience wider mood swings and behavioral changes than the general population. Some of this is hormonally based; some is due to societal pressure and conflict. When adolescents face conflicts, they are often in the disquieting position of dealing with adult-level problems with little more than child levels of maturity. The resulting reactions often seem extreme. It is no accident that the mental diagnoses defining poor ability in relationships (Axis II) may not normally be applied to patients of this age group. Indeed, several observers have defined adolescence as the "borderline/narcissistic years."

ADOLESCENTS AND GROUP TREATMENT

Because the peer group has such salience for adolescents, group therapy offers several advantages not readily available from one-to-one interaction. Group therapy for adolescents has a long history beginning with Moreno (1911). Other pioneers were Aichhorn (1935), Gabriel (1939, 1944), and Slavson (1964) who is called by Rachman and Raubolt (1984) "the father of adolescent group psychotherapy."

Universality of Experience

Adolescents may be able, through participation in group, to gain a sense that their personal experience is not fully unique. They are comforted by knowing that they are heading down a path that has been cleared by previous travelers. Although they commonly take pride in deviating from convention, they are reassured by not being alone in their pursuit of self-sufficiency. In group, members are exposed to common themes, concerns, and actions.

Development of Empathy

Although the development of individuality is crucial, successful adulthood also requires the ability to listen to others and to communicate cognitive and emotional understanding. Sensitivity to others' feelings, thoughts, and experiences are also core group foci.

Problem Resolution

For many adolescents, vicarious learning is as powerful as hands-on approaches. Often, the most fruitful modeling is done by others of similar skills and age. Thus a successful resolution of a problem by a group member may be easier to emulate than similar successes of an adult, with whom the adolescent has a more difficult identification. Again, groups provide ample opportunity for members to see "success stories" from within their midst.

Catharsis

Hormonal, familial, social, vocational, and academic changes dramatically impact adolescent cognitive, psychological, and emotional functioning. If the group environment is established as a safe and caring milieu, the expression of feelings may help to dissipate many of the strong emotions experienced by adolescents.

Acceptance and Support

Adolescence seems a time of paradoxical demands. It is a time to develop a sense of one's own unique identity while simultaneously maintaining acceptance by peers. To accomplish what may appear as metamorphosis from child to adult, adolescents must both remain connected to the group and individuate. Overtly superficial means to achieve group acceptance—such as conformity of hair style, dress, use of alcohol or drugs, sexual behavior—may be offset in a group by more significant means of identification, based on mutual and global acceptance of feelings in the group counseling situation. Similarly, acceptance and support from the group can help individual members experiment with new behaviors in a "lab" setting where they may try out new solutions to common difficulties. By providing a "developmental womb," the effective group offers a powerful medium in which this population can experiment.

Although group psychotherapy can help adolescents cope with academic, social, peer, and family concerns, its overriding benefit is in the amelioration of emotional conflicts, value discrepancies, and strong feelings of insecurity. Adolescents typically use their group participation to help define themselves. As they navigate unfamiliar waters, their ego defenses are activated. Often these defenses are quite primitive in both intensity and style. As the process and pressure develop, reactions to authority are bound to be an issue. Adolescent behavior in group is reminiscent of intensified adolescent behavior outside the group setting.

Groups that focus on process provide adolescents with feedback from authorities and peers and offer opportunities to try out solutions to internal and external conflicts without fear of the usual repercussions of such challenging behavior (Bernfeld, Clark, & Parker, 1984). Group members do not have to "live up to" their victories or defeats. Instead, both are opportunities for learning and experimentation.

Even brief observation of an adolescent group in action leads to the obvious conclusion that adolescents yearn to complete themselves, to feel whole (Ackerman, 1955). That striving to a great extent characterizes the adolescent experience. Facing internal growth changes and rigorous societal requirements, adolescents typically are preoccupied with attempts to define and affirm themselves in preparation for acceptance into the adult community. Because of this, adolescents exhibit extraordinary sensitivity to external judgment of their worth, are quite focused on proving their adequacy, and experience a profound sense of vulnerability. Therapy groups offer opportunities for members to adopt characteristics that individuals perceive as personally lacking and to experiment with self-approval and a reduction of the discrepancy between perceived and ideal self-images (Kraft, 1968).

Relational and Sexual Concerns

Adolescents struggle with their sexual identities and feelings of inferiority, especially those related to physical appearance and prowess. To compensate for their feelings of inadequacy, many teens become overly controlling in their relationships. Although loyalties often shift, they are fervently held. In the sexual terrain, desire for experimentation and novel relationships produces anxiety and often a retreat to the safe turf of family or same-sex alliances. Other teens seek to lock in a single friendship or sexual relationship for both safety and experimentation, yet one that limits chances to know and learn from others.

Leaders of groups must understand and support the needs for security as well as offer opportunities for freedom and alternative choices. Often, sensitivity, transparency, and a gentle sense of humor about teen concerns best facilitate adolescents' exploration of the dance between the safety of the status quo and the danger of the unknown.

For the most part, the adolescents who are in groups have had trouble coping with the stressors in their life without access to sufficient support (Wagner, Compas, & Howell, 1988). Under large or consistent stressors, adolescents may regress to childlike levels of functioning. Such behavior is psychologically designed to elicit parental limit setting and support. The group may offer such limits and additional support as well as an understanding of the depth and import of the stressors through the teenager's eyes. Members may then be able to work through their excessive dependence and defenses.

ADOLESCENT GROUPS AND THE BRIEF TREATMENT MODEL

Some distortion of the basic group model occurs in work with adolescents. Leaders of adolescent groups have to better *prepare* candidates for adolescent groups. In addition, group leaders normally work to *reduce anxiety* to manageable levels instead of structuring the group environment to attain an optimal level of anxiety. They also typically maintain a higher level of *activity* than found in most adult groups. Leadership challenges are generally more pronounced and more frequent than in most adult groups. Termination requires extra sensitivity to the unspoken needs of members and clearer attention to transfer of training.

Group therapy with adolescents is like performing a piece of music with many of the accents and intonations changed. Anticipated quiet passages give way to booming crescendos. Subtleties of timing are replaced as members zoom through certain well-known measures to linger agonizingly at others that are less familiar. One cannot expect adolescents to function as adults in a group or to be as compliant as children.

PREPARATION

Berkovitz (1972) suggests individual sessions to prepare adolescents for the group experience. Corey (1990), working with the later adolescent years (college students), also uses a preparatory period. These sessions can help to establish a one-to-one, therapist-client relationship. Additionally, they allow the therapist to assess prospective participants for pathology and level of motivation. Rachman (1975) recommends that pregroup sessions include education about group interaction and discussion of fears related to group participation. Common foci of anxiety are peer relations, interpersonal relations, initiation, contact, and confrontation.

To ameliorate inordinately high levels of anxiety, preparatory group sessions stress peer support, mutual exploration, analysis of concerns, and emotional bonding among group members. Participants are assured that in group, the leader will be present and supportive.

Screening during Phase 1 must include attention to prospective members' developmental level. Composition of the group must be based on each individual's needs, age, psychosexual level, and diagnosis. As a clear guideline, Sugar (1975) specifies that group members should fit within a three-year age span. With a wider age span, members' developmental tasks may be too different to allow them to work well together. Younger adolescents may do better in unisexual groups whereas middle and late adolescents benefit more from coed groups (Kennedy, 1989).

In addition to chronological age, a therapist must consider levels of maturation and judgment, ability to test reality, sophistication of defenses, state and ease of regression, current levels of ego integration, and potential threats to that integration. Acting-out individuals must be assessed as threats to other group members. Similarly, as Berkovitz and Sugar (1983) indicate, adolescent group treatment is contraindicated for those who exhibit overt psychoses and extreme narcissism, especially in outpatient settings. They also underscore the need to delay entrance into the group for youngsters who clearly refuse to participate because of very high levels of anxiety. Shapiro (1995) recommends that physically violent adolescents be seen only when sufficient controls and safety measures are available, such as inpatient facilities or well-staffed outpatient clinics. He noted that coed groups are likely to be less volatile than single-sex groups (Shapiro, 1994).

During screening, leaders must be especially aware of the likelihood for members to skip, leave, or be tardy for sessions. Progress will be limited in groups with extreme variations in attendance. A common way to forestall such behavior is with contracts and formal agreements to attend.

TRANSITION
Setting Rules

Because everything in adolescent life seems to be bigger than in the therapist's reality, the therapist must set ground rules that are effective without appearing to be heavy-handed. Minimal rules for safety and communication are crucial. Sometimes greater latitude with fewer crucial rules is appropriate in an adolescent group. For example, soft drinks, self-directed "time-outs," or indoor or outdoor activities may be allowed in an adolescent group. Often the preparatory sessions and simple written signed agreements help the members enforce the few important rules. The leader who attempts to use authority as the primary tool of facilitation will usually be met with defiance and possible rebellion. A more effective approach is to be firm and fair and let the group do some of the enforcement itself. Thus, in a group that has a no-interruption rule, speakers who are interrupted may appeal to the group membership to be able to continue after such an interruption has occurred.

Some issues that may require attention are eating and drinking in group meetings, cleanup, and absences. Rather than require attendance at each session and on-time appearance for group, specifying the importance of these behaviors in pregroup sessions coupled with the development of on-time and consistent attendance as a group norm avoids much of the testing and confrontation that can bog the group down.[1]

Leadership Challenges

Adolescents normally challenge authority figures by acting out. It is not unusual for members to challenge group leaders by tardiness, absence, insolent "mouthing off," or "loud" silence. For the leader, the true test is the ability to remain authoritative without being authoritarian. Neither too much permissiveness nor too much rigidity in enforcing rules will be helpful. In the midst of the chaos that often marks transition, leaders should remember that the adolescents are expressing in behavior their internal fears and anxieties. The leader's job is to contain the anxiety and help the group move forward to the point that members' fears may be directly addressed in the group.

Acting out is likely to be most prevalent during the transition phase of the group. Adolescent anxiety related to fears of lack of control, helplessness, sexual and angry impulses and tensions, anxiety about self-disclosure, and mistrust of adults and peers fuels the urge to act out. An inability to tolerate these fears among others makes acting out the grist for the group therapy mill during transition.

Leaders run the risk of being seduced into becoming authoritarian and demanding compliance. This is normally a countertransference reaction to the leaders' own fears of losing control. Remember that adolescents tend to polarize issues to black and white extremes. It is the leaders who must offer the shades of gray. Rachman (1972), for example, defines such a leader as having the ability to function in an active, emotionally involved manner as a positive adult authority, fostering humanistic relationships with adolescents. Phelan (1972) emphasizes the therapist's ability to demonstrate appropriate and spontaneous expression of emo-

---

[1] Many groups for adolescents within institutions have mandatory attendance. If the group leader is also an attendance monitor, clear guidelines must be communicated to the group members prior to the first absence. It is important not to leave grounds for rule altering that would place the group leader in opposition to institution rules. When the leader disagrees with such rules, he or she should negotiate their alteration before the group convenes, not at the request of the members.

tion. He sees as crucial the expression of warmth and affection, a demonstration of care, and the willingness to be cared for. Genuine involvement is essential.

Interaction often begins immediately and intensely in an adolescent group. Often, leaders must assume an active role quickly if they are to orchestrate and model mutual respect in an effective manner. Guidelines about listening to others and the important distinctions between thoughts, feelings, and judgments may need to be demonstrated clearly and enforced firmly if gently. Those counselors and therapists possessing a low frustration tolerance for anxiety or expressed anger and acting out might seriously consider the advisability of initiating group work with this population.

A pioneer in the field, Slavson (1964) underscores the importance of using techniques suitable for adolescents. He notes that adolescents are themselves in a transitional stage, no longer using action as a primary means of communication and not yet using verbal communication as a primary means. Activities that lead to talking are often the most helpful in teaching adolescents how to be members in a counseling or therapy group and how to achieve the greatest benefit from the group. Kraft (1961) suggested that numerous activities—in number and in proportion of group time—should be used with more pathological adolescent populations. Shapiro (1994) reported on the use of basketball or soccer as an integral part of a group of middle adolescents who were incarcerated as delinquents. Kraft (1961) and Shapiro (1978) have also recommended settings conducive to considerable physical activities, such as team sports and games, as an integral component of the group therapy effort.

Nonverbal techniques play a significant role in the early sessions of adolescent group psychotherapy. Role playing (Olsson & Myers, 1972), the "Greek chorus" and split ego technique (Rachman, 1971), and popular music (Frances & Schiff, 1976) have all been used as effective catalysts during the transition phase with this population.

TREATMENT

Adolescence is a time of "becoming." The struggle for personal identity, for a sexual role, and for a sense of self-worth significantly influences group process. Group psychotherapy encourages individual introspection and mutual exploration with peers about personal interests and concerns.

If we consider that the group can serve the function of family in which the adolescent can participate, we see the heightened importance of leaders fulfilling a positive parental role. During the Treatment phase, intense transference reactions to group members and to the leaders are common. It is the leaders' job to help members work through these transferences in an atmosphere in which peer pressures and peer approval are more heavily weighted than in adult groups.

The adolescent group therapist must be more transparent with feelings regarding the group and individuals. Distrust of adults, beginning with parents, makes the peer group an attractive choice for many adolescents. Adolescent group therapists must in many ways fill the role of the parent while drawing a considerable amount of adolescent fire. At the same time, the leaders must demon-strate effective "parenting," providing an atmosphere that leads to insight and understanding.

As things "heat up," regression by one or several group members may become evident. Discernment of this phenomenon is useful for ongoing diagnosis and treat-ment in the group. Rather than permit recrimination or punishment, a savvy group leader will be able to accept regression as protective and begin to explore the mean-ing and function of the defense with the group and with individuals. At times, he or she may also have to approach the teenager as a child, with a child's needs. Alternation between orderly communication and disruption is likely to occur, espe-cially when anxiety-producing material is introduced. If the group leaders can remain aware of a theoretical framework for their interventions, they are less likely to be swept into the fray or into a punitive judgmental counterreactive stance.

Two frameworks that will lead to effective interventions are the understand-ing that adolescents are searching for an ego identity and the recognition that they are in an intense relationship with their social world. Interventions are best if they keep in perspective the member's needs for peer approval and his or her sense of being part child and part adult.

We recommend the following interventions as common and generally effective in a well-functioning adolescent group:

- Description of indicators of feelings (posture, tone of voice, dress, mood, etc.), in order to help members confront emotions, clarify reality, aid in transactions between members or to interpret them
- Well-timed, briefly and clearly phrased educative statements
- Empathy and genuine, appropriate self-revelation of leaders' feelings, especially strong emotions such as anger or affection in response to group behavior

A pioneer in adolescent groups, Ackerman (1955) pointed to the importance of providing an atmosphere conducive to shedding conventional social hypocrisies and stances. Good manners and conformity to perceived adult expectations are of little benefit in the search for personal identity. Ackerman suggested a group envi-ronment that is informal and intimate, reducing business aspects to a minimum. He encouraged adolescents to own the group as theirs, thereby taking responsibility to accept and emulate group norms as modeled by the leaders.

In any group therapy situation, it is necessary to penetrate the facade of words that often functions more to hide than to reveal feelings. During the treatment phase in adolescent groups, this is frequently accomplished by attending to non-verbal behavior when it is discrepant from the verbal. Expecting adolescents to make and to reveal associations by confronting them solely on a verbal level is usu-ally counterproductive. The therapist's consistent attention to nonverbal body lan-guage helps individuals in the group better understand the messages they are sending and receiving. It also helps adolescent members attend to nonverbal mes-sages as a way to better understand themselves and to develop more effective means of encountering each other. Themes such as sexual conflicts, anxieties, and feelings of guilt, shame, or inferiority related to the landscape of the patient's personality may be identified and addressed by tuned-in leaders and increasingly astute members during the treatment phase.

TERMINATION

Because transference and countertransference issues play such a significant role in prior phases of the group psychotherapy experience, it is no surprise that they continue here as a focus of termination. In a closed group, it is important for the leader to work toward closure with the entire group while attending to individual members as necessary. Terminations as a group are quite common for adolescents as they go through school, extracurricular activities, camps, and other activities.

A leader must pay special attention to allowing sufficient time for proper termination when working with this population. Reminding the group that termination is nearing is appropriate and necessary. Termination from group is in fact, quite extraordinary, because it is a transition that is *examined*. Review of goals and the extent to which they have been accomplished serves to clarify members' progress and to point out what more needs to be done. Exploring feelings about leaving also lets the members disclose and examine losses in their lives. Leaders may help members to examine their sense of worth on leaving the group and to affirm their emerging abilities to define themselves as personally unique as well as to develop and maintain relationships with peers, family, authority figures, and others outside the group. Leaders must keep in mind however, that much of the work accomplished in an adolescent group is developmental in nature and many adolescents simply will be unable to report fully on that process.

More than for adults, acting out can and does occur in all phases of the adolescent group when members feel an overwhelming need to escape from intolerable feelings. To the extent that leaders can anticipate the possibility of adolescents terminating membership prematurely, members can be approached to diffuse the need to flee. A co-leadership team is especially helpful in this work so that one leader can focus on the individual at risk while the other tracks the group in preparation for eventually working with other members who are experiencing the same or similar feelings. Because adolescence is a time fraught with separation anxiety, a safe bet is that separation anxiety will emerge in full force during termination.

SUMMARY

Working with adolescents requires attention to their developmental needs. These include being emancipated from childhood dependencies on parents; accomplishing successful attachments to peers; learning to love and value others in addition to themselves; and attaining a durable, consistent sense of identity in family, social, sexual, and work creative arenas (Berkovitz & Sugar, 1983).

Group work with teenagers also requires leaders to be flexible yet clear; to be warm, open, genuine, spontaneous, and empathic in the face of volatile and unpredictable behavior. In addition, to relate to adolescents, leaders need an emotional connection with their own remembered adolescence.

Pragmatically, group therapy is effective in assisting adolescents' management of their school, social, peer, and family lives. Its underlying theme is to help adolescents cope with communication difficulties, overpersonalization, and strong feelings.

CHAPTER 12

INDIVIDUALS WITH EATING DISORDERS

TYPES OF EATING DISORDERS

Bulimia, anorexia, and compulsive overeating are disorders that have been increasingly reported by clinicians since the 1980s (Hendren, Barber, & Sigafoos, 1986).

Bulimia nervosa is defined as "binge eating and inappropriate compensatory methods to prevent weight gain. In addition, the self-evaluation of individuals with Bulimia Nervosa is excessively influenced by body shape and weight" (American Psychiatric Association [APA], 1994, p. 545). Binges, defined as rapid consumption of great quantities of food in a relatively brief (usually less than two hours) period of time are characteristically terminated as a result of abdominal pain, onset of sleep, social interruption, self-induced vomiting, or the use of cathartics or diuretics. Alternately binging and fasting are associated with repeated attempts to reduce weight. Fluctuations greater than 10 pounds are common as a result of dieting restrictively, vomiting by self-induced means, fasting, and using cathartics or diuretics. Often, people with this disorder are aware that their eating patterns are abnormal; at the same time, they are afraid they won't be able to stop eating voluntarily. Depressed mood and negative self-perception are known frequently to follow binges.

The essential features of *anorexia nervosa* "are that the individual refuses to maintain a minimally normal body weight, is intensely afraid of gaining weight, and exhibits a significant disturbance in the perception of the shape or size of his or her body." (APA, 1994, p. 539). Other criteria include a fear of obesity that does not diminish in response to weight loss, a distorted body image (seeing oneself as fat) regardless of objective reality (one is actually thin or emaciated), 25% loss of original body weight, refusal to maintain normal body weight, and no known physical illness that would account for the weight loss.

Siegal, Brisman, and Weinshel (1988) define *compulsive overeaters* as having the same characteristics as bulimics with the exception of purge behavior.

Diagnosis

Despite numerous theoretical hypotheses, the etiology of eating disorders remains unknown and may well be polydetermined. In the 19th century, attention was focused on psychological causes of anorexia nervosa. The early 1900s saw a shift toward consideration of endocrine abnormalities. This trend was followed in the 1930s by a psychoanalytical countershift toward psychological etiology (Webb, 1988).

Not until the early 1980s was bulimia nervosa diagnosed. Today the focus on psychological causation of all eating disorders is tempered with the view that biological factors play a significant role (Connors, Johnson, & Stuckey, 1984).

Larson and Johnson (1985) brought attention to the disrupted family environments in which many eating-disordered (bulimic) patients developed. Enmeshed family systems, characterized by faulty or nonexistent boundaries, were thought to hinder the children's ability to develop an internal sense of an autonomous self. Disengaged family systems, characterized by parental apathy and/or lack of involvement, were also thought to hinder development of autonomy. In our experience, chaotic family histories and boundary difficulties frequently accompany eating disorders. By contrast, Bruch (1982) described the historical family environment of anorexics as seemingly well functioning. She noted, however, that little attention is paid in these families to the child's expression of needs, wants, and emotions.

Most specialists view eating disorders as multidimensional problems that commonly surface at transitional phases in women's development (i.e., onset of adolescence, leaving home for college or job, etc.). Logically, patients with poorly formed ego boundaries would have special problems in new environments and with shifting demands. An eating disorder may help to maintain a semblance of stability, however problematic, in a time of perceived increasing chaos.

Treatment

Bruch (1982) noted the effectiveness of active patient/therapist collaboration unhindered by theoretical orientation. Individual psychological empowerment within the context of attention to life-threatening biological/physiological realities remains a common focus of treatment. Despite numerous descriptive analyses of eating disorders, few identify specifics for psychotherapeutic attention (Inbody & Ellis, 1985). Practically none assess specific outcomes from identifiable interventions (Yates & Sambrailo, 1984). Although the prognosis for recovery is not particularly optimistic at present (Elston & Thomas, 1985), all therapeutic orientations seem to help some patients in ameliorating their binge/purge behaviors.

Among the recommended treatments for eating disorders are psychodynamic, experiential, cognitive-behavioral, transactional, rational emotive, family systems and a host of medical/psychotropic approaches. On the group treatment level, psychodynamic and behavioral approaches have predominated. Multimodal treatment is increasingly employed as therapists try to address the multiplicity of factors requiring attention. It is not uncommon to see medical management, behavioral therapy, inpatient and outpatient group therapy, personal therapy, and family therapy employed in attempts to impact these disorders, which are particularly resistant to intervention.

Although the research evidence on outcomes is minimal, group therapy for patients with eating disorders is gaining acceptance as a treatment of choice for several reasons. Piazza, Carni, Kelly and Plante (1993) focus on mutual support and socialization as factors in reducing relapse. Rollins and Piazza (1981) also stressed the importance of peer support. Lacey (1983) noted the value of education about the disorder. Not least among the advantages of group therapy are relatively low cost and influence of peer interaction for the adolescents and young adults most frequently afflicted. To the extent that life transitions exacerbate these symptoms, group therapy offers particular advantages.

The accelerated unfolding of process and transitional stages in the group affords eating-disordered participants an opportunity to replicate, simulate, and resolve individual transitional issues. In addition, the group setting allows members to bring up historic and present family of origin issues that bear on the condition. Group leaders tend to draw the parent-child transference, and other members often serve as substitute family members. The group may become a setting in which to identify, work through, and ultimately resolve family of origin issues directly affecting the development and progression of eating disorders.

In a sense, the well-functioning group may function as an alternative cognitive and emotional mirror for its members. In this way the group serves as a replacement for members' bodies as the instrument of self-definition and worth (Laube, 1990). The group reflection is more reality based, allowing members to gain a more normalized view of themselves. Members borrow from each other and the leaders a more realistic self-percept and ego strength.

Here-and-now brief group treatment makes it difficult for members to avoid the immediate experience of emotion. Members can use the group to draw parallels between individual and group methods of anxiety regulation.

Between-session assignments may be used as an effective way to maintain a here-and-now, therapeutically positive focus from one session to the next. Members may experiment outside the group environment with dynamics that emerged during sessions. Group experiences can be linked with specific individual member behavioral responses in the group ("lab") setting. Observation of feelings and resultant behaviors can then be addressed in back-home settings. Experimentation with alternatives to eating-disordered responses to emotional stimuli can be attempted as well. Suggestions might typically be made by the leaders at the end of each session, after commenting on an emerging central dynamic theme. Connections between this identified theme in the group process and members' back-home experience may then be explored. Further opportunity to generalize development to outside-of-group environments strengthens the value of the group experience.

Unique Characteristics of the Population

Among people with anorexia, high introversion and narcissism coupled with low self-esteem are associated with difficulty in identifying and expressing feelings, hypersensitivity to real and perceived judgments of others, and extreme perfectionism. These individuals often have difficulty with sexual identity including disinterest or disgust with their own sexuality. A symptom of anorexia nervosa with potential secondary gain among postpubescent females is amenorrhea. Because these individuals appear more girl-like than womanly, they are able to avoid dealing with personal feelings of adult sexuality and sexual advances from others. Distortion of body image (Vandereycken, Depreitere, & Probst, 1987), depression, and low assertive skills are also common in the psychological profile of the generic anorexic (Yates & Sambrailo, 1984).

Compared to those with anorexia, denial is less an issue among individuals with bulimia. Although they sense that something is wrong, they surround their symptomatic behavior with secrecy. Unlike those with anorexia, people with bulimia often display great sociability and a high interest in sexuality. Poor impulse control has been described as characteristic of the condition (Thornton & DeBlassie, 1989). Although the progression from bulimia to anorexia is rare, people with anorexia frequently display characteristics of both disorders and are known to progress from anorexia to bulimia.

Research and Practice

Like many of the clinical applications of group therapy, group treatment of eating disorders suffers from a lack of clear research support. Oesterheld, McKenna, and Gould (1987), among others, have noted problems in many studies of the group psychotherapy of bulimia. These include lack of accepted uniform diagnostic criteria, numerous sampling errors, omission of control groups, inadequate sample size, and absence of uniformity in testing. Variations in goals, intensity, and length of treatment muddy the waters even further. These problems are common to research in group psychotherapy generally.

Selection criteria for participation in group research studies invariably omit eating-disordered subjects who are poorly motivated. Cox and Merkel (1989) have noted the wide range of subjects who are included in eating-disorder studies, often making comparisons across studies questionable. Thus, participants in one group may be functioning relatively well except for the eating disorder whereas participants in a comparison group may carry dual diagnoses and a third group may have mixed pathology and levels of ego strength. The only commonality among the groups is the eating disorder. This factor is particularly troubling in evaluating results, specifically because eating-disordered clients are often significantly less motivated toward change than the general population.

Hendren, Atkins, Sumner, and Barber (1987), conducting mixed bulimic and anorexic open group therapy for inpatients and outpatients, stressed the importance of long-term therapy to support social change. They advocate mixed groups because many of these patients share the same fears, varying in terms of their social perspective. Selection criteria include age and transitional issues. Hendren et al. recommend separate groups for high school age, college age, mid-twenties, and older members.

When a patient has a simultaneous psychoactive drug dependency, the two disorders must be treated at the same time. Yeary and Heck (1989) propose the use of an addiction model emphasizing abstinence. They also consider eating disorders as addictions in their own right. The implications of this view can dramatically affect decisions regarding selection and inclusion of members in group treatment.[1]

In spite of its weaknesses, the clinical literature reports at least limited success with a variety of time-limited group interventions. Group therapies emphasizing behavioral theory and technique report the benefits of symptom reduction (Gray & Hoage, 1990). Those that used cognitive group treatment modalities report intrapsychic changes (Connors, Johnson, & Stuckey, 1984). After summarizing published studies using antidepressant drug therapies and resultant affective changes, Freeman and Munro (1988) concluded that combined individual and group therapies are more effective than either alone. In general, clinicians and researchers recommend active group leadership and eclectic approaches.

Currently there is a trend emphasizing multifaceted group therapy approaches (Thornton & DeBlassie, 1989) and incorporation of specific behavioral prescriptions. The immediacy afforded by concrete instruction and task fulfillment may strengthen beginning group members' and leaders' faith that change is attainable. Stronger confidence may improve members' motivation and stamina to attain longer-term success.

Why Group Treatment Is Advantageous

By attending to group content and process, the group can be used to identify and resolve physical, psychological, and social issues associated with the disorder.

Because of the safety individuals feel in exploring in a group, they are often willing to investigate the social situations in which their disorders emerged and developed. As self-disclosure increases, members are able to re-create and examine family patterns that may have contributed to their symptom formation. Relief from secrecy and isolation through sharing of experiences and the discovery of ubiquitous "skeletons in the closets," may serve to diminish shame. Modeling for and receiving feedback from others with whom they can identify as fellow sufferers offers the possibility to learn effective communication of emotion. It also gives them

---

[1] The notion of co-dependency as the core of all addictive processes is addressed in Chapter 10. It is important to consider the potential viability of an addiction-centered or addiction-augmented approach to the treatment of anorexia and bulimia and compulsive overeating.

the opportunity to test their distorted individual beliefs and views of reality. Through the mirroring and confrontation that take place in the group, they can form a more accurate self-view. Finally, social skills that would likely not be attempted in the larger society can be practiced.

PREPARATION

Eating disorders must be considered as possibly life threatening. It is therefore imperative to evaluate potential group members to determine whether they need immediate medical treatment. For example, assignment to an outpatient brief group would be inappropriate and potentially dangerous as a primary therapeutic treatment for an anorexic client in immediate physical danger because of the severity of the condition. Assessment for suicide and failure at prior outpatient treatment attempts might also point toward referral for inpatient care (Yeary & Heck, 1989). Medical consultation and evaluation should be standard preparatory and continuing practice in working with eating-disordered clients.

A patient's level of motivation must be considered as well (Lenihan & Sanders, 1984). Clients who are so attached to their symptoms that they are unwilling to consider alternatives to retaining them are unsuitable for brief group treatment. Individual support to gain the client's willingness to engage in treatment necessary for survival may well be the first step in preparation for future group treatment. For many, group participation is far too threatening and conceivably destructive. Patients must achieve sufficient ego strength before they can reach a threshold for inclusion in the group environment.

A number of issues are common to people who suffer from anorexia, bulimia, compulsive overeating, and psychoactive substance dependence (Yeary & Heck, 1989). These include fears of loss of control, inordinate attention to and involvement with the abused substance, use of the substance to medicate stress and emotions, secrecy, denial, and attachment to behaviors despite their negative consequences. Screening for addictions, dependencies, or abuse of other substances (drugs, alcohol, etc.) is routine in evaluating potential members. Inclusion in group treatment, according to the proposed model, is not appropriate for those who are not consistently clean and sober (see Chapter 10). Such individuals should be referred to recovery programs before attempting any brief outpatient group work.

Leaders must decide whether to have separate groups or to include individuals with anorexia, bulimia, and compulsive overeating in the same group. Screening procedures should help to ensure that selected members will be roughly equivalent in ego strength, age, and stage of life to cope with variations in the group population while benefiting from exposure to a range of individuals and symptoms similar to their own. In general, as ego boundaries become weaker, homogeneity tends to be favored by group leaders. An individual with anorexia who has poor interpersonal boundaries and a weak ego may be far more prone to add through "contagion" symptoms such as those of bulimia.

TRANSITION

Resistance to treatment is a primary consideration in the preparation phase of group work. It remains a central theme in transition. During this phase, members routinely focus on commonalities among themselves while attempting to discover and comply with the leaders' and other members' expectations. At the same time, defense against threats of loss of control may lead members to subtly resist the very expectations they are apparently "trying" to meet. Frequently, their challenges to the leader take the form of *seemingly* passive aggressive behavior. However, the resistance is far more amenable to treatment than that of truly passive aggressive personality-disordered individuals. According to Bruch (1982), attempts to interpret the resistance are bound to fail with this population, especially at this phase of treatment. Instead, leader willingness to model appropriate group behavior helps members begin to trust the leaders and other members. The stage may then be set for incremental significant risk taking as the group develops.

Differences are significant between individuals with anorexia and those with bulimia. First, there are age and lifestyle differences: Those with anorexia are generally younger girls with a reticence about growing up; individuals with bulimia tend to be older, struggling in the larger world. In addition, there are differences in awareness and acceptance of their eating-disordered conditions. Whereas bulimia sufferers generally know something is wrong, people with anorexia who are beginning treatment are usually in denial of their problem. To approach an individual who believes that her behavior is normal and acceptable with demands or invitations to change can be confusing at best and decidedly destructive at worst. During transition, leaders must create an alliance with members to explore who they are in an atmosphere of acceptance and support.

During transition, food and eating behaviors tend to monopolize group interest and time. Addressing something less threatening than feelings and self-image helps members to learn group norms more safely while they focus on manageable content. A treatment plan that directly addresses eating problems while supporting the growth of healthier ego functioning is an aspect of brief group treatment during transition that continues through sequential treatment phases.

Brisman and Siegel (1985) are representative of researchers and clinicians who believe that the time constraints of group psychotherapy and the slow formation of group cohesion make transition with this population an unacceptably long process. The authors advocate intensive weekend group treatment followed by a three-hour follow-up session to deal with difficulties encountered in implementing the eating-disorder specific treatment plan. Simultaneously, the leaders reinforce successful behavior as they encourage continuing support among members. A third phase of Brisman and Siegel's model takes place without leaders. A format is provided, however, to encourage peer support, delineation and evaluation of contracts, and expression of feelings. It seems that intensive treatment could be provided to facilitate transition more effectively; this would be consistent with our brief group treatment model. Brief group content in the meeting subsequent to an intensive treatment day or weekend could very well focus on those issues prescribed by Brisman and Siegel. However, we do not advocate a group meeting without leaders present. Issues of group safety as well as difficulties with continuity of care in the absence of leader access to important group interaction are seen to outweigh potential benefits.

TREATMENT

Treatment goals for this population include behavioral and psychodynamic changes. Without attention to both, the possibility of lasting change is diminished. Behavioral changes involve the attainment of normal weight for people with anorexia, cessation of binging and binge/purge cycles for those with bulimia, and eating primarily in response to physiological need for those who are compulsive overeaters. Among the psychological changes are improvement of dysphoric mood; elevation of self-esteem level; reduction in obsessive ideation relative to food; accurate perception of body image; increased social skills correlated with a decrease in social isolation; improvement in abilities to identify, experience, and express emotion; reduction in impulsivity; and development of internal and external limits (ego boundaries) and a sense of autonomy.

Behavioral Strategies

Pyle, Mitchell, Eckert, Hatsukami, and Goff (1984) list a host of behavioral techniques for eating-disorder groups. These include education, self-monitoring of behavior, adoption of adaptive eating behaviors, interruption of routinized behavioral chains of events, desensitization, response prevention, positive reinforcement, and mastery of adaptive skills. In addition, relaxation training, problem solving, incrementally defined behavioral tasks, development of coping strategies, and self-monitoring diaries are commonplace (Freeman, Sinclair, Turnbull & Annadale, 1985). Kirkley, Schneider, Agras, and Bachman (1985) also use systematic modification of eating behavior, group interaction focused on the disorder, weekly graphing of eating-disordered behavior, and daily self-monitoring.

Yates and Sambrailo (1984) add cognitive-behavioral techniques such as identification, record keeping, and Socratic questioning of automatic thoughts; arriving at realistic perceptions of weight gain; assertiveness training; and provision of accurate medical information.

During treatment all behavioral and cognitive-behavioral therapists focus on education and support. Sometimes this takes the form of lecture and homework assignments (Pyle et al., 1984). At other times, more open discussions occur with leader guidance and reinforcement. Leaders encourage group members to support each other outside the group as well as within, reinforce reports of success (e.g., freedom from bulimic episodes), and discourage talk of deviant behavior (Freeman et al., 1985). The content themes are centered on transfer of training (e.g., nutrition, stress management, assertiveness, etc.).

Psychodynamic Approaches

The dynamic approaches focus more on the underlying concerns, especially those dealing with the boundary issues and fallout from chaotic families of origin. The basic issues of separation and individuation, control, identification of internal states (emotions) and assumption of responsibility for behavior (Weinstein & Richman, 1984) have been identified as central themes in group therapy with an eating-disordered clientele.

The group leaders' psychodynamic tasks include assessing members in identifying their feeling states. Leaders can accomplish this by modeling and gently probing to elicit feeling responses. Clarifying issues of control as they are identifiable in the group is another essential function. One reemerging theme during treatment is members' perceived helplessness and the power of passivity as it is enacted in the group environment. Leaders may encourage members to experiment with alternative, healthier means of empowerment. Other frequent psychodynamic interventions are interpretation of fears of rejection and abandonment and support for the identification and expression of feelings and perceptions. Gentle assertive leader encouragement and supportive confrontation to facilitate member experimentation seem particularly effective in helping members combat their distorted perceptions.

The Addiction Model

The addiction model for the treatment of eating disorders focuses on psychodynamic and behavioral considerations in a unique manner. Initial interruption of the eating disorder is followed by attention to maintaining abstinence (Yeary & Heck, 1989). Success is measured by abstention from compulsive overeating (Overeaters Anonymous, 1980) for compulsive overeaters, interrupting the dysfunctional eating pattern for those with anorexia, and ending the binge-purge cycle for individuals with bulimia.

Group psychotherapy that focuses on abstinence and psychological development is often an important component of a more comprehensive treatment plan. The plan may also include education, medical evaluation, nutritional consultation, individual therapy, family therapy, 12-step support, and relapse prevention.

Potential benefits of an addiction-based group treatment model include members' sense of identification and belonging, development of healthy interpersonal skills, and interruption of the denial process. Advocates of the addiction model caution that therapy should be appropriately paced. Abstinence counseling, beginning with interruption of the eating disorder and its concomitant psychoactive dependence, should be followed by attention to more complex psychotherapeutic issues. This process is dependent on medical stabilization of the patient (Yeary & Heck, 1989).

TERMINATION

Aside from the standard termination issues and tasks that occur in any brief treatment group, the possibility of relapse stands out as a central issue for eating-disordered populations. Despite any psychological, emotional, cognitive, or behavioral gains, long-term recovery from potentially life-threatening conditions must be a focus of treatment and must be particularly addressed in termination.

Consideration of group treatment as a component of a lifelong process to cope with compulsive behavior helps to put into perspective the very real threat of relapse. If the group experience has been effective, members will be able to use "slips" to gain additional data with which to confront denial about their disorders. Members often have lapses after termination as a way to test their gains. These are not to be encouraged.

As their group experience draws closer to completion, members will ideally grapple with the continuing task of maintaining achieved gains. Reinforcement of cognitive, behavioral, and psychodynamic development helps members anchor these gains in support of continuing success. Exploration of future plans and perceived difficulties that might emerge helps members to gain security and a feeling of greater competence to cope with after-group living. Reaffirmation of available resources (including continuing contact with group members) and referral alternatives contributes significantly toward long-term stability.

SUMMARY

Group treatment for eating-disorder populations requires attention to physiological, psychodynamic, behavioral, environmental, and cultural considerations. The etiology of the disorders is still unconfirmed, and a number of treatment types are used. Leaders who are proficient and flexible in using different theories and techniques will be in the best position to provide effective service. It is likely that in the foreseeable future, a multidimensional approach toward treatment will prevail.

Although the basic model favored in this text is viable, some therapists believe that longer treatment is necessary. We maintain, however, that the exigencies of a managed care environment demand the provision of high-quality, brief group treatment for these populations. Treatment can be cost effective and therapeutic on a brief, intensive basis. Leaders must pay attention, however, to the need for continuing care such as follow-up therapy and self-help groups. Adequate knowledge of and availability of local resources are a mandatory component of an individual's continuing recovery.

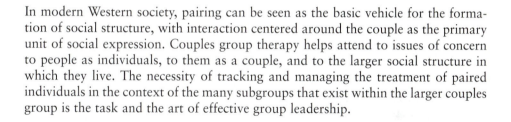

CHAPTER 13

COUPLES

In modern Western society, pairing can be seen as the basic vehicle for the formation of social structure, with interaction centered around the couple as the primary unit of social expression. Couples group therapy helps attend to issues of concern to people as individuals, to them as a couple, and to the larger social structure in which they live. The necessity of tracking and managing the treatment of paired individuals in the context of the many subgroups that exist within the larger couples group is the task and the art of effective group leadership.

HISTORY

It is not surprising that attention turned to couples treatment during the 1960s, a time of tremendous social and political upheaval and change. Clinicians and researchers in family and group therapy reported numerous innovations beginning in this period. In 1960, Jackson and Grotjahn emphasized the value of reenacting the dysfunctional marital relationship in a group setting. In 1962, Van Emde Boas suggested that long-term groups with fixed membership be formed for couples whose marriages had a poor prognosis. In the same year, Leichter (1962) reported on her use of therapy to help couples with problems of separation and individuation. McGee and Kostrubala (1964) described the disequilibrium in relationship patterns that would propel a couple into group therapy.

Emphasizing the therapeutic process for couples, Hastings and Runkle (1963) argued that learning to control the "marriage neurosis" in the group was "ego-strengthening and a corrective emotional experience." Blinder and Kirschenbaum (1967) were among the first to single out one couple as a focus of group discussion.

They approached the problem from an interpersonal rather than an intrapsychic viewpoint and found that communication distortions were easier to demonstrate and change by this method. Responding to fears from the therapeutic community of "emotional contagion," Gottlieb and Pattison (1966) noted that neurotic marital patterns, played out in a group, were not detrimental to group dynamics. Indeed, the group provided considerable reality testing for the couples' personal neurotic distortions.

During these early years, marital group therapy was something of an interface between traditional group psychotherapy and family therapy. Following the explosion in popularity of a number of group therapies during the early 1970s, there was an equally powerful burgeoning of interest in the study and utilization of dynamically oriented and systems-oriented marriage and family therapy. An increased understanding of the dynamics and structure of the small group provided additional understanding of family and marital functioning. This understanding, combined with the therapeutic dictum of the late 1970s and early 1980s—"by the family they have been broken, by the family they shall be healed"—generated increased interest in the small group treatment of natural (i.e., couples, families) groups.

A number of authors described methods for altering couples' systemic and dynamic patterns. Markowitz and Kadis (1972), for example, postulated that a relationship in which each spouse is projecting on the other the demand to play his or her omnipotent parent from childhood is both growth-stopping and dysfunctional. Group process was employed first to encourage such projections and then to work them through in the more public, more supportive setting of the group. Similarly, Grunebaum, Christ, and Neiberg (1969) used the group process to enhance movement when one of the partners acted out in anticipatory fear of change in the other. In the group, the focus was shifted to the anxious partner and support was offered to him or her as the psychological separation was achieved.

Bowen (1971), an early spokesman for the family system orientation, emphasized the value of working with the nuclear family in depth as a way of altering rigid patterns of interaction. Often this work would be done in a multiple-family group context with active group leadership. Low and Low (1975), employing Blinder and Kirschenbaum's (1967) techniques, applied many of Bowen's principles directly to the treatment of married couples. The treatment team would spend 30 minutes each session discussing one couple while the other couples in the group observed. The process would be repeated in turn for each couple in the group.

Following Bowen, Framo (1973) placed treatment priority on individuals differentiating "from the marital symbiosis." He asserted that couples groups were the treatment of choice for marital problems. Like Low and Low, he used a technique that deemphasized cross-relation and intragroup issues while concentrating primarily on the marital relationship. Two other important aspects of his technique were the introduction of an opposite-sex co-therapy team and the attention given to role modeling by the therapist.

Eclectic approaches, emphasizing group dynamics as well as couples systems, were underscored by Alger (1976) and Spitz (1978). Three themes can be identified in these authors' works: (1) Psychotherapy with couples in groups appeared to be a viable treatment method, worthy of further study and experimentation. (2) Many of the objections to the couples group format that had been raised theoretically (i.e., fears of emotional contagion, confused transferences) did not materialize in actual practice. (3) Specific problems inherent in working with groups of married couples came to be seen more clearly.

The emphasis on couples and family treatment has continued into the 1990s (cf. Marett, 1988; Coche & Coche, 1990). By 1990, Reighline and Targow claimed that group psychotherapy is the most effective treatment for troubled couples. Group treatments of natural groups have also grown in use in clinical and training settings. Today in various forms, couples groups are a popular and important treatment modality.

CHARACTERISTICS OF THE POPULATION

The most important difference between couples[1] and individual groups is the existence of built-in subgroups. Jacobs, Harville, and Masson (1994) note that "groups for couples offer some special challenges to the group leader. The leader is not only dealing with the dynamics among six or eight members, but also with three or four relationships that have their own (internal) dynamics" (p. 384)

Every couples group has multiple subgroups: the marital dyads; the husbands' group; the wives' group; the more compulsive subgroup; the quieter subgroup; and so on. Emotional alliances are often based on shared in-group and out-of-group experiences and valences of affiliation. In addition, confidentiality rules are stretched more in such groups. Thus, each subgroup couple can be expected to discuss the group between sessions.

Although subgroups develop and exist in every group treatment population, a sophisticated understanding of the quantity, complexity, and centrality of the subgrouping dynamic in couples group treatment is essential for effective leadership.

PREPARATION

Because of the complex nature of couples groups, preparation for treatment is especially important. Perhaps the most essential preparatory decision couples group leaders must make is the choice of their own partner in the group: a co-leader.

---

[1] The groups defined in this section are all characterized by Cookerly (1973) as conjoint couples groups in which both spouses are in the same group. Concurrent groups (usually of one sex) are discussed in Chapter 15.

Co-Leadership

Although we strongly recommend co-therapy for all groups, many authors reserve the mandate of co-leadership for couples group. An almost universal suggestion is for one male and one female leader.[2]

The role of the group leaders has been addressed by a number of authors. Gottlieb and Pattison (1966) point to two particular advantages of co-therapy in couple groups: the co-therapists serve as checks on each other's countertransference and inevitable marital blind spots, and they also provide a couple model for the group. Echoing this observation, Markowitz and Kadis (1972) view the therapists' task as twofold: working with and interpreting the group process and serving as models of realistic and mature behavior. They observed that the group was advantageous to the therapists and ultimately to its members because it made dealing with countertransference issues easier.

Morrison (1986) also noted that group leaders are presented with the task of modeling effective resolution and compromise. He adds the caution that group leaders are inevitably influenced by the projective identifications of the couples and need to maintain an awareness of this to make effective interventions. It is common for the co-leadership team to disagree, negotiate, and resolve differences of perspective, opinion, or concern in front of the group. This modeling serves as a very powerful example of successful conflict resolution for members. Of course, leadership teams with continuing and severe interpersonal conflicts are well advised to negotiate the bulk of such conflicts out of, and preferably prior to, the group meetings. The most compatible teams seem to have long personal relationships, sufficient time together outside the group, and well-oiled methods for conflict resolution. It is not unusual to find married couples as co-therapists of these groups.

Format

Brief treatment couples groups typically span 8 to 12 sessions of approximately 1.5 to 3 hours each, over 2 to 3 months. Corey and Corey (1992) recommend extended sessions (marathons) as well as regular sessions for this population. In addition, Marriage Encounter and Marriage Enrichment procedures and weekends or similar lay workshops are used adjunctively. We also favor a combined extended and marathon group format. Thus, members meet for 8 to 10 two-hour sessions with an eight-hour weekend marathon session occurring during the fourth week (timed for the anticipated movement in group process from Transition to Treatment). The total amount of contact would thus be just under 30 hours spanning three months. We believe there are several advantages to working with couples in a group format on an intensive basis.

---

[2] The most common exception from this rule of thumb is in gay and lesbian groups for which two male or two female leaders may better reflect the composition of the group. However, because relaionship dynamics seem to span groups regardless of gender, two disconnected leaders of the same gender may not be as great an advantage as might be assumed. The relationship between the leaders may be more important than their genders. An atypical number of husband-wfe therapist teams do seem to co-lead groups.

Recently, Peltz, and Galin (1996) have developed a unique experimental format for at least one group consisting of six couples. The carefully screened members drawn from the clientele of the male and female leaders met for two consecutive, 8-hour sessions, once per quarter, over a period of two years.

The three-month gap between group sessions allowed members to integrate, practice, and address with their own therapists material that surfaced in the group. The time gap also enabled members to gauge their progress by incremental feedback from other members and from the leaders. Each couple was able to relate to the others from the perspective afforded by a three-month latency period. Progress or lack thereof was evident against the backdrop of a significant intervening life experience. Although this experimental quarterly group was employed as an adjunct to ongoing individual couples therapy, it is a model that may be interesting as a stand-alone format for future groups.

Screening

Screening is very important in couples groups. Frequently, partners come to the group with different agendas. Thus, if one couple is there to effect an easier divorce, they may have a negative impact on couples who are trying to repair their relationships. Coche and Coche (1990), who primarily recommend intermediate term (11-month) closed-ended groups suggest a motivation requirement. In their groups, all members must have an "evident desire" to work out differences in the relationship. While the Coches recommend heterogeneity of age, problem type, and severity, they try to match member couples for fit with each other and "cognitive homogeneity"—that is, similarity in intellectual functioning.

Lieberman and Lieberman (1986) report that differences in symptoms, socioeconomic status, education level, job status, ethnicity, and religion may enhance the group. In her therapy groups, Leichter (1975) prefers couples who are at similar life cycle stages.

Our own position is closest to that of the Coches and Liebermans. We prefer couples from different life cycle stages, avoiding inclusion of isolates. For example, five couples ranging in age from their twenties to their sixties would be acceptable. However, four couples in their twenties involved in the early parenting years would not be mixed with a couple in their sixties who had grown children. Aside from the "no-isolate rule," our most salient criterion is level of ego strength. When this is discrepant either within or between couples, the group task may be compromised.

ADDITIONAL SCREENING CONSIDERATIONS   A predominant criterion is that couples groups be primarily geared for clients for whom the *relationship* is the primary cause of distress (Papp, 1976). Members for whom individual pathology is dominant and whose level of ego strength is different from that of others may well be helped by a group, but a *couples* group is generally counterindicated. Kaslow (1981) and Lieberman and Lieberman (1986) screen out individuals with "severe" psychopathology, such as psychotic disorders, significant substance abuse, active suicidal or homicidal ideation, and severe personality disorders.

Schindler, Halweg, and Revenstorf (1983) reported that one or two severely distressed couples in their Communication Training Conjoint Group therapy "tainted the group atmosphere." As the couples in the group saw each other not improving or improving only slightly, their overall dissatisfaction intensified and the improvement of the healthier couples was limited.

Spitz (1979) suggests that younger couples, couples for whom a marital homeostasis has yet to be reached, couples for whom a relationship pathology is chronic and ego-syntonic, and couples in which there is scapegoating and/or role confusion will respond best to the confrontation available in a group of peers. Luthman and Kirschenbaum (1974) also recommend group for couples with a mutual blaming or blaming-placating pattern. Grunebaum, Christ, and Neiberg (1969) suggested groups for marital problems that seem to be a way of life. Paolino and McCready (1978) focused on couples who are best served by the recognition and alleviation of reciprocal enmities and an understanding of universality.

One unique characteristic of membership in a couples group is prior experience in therapy. Most of the time, couples are referred to a couples therapy group from other individual, family, or couples therapy. Some clinicians *require* prior therapy experience (Coche & Coche, 1990).

Group composition is central to the success or failure of marital group therapy. A cardinal goal in every group is a balance between similar and dissimilar elements. The optimum group has membership that is homogeneous enough for trust and identification with one another and at the same time sufficiently diverse to encourage interaction with one another and to create interpersonal tension (Spitz, 1979).

Orientation

No special orientation or pregroup session is necessary for the normal outpatient groups. However, couples should be told of the special limits to confidentiality when their partners are also in the room. Even apparently small changes in session may carry over directly into members' normal living. Thus, it is often important to warn couples to be careful and moderate in their personal revelations and particularly aware of the implications on marital loyalty of disclosing a partners' personal concerns or behaviors.

TRANSITION

In the early stages of the couples group process, anxiety coalesces around issues of acceptance and rejection as well as ambivalence about participation. As in any group, expectations are high that the leaders will provide exercises or answers to problems. Coche and Coche (1990) see this stage characterized by much social politeness and propriety. Early self-disclosure is limited by the presence of the partner. Often, members present a "couples face," avoiding any semblance of serious conflict. Expressed disagreements usually center around established and well-worn complaints.

When complaints about their partners are aired, there is often an expectation that the other members and especially the leaders will "take their side" and judge their partner "the problem." As in all couples therapy, it is essential that the leaders resist the temptation to fall into this trap. In couples therapy, the *relationship* is the client and the core of the therapy. Judging one member of the couple as the problem and the other as the victim causes issues to be missed that may be addressed in such a group and likely replicates out-of-group experiences.[3]

The *unsolvable problem* in couples groups may center around in-laws, finances, or the inability of one partner to change the other. It may also emerge in the expression of *The Fight*, a characteristic, unchanging struggle each couple employs to regulate interpersonal distance. The fight script uses clear and well-known verbal lines and emotional expressions to bring about predictable end results.

Finding an Appropriate Level of Disclosure

Couples groups are different from groups of individuals, primarily because of the need to trust one's partner as well as the need to be personally trustworthy. To determine an acceptable level of self-disclosure, each partner must account for the other's needs for disclosure and privacy at any given time. During Transition, couples experiment with what and how much they may disclose. Often, one member's tolerance for vulnerability is different from his or her partner's or from the tolerance of other group members. Similarly, one couple may be able to self-disclose more or less than other couples. The discrepancies in such abilities and timing create tension within the group.

The leaders must support the group members' attempts to find an acceptable level of anxiety in the group. This is usually done in an unconscious trial-and-error process by the members with intentional guidance by the leaders. Ultimately, the group will settle on a range of self-disclosure that is acceptable to the members. It is within this broad range that the group will work until termination. The level of depth and amount of personal disclosure normally increases through the Treatment phase as the group level of trust grows.

It is essential that each member find a personal level of self-disclosure within the parameters appropriate for his or her primary relationship and the group. By the end of the Transition phase, members begin to emerge as individuals with their own style and problems instead of being identified solely as a part of a couple.

TREATMENT

Treatment in couples groups is usually initially characterized by each partner discussing dissatisfaction with the other. This is often expressed by instigation of *The Fight*. It is the leaders' job to help couples identify and understand the

---

[3] This notion of equivalent pathology is predicated on careful screening of members that has ruled out a couple in which one member is severely disturbed or one where there is abuse or potential harm.

psychological function of The Fight (distance regulation) and to encourage the couple to experiment with less predictable responses. The resulting anxiety about the unknown often precipitates expressions of dissatisfaction, scapegoating, or co-dependence, and a significantly larger conflict emerges before partners can approach greater intimacy. As they take more risks and struggle with increasing feelings of intimacy, self-disclosure becomes deeper and work begins on more painful and embedded marital problems. In addition, each member of the group may begin to work on personal family of origin issues.

Leaders must be careful to keep the group interactions at roughly the same level of depth. For example, family of origin revelations and therapeutic intervention may have to be somewhat truncated until the group as a whole is ready.[4] Member resistance will indicate when the anxiety about progressing to greater depth and intensity goes beyond manageable limits. Often this is indicated by a member's attempts to test the level of trust in the group.

During this phase, fear-induced concerns about trust and psychological resistance frequently emerge in response to attempts to alter the boundary between couples. Thus, in a couples group, one partner may discuss the other's impressions of comments about another member of the group. Loyalty conflicts and a sense of betrayal are likely to ensue. In one group, for example, Brad disclosed that his wife Brenda was very critical of the weight of another woman in the group. The resulting conflict focused on the two women with other members rushing to support one or the other. The more significant concern of loyalty and the power struggle within Brad and Brenda's relationship was temporarily lost.

Interpersonal attraction may also feed these conflicts. Thus, when Sandra displayed a strong admiration and attraction for Matt, Mary's husband, it was threatening to *her* husband, to Matt, and to Mary. The resulting discussion underscored her own husband's abandonment fears as well as concerns of betrayal and disloyalty. For Mary, it also raised issues of jealousy, even though Matt politely yet clearly rebuffed Sandra's attention.

During such times, the therapists must be able to help individuals explore resistance to looking within their relationships for solutions to their problems and to help each couple refocus on intracouple concerns.

As the group moves to greater depth, cohesion among members increases as does warmth, genuine caring, and helpfulness. The group will become ready to tackle the issues of power, maturity, and intimacy in marriages as well as in the larger group context. In a sense, the members experience a process of movement—from being part of a couple, to self-exploration and development, and finally to bringing a more developed individual self to the couple relationship with enhanced integration. In the words of one former member of a couples group, "We went from co-dependence to independence to interdependence in three months."

---

[4] In many brief treatment groups, the members will not reach this level of readiness nor will there be adequate time to explore such issues in sufficient depth. In these cases, a clear referral for continuing work in couples therapy is mandatory.

TERMINATION

As in most groups, Termination elicits a host of reactions from the members. Most common in couples groups is a regression to former patterns of behavior and reemergence of the pre- and early group arguments that were characteristic prior to members' work on their relationships. As the leaders support the members' feelings of impending loss of the group, they are able to regain much of the learning that previously occurred and to then practice more in their lives at home.

Two unique and significant differences exist in couples groups. The first is that transfer of training in such groups is more direct. After all, one's significant other is present for and is part of all the group-induced changes; he or she is also present at home. In such situations, even small behavioral and attitudinal alterations have potentially far-reaching implications. Changes in communication, self-disclosure, and problem solving that occurred for the couple in group are undeniably existent and available for practice at home as well.

Second, because couples group members return to their out-of-group lives with their partners, feelings of loss of the group are somewhat tempered: Each individual is going home with another member of the group. Thus, the group process may well continue for each couple. Because of this, the "alohas" are not as stark and members not as lonely after the group ends.

In addition, it is more common than in other groups for couples group members to socialize and support each other after termination. Perhaps this is because of the built-in support systems that participants enjoy. An example was provided earlier of a group that became a bowling team that for years met, bowled, and socialized on their former group night.

PREMARITAL GROUPS

Premarital groups merit special attention. Predominantly the purview of pastoral counselors and clergy, these much-needed yet sparsely available couples groups are designed as preventive measures for a "healthy and happy" population. As such, they are often primarily psychoeducational in nature. Leaders walk a fine line between helping members explore potential problem areas in their relationships and exercising caution not to create or prematurely expose such conflicts.

In Kilgo's (1975) definition, the overall goal of the premarital counseling group is to enhance the premarital relationship so that it will develop into a satisfactory and stable marital relationship. This is done by a combination of information dissemination, a focus on communication and skill development, exploration of conscious and unconscious expectations, and family of origin considerations. Group process is used to facilitate self-understanding, development of support systems, uncovering of personality styles, and unconscious motivation as well as to elicit feedback from members.

Like all couples groups, premarital groups have a dual focus: individuals, and couples as units. Because this population is approaching marriage (presumably anxious, excited, and happy about their upcoming wedding and life together), the leaders must take an approach that stresses education and looks at deeper psychological levels only as they emerge naturally in group process.

The most commonly employed facilitative methods are cognitive/behavioral. They follow Guerney's (1977) Relationship Enhancement Program in which group leaders often model and encourage the development of communication skills and interpersonal empathy. A similar set of techniques is derived from Marriage Enrichment Programs (Zimpfer, 1988). However, leaders must realize that members may not develop such skills sufficiently to be able to generalize or maintain them unless there is also significant attention to deeper psychological concerns and family of origin issues.

In addition to self-understanding and personal growth, other advantages of premarital groups include the value of peer influence and modeling, consensual reality, direct education about conflict potential and resolution, opportunity to generate topics of import for later couple discussion, and altruism (Gleason & Prescott, 1977; Glendening & Wilson, 1972; Horejsi, 1974; Mace & Mace, 1977; Rolfe, 1977; Ross, 1977).

Preparation

SCREENING   Normally couples are identified for premarital groups by preparatory interviews with the member of the clergy who will marry them or as part of a mandatory program. Other couples will see a couples therapist "just to make sure there isn't something wrong that we are missing."[5]

The couple should attend the screening interview together and the therapist or counselor should not only explain expectations of group process but should also ascertain whether the couple will be appropriate for the process. Couples for whom group may be less appropriate include those in which one spouse is particularly sensitive to privacy issues or is emotionally inhibited, the problems are deviant in the particular setting or group constellation, and/or there is individual psychopathology. Other couples unlikely to benefit from these groups are those with a primary relationship dysfunction, those opposed to a group context, and couples who are not at least nominally voluntarily committed to the counseling process itself.

Stahmann and Hiebert (1980) suggest several screening criteria for groups of younger couples (late teens to late twenties). We believe the criteria generalize to older couples as well. Stahmann and Hiebert recommend a screening interview with each prospective couple by *both the male and female co-leaders;* a size of five couples per group; an initial commitment for *five 2 1/2 hour, consecutive weekly sessions;* a minimum of *three months in the present relationship* prior to group; and *voluntary participation* with a goal of strengthening their current and future relationship.

---

[5] Generally, these "fully voluntary" participants are more mature, are often divorced or widowed, are entering into blended or stepfamily situations, come from diverse cultures, and/or are professionals in mental health and human services fields.

   Most authors agree on a group size of four to six couples and a five-to-eight-week duration. Sessions normally span 90 to 180 minutes. It is often advisable to complete such groups before the wedding preparations become too time-consuming.

CONFIDENTIALITY   Because these groups are not defined as therapy, members' expectations about privacy may vary considerably. Confidentiality needs to be explained in the precounseling screening interview and reinforced throughout the counseling process.

CO-THERAPY   As for other couples groups, a male-female co-leadership team is strongly encouraged to enhance the impact of normal male-female modeling and conflict resolution. This combination is especially valuable when one of the leaders is a member of the clergy. An unmarried minister leading the group may well invite projections and perceptions of "standards" that are unrealistic. Thus, in groups led by a Catholic priest, members may well question his personal understanding of intimate sexual marital relationships. Married clergy often report that members idealize their marital relationships. One Protestant minister and his co-leader wife were seen as having a "perfect" relationship, living up to standards that were "impossible for normal people," or not knowing about some of the more unpleasant aspects of relationships.

Transition

Because these groups are geared primarily for prevention and have a strong educational component, it is common for early sessions to involve specific, structured exercises designed to enhance intracouple communication. In addition, homework assignments for each couple to complete between sessions are also normal (Bernard & Corrales, 1979; Rappaport, 1976). The groups in general are more structured, especially in the early sessions. Often leaders or members select themes for individual sessions. Early themes may focus on expectations of marriage; communication or problem-solving skills; or members' thoughts about religion, children, money, sexual fulfillment, decision making, the nature of commitment, or sex-roles.

LEADERSHIP TESTS   Tests of leadership usually involve the leaders' personal relationships. Leaders who are divorced, single, gay, or celibate may present a particular lightning rod for challenges. Expressed concerns that a leader's personal relational abilities will impact negatively on his or her understanding of members' problems are common. Tests of leadership limitations often focus around future in-law problems, step- or blended family concerns, or other out-of-group or extra-couple concerns.

Treatment

The most common leadership focus during this stage is the shift from skill building to more intrapsychic concerns. These group members are often reticent to delve into potentially problematic areas. It is the leaders' job to gently open the door and invite members to consider deeper issues. Among the most common defenses during treatment is *denial*. Many couples in the throes of pre-wedded bliss, fearing the loss of this feeling or the relationship itself, will deny the existence of potential conflicts. The leaders must create an environment in which such concerns might be addressed with maximum sensitivity and safety. Ultimately, premarital couples will be able to express discomfort, dissatisfaction, or worry without bringing such concerns to the relationship level. Thus, problems or differences may be addressed with the assumption that such exploration will expand rather than break the relationship.

The predominant leadership task is to help members develop clearer boundaries. Successful premarital groups allow for the establishment of each member's personal identity as well as the couples' identity. Members will also learn how to identify and articulate differences and similarities between themselves and their partners.

Termination

Termination in premarital couples groups is not as distinct as for groups of unrelated individuals. Each member, after all, has a partner with whom she or he is making a new life, and couples often continue to meet socially after the group's ending. Some leaders encourage "self-help" follow-up meetings by members for mutual support. Leaders work to enhance transfer of training by underscoring techniques and successes in communication, problem solving, and conflict resolution skills. Continuing homework assignments are not uncommon (Wagner, Compass, & Howell, 1988; Whitaker, 1982; Darongkamas, Madden, Swarbrick, & Evans, 1995).

Follow-Up

Premarital groups are particularly well suited to postmarital follow-up. Leaders commonly have either individual couple sessions or "graduate" group meetings at intervals after marriage. These sessions may be particularly valuable in groups in which in-depth work was absent or minimal. At least one study (Ridley & Bain, 1983) indicated that the postgroup effects of a cognitive behavioral approach were non existent after six months. Many pastoral counselors (Hall, 1992) also recommend a Marriage Enrichment Program at one year after marriage to "review and reinforce" the lessons of the premarital group. These findings would suggest that effects of the psychoeducational groups are mitigated by the premarital emotional state and the cold light of marital realities. Follow-up sessions, six to twelve months after marriage, are often very valuable in helping couples to cope with the transition from newlywed to young married status. In these follow-up sessions, members often talk more openly about their "disillusionment" with the "happily ever after expectation" and about their partner as a real person.

CROSS-CULTURAL COUPLES

Because premarital groups have occurred so frequently within religious settings, couples from different religious backgrounds often have limited access to them. With the incidence of interracial and interreligious marriages on the rise, these populations have increasing needs for such groups.

Bernadett (1981) notes that couples with members from widely divergent (interracial) cultural backgrounds have unique needs. Early in the relationship, she reports, they tend to experience greater harmony, primarily because they attribute certain conflicts to the cultural differences. Later adjustment is more problematic when the cultural differences interact with personal differences as well. By contrast, couples with apparently similar backgrounds (e.g., two different Christian denominations) have a more difficult early adjustment with more harmony later.

Because of a reluctance to appear insensitive to cultural or religious backgrounds, members of the couple will both attribute problems to such factors and be reticent to confront them at that level. Major discrepancies in values or personality may be dismissed as acceptable cultural differences. It is the leaders' job to hold up these differences and encourage the couple to react, negotiate, and compromise instead of considering any culturally based trait to be immutable.

Shapiro (1992), reporting on a group of Christian-Jewish interfaith couples, concluded

> that there was a strong tendency for each member of the couple to avoid and deny differences for fear that the expression of such divergences could be explosive. The core issue wasn't about attending religious services or whether to have a Christmas tree. For each member of this eight-person group, the biggest fear was that they would have to relinquish their past and their identity to stay in the relationship.

For such groups, having an interreligious leadership team is helpful. Leadership tests will often center around a theme of preference for one member's "side." Leaders must respect the importance of each person's background, being especially careful of countertransference issues. Often parallel conflicts may arise between the leaders, indicating a need for greater sensitivity within the group.

Throughout the treatment phase of the group, the leaders must shine a light on these dark corners and have the couples confront their fears. Having the members educate each other about the personal importance of their religious/cultural beliefs and practices often allows for greater understanding and less fear of loss; frequently, it prevents much bigger, later battles.

SUMMARY

In Western culture, people are generally free to pair with anyone they wish. Yet despite careful consideration in choosing a partner, the majority of marriages end in divorce. The causes of marital unhappiness and disequilibrium have been extensively examined. They vary, extending from cultural dissimilarities to differences in personality. To be of help to couples, leaders must be fully aware of the cultural, individual, and relational complexities and intricacies in treating this population.

The term *relationship* is key to understanding paired individuals in the context of group psychotherapy with others similarly paired. Each member brings a unique individual personality, family history, and level of personal development to the group. Each also comes to group treatment with characteristic, habitual ways of interacting with her or his partner. Adding to this existing complexity is the intricate dynamic of relating to other individuals and couples. In essence, the task of couples group psychotherapy is the development, enhancement, and maintenance of optimally functioning individuals in the context of intimate relationships. Dynamically and interactionally rich, brief couples group treatment is particularly well mated to the task.

CHAPTER 14

GROUPS FOR PERPETRATORS AND SURVIVORS OF DOMESTIC VIOLENCE

DOMESTIC VIOLENCE

In recent years, domestic violence has become increasingly evident in both lay and professional arenas. Although jurisdictional definitions vary, domestic violence is often defined as "the infliction of corporal injury resulting in a traumatic condition upon a family or household member" (Conideris, Ely, & Erikson, 1991; p. 198). Family courts and penal codes have extended the definition to include sexual assault; unlawful entry; destruction or theft of personal property; keeping someone prisoner or kidnaping; murder: psychological intimidation or control (through such means as stalking, harassment, threats, violence against pets, etc.).

It is a serious and apparently growing problem. Straus and Gelles (1986) reported that 20% of couples report violence in a given year and they estimate that fully one third of couples will behave violently during their relationship. Bryant (1994) reports a high incidence of repeat violence in families. The incidence of violence in a relationship is serious, dangerous, and likely to permanently change the nature of the relationship. It also has an impact on others in the environment, such as children.

On one hand, the clear mandate is that the violence in a relationship must be ended as quickly as possible. On the other, the occurrence of such an escalated domestic dispute is quite complex in terms of its origins, maintenance, and termination. Deschner and McNeil (1986) argue that the use of psychological or physical force must be understood within the domestic environmental system in which it occurs. However, although violence occurs between members of a household, we rarely treat them together or in the home environment. Routinely, treatment programs separate men, women, and children, with little overlap. The necessity for helping those involved in the violence gain authority and responsibility for themselves, develop greater self-esteem, and learn personal control are the reasons most often given for this strategy.

Group therapies for victims and perpetrators of violence are no exception: Perpetrators are treated separately from victims. Group-based programs are available in almost every community. According to Russell (1988), most of these group programs use an educational approach based on the premise that violent behavior is learned.

TWO-STAGE PROCESS

Groups for both perpetrators and victims necessarily have two stages. The first is geared to stopping the cycle of violence. The second is more reconstructive and ego centered. The general assumption is that the violence must be arrested before existential issues can be explored and deeper psychotherapeutic work can occur. Eventually the self-destructive aspects of violence and abuse can be identified and examined as a base from which those involved in violence can learn better coping skills similar to addiction treatment, it is appropriate to have basic groups and more advanced groups. In the basic groups, the violent behavior needs to be addressed and ways found to stop it. In advanced groups, understanding and deeper exploration into personal victimhood might be explored. Group counseling and therapy as described in this text are primarily geared to the advanced or secondary groups.

ANGER MANAGEMENT GROUPS

Typically, anger management groups combine or sequence education and group process. The focus of such groups is each individual's situation and the consequences of the violence for that person. Normally, a predominant emphasis is placed on how violence is used for control. The primary goal of such groups is to change behavior, with an assumption that attitudes will change secondarily. Group members' denial and minimizing of their violent behavior are routinely confronted. *Power* and *control* are prominent "buzzwords" in most programs. When group members begin to understand power and control issues as well as cues to violence, they can often understand and address the progression of events that occurs in escalating violent situations. Then they can begin to learn the concept of self-control. To accomplish this, they are taught behavioral skills—such as time out and relaxation techniques—and cognitive skills that help them analyze violent incidents. With these and similar strategies, they begin to learn acceptable, nonviolent responses to life events.

Frequently, a powerful and directive group leader acts as combined parent, authority figure, coach, and friend devoted to a single purpose: stopping the violent behavior. Once the work has progressed sufficiently to ensure safety of their former victims, the stage can be set for inclusion in "second order" groups which focus on the whole person. It is through structured group work, where consistent support is available, that bonding among members often develops. In these "second order" groups, attention turns to the higher goal of effectively and adequately nurturing oneself.

ADVANCED GROUPS FOR PERPETRATORS

Groups for perpetrators (usually male) focus primarily on the development of communication skills, conflict resolution skills, and anger and stress management. Typically, a male abuser's program is focused on helping him learn to identify personal cues preceding violent behavior and learn behavioral alternatives. Tension reduction and systematic desensitization techniques often accompany such treatment. Once these basic goals are met, the men are exposed to assertion skills, cognitive restructuring (self-talk), and consciousness raising related to the roots of violence (Saunders & Hanusa, 1986).

Group discussion explores violent feelings and impulses. Along with identifying destructive self-talk, members are encouraged through role playing and homework to develop their communication skills (Brygger & Edelson, 1987). Through these discussions, education, and the identification of methods to control violent impulses, members are supported to take increasing personal responsibility for their behavior and to minimize or eliminate their violent outbursts.

Treatment models of choice have generally been structured groups focusing specifically on controlling violence through cognitive-behavioral means combined with education. These sessions address the ways abuse happens; its impact for the abuser and the abused; why abuse has become a part of the participant's life; and ways the abuser can change (Edelson & Syers, 1990; Faulkner, Stoltenberg, Cogen, Nolder, & Shooter, 1992). It is likely that the initial experience of mastering violence better prepares members for advanced group work.

Note that controlling the violence is necessary but insufficient for durable change in the violence cycle. The shift from effective survival strategies to development and growth usually requires *therapeutic intervention and support*. Long-term self-help support programs focusing on maintaining the nonviolent behavior often act as stepping stones from which members seek further options for their personal development.

Participation in such a theme-centered and psychoeducational group often lets members view themselves and others with increasing levels of esteem and respect. Establishing a minimal, viable level of self-esteem in beginning anger management programs frequently paves the way toward a deeper exploration of self and the possibility of greatly enhanced self-development for members.

The Inclusion of Partners

Some programs, particularly those conducted by systems-oriented therapists, include partners and focus on the violence as a product of interaction. The rationale for including significant others in treatment is to identify and ameliorate characteristic patterns of dysfunctional interaction. Theoretically, anger management skills can be learned and specific issues between partners can be uncovered and resolved in group treatment; but this happens in reality only if sufficient personal resources exist and can be mobilized by each partner in the service of conflict resolution. In general, therapists who stress the importance of people taking personal responsibility for their own thoughts, feelings, and behavior will advocate joint treatment for partners after individual and separate treatment for each. Almost all such groups require partners' reports of behavior to ensure that violence is not recurring in the home.

Preparation Considerations

Advanced prospective psychotherapeutic group members absolutely must be adequately screened to ensure that those with diagnoses of psychopathic, sociopathic, or antisocial personality; Axis II disorders; and active drug or alcohol addiction are placed in separate treatment and not mixed with the general population of abusers. Such participants could wreak havoc in the group and render it unable to accomplish its aims because it would be incessantly focused on one discomfited member. These members might also be prone to violent behavior in the group, or to self-destructive behavior.

Another screening consideration is the requirement that prospective members be currently nonviolent and preferably possess a significant history (perhaps one year, at least) in which they have done no violence. Members who revert to violent behavior during participation in group therapy might be counseled into more appropriate treatment to address directly the reemergent, immediate crisis. Often family members' reports of violence are sought during the group duration.

Because those engaged in domestic violence have frequently become habituated to crisis, screening for advanced group work should include an exploration of prospective members' current life situation. Consistent involvement in crisis and participation in a group focused on development and growth are incompatible.

Transition

The ground rules for anger management groups are different from the rules for the other types of groups we have discussed. For example, the focus on expression of feelings as they occur in the here-and-now between group members and leaders, customary in most groups, is in stark contrast to the goal of controlling feelings and behavior in potentially abusive situations.

Furthermore, confidentiality is often limited or partially compromised in many anger management programs. Partners of abusers are routinely consulted in many programs to corroborate or refute reports by program members regarding their violent behavior. In addition, government agencies such as the courts, probation officers, children's protective service agencies, and others are frequently apprised of participant behavior and progress in the program.

The customary rights of a member to refuse to participate in a given interaction or exercise are limited in anger management groups. Nonparticipation may be seen in such groups as avoidance or refusal. Direct and indirect pressure may be brought to bear on members to perform regardless of their personal preference.

Members must be clearly informed that if their violent behavior recurs, the automatic response will be a transfer out of the advanced group back to anger management groups and/or individual help to stop the behavior and to extend basic skills training. This action is necessary for both the violent member of the group and the remaining "recovering" members. Simply stated, the group must have a sustained base level of safety to encourage the creation of trust necessary to support members in tolerating their explorations of uncharted territory.

Normally during Transition, group members must deal with quite unstructured group environments. However, the crisis intervention types of anger management treatment, which commonly precede the group work, are of necessity quite tightly controlled and structured. By the time the participants reach the group, they have an expectation for leaders to be directive. It is not surprising that during transition in a less-structured group environment, members may have great difficulty with ambiguity.

Leaders working with this homogeneous group should prepare its members for a less-structured approach prior to including them in a group; they should also take care to gradually decrease structure as the group progresses. The result of moving too fast with this population is the danger of exposing them to unmanageable levels of anxiety which could lead to a reemergence of their uncontrollable demanding behavior and violent acting out.

Rather than take on responsibility for group member behavior, the leader's responsibility is to manipulate the level of anxiety in group sessions to facilitate members' working through issues. Too much anxiety too soon does nothing to prepare members to work during the therapy phase and may inhibit the group's ability to move forward. The level of ambiguity must match the group's level of tolerance. Failure of leaders to recognize and address this fact may lead to regression and reemergence of symptoms among members.

During transition, there is usually great pressure for leaders to take charge. The inexperienced leader may think she or he is about to be "eaten alive" during transition as members' coping strategies are played out in tests and challenges. The temptation to "lay down the law" and alternately to wish to flee are not uncommon among leaders.

Because the group cannot tolerate the result of "killing" its leader, the reality of truly destroying the leaders' ability to function is remote. Remember, though, that an abusing population's defenses will be activated quickly under stress. The characteristic defenses of abusers are aggression and threats of aggression. An effective group leader must find alternatives to "fight or flight," modeling those he or she wishes the group members to master.

These skills include the ability to identify, set, and maintain appropriate personal limits; to state personal reality in ways that are not extreme; to meet one's own needs and wants; and to focus on self-esteem as an alternative to predominantly seeking approval from others (Mellody, 1989).

Treatment

If the group members have managed to assert some mastery over their abusive behavior, the psychological treatment in group must focus on members' underlying low self-esteem and hostile worldview. Describing common psychological char-acteristics of batterers, Star (1978) included feelings of low self-worth; rigid role values; projection used as a defense for unacceptable behavior; pathological jeal-ousy; operating at the poles (violence versus contrition); reacting to severe stress by self-medication with drugs or alcohol in an attempt at self-control—or alterna-tively, by behaving violently; sex used aggressively to bolster self-image; unwilling-ness to accept the concept of consequences for violent behavior; social isolation; vigilance and intense sensitivity to others' behavior; and the emergence of paranoia under stress.

The predominant therapeutic goal, once the violence has terminated, is to help members move from external to more internal valuations of self. In doing so, the leaders must be constantly aware that the impulses formerly leading to violence will arise frequently. In the face of these impulses, members must learn to substitute thought and internalization for impulsive action or reaction. Often, members will attempt to control their destructive impulses with alcohol or drugs.

Each intervention is designed to help members to take increasing personal responsibility for themselves, as the concept of self-worth is identified, articulated, and accepted. Gaining a sense of internal self-worth (as opposed to self-worth determined by displays of power to gain mastery over a frighteningly intimidating world) helps members develop a basis from which to present them-selves (purposely hyphenated) in relationship to others.

Termination

As for all groups, termination involves transfer of training. It is essential in per-petrators' groups to help the members devise a *workable* nonviolent plan of action for dealing with stress. A great deal of "what if?" role playing is common in such groups. Among the special requirements of termination are follow-up sessions with the group or individually with members, and continued reporting from the spouse.

TREATMENT FOR SURVIVORS OF FAMILY VIOLENCE

Of primary importance is the immediate protection of emotionally, physically, or sexually battered spouses (usually women) and children. Support and advocacy dur-ing this time of crisis are also mandatory. At the same time, previously discussed treatment and accountability for violent partners is necessary (Brygger & Edleson, 1987).

Often such groups have a large educational and case work component. The physical safety of the women[1] must first be assured. Underlying dynamics and future plans may be explored only after the basic survival needs are secured.

---

[1]The vast majority of such groups are for women only. Abuse against men is widely underreported and undertreated. Often, abused male spouses are simply not believed or their pain and suffering are mini-mized. Groups for battered men or mixed groups are becoming more common but still represent a small fraction of the total population.

Screening

Battered women have typically been self-referred or referred to treatment by social and/or government agencies. The very fact that a battered woman presents herself for treatment usually guarantees her inclusion. The luxury of selecting women for a good match with services offered or for equivalent ego strength is, in the real world, usually sacrificed to the exigencies of providing crisis intervention. Obviously, women who are functionally impaired to the point of being unable to understand or integrate information offered in an education-support group are best served by alternative treatment modalities. At times of a personal crisis of this magnitude, some women will eschew group treatment in favor of individual consultation, hospitalization, milieu therapy, or residence in a safe house.

Transition

Leadership challenges for this group may be slow to develop; when they do, they contain a great deal of (often hostile) dependency. Great power is often attributed to leaders as authority figures; they are also seen frequently as agents of potentially substantive punishment. More support and information dissemination characterize the transition phase of this group. Remember that while members are making this transition in the group, they are simultaneously going through a life transition of far greater consequence. The members' uncertainty about what to expect in the group is likely to activate a host of ambiguities about their futures.

In these groups, the testing aspect of transition may well continue throughout the group process. As members master each new level and approach another, the testing may recur as a way for them to build courage and support for the next therapeutic endeavor. This is different from what happens in other populations, primarily in degree. All groups test throughout, but in victims' groups, the testing is more visible for leaders. Willing participation is almost always a temporary phenomenon. One predominant goal of transition is for members to develop a sense of universality. Members grow to understand that they are not alone. They begin to emerge from social isolation with the support of each other and the leaders. This emergence serves as a prototype for later support systems in their back-home world. Trimprey (1989) underscores the significance of focusing on underlying anxiety and building of self-esteem during the early phases of the group.

Treatment

For the basic group treatment, Brygger and Edleson (1987) provide a normative sequence of treatment concerns for this population. Beginning group sessions usually focus on developing and tailoring protection plans that have been rudimentarily discussed in intake interviews (Brygger & Edleson, 1987). These are followed by discussions of some of the myths of battering (i.e., women are to blame for their situation and the physical punishment resulted from their failure to perform well or to respect the perpetrator's authority). The survivors are taught that violence and threats are progressive in nature, and they learn to identify the clues that point to escalating violence. Their legal rights are also identified and reinforced. Lewis

(1983) recommends a similar combination with behavioral, insight, and feminist therapies.

Many authors, including Cooper-White (1990), argue that the group counseling will be most helpful after the crisis has been adequately addressed and violence-free living has been attained. Keep in mind that survivors of abuse must develop a sense of an autonomous self. Until they have learned to live by their own personal standards and values, the risk remains that they will adopt someone else's values, commonly those values least able to support the development and maintenance of a healthy self-concept.

Consistent support and experimentation in the group encourages the process of building new social networks. These networks are especially important in helping members confront the pressure to remain in or return to abusive relationships, assuming full responsibility for their repair.

Initial support and education provide the foundation for work during this group phase. Normally, in such groups, much individual exploration of family (and culture) of origin takes place. The themes of fear, shame, and guilt often are accompanied by a great deal of expressed affect. Additional time is typically spent on developing communication skills, assertiveness training, exploring sexuality, and focusing on parenting. Finally, members are encouraged to be pragmatic in dangerous situations, eschewing opportunities to make a verbal point if the verbal parry has a great personal cost.

Termination

Similar to the abusers, the abused members are encouraged to practice dealing with stress. Role playing and observing examples of alternative responses are common in promoting transfer of training. Follow-up sessions are also advisable. During termination the loss of the group process provides another opportunity for the abused members to work through the loss of the primary relationship with the abuser or certain aspects of that relationship.

THE CHILDREN

Minimal research has been directed toward the group treatment of physically or emotionally abused children. Some research has focused on sexually abused children, and these studies help to support assumptions regarding effective group procedures with the child survivor population in general.

Group treatment for abused children seems to offer the following potential benefits: mitigation of the child's sense of responsibility for the abuse and the abusive situation; inclusion of the child in a supportive group environment to reduce isolation; opportunity for the child to learn socialization skills; and promotion of the emergence of the child's experience of the abuse.

Wagar and Rodway (1995) present at least one approach for helping children who have witnessed spousal abuse. An inference from their work is that groups for child witnesses may reduce the probability that they will grow up to be abusers or victims. Similarly, Peled and Edleson (1992) found that group work with these children helped them improve their school performance and socialization.

It is, of course, crucial that the child's physical needs for safety and security are met prior to group treatment. The development of a peer group seems particularly salient in such treatment. For this reason, group leaders are encouraged to have longer durations for their groups treating abused children.

SUMMARY

Domestic violence is a serious and present danger in American culture. Group therapy will continue to be an important therapeutic intervention for both perpetrators and survivors of abuse.

Treatment for perpetrators requires a two-stage process consisting of an anger management group followed by a more advanced process group in which members may address deeper, underlying psychological issues.

Groups for survivors also involve two stages. Basic survivor groups focus on safety, education, and support. In more advanced groups, survivors of domestic violence are encouraged to develop life skills, such as assertiveness, communication, and parenting. Both victims and perpetrators need to develop support systems and healthy methods of coping with stress. Groups specifically designed for this population are particularly effective.

CHAPTER 15

SINGLE-GENDER GROUPS: WOMEN'S GROUPS, MEN'S GROUPS

The literature on groups raises questions about the benefits and liabilities of homogeneous versus heterogeneous group membership. In forming the brief treatment groups that are the focus of this text, we have repeatedly recommended that group leaders pay attention to selection of members to ensure homogeneous ego strength and commonalties of need. Conversely, heterogeneity regarding race, gender, and culture is generally desired. In this chapter, we explore a partial exception to this rule: groups specifically designed for a single gender.

By default single-sex groups have existed for years for certain populations. Some treatment centers admit individuals of only one sex. For example, although there are large numbers of male victims of sexual assault and violence (Steinmetz, 1978; Strass, 1985; Strauss & Gelles, 1986), group and individual treatment for survivors seems to be focused almost universally on females. Similarly, females are rarely members of abuser groups. Members of groups that focus on eating disorders are universally female as well (Burch, 1982; Gendron, Lemberg, Allender, & Bohanske, 1992; Crosby, Mitchell, Raymond, & Specker, 1993; Blouin et al., 1994; Gowers, Norton, Halek, & Crisp, 1994).

For years, there have been groups of combat veterans at VA facilities that have primarily been all male. Some illnesses also are clearly gender related, such as breast, uterine, or prostate cancer, and victims of these diseases would naturally form single-sex groups. Although such groups are made up of members of the same sex, however, gender is something of an artifact in them rather than a focus of attention.

This chapter focuses on groups specifically designed to engage members in exploring issues from a gender perspective. In such groups, men and women are separately encouraged to explore meaning, experiences, and confusions in intrapsychic and interpersonal development in a way that encourages input from other members of the same sex. The perspective is not new. It was traditional in most cultures for boys and girls to be separated for some time to be trained in cultural roles by elder members of the tribe. Older women were looked to as experts for females and older men were the mentors for males. In psychology, early writers such as Horney (1935) and Thompson (1941), wrote convincing (if unheeded) statements about the importance of sensitivity to cultural demands and pressures in treating women patients in psychodynamic psychotherapy.

WOMEN'S GROUPS

Women's groups, particularly consciousness-raising groups, were a key component of the women's liberation movement that was spawned from the civil rights movements in the late 1960s and early 1970s. In both traditional, professionally led groups and in leaderless support groups, women all over North America provided each other normalization, mutual support, and encouragement to experiment with new roles and attitudes. These groups were primarily successful in raising women's consciousness of novel roles and expectations in both work and home realms.

By the late 1970s, these groups had proliferated into what are now known as women's therapy, discussion, parent-education, and theme support groups for mothers, single mothers, displaced homemakers, and women in general. Members addressed concerns inherent in mothering, feminine identification, and sex-role-restricted behavior (e.g., assertiveness) in the modern world. In the original consciousness-raising groups, the primary focus was on external pressures, ideology, and political/social influences on women's personal experiences and self-esteem. More modern groups have a core psychotherapy component as well (Kravetz, 1987). Currently, women's therapy groups focus more on members' internal worlds and interpersonal dynamics without losing sensitivity for the sociocultural context. In group psychotherapy there are clearer boundaries between members and leaders. This makes intrapsychic change more probable. According to Doherty and Enders (1993), the women's therapy group provides a laboratory in which women can experiment with new behavior and examine and reorganize character traits and defenses as these are played out in the group context.

Several authors have reported advantages in women's only groups for women making post-divorce adjustments (Coche & Goldman, 1979), single mothers (Rosenthal & Hansen, 1980; Siegler, 1983), survivors of child sexual abuse (Voigt & Weininger, 1992; Turner, 1993; Darongkamas, Madden, Swarbrick, & Evans, 1995), women exploited by health care providers (Brownlee, 1994), adult survivors of childhood incest (Goodman & Nowak-Scibelli, 1985; Herman & Schatzow, 1984), mothers of incest victims (Landis & Wyre, 1984), and low-income mothers (Bumagin & Smith, 1985).

Feminist writers claim that the unique advantages of women-only groups include a decrease in "unconscious sexism" and isolation, reduced competition, opportunities for assertiveness, attention to the political context for women, and more freedom to talk openly, especially about "taboo" subjects.. These authors believe that such gains are not as readily possible in mixed gender groups (Durkin, 1954; Brodsky, 1973; Walker, 1987).

Reliable empirical support for such assertions is still lacking. However, clinical observations, self-reports of members, and theoretical logic suggest that women-only groups have a unique and important place. In particular, single-sex groups are recommended when inclusion of males might impede or impair member and group functioning. Specific populations include early adolescents (Kennedy, 1989), women dealing with self-esteem and assertiveness concerns, and abuse survivors.

Doherty and Enders (1993) also note that the particular advantages of women's groups can lead to potential problems such as

> perpetuation of gender polarities with unwitting (at best) support for the continuation of gender-role mythology; a tendency to encourage blaming the absent gender for one's problems; increased susceptibility to fusion either between members or with the same-sex leader; and the fact that single-sex groups do not resemble the real, heterogeneous world in which we live. (p.379)

Preparation

The process of single-gender groups is not significantly different from the process of other groups. However, the screening may be deceptively more complex. In attempting to keep ego strength relatively level in a gender-oriented group, leaders should not mix therapy and growth clients. For example, a false assumption about gender-oriented growth groups is that they are free from concerns about individual member pathology. Yet in such groups, lower-functioning members, particularly those with Axis II diagnoses (APA, 1994), may severely and adversely affect the process. It is crucial for leaders to understand that the core process in growth groups is enhancement of the individual member's self-esteem (as a woman and as a person).

Another issue to attend to in selection is political orientation. Members should have at least a nominal willingness to consider the views, opinions, and feelings of other members as worthy of examination and respect. Political zealots, although sometimes quite effective in others arenas, can be quite destructive in treatment and growth group environments.

Transition

One of the most interesting aspects of single-sex groups is the nature of the leadership challenges. Leaders are often tested more personally in such groups. Conflicting, somewhat unconscious, desires to relate to the leader as sister and as mother create tensions and ambivalence for group members. Behavior intended to bridge the distance between member and leader (as sister) often alternates with efforts to act out against her (as parent). McWilliams and Stein (1987) have described an interesting pattern of leadership challenge: group participants engage in a "collusion to expose what they believe is the therapist's incompetence and then console her for it" (p. 139). This particular kind of challenge is often expressed covertly and in the guise of maternal or sisterly concern for the leader's feelings. Concurrent with the deprecating communications, which group members usually do not consciously perceive as devaluing, are equally subtle efforts to render the leader impotent. It is not unusual for the leader's competence as a mother to be challenged. As MacWilliams and Stein suggest, women often are attracted to such groups at times when their self-esteem is low, when they are particularly stressed by their multiple roles or by relationship problems—times when unfinished family of origin issues are also activated and projective defenses triggered. They conclude:

> Many women come into a group like the ones we have worked with having suffered profound narcissistic injuries as wives and parents. In many instances, the devaluing dynamic seems to be a product of severe stress and might be expected to be temporary. (p. 144)

These challenges have a very elusive quality, are initially quite inaccessible to interpretation, and have the effect of inducing in the group leaders feelings of confusion, depression, and incompetence. Leaders have a difficult time identifying this behavior as a leadership test for several reasons. First, in most women's groups, the prevailing ethic is for connection rather than individuality. In such situations, there is no place for overt intragroup hostility. In such groups, women do not frequently confront one another directly, especially at such early stages. Indeed, prior to the leadership tests, it is common for such groups to define themselves as the *in group*, of victims or survivors, and to portray men as the dangerous *out group*. Questioning the behavior of a victim in the group in any way may lead other members to see the confronter as a perpetrator. Second, the leaders commonly also hunger for the kind of emotional sisterhood the group seems to offer. Countertransference needs for sharing in the process may diminish the leaders' professional distance and ability to access the already meager cues. Another type of countertransference—leaders' feminist sensitivity—may also make differentiation between leaders and members more difficult.

Whether one takes MacWilliams and Stein's position that this ethic is generated by a profound narcissistic injury suffered by the women prior to entering the group or as a test of leadership strength that reflects an unconscious attempt to enhance their own self-esteem, leaders must be prepared to identify this process and to respond to it. Leaders must help the members move from initial dependence and connection to being able to express negative emotions toward one another. Wolman (1976) warns that when anger or disappointment is expressed in women's groups, attrition is likely to be high. When leaders demonstrate that competition and conflict may be expressed and that the group can cope with it, members are more likely to remain and to move to deeper intrapsychic levels.

Treatment

In process terms, women's difficulty with confrontation can inhibit some facets of their treatment as well as their transition within a group. More accustomed to nurturing and supporting roles, women are often uncomfortable with the constructive encounter and challenge that occur during the treatment phase. It may be the leaders' responsibility to model and provide much of the confrontation within the group. The leaders must also seek out and encourage budding assertiveness and confrontation between members.

Women's groups tend to focus more during this period on nontraditional female roles: assertiveness, independence, and healthy competition. Members are encouraged to articulate their desires and to develop pathways to fulfilling these. The responsibilities and fear that accompany increased freedom also become a focus of attention.

Termination

It is crucial during the transfer of training phase of termination that leaders help members take what they have learned in group and use it successfully in interactions with men and other women outside the group. One danger of a same-sex group is that it can subtly encourage stereotypes. Thus, if a member leaves a group believing that only other women will understand her and she needs to avoid close relationships with men, the group has not been a success. Leaders must be especially circumspect to assure that the benefits of richly enhanced sisterhood are not gained at the expense of intimacy with men. Unlike the members of most mixed-sex groups, many members in single-sex groups pursue enduring friendships or future get-togethers after the group terminates.

MEN'S GROUPS

Following the success of women's groups, men's groups were also formed around a consciousness-raising motif. For the most part these groups had little success or impact. Membership was unstable and the men themselves seemed not to bond around these issues the way women did. Many hypotheses have been offered to explain this discrepancy. Perhaps the issues did not hit a special sensitivity for men. Perhaps men do not experience cultural and sexist oppression as personally as women. Perhaps the outcome goal of accepting politically correct feminism was inappropriate or distasteful to men. Perhaps men don't learn the same way women do. Whatever the reason, these groups had far less impact than women's groups and never achieved much popularity in the 1970s.

With the revival of the men's movement in the 1980s, men's groups again began to appear in major cities around the United States and Canada. These groups had wide-ranging motifs from the "wild man" to "feminist men." Somewhere in between, a format arose for men's therapy groups that is quite masculine, yet untraditional. These are the groups described in this chapter.

Men's consciousness raising was primed in the late 1980s by Robert Bly (Bly, 1990; Bly & Moyers, 1989), Sam Keen (1991), and others. In addition to consciousness-raising groups, men have joined in increasing numbers psychoeducational, behavioral, psychodynamic, existential, and workshop-oriented groups. In a way, these groups are diametrically opposed to the typical male gender role socialization.

In men's groups, participants struggle with the conflicting modern role restrictions and expectations demanded of men. Stein (1983) identified five areas of gender role conflict for men: a generalized difficulty and anxiety relating to the changing role of women in society, changes in the fathering role, examination of the male role in work and recreation, a wish by men to express their feelings verbally while being respected for "male styles" of connecting in adult relationships, and changing patterns of sexual functioning.

One way that men's groups approach these concerns is by encouraging mutual support, cooperation, encouragement, and identification. They strive to counter the traditional alienation of men from other men and to encourage relating between men versus the tendency to rely on women for relating. Men have traditionally had difficulty expressing their emotions and prefer to intellectualize, particularly within a group setting. Normally, men have felt the necessity to present a strong independent facade externally and find it difficult to admit weakness and dependence.

Why Men's Groups?

A number of authors have identified advantages of men-only groups. Van Wormer (1989) and others emphasized the importance of an absence of women, including the following:

1. Men relate to other men without the distraction of competition to impress women.
2. Men learn to assume some of the caretaking roles commonly played by women in a mixed setting.
3. Men discuss controversial topics (such as child custody, dating, cohabitation patterns) without being sidetracked into political arguments or having to be sensitive to feminist concerns or oppositions.
4. Men face and work on destructive and restrictive aspects of the masculine gender role. Together, men can explore relationships with the opposite sex and thereby learn new patterns of relating to women.
5. Highly personal topics such as male health problems and sexual needs and dysfunctions are more easily explored.
6. Members of the men's group can become sensitized to their feminine as well as masculine characteristics; they can learn to become more flexible in their sex-role definitions.

Other authors such as Stein (1983) focus more on the direct advantages of being in a group of men. In such groups, it is argued, members may more easily

1. Pursue mutual goals and concerns.
2. Support caring and friendship among men.

3. Engage in the exploration of nontraditional masculine values and find support for desirable changes among those with similar values and interests.

4. Be nurturing and nurtured with less concern for performance-based return.

5. Examine their masculine-associated characteristics, such as competitiveness, aggressiveness, and independence, and experiment with alternative forms of expression and relating.

6. Contemplate the ways they have related to the significant men in their lives. In the "here and now" male-male context group members may acquire a greater understanding of the ways in which they, both as individual men and men in groups, are encouraged to interact with other men.

7. Discuss difficult topics such as dependency, homosexuality, and concerns about gender identity. The open acknowledgment of such topics within a group of men may serve to reinforce a greater openness in sharing a wider range of other feelings as well.

8. Develop an understanding of special problems for men, such as male diseases, an excessive need to achieve, reactions to divorce, and difficulties in parenting. The opportunity to hear from contemporary models and peers is particularly helpful.

9. Learn new patterns of relating to women and develop more social and political awareness of individual and institutional sexism.

Nahon (1992) and Rabinowitz (1991) discuss the importance for men of developing the ability to touch other men without homophobia. Nahon (1992) also underscores the concerns of Meth and Pasick (1990) that men will avoid therapy and are most likely to utilize a group that is sensitive to the male role.

Finally, Kaufman (1983) and MacNab (1990) view the men's group process as a modern opportunity to help provide for lost or missing cultural functions that demarcate the passage into adult masculinity. These groups may replace some of what traditional initiation rites offered men: a deeper sense of maleness. MacNab (1990) delineates a four-phase process of gender discovery in men's groups: setting boundaries with women, forming male subgroups, finding and awakening the father, and finally, reentering the larger group as a different person.

In the authors' experience of leading and co-leading men's groups over the past 25 years, men's groups offer some additional advantages that mirror the advantages in women's groups. For many men, such groups are simply safer than mixed groups. Participants in our men's groups consistently underscore their greater degree of comfort in an all-male group in disclosing and exploring emotional, physical, and cognitive vulnerability. As the leaders model self-disclosure and the ability to contain and manage sensitive material, members feel sufficiently supported to be able to address such issues as dependency, doubts about the worthiness of their innermost feelings, fears about individuation and separation from significant others, and similar topics. These concerns tend to emerge in any well-led group, but they are more likely to emerge earlier and to be explored in greater depth in the safety of the men's group environment.

Preparation

As in women's groups, the primary screening concern is keeping ego strength relatively level. For example, men struggling with conflicting roles at work and as fathers of small children will not have the same needs as men who are struggling to break addictive or violent patterns of interaction. The screening process is often complicated for leaders by low numbers of applicants. It is not always easy to get a men's group started or to retain membership during the early phases of the group.

To some extent, there are advantages for men's groups of including members across the spectrum of life stages. For example, groups whose members range in age from their twenties through their sixties can offer a context for the development of a community of men able to provide mutual assistance. Some younger men may be mentored by older members, and older men may have the opportunity to be altruistic and honored for their experience.

Transition

Silverberg (1986) reports that initial concerns exhibited by men in men's groups include a persistent anxiety about their ability to interact with each other in the absence of women, fear of self-disclosure, issues around homophobia, and a desire to appear physically strong to other members. He argues that before members can open up to new feelings and disclosure, they need a clear set of ground rules and structure. Heppner (1983) agrees and proposes structured exercises as crucial components to alleviate anxiety.

Equally as important as providing safety through form is the task of weaning members from the known to explore the less familiar. As the expectation for self-disclosure becomes clear to the men in the group, they have to confront a deep sociocultural conflict. The open expression of feelings brings forth a sense of vulnerability and dependency. For most men in Western society, having to acknowledge dependency on others is particularly humiliating. Anxiety over feeling dependent and being seen as dependent often emerges as a sense of shame and diminished masculinity (Osherson & Krugman, 1991). When this threat to members' masculinity surfaces, they tend to protect themselves by acting out in more aggressive ways.

Whereas in women's groups direct challenges are rare, in men's groups the leadership test will likely be more direct, aggressive, and competitive. The usual precursor to the most potent leadership challenges is the vulnerability members feel around the expectation for self-disclosure and affective expression (Osheron & Krugman, 1991). Leaders must be prepared to play the firm, fair fatherhood role, both to contain the group members' anxiety and to provide a safe environment for the work to continue.

Treatment

Although the following two crucial issues are likely to emerge first during transition and must be partially resolved to move the group forward, both concerns will reemerge in the treatment phase of gender-oriented men's therapy groups. In each men's group, attention will likely turn to discussions of friendship and fathers. Three important subthemes—self-disclosure, competition, and affection—have also been identified (Washington, 1979, 1982).

FRIENDSHIP   For many men, friendship is quite complex. Shapiro (1995) reports that a majority of men stop making close friends when they mature and have families. It is not uncommon for men to report that their best friends came from school or military days. Work friendships are often complicated by competition. A large number of North American men reported that their best friends as adults were their wives or other women or men that they had known for decades. This phenomenon produces in most men a longing for connection with other males, yet this longing often brings with it a form of homophobia. The Western ideal of man as the rugged individualist plays no small role in keeping men from close interactions with their peers. The scars if not the actual pain of childhood and adolescent wounds sustained in the process of forming relationships also play a large part in the reluctance of many men to seek the rewards of greater male intimacy.

In group, as the distance between members dissolves, competitive and sexual fears may arise. In groups where one or more members are openly gay, the sexual fears may come to a head quite quickly. It is important for leaders to underscore and encourage the development of nonsexual intimacy between members. Often the team metaphor is a good starting place.

FATHERHOOD: THE CORE OF MASCULINITY   Shapiro, Diamond, and Greenberg (1995) have described the essential place of a man's fatherhood in his self-definition. In addition, Osherson (1986), Corneau (1991), and Shapiro (1995) have all underscored the influence of a man's father on his own subsequent development. In men's groups, the highest levels of affect often accompany discussions of a member's relationship with his distant or dead father. In addition, members commonly express powerful feelings and regrets about their relationships with their children. This is especially true for men who are not living with their children and/or have limited access to them.

Projections onto the leader as good father and bad father are likely. The leader must maintain a powerful, positive masculine role in these groups. Successful leaders are seen as firm, fair older men who contain the emotion, support its expression, and help guide members to understanding and resolution. The leaders serve both as models of the father these men want to become and as the ideal personal fathers with whom members may confront unresolved family of origin issues about their own fathers. When members can become vulnerable enough to express their needs for "a real father," the emotionality in the room surges. In this setting, leaders provide the opportunity for corrective emotional experiences.

CRUCIAL MALE ISSUES   Across the life cycle, boys and men struggle with conflicts around attachment, aggression, and self-esteem (Levinson, 1978; Osherson, 1986). They seem to coalesce around the sense of self in performance. Wright (1987) observed that "most men have had a major separation-induced emotional trauma inflicted on them in early life, and carry a serious shame and humiliation based handicap with them forever after" (p. 242). The psychological movement away from mother as a source of primary identification and toward father requires an engaged and emotionally available father (Diamond, 1995). For most boys, such a male figure is not fully available; thus, the child turns to accomplishment and peers for support and identification. Such attachments are fraught with competitiveness and losses. Lacklin (1989) has underscored the salience of these peer relationships. Yet as Diamond (1995) has indicated, without the watchful guardianship of adult males, these peer relationships commonly lead to chaotic, primitive social organizations and violence, as so powerfully depicted in Golding's *Lord of the Flies.*

Krugman and Osherson (1993) see the difficulty of integrating aggression with attachment as the heart of the male developmental struggle. In western culture, successful socialization for males requires denial or repression of dependency, replacing it with competitiveness. In the Treatment phase of group, men begin to seriously confront their aggressive-competitive impulses as reactions to fears of dependency and needs for attachment. Leaders must provide a slow steady hand on the level of anxiety that emerges with these concerns.

REJECTION AND ABANDONMENT   Underscoring both the friendship and fathering themes is a profound sense of psychological abandonment or rejection. Male group members tend to defend most against being wrong, shamed, or dismissed. In groups that develop the greatest depth, the issue of fear of abandonment and rejection emerges late in the process. This is an extremely sensitive and volatile topic. Many men describe their earliest memories of being embarrassed or rejected. They talk about their worth based on a performance standard: emotionally living and dying with successes and failures. Leaders must be very sensitive to members' fears of rejection and shame. These concerns need to be teased out with support.

Termination

Men's groups provide a sense of brotherhood, a heightened sense of emotional connection, and an opportunity to confront normally taboo topics. The uniqueness of this situation allows members to behave in quite atypical ways. The relief and "high" that often accompany the opening up of such feelings may tempt the members to release them out of group as well. In any group, the temptation to generalize is a danger, but it is especially so in men's groups because the sharing is so atypical for many members. Leaders must be especially careful, encouraging men to identify relevant cues and safe environments in which to transfer their learning.

Having found an opportunity to escape normal social demands, many men are reluctant to let the group end. Often group members continue to meet after termination without the leaders to hold off the pain of separation from this source of nurturance and to keep the close relationships going. Plans to continue meeting after the formal sessions end also let members avoid dealing with their abandonment fears. It is important for leaders to keep members focused on the loss of the group and on careful transfer of training, even when the members subsequently will reconstitute another type of meeting.

SUMMARY

Single-gender groups seem to have a special place. They provide a form of safety, reduced competitiveness, and a unique opportunity for members to come to grips with deeper gender awareness. The most powerful men's and women's groups take heed of socialization, political, and cultural pressures, but they focus primarily on the members' incorporation of these demands and their attribution of meaning to their sex roles. Leaders in such groups are most appropriately the same sex as members. They must be able to withstand powerful leadership tests and be especially aware of their own countertransference. At the current time, such groups seem to be growing in popularity.

CHAPTER 16

WHITHER BRIEF GROUP TREATMENT?

Characterizing the events of one's own times is always a dubious enterprise. Even more questionable is predicting confidently the future of one's field of expertise. Nonetheless, in this chapter we extrapolate from our understanding of the times, the historical realities of the field, research, and practitioners' intuition to project a course. If at times, we seem to be too involved with trees, those who join us on our journey will have to presume the presence of a forest.

HISTORICAL AND RECENT TRENDS

From Pratt's (1906) early work with tuberculosis patients involving ministers, Marsh's (1931) early experiments with what later became known as *milieu therapy,* and Moreno's (1932) classification of the "group method," to the present, group work has paralleled social needs and changes. For most of its history, group work has been particularly responsive to the interaction of personal and social needs. Not only has the content of group discussion followed social trends, beliefs, myths, and feelings, but group solutions have typically been predicated on changes in contemporary ways of responding to dilemmas in individuals' lives.

Thus, with apologies to stereotypical characterization of large bodies of time and numbers of people, we explore the interaction of social trends and corresponding individual needs. The 1950s, following the immediate postwar period, was seen as a time of personal conformity and economic growth. In these years, people could get ahead by "playing the game." Correspondingly, group work was primarily centered on *adjustment to broader social norms,* with members focused on becoming "team players." Sociopsychological approaches centered on an understanding of the process of the group and its application to a wider environment.

Group research was primarily descriptive and theorizing, dominated by psychoanalytic thinking; it involved the application of individual psychological approaches to the group setting.

The decade of the 1960s (1964–1973) can be viewed as the period of rebellion. In the West, it was an era of political unrest, marked by a diminution of trust in established authority and considerable questioning of traditional values. Groups during this period focused on questions of power, social integration, and alternative (Eastern) philosophies. Encounter groups emphasized alternative rather than traditional solutions to social and interpersonal problems. Therapy groups began to incorporate social as well as intrapsychic and physiological diagnoses and treatments. The political theme of the 1960s was confrontation between people of different cultures (e.g., black versus white, "cops" versus "hippies," young versus old). Group work responded by attempting to develop *bridges between people* based on common ground and mutual learning. Research was primarily limited to descriptive and "black box" (outcome) studies.

The decade of the 1970s (1973–1982) has been labeled by many as the "me" generation. The primary social focus was on *self-actualization*. The sexual revolution, popularization of mind-altering substances, and other means of self-exploration and/or escapism all represent part of a greater consumerism that often followed the maxim, "If it feels good, do it." As usual, group work addressed the needs of the times. Primary themes in groups were *identity* and *self-esteem*.

Gender became a dominant theme in the 1970s as well. The women's movement became a significant social catalyst, influencing mores, values, attitudes, and behavior in virtually every realm of Western society. Attention to and consideration of gender issues occurred in group work also. Curiously, not until the late 1980s did men's groups emerge in full force, spurred by women's group outcomes and the popularity of authors such as Robert Bly and Sam Keen.

Group technology also found its way into the workplace, salesroom, and classroom to a much greater extent. The small group format and technology often gave way to larger groups (e.g., community groups, "est" seminars) or to different settings (classrooms, sales enhancement classes, limited partnership sales), but the technology that had developed in the small group was still dominant. In research, the beginnings of comparative outcome studies and serious studies of group process appeared.

In the 1980s, family roles were examined in new ways. Women's roles in particular were reconsidered and expanded. As the "baby boomer" generation progressed through their thirties, they began to add *family* to *career* and *self-actualization*. The resulting combination produced a "we can do it all" attitude among an expanding middle class. Women's and minority considerations were powerful themes in the culture in general and in groups. Along with a revision of women's roles came a greater awareness of a multiplicity of family formats. Group work commensurately took a giant turn in that direction by incorporating family therapy into the group literature, including family therapy research for the first time in the annual review of groups in the *International Journal of Group Psychotherapy*. The technology from natural groups, best exemplified by marital and family therapy and industrial psychology, were increasingly integrated into group work. In addition, considerations regarding family of origin have merged with more classical intrapsychic explorations in current therapy and growth groups. Research was increasingly process centered.

As the 1990s rapidly disappear into the millennium, dominant social trends include single issue politics, predominance of fiscal over social considerations, a wider divergence between the "haves" and the "have-not's," and reduced availability and reliance on extended families for support. Commensurate cutbacks in governmental economic support, medical coverage and community props have propelled individuals and nuclear families to become the primary social entity. Within this framework, *diversity* and the need for personal *choices* have become central.

With these social factors coalescing to support individualism, a contradictory need for connection and association with like-minded individuals is emerging. As traditional avenues of connection are less available, non-traditional means are emerging for people to find support and community. Some of these are technological in nature. Using the Internet for example, individuals are communicating regularly with friends, colleagues, and acquaintances who share interests without regard for physical proximity.

Offering both diversity and personalized support, groups have focused more and more on specific needs of a host of diverse cultural and interest clusters. Specialty groups for people with similar interests, diagnoses, cultural backgrounds, and gender orientations represent the areas of greatest growth.

An outgrowth of this increasing specialization has been a growing realization that "we can't have it all," at least not without a perspective of the limits and value of time. Indeed, in the middle class, time recognized as a limited commodity, is becoming the dominant currency. Downsizing, a growing acknowledgment of the limitations of institutional support for the individual, and a contrasting empowerment through the high-tech revolution have all pushed individuals to make significant choices (e.g., time versus money).

Nowhere is the impact of downsizing and choices more evident than in health care. Medical advances that allow for greater longevity present us with opportunities and choices. Longer life after the productive years produces an inevitable dilemma: Who gets the expensive, life-extending, and limited services? The field of medical ethics has grown dramatically. Even more evident has been the dramatic growth of managed health care, in which budgetary considerations play an increasing role in determination of what services are covered by third party (insurance) payment and what are considered unnecessary and hence, unreimbursable. By providing cost-effective and specific solutions, theme-centered specialty groups are increasingly offered as a means to address managed care and client needs simultaneously.

INTO THE MILLENNIUM
Social Trends

The 1950s showed us the *individual in society;* the 1960s presented the *individual against society;* the 1970s gave us the *individual's conflict with self;* the 1980s saw the *individual's integration into the new family;* and the 1990s showed *a growing realization of the price of individual freedom and choice.* The first decade of the 21st century will likely involve reintegration of the individual in society in the *age of information.*

The trends of the nineties play in an interesting way into the expansion of group technologies in the foreseeable future. For the past 40 years, the extended family has been a diminishing resource. In addition, the positive, stabilizing influence of other traditional major institutions such as schools, churches, and government have also been less supportive to individuals.

Changes in the workplace exemplify and exacerbate these shifts. Decentralization, downsizing, extended hours for those who are employed; deterioration in benefit plans; and a general reduction of security and loyalty have ushered in a new era with new needs for individuals. As available information grows at a geometric pace, specialization becomes more salient. Individuals with computers, fax machines, cell phones, and an Internet connection may do the work formerly done by entire companies.

Naisbitt and Aberdene (1990), in their *Megatrends 2000,* concluded:

> The great unifying trend at the conclusion of the 20th century is the triumph of the individual. . . . It is an individual who creates a work of art, embraces a political philosophy, bets a life savings on a new business, inspires a colleague or family member to succeed, emigrates to a new country, has a transcendent spiritual experience. . . . Individuals today can leverage change far more effectively than most institutions. (p. 298)

Such individual power, of course, engenders greater social fragmentation and pressing psychological needs. If I can no longer rely on my job to guarantee my retirement and health care, if I can no longer count on the schools to educate well my children, if I cannot count on government to provide sufficient resources for everyone of my generation, I must rely on myself, my co-workers, my family, and my friends. Yet, extended families are no longer omnipresent sources of security. Even the form of the family has changed dramatically. If one is to believe middle-class clients in dual-earner families, there is decreasing time for friends and community. Too much freedom without sufficient security or time is a prescription for certain unconscious fears of abandonment and isolation.

What are the antidotes to these fears? From our perspective, barring a sociopolitical revolution rivaling that of the 1960s in power and scope, the answer is intimacy in its broadest sense. Where may individuals find intimacy in the world of telecommunication, telecommuting, the Internet, and the isolated nuclear family? It is curious that one of the dominant themes to emerge from the worldwide web is its value in creating groups of people of similar interest and finding ways to connect them. Indeed, dating services have also been an integral part of the computer generation. Is this a way that individuals may satisfy their yearnings for connection, albeit through telephone wires, e-mail, and modems?

In the therapy realm, group therapy may be much better suited than individual work to the needs of individuals who feel isolated. Although the intimacy of a transference relationship may promote greater self-understanding, it is the group interactions with peers that provide intimate connection between equals. Adolescents who are depressed or feeling isolated at school seem to respond much more positively to group interaction. Company CEOs and presidents who have no peer group at work similarly are offered special opportunities in a group of others who might understand their pressures and isolation.

A natural conclusion is that as the individual becomes more independent, his or her needs for connection will move more to the forefront. Groups of individuals who share certain values or needs will be especially useful. This trend has already been in place for several years. The popularity of theme-oriented groups, self-help groups, and diagnosis-related groups has been burgeoning and is likely to continue.

This is all an argument that group counseling or therapy will often be *the treatment of choice*. Groups may provide both prevention and treatment for the alienation disorders of our times. Moreover, economic factors have also coalesced to make groups more desirable to those who pay for mental health treatment. Whether groups are to occur in a managed care system emphasizing cost containment or paid for directly by consumers who will demand affordable effective treatment, brief groups are very likely to proliferate in the foreseeable future.

PROFESSIONAL ISSUES IN GROUPS OF THE FUTURE

In the May 1985 special issue of the *Journal of Specialists in Group Work*, several experts in the field of group work predicted trends for the year 2001. The editors of this special edition of the journal summarized these contributions:

> For the most part, . . . the future of group work seems robust to the authors. Groups will abound. They will become major forces for combating the increasing depersonalization and anomie that are likely to accompany the computer and "high-tech" revolution. As Gazda illustrates, group work will be directed much more extensively to the well population as a major means to prevent excessive life stress and situational problems and to promote life skills. Group methods will be used increasingly with families, with diverse populations, within organizations, and even, according to Klein, to achieve social change across all levels of systems: in groups, organizations, communities, regions, nations, and the world. (Conyne et al., 1985, p. 114)

Three-fourths of the time between their predictions and the new millennium has passed, and most of the predictions remain on target. However, there are forces that continue to prevent group therapy from becoming the therapy whose time has come. Chief among these are the dilemma of adequate training for leaders, a need for leaders to better understand and respond to diversity, and a dearth of compelling *process* research evidence.

A Call for Leadership

Who will lead the groups that are necessary in the 21st century? The history of group therapy is littered with reports of well-meaning but untrained professionals applying individual therapy, family therapy, and education skills to group work. Historically, in many institutions, group treatment has been assigned to a variety of professional and paraprofessional staff members, often without regard to their background and training. Because it is the least understood of the therapy methods, and because individuals are least well trained in offering it, group treatments have often been denigrated. An unfortunate cycle ensues.

Once group treatment is considered an inferior form of care, many institutions customarily consign group treatment to staff members with the least training. Thus, in a typical inpatient setting, it is normal to see a group led by nurses, aides, occupational therapists, and social workers on a rotating and irregular basis. Many groups have different leaders on consecutive days. Furthermore, patient attendance is often not supported or is even sabotaged by staff. The groups run by leaders untrained in group process are then evaluated accurately to be inferior methods of treatment. The self-fulfilling prophecy continues, with groups being further denigrated. Group treatment per se is *not* being judged, however. The evaluation is of groups led by those with inadequate understanding and training in group methods. An unfortunate reality is that in untrained hands, the very tools that produce most growth in groups can be dangerous for members. Corey and Corey (1992), Haeseler (1992), and Lakin (1991) among others describe a number of unfortunate results that can come from poorly led groups: scapegoating, diffusion of responsibility, pressures toward uniformity, premature vulnerability, unreasonable demands for inappropriate affect, and promotion of impulsivity.

Group leaders of the future must be specifically trained in group process and group methods. Simply because an individual is licensed or has a staff position at an institution that holds groups is insufficient to qualify him or her as a group leader. Indeed, there are serious ethical considerations in using untrained leaders. Each of the mental health professional organizations has a code of ethics that defines the scope of practice. In line with the "do no harm" injunction is a demand that practitioners recognize the boundaries and limitations of their training and competencies. Individuals who are not qualified by education, training, or experience, are in violation of ethical codes when they lead groups. Newman and Levant (1993) note that the generic practitioners' license is such that each individual counselor's or therapist's scope of competence is necessarily less than the scope permitted by license.

It is incumbent on each practitioner to obtain the requisite training, work under direct supervision of a qualified group leader, work with an experienced co-leader, or resist employer or economic pressure to practice group leadership when doing so is beyond the scope of his or her training. Equally essential is that well-trained group leaders educate their professional colleagues and the public to understand and appreciate the value of group process and professional leadership. Practitioners also need to address an unfortunate countertrend toward both leaderless groups and a proliferation of "psycho-educational" groups (classes) run by novice counselors hired by employee assistance programs and agencies contracted by managed care organizations, primarily on the basis of economic convenience.

What Is Appropriate Training?

There is no current, special credentialing for group leaders that has any *legal* standing. A licensed therapist is not specifically barred from practicing group therapy. Only ethical guidelines limit the scope of practice in this regard. At least one attempt for a national standard is being supported by the National Registry of Certified Group Psychotherapists in association with the American Group Psychotherapy Association. However, this standard is voluntary, and the registry is a professional, not a licensing organization.

In this text, we have described what we believe to be *minimal* training for group leaders if they are to use group process effectively. We believe that group training is best taught as a specialization in graduate school and continuing education classes. Certainly, the training should include a basic course, extensive supervised practice, personal group experience as a member, observation and/or co-leadership with experienced professional group leaders, and licensure. We also recommend strongly personal individual or group therapy, and continuing education in theory and group methods. Such training could allow for a new group therapist specialization in mental health—one that would promote a higher status for group work and attract better-qualified practitioners.

The goal of appropriate training is to produce leaders who are more master craftspersons than technicians. Particularly in an age so influenced by technology, the irreplaceable value of human interaction is what counters isolation and fosters growth. Leaders who know themselves and are courageous and ethical in bringing that self-knowledge to group interventions are best suited to have maximum impact on group members. It is also important that leaders become aware of and sensitive to the personal backgrounds of members of their groups.

Diversity

In addition to training in group process, leaders need training in knowledge of diversity. Groups are made up of individuals who bring a personal history and culture to each meeting. In any group, there may be members with different needs, backgrounds, religions, races, ethnicity, and cultures. Leaders must be sensitive to and aware of these differences.

In some ways, comprehensive knowledge of diversity is becoming increasingly complex to obtain as the American population in general becomes more varied. Commentaries on data from the 1990 U.S. Census indicate that the percentage of ethnic minorities will dramatically increase and that by the year 2025, Caucasians will become a numerical minority. Doubtlessly, sociocultural value differences will mandate alternative intervention styles and possibly even group values. For example, the supremacy of independence that guides many therapeutic interventions is not highly valued in some ethnic groups.

Immigrant groups with a variety of Asian, Hispanic, or Russian backgrounds may need to be treated differently. It is insufficient to assume that a Chinese immigrant from Hong Kong will be similar to an Irish immigrant simply because they are both immigrants. Indeed, it is equally important to realize that two Chinese immigrants from Hong Kong may have widely divergent needs and respond quite differently to the same intervention.

Sensitivity to diverse groups of individuals often does not come easily. Stereotyping and overgeneralization are as problematic as is assumed similarity. Thus, if the leader of the group is a 49-year-old African American woman with a degree in social work from a major university in New York, she must be cautious about assuming that a member of her group who shares all those anamnestic criteria will be like her. She must also be wary of assuming that the Samoan woman, African American man, or Japanese American social worker in the group are different from her, similar to her, or like each other is some specific way.

Of course, individual leaders will never be able to know fully a host of different cultures and the driving forces of cultural values within those cultures. It is essential to develop a sensitivity to cultural, ethnic, gender, religious, and lifestyle differences and to learn to approach within parameters offered by the members of the group.

There is little question that any counselor or therapist must constantly learn about the basic values and styles of behaviors customary in the diverse cultures of members. It is inevitable, for example, that members of a minority culture will view potential for change and influence differently from members of a dominant culture. It is also very important, to recognize the differential value placed on traits such as independence in non-Western cultures. The differences between a "guilt" culture and a "shame" culture may have a large impact on the style of intervention required. Similarly, the power of nuances of language and emotion may be mitigated with clients who are engaging in the group using their second, third, or fourth language. Several authors have discussed the dangers of misunderstanding progress (Leong, 1992) or underutilizing group methods (Sue & Sue, 1990) in Asian populations. Without understanding the interaction of the cultural values and the treatment method, a leader can easily misinterpret the behaviors, implications, progress and meaning of groups with minority culture members (Pederson & Marsella, 1982; Brislin, 1990).

DANGERS OF A DIVERSITY FOCUS　In addition to the great value a focus on diversity brings, there are also potential dangers to a diversity focus. One danger is to minimize the value of common human needs. In the rush to avoid stereotyping, a group leader may also lose sight of the intrinsic similarities for affiliation, attachment, creativity, and suffering that surpass all boundaries. In addition, group members in any voluntary group will have subscribed at least partially to the group values or they would not have joined at all.

A second danger involves the tyranny of political correctness. When form subsumes substance, political correctness may in some circumstances be used not as the protector of minorities but rather as another form of intolerance. Any belief that a group is correct because of skin color, gender, or national origin is prejudice. A group leader may be frozen into inaction or stuck in blandness because of an excessive fear of offending someone.

"I DON'T HAVE A CULTURE; I'M FROM THE MIDWEST"　A delicate line separates true sensitivity to others from stereotypic limits of action that actually cheat members from much of what a leader may offer. To walk that line a leader must be willing to be educated by each member of a group as to what particular intervention will best support change and to become increasingly aware of his or her personal cultural influences. Perhaps the most significant culture a group leader will ever need to know is his or her own. Rappaport (1994) strongly urges therapists to

acknowledge and explore their personal culture and value systems and to give up the notion that therapy is value free or neutral. What is important is awareness of the automatic, unconscious translations of input that provide meaning to the therapist, and to understand other people's responses to one's self.

The leaders' values have a potentially powerful impact. In at least one study, Shapiro and Siu (1976) demonstrated that members of groups at least temporarily tended to take on behaviors, forms of speech, and cultural values of their leaders through subconscious modeling. From pretest to posttest, members showed a significant tendency to give responses more similar to responses of the leaders of their groups. Thus, when both leaders were Caucasian, the members of a multiethnic group had developed values and responses more characteristic of Caucasians by posttest. Similarly, in groups led by co-leaders of Japanese and Hawaiian descent, the members' responses emulated the values characteristic in those cultures. In groups led by co-leaders who were not of the same ethnic origin, less modeling of this kind was shown. An important note is that these value differences did not continue into the six-month follow-up.

TRAINING FOR DIVERSITY The biggest problem to overcome is the "one size fits all" therapy and develop instead a multicultural viewpoint. Such a perspective honors what actions, thoughts, and feelings mean to an individual within the context of culture, gender, and family of origin. This is a *true advantage for group treatment*. Each member can teach others how a particular intervention might work for him or her.

Leaders are specifically encouraged

1. To became informed about members' cultures but not try to be an expert
2. To help members define how the group will fit and serve them personally
3. To respect differences and break down stereotypes
4. To focus explicitly on cultural issues; not to act as if culture is invisible
5. To focus more interpersonally as multiculturalism increases
6. To have a co-leader who is from a different ethnic group, especially when the group members come predominantly from a similar ethnic background that differs from that of the leader.

Psychology has always been defined as the science of the individual. Clearly, psychologically based treatment cannot take a *one-size-fits-all* approach to groups, even when group process is the cornerstone of that approach. Group treatment is ultimately treatment for *individual members*. Success cannot be defined by a group plan of action for all members. Each individual contributes something unique to the group process and each takes something personal away from the group.

The Issue of Research

There is a long history of research on groups of all types. Some of the studies are remarkably sophisticated empirically whereas others rely more on the "your group made a new man of me, Doc" levels of data.

If brief group treatment is to claim eminence as a therapeutic modality its claim must be supported by hard data.

> Recent developments demonstrate that clinicians and researchers can no longer afford to maintain their mutual dissociation. Many experts have argued, in fact, that the survival of psychotherapy as a profession depends on the active integration of research and practice. (Dies, 1985, p. 72)

The challenges we face in the future are not new. Professional group leaders are in the best position to identify and evaluate the sophisticated process and outcome dimensions which will be most fruitful to investigate. If we leave the empirical research to others, nonclinical factors, such as cost containment or conventionality, may dominate future research. It is up to us to set up programs to study ongoing groups in private sectors, universities, and agencies and to press for appropriate grants to support more complex and comprehensive research. The ball is clearly in our court.

SUMMARY

As we move into the new millennium, we will need to integrate 21st-century individualization and corresponding needs for affiliation into an information-age society. This will likely require greater sensitivity to increasingly diverse, multicultural membership in our groups. We believe that groups can provide an excellent antidote to feelings of isolation, disconnection, and alienation. To reach this goal, leaders must be well trained in generic group process, such as the one delineated in this text, and be ready to make adjustments for particular group populations. It is, after all, the *process focus* that allows group progress and crosses many cultural and socioeconomic barriers.

References

Ackerman, N. W. (1955). Group psychotherapy with a mixed group of adolescents. *International Journal of Group Psychotherapy, 5,* 249–260.

Ackerman, R. J. (1987). *Same house, different homes.* Pompano Beach, FL: Health Communications.

Adam, P. (1982). *A primer of child psychotherapy.* Boston: Little, Brown.

Adelson, J., & Doehrman, M. (1980). The psychodynamic approach to adolescence. In J. Adelson, *Handbook of adolescent psychology.* New York: Wiley.

Aichhorn, A. (1935). *Wayward youth.* New York: Viking Press.

Alger, I. (1976). Multiple couple therapy. In P. Guerin (Ed.), *Family therapy theory and practice* (pp. 364 387). New York: Gardner Press.

Alonso, A. (1993). Training for group psychotherapy. In A. Alonson & H. I. Swiller (Eds.), *Group psychotherapy in clinical practice* (pp. 521–532). Washington, DC: American Psychiatric Press.

Alonso, A., & Swiller, H. I. (1993). *Group therapy in clinical practice.* Washington, DC: American Psychiatric Press.

American Association for Counseling and Development. (1988). *Ethical standards of the American Association for Counseling and Development.*

American Association of Marriage and Family Therapy. (1988). *Ethical guidelines.* Washington, DC: Author.

American Group Psychotherapy Association. (1978). *Guidelines for the training of group psychotherapists.* New York: Author.

American Psychiatric Association. (1981). *Code of ethics.* Washington, DC: Author.

American Psychiatric Association. (1994). *Diagnostic and statistical manual of mental disorders* (4th ed.). Washington, DC: Author.

Anderson, B. N., Pine, L., & Mae-Lee, D. (1972). Resident training in co-therapy groups. *International Journal of Group Psychotherapy, 22,* 192–198.

Appley, D. G., & Winder, A. E. (1973). *Groups and therapy groups in a changing society.* San Francisco: Jossey-Bass

Association for Specialists in Group Work. (1990). ASGW Ethical guidelines for group counselors. *Journal for Specialists in Group Work, 15*(2), 119–126.

Bandura, A., & Walters, R. H. (1963). *Social learning and personality development.* New York: Holt, Rinehart & Winston.

Battegay, R. (1989). Apparent and hidden changes in group members according to the different phases of group psychotherapy. *International Journal of Group Psychotherapy, 39*(3), 337–353.

Beletsis, S. G., & Brown, S. (1981). A developmental framework for understanding the adult children of alcoholics. *Journal of Addictions and Health, 2,* 188–199.

Benjamin, S. E. (1972). Cotherapy: A growth experience for therapists. *International Journal of Group Psychotherapy, 22*(2), 199–209.

Berkovitz, I. H. (1975). On growing a group: Some thoughts on structure, process and setting. In I. H. Berkovitz, *Adolescents grow in groups*. New York: Brunner/Mazel.

Berkovitz, I. H., & Sugar, M. (1983). Indications and contraindications for adolescent group psychotherapy. In A. H. Esman, *The psychiatric treatment of adolescents*. New York: International Universities Press.

Bernadett, S. T. (1981). *Cross cultural counseling*. [Workshop]. Clark Air Force Base, Republic of the Philippines.

Bernard, C. P., & Corrales, R. O. (1979). *Theory and technique of family therapy*. Springfield, IL: Charles C Thomas.

Bernard, S., & Mackenzie, K. R. (Eds.). (1994). *Basics of group psychotherapy*. New York: Guilford.

Bernfeld, G., Clark, L., & Parker, J. (1984). The process of adolescent group psycho-therapy. *International Journal of Group Psychotherapy, 34*(1), 111–126.

Beymer, L. (1969). Confrontation groups; hula hoops? *Counselor Education and Supervision, 9*, 75–86.

Black, C. (1981). *It will never happen to me*. Denver: M.A.C.

Blinder, M., & Kischenbaum, M. (1967). The technique of married couples group therapy. *Archives of General Psychiatry, 17*, 44.

Blouin, J. H., Carter, J., Blouin, A. G., Tener, L., Schnare-Hayes, K., Zuro, C., Barlow, J., & Perez, E. (1994). Prognostic indicators in bulimia nervosa treated with cognitive-behavioral group therapy. *International Journal of Eating Disorders, 15*(2), 113–123.

Bly, R. (1990). *Iron John*. Reading, MA: Addison-Wesley.

Bly, R., & Moyers, B. (1989). *A gathering of men*. New York: Mystic Fire Video.

Bogdaniak, R. C., & Piercy, F. P. (1987). Therapeutic issues of adolescent children of alcoholics (AdCA) groups. *International Journal of Group Psychotherapy, 37*(4), 569–588.

Bohman, M., Sigvardsson, S., & Cloninger, R. (1981). A developmental framework for understanding the adult children of alcoholics. *Journal of Addictions and Health, 38*, 965–969.

Bowen, M. (1971). Family therapy and family group therapy. In H. Kaplan & B. Sadock (Eds.), *Comprehensive group therapy*. Baltimore: Williams & Wilkins.

Bradford, L., Gibb, I., & Benne, K. D. (1964). *T-group theory and laboratory method in re-education*. New York: Wiley.

Brislin, R. W. (1990). *Applied cross cultural psychology*. Huntington Park, CA: Sage.

Brisman, J., & Siegel, M. (1985). The bulimia workshop: A unique integration of group treatment approaches. *International Journal of Group Psychotherapy, 35*(4), 585–601.

Brodsky, A. M. (1973). The consciousness raising group as a model for therapy with women. *Psychotherapy: Theory, practice and research, 10*, 24–29.

Brown, S. (1988). *Treating adult children of alcoholics: A developmental perspective*. New York: Wiley.

Brown, S., & Yalom, I. D. (1977). Interactional group therapy with alcoholics. *Journal of Studies on Alcohol, 38*, 426–456.

Brownlee, J. (1994). Group psychotherapy for women exploited by health care providers. *American Journal of Psychotherapy, 48*(2), 262–279.

Bruch, H. (1982). Anorexia nervosa: Therapy and theory. *American Journal of Psychotherapy, 139*, 1531–1538.

Brygger, M. P., & Edelson, J. L. (1987). The domestic abuse project. *Journal of Interpersonal Violence, 2*(3), 324–336.

Bryant, N. (1994). Domestic violence and group treatment for male batterers. *Group, 18*, 235–242.

Budman, S. H. (1992). Models of brief individual and group psychotherapy. In J. Feldman & R. Fitzpatrick (Eds.), *Managed mental health care: Administrative and clinical issues* (pp. 231–248). Washington, DC: American Psychiatric Press.

Budman, S. H., & Gurman, A. S. (1988). *Theory and practice of brief therapy.* New York: Guilford Press.

Budman, S. H., Demby, A., & Randall, M. (1980). Short term group psychotherapy. Who succeeds? Who fails? *Group, 4,* 3–16.

Budman, S. H., Simeone, P. G., Reilly, R. & Demby, A. (1994). Progress in short term and time-limited group psychotherapy: Evidence and implications. In A. Fuhriman & G. M. Burlingame (Eds.), *Handbook of group psychotherapy: An empirical and clinical synthesis.* New York: Wiley.

Bumagin, S., & Smith, J. M. (1985). Beyond support: Group psychotherapy with low-income mothers. *International Journal of Group Psychotherapy, 35*(2), 279–294.

Capuzzi, D., & Gross, D. R. (1992). *Introduction to group counseling.* Denver: Love.

Carkhuff, R. R., & Berenson, B. (1967). *Beyond counseling and therapy.* New York: Holt, Rinehart & Winston.

Carroll, M. R., & Wiggins, J. (1990). *Elements of group counseling: Back to the basics.* Denver: Love Publishing.

Cermak, T. L. (1985). *A primer on adult children of alcoholics.* Pompano Beach, FL: Health Communications.

Cermak, T. L. (1986). Diagnostic criteria for codependency. *Journal of Psychoactive Drugs, 18*(1), 15–20.

Cermak, T. L., & Brown, S. (1982). Interactional group therapy with adult children of alcoholics. *International Journal of Group Psychotherapy, 32,* 375–389.

Coche, E. (1983). Change measures and clinical practice in group psychotherapy. In R. R. Dies & K. R. MacKenzie (Eds.), *Advances in group psychotherapy: Integrating research and practice.* New York: International Universities Press.

Coche, E., & Goldman, J. (1979). Brief group psychotherapy for women after divorce: Planning a focused experience. *Journal of Divorce, 3,* 153–160.

Coche, J., & Coche, E. (1990). *Couples group psychotherapy.* New York: Brunner/Mazel.

Coleman, J. (1980). Friendship and the peer group in adolescence. In J. Adelson, *Handbook of adolescent psychology.* New York: Wiley.

Conger, J., & Petersen, A. (1984). *Adolescence and youth, psychological development in a changing world.* New York: Harper & Row.

Conideris, M. G., Ely, D. F., & Erikson, J. T. (1991). *California laws for psychologists.* Gardena, CA: Harcourt Brace Jovanovich.

Connors, M. E., Johnson, C. L., & Stuckey, M. K. (1984). Treatment of bulimia with brief psychoeducational group therapy. *American Journal of Psychiatry, 141,* 1512–1516.

Conyne, R. K., Dye, A., Gill, S. J., Leddick, G. R., Morran, D. K., & Ward, D. E. (1985). A retrospective of "critical issues." *Journal of Specialists in Group Work, 10*(10), 112–115.

Cookerly, J. R. (1973). The outcome of the six major forms of marriage counseling compared: A pilot study. *Journal of Marriage and the Family, 35,* 608–611.

Cookerly, J. R. (1974). The reduction of psychopathology as measured by the MMPI clinical scales in three forms of marital counseling. *Journal of Marriage and the Family, 36,* 332–335.

Cookerly, J. R. (1980). Does marital therapy do any lasting good? *Journal of Marital and Family Therapy, 6*(4), 393–397.

Cooper, C. L., & Mangham, I. L. (1971). *T-groups: A survey of research.* London: Wiley Interscience.

Cooper, L. (1976). Co-therapy relationships in groups. *Small Group Behavior, 7,* 473–498.

Cooper-White, P. (1990). Peer vs clinical counseling: Is there a place for both in the battered women's movement? *Response to the Victimization of Women and Children, 13*(3), 2–6.

Corey, G. (1985). *Theory and practice of group counseling* (2nd ed.). Pacific Grove, CA: Brooks/Cole.

Corey, G. (1990). *Theory and practice of group counseling* (3rd. ed.). Pacific Grove, CA: Brooks/Cole.

Corey, G., & Corey, M. S. (1982). *Groups process and practice* (2nd ed.). Pacific Grove, CA: Brooks/Cole.

Corey, G., & Corey, M. S. (1987). *Groups process and practice* (3rd ed.). Pacific Grove, CA: Brooks/Cole.

Corey, G., & Corey, M. S. (1992). *Groups process and practice* (4th ed.). Pacific Grove, CA: Brooks/Cole.

Corneau, G. (1991). *Absent fathers; lost sons.* Acton, MA: Shambala.

Corsini, R. (1957). *Methods of group psychotherapy.* New York: McGraw-Hill.

Corsini, R. J., & Lundin, W. H. (1995). Group psychotherapy in the midwest. *Group Psychotherapy, 8,* 316–320.

Coulson, W. R. (1972). *Groups, gimmicks and instant gurus.* New York: Harper & Row.

Cox, G. L., & Merkel, W. T. (1989). A qualitative review of psychosocial treatments for bulimia. *Journal of Nervous and Mental Disease, 177*(2), 287–301.

Crosby, R. D., Mitchell, J. E., Raymond, N., & Specker, S. (1993). Survival analysis of response to group psychotherapy in bulimia nervosa. *International Journal of Eating Disorders, 13,* 359–368.

Dacey, J., & Kenny, M. (1994). *Adolescent development.* Madison, WI: Brown & Benchmark.

Darongkamas, J., Madden, S., Swarbrick, P., & Evans, B. (1995). Touchstone therapy group for women survivors of child sexual abuse. *Journal of Mental Health, 4*(1), 17–29.

DeLeon, P. H., VandenBos, G., & Bulatoa, E. O. (1991). Managed mental health care: A history of federal policy initiatives. *Professional Psychology, 22,* 15–25.

Deschner, J. P., & McNeil, J. S. (1986). Results of anger control training for battering couples. *Journal of Family Violence, 1*(2), 111–120.

Diamond, M. J. (1995). The emergence of the father as the watchful protector of the mother-infant dyad. In J. L. Shapiro, M. J. Diamond, & M. Greenberg (Eds.), *Becoming a father,* New York: Springer.

Diamond, M. J., & Shapiro, J. L. (1973). Changes in locus of control as a function of encounter group experience. *Journal of Abnormal Psychology, 83*(3), 514–518.

Dick, B., Lessier, K., & Whiteside, J. (1980). A developmental framework for cotherapy. *International Journal of Group Psychotherapy, 30,* 273–285.

Dies, R. R. (1979). Group psychotherapy: Reflections on three decades of research. *Journal of Applied Behavioral Science, 15,* 361–374.

Dies, R. R. (1980). Current practice in the training of group psychotherapists. *International Journal of Group Psychotherapy, 30,* 169–185.

Dies, R. R. (1985). Research foundations for the future of group work. *Journal of Specialists in Group Work, 10*(2), 68–73.

Dies, R. R. (1992). The future of group therapy. *Psychotherapy 29,* 58–64.

Dies, R. R., & Dies, K. R. (1993). The role of evaluation in clinical practice: Overview and group treatment illustration. *International Journal of Group Psychotherapy, 43,* 77–105.

Dies, R. R., & MacKenzie, K. R. (1983). *Advances in group psychotherapy: Integrating research and practice.* New York: International Universities Press.

Dinkmeyer, D. C., & Muro, J. J. (1971). *Group counseling: Theory and practice*. Itasca, IL: Peacock.

Dreikurs, R. (1950). Techniques and dynamics of multiple psychotherapy. *Psychiatric Quarterly, 24*, 788–799.

Driekurs, R. (1951). The unique social climate experienced in group psychotherapy. *Group Psychotherapy, 3*, 292–299.

Dreyfus, E. A., & Kremenliev, E. (1970). Innovative group technique: Handle with care. *Personnel and Guidance Journal, 49*, 279–283.

Doherty, P., & Enders, P. L. (1993). Women in group psychotherapy. In A. Alonso & H. I. Swiller (Eds.), *Group therapy in clinical practice*. Washington, DC: American Psychiatric Press.

Durkin, H. E. (1954). Group dynamics and group psychotherapy. *International Journal of Group Psychotherapy, 4*, 56–64.

Edelson, J. L., & Syers, M. (1990). Relative effectiveness of group treatment for men who batter. *Journal of Social Work Research and Abstracts, 26*(2), 10–17.

Egan, G. (1976). *Interpersonal living*. New York: Wadsworth.

Elkind, D. (1980). Strategic interactions in early adolescence. In J. Adelson, *Handbook of adolescent psychology*. New York: Wiley.

Elston, T., & Thomas, J. B. (1985). Anorexia nervosa. *Child Care, Health and Development, 11*, 355–373.

Erickson, R. C. (1975). Outcome studies in mental hospitals: A review. *Psychological Bulletin, 82*(4), 519–540.

Esman, A. H. (1983). *The psychiatric treatment of adolescents*. New York: International Universities Press.

Family Court Services, Santa Clara County Superior Court. (1993). Family Court Services Orientation Program.

Faulkner, K., Stoltenberg, C. D., Cogen, R., Nolder, M., & Shooter, E. (1992). Behavioral group treatment for male spouse abusers. *Journal of Family Violence, 7*(1), 37–46.

Fiebert, M. S. (1968). Sensitivity training: An analysis of trainer interventions and group process. *Psychological Reports, 22*(8), 829–838.

Finn, B. & Shakir, S. A. (1990). Intensive group psychotherapy of borderline patients. *Group, 14*(2), 99–110.

Foulds, M. (1971). Changes in locus of internal-external control. *Comparative Group Studies*, 293–300.

Foulds, M., & Hannigan, P. (1976). Effects of gestalt marathon workshops on measured self-actualization: A replication and follow up. *Journal of Counseling Psychology, 23*, 60–65.

Framo, J. (1973). Marriage therapy in a couples group. In D. Block (Ed.), *Techniques of family psychotherapy: A primer*. New York: Grune & Stratton.

Frances A., & Schiff, M. (1976). Popular music as a catalyst in the induction of therapy groups for teenagers. *International Journal of Group Psychotherapy, 26*, 393–398.

Frankl, V. (1963). *Man's search for meaning*. New York: Simon & Schuster.

Freeman, C., Sinclair, F., Turnbull, J., & Annadale, A. (1985). Psychotherapy for bulimia: A controlled study. *Journal of Psychiatric Research, 19*, 473–478.

Freeman, C. P. L., & Munro, J. K. M. (1988). Drug and group treatments for bulimia/bulimia nervosa. *Journal of Psychosomatic Research, 23*(6), 647–660.

Freud, S. (1924). *Collected papers*, Vol. II. New York: International Psychoanalytic Library.

Gabriel, B. (1939). An experiment in group therapy. *American Journal of Orthopsychiatry: Neuropsychiatry, 9*, 593–602.

Gabriel, B. (1944). Group treatment for adolescent girls. *American Journal of Orthopsychiatry, 14*, 592–602.

Gallatin, J. E. (1975). *Adolescence and individuality*. New York: Harper & Row.

Gans, R. W. (1957). The use of group co-therapists in the teaching of psychotherapy. *International Journal of Group Psychotherapy, 9,* 618–628.

Garfield, S. L., & Bergin, A. E. (Eds.) (1986). *Handbook of psychotherapy and behavior change* (3rd ed., pp. 627–670). New York: Wiley.

Gazda, G. M. (1989). *Group counseling: A developmental approach* (4th Ed.). Boston: Allyn & Bacon.

Gendron, M., Lemberg, R., Allender, R., & Bohanske, J. (1992). Effectiveness of the intensive group process-retreat model in the treatment of bulimia. Special Section: The use of group therapy in the treatment of eating disorders. *Group, 16*(2) 69–78.

Getty, C., & Shannon, A. M. (1969). Co-therapy as an egalitarian relationship. *American Journal of Nursing, 69,* 767–771.

Glass, T. A. (1997). Ethical issues in group therapy. In R. Anderson, T. Needles, & H. Hall (Eds.), *A practitioners guide to ethical issues in psychology specialty areas*. Springfield, IL: Charles C Thomas.

Gleason, J., & Prescott, M. R. (1977). Group techniques for premarital preparation. *Family Coordinator, 20,* 277–280.

Glendening, S. E., & Wilson, A. J., III. (1972). Experiments in pre-marital counseling. *Social Casework, 53,* 551–562.

Goodman, B., & Nowak-Scibelli, D. (1985). Group treatment for women incestuously abused as children. *International Journal of Group Psychotherapy, 35,* 531–544.

Goodwin, D., Schulsinger, F., Hermansen, L., Guze, S., & Winokur, G. (1973). Alcohol problems in adoptees raised apart from biological parents. *Archives of General Psychiatry, 28,* 238–243.

Gottlieb, A., & Pattison, E. M. (1966). Married couples group therapy. *Archives of General Psychiatry, 14,* 143–152.

Gowers, S., Norton, K., Halek, C., & Crisp, A. H. (1994). Outcome of outpatient psychotherapy in a random allocation treatment study of anorexia nervosa. *International Journal of Eating Disorders, 15*(2), 165–177.

Gravitz, H. L., & Bowden, J. D. (1984). Therapeutic issues of adult children of alcoholics. *Alcohol Health and Research World, 8*(4), 25–36.

Gray, J. J., & Hoage, C. M. (1990). Bulimia nervosa: Group behavior therapy with exposure plus response prevention. *Psychological Reports, 66*(2), 110–121.

Greenleaf, J. (1981). *Co-alcoholic/para-alcoholic: Who's who and what's the difference?* Denver: M.A.C.

Grotjahn, M. (1951). Special problems in the supervision of group psychotherapy. *Group Psychotherapy, 3,* 308–313.

Grotjahn, M. (1971). The qualities of the group therapist. In H. I. Kaplan & B. I. Sadock (Eds.). *Comprehensive group treatment*. Baltimore: Williams & Wilkins.

Grunbaum, H. (1986). Inside the group. In A. S. Gurman (Ed.), *Casebook of marital therapy* (pp. 742–775). New York: Guilford Press.

Grunebaum, H., Christ, J., & Neiberg, J. (1969). Diagnosis and treatment planning for couples. In H. Grunebaum & J. Christ (Eds.), *Contemporary marriage: Structure, dynamics and therapy*. Boston: Little, Brown.

Guerney, B. G., Jr. (1977). *Relationship enhancement*. San Francisco: Jossey-Bass.

Gurman, A. S., & Kniskern, D. P. (1981). Family therapy outcome research: Knowns and unknowns. In A. S. Gurman & D. P. Kniskern (Eds.), *Handbook of family therapy* (pp. 742–775). New York: Brunner/Mazel.

Hadden, S. B. (1947). The utilization of a therapy group in teaching psychotherapy. *American Journal of Psychiatry, 103,* 644–651.

Hadden, S. B. (1955). Historic background of group psychotherapy. *International Journal of Group Psychotherapy, 5,* 162–168.

Haeseler, M. P. (1992). Ethical considerations for the group therapist. *American Journal of Art Therapy, 31*(1), 2–9.

Haley, J. (1963). *Strategies of psychotherapy.* New York: Grune & Stratton.

Hall, Z. M. (1992). Group therapy for women survivors of childhood sexual abuse. *Group Analysis, 25*(4), 463–474.

Hansen, J. C., Warner, R. W., & Smith, E. J. (1980). *Group counseling: Theory and process* (2nd ed.). Chicago: Rand McNally.

Harari, C., & Harari, C. (1971). The co-therapist encounter: A catalyst for growth. In L. Blank, G. B. Gottsegen, & M. G. Gottsegen (Eds.), *Confrontation.* New York: Macmillan.

Hastings, P. R., & Runkel, R. L. (1963). Married couples with severe problems. *International Journal of Group Psychotherapy, 13,* 84–92.

Hedlund, J., & Viewig, R. (1984). Michigan Alcoholism Screening Test: A comparative review. *Journal of Applied Psychiatry, 84,* 55–65.

Heilfron, M. (1969). Co-therapy: The relationship between therapists. *International Journal of Group Psychotherapy, 19,* 366–381.

Hendren, R. L., Atkins, D. M., Sumner, C. R., & Barber, J. K. (1987). Model for the group treatment of eating disorders. *International Journal of Group Psychotherapy, 37*(4), 589–602.

Hendren, R. L., Barber, J. K., & Sigafoos, A. (1986). Eating disordered symptoms in a non-clinical population: A study of female adolescents in two private girls' schools. *Journal of the American Academy of Child Psychiatry, 25,* 836–840.

Henry, S. (1981). *Group skills in social work: A four dimensional approach.* Itasca, IL: Peacock.

Heppner, P. (1983). Structured group activities for counseling men. *Journal of College Student Personnel, 24*(2), 275–277.

Herman, J., & Schatzow, E. (1984). Time limited group therapy for women with a history of incest. *International Journal of Group Psychotherapy, 34*(4), 605–616.

Hollis, J. W., & Wantz, R. A. (1990). *Counselor preparation 1990–1992* (7th ed.). Muncie, IN: Accelerated Development.

Horejsi, C. R. (1974). Small group sex education for engaged couples. *Journal of Family Counseling, 2,* 23–27.

Horney, K. (1926). *Feminine psychology.* New York: Norton, 1967.

Horney, K. (1935). The problem of feminine masochism. *Psychoanalytic Review, 22,* 241–257.

Huston, K. (1986). A critical assessment of the efficacy of women's groups. *Psychotherapy, 23,* 283–290.

Hulse, W. C. (1950). The therapeutic management of group tension. *American Journal of Orthopsychiatry, 20,* 834–838.

Hulse, W. C., Ladlow, W. V., Rindsberg, B. K., & Epstein, N. B. (1956). Transerence relations in a group of female patients to male and female co-leaders. *International Journal of Group Psychotherapy, 6,* 430–435.

Hymovitz, C., & Pollock, E. J. (1995, July 13). Cost cutting firms monitor couch time as therapists fret. *The Wall Street Journal,* p. AI.

Inbody, D. R., & Ellis, J. J. (1985). Group therapy with anorexic and bulimic patients: Implications for therapeutic intervention. *American Journal of Psychotherapy, 39,* 411.

Ivey, A. E. (1990). *Developmental strategies for helpers: Individual, family and network interventions.* Pacific Grove, CA: Brooks/Cole.

Jacklin, C. L. (1989). Female and male issues of gender. Special issue: Children and their development: Knowledge base, research agenda, and social policy. *American Psychologist, 44*(2), 127–133.

Jackson, J., & Grotjahn, M. (1958). Reenactment of the marriage neurosis in group psychotherapy. *Journal of Nervous and Mental Disorders, 127*, 503–510.

Jacobs, E. E., Harvill, R. L., & Masson, R. L. (1994). *Group counseling: Strategies and skills* (2nd ed.). Pacific Grove, CA: Brooks/Cole.

Kaplan, H. I., & Sadock, B. J. (1971). *Comprehensive group psychotherapy*. Baltimore: Williams & Wilkins.

Kaplan, H. I., & Sadock, B. J. (1983). *Comprehensive group psychotherapy* (2nd ed.). Baltimore: Williams & Wilkins.

Kaslow, F. W. (1981). Group therapy with couples in conflict: Is more better? *Psychotherapy: Theory, Research and Practice, 18*(4), 516–524.

Kaslow, F. W., & Lieberman, E. J. (1981). Couples group therapy: Rational, dynamic and process. In G. P. Sholevar (Ed.), *Clinical handbook of marital therapy* (pp. 175–191). New York: Jason Aronson.

Kaslow, M. J., & Suarez, A. F. (1988). Treating couples in group therapy. In J. C. Hansen & F. W. Kaslow (Eds.), *Couples therapy in a family context: Perspective and retrospective*. Aspen.

Kaufman, J., & Timmons, R. L. (1983). Searching for the hairy man. *Social Work with Groups, 3*, 163–175.

Keen, S. (1991). *Fire in the belly*. New York: Bantam.

Kemper, S., Kibel, H., & Mahler, J. (1993). On becoming oriented to inpatient addiction treatment: Inducting new patients and professionals to the recovery movement. *International Journal of Group Psychotherapy, 43*, 285–300.

Kennedy, J. F. (1989). Therapist gender and the same sex puberty age psychotherapy group. *International Journal of Group Psychotherapy, 39*, 255–265.

Kilgo, R. D. (1975). Counseling couples in groups: Rationale and methodology. *Family Coordinator, 24*(3), 337–342.

Kirkley, B., Schneider, J., Agras, W. S., & Bachman, J. A. (1985). Comparison of two group treatments for bulimia. *Journal of Consulting and Clinical Psychology, 53*, 43–48.

Kirschenbaum, M. J., & Blinder, M. G. (1972). Growth processes in married-couples group therapy. *Family Therapy, 1*, 85–104.

Kline, N. S. (1952). Some hazards in group psychotherapy. *International Journal of Group Psychotherapy, 2*, 111–115.

Koss, M. P., & Butcher, J. N. (1986). Research on brief psychotherapy. In S. L. Garfield and A.E. Bergin (Eds.), 3rd ed. *Handbook of psychotherapy and behavior change*. New York: Wiley.

Kottler, J. A. (1982). Unethical behaviors we all do and pretend we do not. *Journal of Specialists in Group Work, 7*, 182–186.

Kraft, I. A. (1961). Some special considerations in adolescent group psychotherapy. *International Journal of Group Psychotherapy, 11*, 196–203.

Kraft, I. (1968). An overview of group therapy with adolescents. *International Journal of Group Psychotherapy, 18*, 461–480.

Kravetz, D. (1987). Benefits of consciousness-raising groups for women. In C. M. Brody (Ed.), *Women's therapy groups: Paradigms of feminist treatment* (pp. 55–66). New York: Springer.

Krugman, S., & Osherson, S. (1993). Men in group therapy. In A. Alonso & H. I. Swiller (Eds.), *Group therapy in clinical practice*. Washington, DC: American Psychiatric Press.

Lacey, J. H. (1983). Bulimia nervosa, binge eating and psychogenic vomiting: A controlled treatment study and long-term outcome. *British Medical Journal, 266,* 1609–1613.

Lakin, M. (1969). Some ethical issues in sensitivity training. *American Psychologist, 42,* 923–931.

Lakin, M. (1972). *Interpersonal encounter.* New York: McGraw-Hill.

Lakin, M. (1991). *Coping with ethical dilemmas in psychotherapy.* New York: Pergamon Press.

Landis, I. L., & Wyre, C. H. (1984). Group treatment for mothers of incest victims: A step by step approach. *Journal of Counseling and Development, 63,* 115–116.

Larson, R., & Johnson, C. (1985). Bulimia: Disturbed patterns of solitude. *Addictive Behaviors, 10,* 281–290.

Laube, J. J. (1990). Why group therapy for bulimia? *International Journal of Group Psychotherapy, 40*(2), 222–235.

Leichter, E. (1962). Group psychotherapy of married couples group: Some characteristic treatment dynamics. *International Journal of Group Psychotherapy, 12,* 154.

Leichter, E. (1975). Treatment of married couple group. In A. S. Gurman & D. G. Rice (Eds.), *Couples in conflict* (pp. 175–191). New York: Jason Aronson.

Lenihan, G. O., & Sanders, C. D. (1984). Guidelines for group therapy with eating disorder victims. *Journal of Counseling and Development, 63,* 252–254.

Leong, F. T. (1992). Guidelines for minimizing premature termination among Asian American clients to group counseling. Special Issue: Group counseling with mulicultural populations. *Journal for Specialists in Group Work, 17*(4), 218–228.

Levine, B. (1980). Co-leadership approach to learning group work. *Social Work with Groups, 3*(4), 35–38.

Levinson, D. (1978). *Seasons of a man's life.* New York: Knopf.

Lewis, B. (1978). An examination of the final phase of a group development theory. *Small Group Behavior, 9,* 507–517.

Lewis, E. (1983). The group treatment of battered women. *Women and Therapy, 2*(1), 51–59.

Lieberman, E. J., & Lieberman, S. B. (1986). Couples group therapy. In N. Jacobson & A. Gurman (Eds.), *Clinical handbook of marital therapy* (pp. 237–251.) New York: Guilford Press.

Lieberman, M. A., Yalom, I. D., & Miles, M. B. (1973). *Encounter groups: First facts.* New York: Basic Books.

Lifton, W. M. (1966). *Working with groups.* New York: Wiley.

Long, S. (1988). *The six group therapies compared.* New York: Plenum.

Low, P., & Low, M. (1975). Treatment of a married couple in a group run by a husband and wife. *International Journal of Group Psychotherapy, 25,* 54–66.

Lubin, B., & Lubin, A. L. (1987). *Comprehensive index of group psychotherapy writings.* Monograph. Madison, CT: International Universities Press.

Lundin, W. H., & Aranov, B. M. (1952). The use of co-therapists in group psychotherapy. *Journal of Consulting Psychology, 16,* 76–80.

Luthman, S. G., & Kirschenbaum, M. (1974). *Dynamic family.* Palo Alto, CA: Science and Behavior Books.

Mace, D. R., & Mace, V. (1977). *How to have a happy marriage.* Nashville, TN: Abington Press.

MacKenzie, K. R. (1987). Therapeutic factors in group psychotherapy: A contemporary view. *Group, 11,* 26–34.

MacKenzie, K. R. (1990). *Introduction to time limited group psychotherapy.* Washington, DC: American Psychiatric Press.

MacKenzie, K. R. (1993). Time limited group theory and technique. In A. Alonso & H. I. Swiller (Eds.), *Group therapy in clinical practice.* Washington, DC: American Psychiatric Press.

MacKenzie, K. R. (1994). The developing of the therapy group structure. In H. S. Bernard & K. R. MacKenzie (Eds), *Basics of group psychotherapy.* New York: Guilford.

MacLennan, B. W. (1965). Co-therapy. *International Journal of Group Psychotherapy, 15,* 154.

MacNab, R. T. (1990). What do men want? Male rituals of initiation in group psychotherapy. *International Journal of Group Psychotherapy, 40,* 139–155.

Marett, K. M. (1988). A substantive and methodological review of couples group therapy outcome research. *Group, 12,* 241–246.

Markowitz, M., & Kadis, A. L. (1972). Short term analytic treatment of married couples in a group by a therapist couple. In C. Sager & H. S. Kaplan (Eds.), *Progress in group and family therapy* (pp. 463–482). New York: Brunner/Mazel.

Marsh, L. C. (1931). Group treatment of the psychoses by the psychological equivalent of the revival. *Mental Hygiene, 15,* 328–349.

McCallum, M., & Piper, W. (1990). A controlled study of effectiveness and patient suitability for short-term group psychotherapy. *International Journal of Group Psychotherapy, 40,* 431–452.

McGhee, T. F., & Kostrabula, T. (1964). The neurotic equilibrium in married couples applying for group psychotherapy. *Journal of Marriage and the Family, 26,* 77–88.

McGhee, T. F., & Schuman, B. N. (1970). The nature of the cotherapy relationship. *International Journal of Group Psychotherapy, 20,* 25–36.

McWilliams, N., & Stein, J. (1987). Women's groups led by women: The management of devaluing transferences. *International Journal of Group Psychotherapy, 37,* 139–153.

Mellody, P. (1989). *Facing codependence.* New York: HarperCollins.

Meth, R. L., & Pasick, R. S. (1990). *Men in therapy.* New York: Guilford.

Moreno, J. L. (1911). *Die gottheit als komediant.* Vienna: Anzangruber Verlag.

Moreno, J. L. (1932). *Application of the group method to classification.* National committee on prisons and prison labor.

Morrison, A. P. (1986). On projective identification in couples' groups. *International Journal of Group Psychotherapy, 36*(1), 55–73.

Nahon, D. (1992). A challenge for men. *Journal of Mental Health Counseling, 14*(3), 405–416.

Napier, R., & Gershenfeld, M. (1983). *Making groups work: A guide for group leaders.* Boston: Houghton Mifflin.

National Association of Social Workers. (1979). *Code of ethics.* Washington, DC: Author.

National Training Laboratories. (1970). *Personal growth and social change.* Institute for Applied Behavior Science, Pamphlet 1–26.

Newman, R., & Levant, R. (1993). Proficiency certification: A useful tool in today's marketplace. *Independent Practitioner, 13*(6), 248–249.

Nicholas, M. W. (1984). Change in the context of group therapy. New York: Brunner/Mazel.

Norcross, J. C., Alford, B. A., & DiMichele, J. (1992). The future of psychotherapy: Delphi data and concluding observations. *Psychotherapy, 29,* 150–158.

Oesterheld, J. R., McKenna, M. S., & Gould, N. B. (1987). Group psychotherapy of bulimia: A critical review. *International Journal of Group Psychotherapy, 37*(2), 163–184.

Olsson, P., & Myers, I. (1972). Nonverbal techniques in an adolescent group. *International Journal of Group Psychotherapy, 22*(2), 186–191.

Orlinsky, D. E., & Howard, K. L. (1986). Process and outcome in psychotherapy. In S. L. Garfield & A. E. Bergin (Eds.), *Handbook of psychotherapy and behavior change* (3rd ed., pp. 311–381). New York: Wiley.

Osherson, S. (1986). *Finding our fathers*. New York: Free Press.

Osherson, S., & Krugman, S. (1991). Men, shame and psychotherapy. *Journal of Psychotherapy, 27*, 327–337.

Overeaters Anonymous. (1980). *The tools of recovery*. Torrance, CA: Overeaters Anonymous World Service Office.

Paolino, T. J., & McCrady, B. S. (1978). *Marriage and marital therapy; Psychoanalytic, behavioral and system theory perspectives*. New York: Brunner Mazel.

Papp, P. (1976). Brief therapy with couples group. In P. J. Guerin (Ed.), *Family therapy: Theory and practice* (pp. 350–363). New York: Gardner Press.

Parloff, M. B., & Dies, R. R. (1977). Group psychotherapy outcome research, 1966–1975. *International Journal of Group Psychotherapy, 27*, 281–319.

Pedersen, P. B., & Marsella, A. J. (1982). The ethical crisis for cross cultural counseling and therapy. *Professional Psychology, 13*(4), 492–500.

Peled, E., & Edleson, J. (1992). Multiple perspectives on groupwork with children of battered women. *Violence and Victims, 7*, 327–342.

Pfeffer, A. A., Friedland, P., & Wortis, S. B. (1949). Group psychotherapy with alcoholics. *Quarterly Journal of Studies in Alcohol, 10*, 198–216.

Phelan, J. (1972). The psychoanalytic approach to group therapy with older teenagers in private practice. In I. H. Berkowitz, *Adolescents grow in groups*. New York: Brunner/Mazel.

Pinney, E. L., Jr. (1983). Ethical and legal issues in group psychotherapy. In H. I. Kaplan & B. J. Sadock, *Comprehensive group psychotherapy* (pp. 301–304). Baltimore: Williams & Wilkins.

Piper, W. E., McCallum, M., & Hassan, A. (1992). *Adaptation to loss through short-term group psychotherapy*. New York: Guilford.

Piper, W. E., & Perrault, E. L. (1989). Pretherapy preparation for group members. *International Journal of Group Psychotherapy, 39*, 17–34.

Pollock, E. J. (1995, December 1). Managed care's focus on psychiatric drugs alarms many doctors. *The Wall Street Journal*, p. AI.

Powdermaker, F., & Frank, J. D. (1953). *Group psychotherapy*. Cambridge, MA: Harvard University Press.

Pratt, J. H. (1906). The home sanitarium treatment of consumption. *Boston Medical Surgeons Journal, 154*, 210–216.

Pratt, J. H. (1907). The class method of treating consumption in the homes of the poor. *Journal of the American Medical Association, 49*, 755–759.

Pratt, J. H. (1908). Results obtained in the treatment of pulmonary tuberculosis by the class method. *British Medical Journal, 2*, 1070–1071.

Pratt, J. H. (1911). The class method in the homes of tuberculars and what it has accomplished. *Transactions of the American Climatic Association, 27*, 87–118.

Pratt, J. H. (1934). The influence of emotions in the causation and cure of psychoneuroses. *International Clinics, 4*, 1–16.

Pyle, R., Mitchell, J., Eckert, E., Hatsukami, D., & Goff, G. (1984). The interruption of bulimic behaviors: A review of three treatment programs. *Psychiatric Clinics of North America, 7*, 275–286.

Rabinowitz, F. E. (1991). The male-to-male embrace: Breaking the touch taboo in a men's therapy group. *Journal of Counseling and Development, 69*(6), 574–576.

Rachman, A. W. (1971). Encounter techniques in analytic group psychotherapy with adolescents. *International Journal of Group Psychotherapy, 21*, 317–328.

Rachman, A. W. (1972). Group psychotherapy in treating the adolescent identity crisis. *International Journal of Group Psychotherapy, 22*, 97–119.

Rachman, A. W. (1975). *Identity group psychotherapy with adolescents*. Springfield, IL: Charles C Thomas.

Rachman, A. W., & Raubolt, R. P. (1984). The pioneers of adolescent group therapy. *International Journal of Group Psychotherapy, 34,* 387–414.

Rappaport, A. S. (1976). Conjugal relationship enhancement program. In D. H. L. Olson (Ed.), *Treating relationships.* Lake Mills, IA:

Rappaport, R. L. (1994). Culture, values, and therapy. *Family Psychologist, 10*(2), 7.

Reighline, P. B., & Targow, J. F. (1990). *Group psychotherapists handbook.* New York: Columbia University Press.

Ridley, C. A., & Bain, A. B. (1983). The effects of a premarital relationship enhancement disclosure. *Family Therapy, 10*(1), 13–24.

Rogers, C. R. (1969). *On encounter groups.* New York: Harper & Row.

Rolfe, D. J. (1977). Techniques with premarriage groups. *British Journal of Guidance and Counseling, 5,* 89–97.

Rollins, N., & Piazza, E. (1981). Change in anorexia nervosa. *Adolescence, 16,* 293–305.

Rosenbaum, M. (1971). Cotherapy. In H. I. Kaplan & B. J. Sadock (Eds.), *Comprehensive group psycotherapy,* Baltimore: Williams & Wilkins.

Rosenbaum, M., & Hartley, E. (1962). A summary review of current practices of ninety-two group therapists. *International Journal of Group Psychotherapy, 12,* 194–198.

Rosenberg, S. A., & Zimet, C. N. (1995). Brief group treatment and managed health care. *International Journal of Group Psychotherapy, 45*(3), 367–379.

Rosenthal, D., & Hansen, J. (1980). Working with single-parent families. *Family Therapy, 7,* 73–82.

Ross, I. (1977). The intuitive psychologist and his shortcomings: Distortions in the attribution process. In L. Berkowitz (Ed.), *Advances in experimental social psychology* (Vol. 10). New York: Academic Press.

Ross, J. H. (1977). The development and evaluation of a group premarital counseling workshop. Unpublished doctoral dissertation, University of North Colorado.

Russell, M. (1988). Wife assault theory, research and treatment: A literature review. *Journal of Family Violence, 3*(3), 193–205.

Rutan, J. S., & Stone, W. N. (1984). *Psychodynamic group psychotherapy.* New York: Macmillan.

Saunders, D. G., & Hanusa, D. (1986, December). The short-term effects of group therapy. *Journal of Family Violence,* pp. 357–372.

Schaffer, J. B., & Galinsky, M. D. (1989). *Models of group therapy and sensitivity training* (2nd ed.). Englewood Cliffs, NJ: Prentice Hall.

Scheidlinger, S. (1994). *Nine decades of group psychotherapy—an overview.* Paper presented at the annual meeting of the American Psychological Association, Los Angeles.

Schindler, L., Halweg, K., & Revenstorf, D. (1983). *The American Journal of Family Therapy, 11*(3), 54–64.

Schuckit, M. A., Li, T. K., Cloninger, C. R., & Dietrich, R. A. (1985). Genetics of alcoholism. *Alcoholism: Clinical and Experimental Research, 1*(4), 123–132.

Schutz, W. C. (1967). *Joy: Expanding human awareness.* New York: Harper & Row.

Schutz, W. C. (1973). *Elements of encounter.* Big Sur, CA: Joy Press.

Selzer, M. L. (1971). The Michigan Alcoholism Screening Test: Quest for a new diagnostic instrument. *American Journal of Psychiatry, 127,* 1653–1658.

Selzer, M. L., Vinokur, A., & Van Rooijen, L. (1975). A self-administered short Michigan Alcoholism Screening Test (MAST). *Journal of Studies in Alcoholism, 36,* 117–126.

Seixas, J. (1982). Children from alcoholic families. In N. Estes & M. Heinemann (Eds.), *Alcoholism: Development, consequences and intervention* (pp. 193–201). St. Louis, MO: Mosby.

Shapiro, J. L. (1973, June 26). Encounter in Hawaii. *Hawaii Observer,* pp. 8–9.

Shapiro, J. L. (1975). Process, progress, and concerns for encounter groups. Paper presented at Hawaii Association of Humanistic Psychology.

Shapiro, J. L. (1976). *The use of videotape in group leader training.* Paper presented at the World's Educators Conference, Honolulu.

Shapiro, J. L. (1978). *Methods of group psychotherapy and encounter: A tradition of innovation.* Itasca, IL: F. E. Peacock.

Shapiro, J. L. (1992, March 21). *Group therapy: The treatment of choice in the 90's.* [Workshop.] San Francisco.

Shapiro, J. L. (1993). *Brief group treatment: A training manual for counselors and therapists.* Santa Clara, CA: Santa Clara University Counseling Psychology and Education.

Shapiro, J. L. (1994). *Brief treatment groups.* [Workshop.] Santa Clara, CA.

Shapiro, J. L. (1995). When men are pregnant. In J. L. Shapiro, M. J. Diamond, & M. Greenberg, (Eds.), *Becoming a father: Contemporary social, developmental and clinical perspectives* (pp. 118–134). New York: Springer.

Shapiro, J. L. (1996). *A semi-formal review of North American group training programs.* Unpublished document.

Shapiro, J. L., & Bernadett-Shapiro, S. T. (1985). Group work to 2001: Hal or Haven (from isolation)? Special issue. *Journal of Specialists in Group Work, 10*(2), 83–87.

Shapiro, J. L., & Diamond, M. J. (1972). Increases in hypnotizability as a function of encounter group training. *Journal of Abnormal Psychology, 79*(1), 112–115.

Shapiro, J. L., Diamond, M. J., & Greenberg, M. (1995). *Becoming a father: Contemporary social, developmental and clinical perspectives.* New York: Springer.

Shapiro, J. L., Marano, P. J., & Diamond, M. J. (1973). *An investigation of encounter group outcome and its relationship to leadership experience.* Paper presented at the 19th annual convention of the Southeastern Psychological Association, New Orleans.

Shapiro, J. L., & Siu, P.K. (1976). *Potential subtle modeling influences in group training: The impact of minority culture group leaders on members' identification and behavior.* Unpublished paper, University of Hawaii.

Shore, K. (1996). Beyond managed care and managed competition. *The Independent Practitioner* 24–25.

Shostrom, E. L. (1969). Group therapy: Let the buyer beware. *Psychology Today, 2,* 36–40.

Siegel, M., Brisman, J., & Weinshel, M. (1988). *Surviving an eating disorder.* New York: Harper & Row.

Siegler, A. (1983). Changing aspects of the family: An analytic perspective on single mothers of oedipal children. In L. P. Wolberg & M. L. Aronson (Eds.), *Group and family therapy.* New York: Brunner/Mazel.

Silverberg, R. A. (1986). *Psychotherapy for men.* Springfield, IL: Charles C Thomas.

Slavson, S. R. (1951). *The practice of group therapy.* New York: International Universities Press.

Slavson, S. R. (1964). *A textbook in analytic group psychotherapy.* New York: Grune & Stratton.

Solomon, J., & Solomon, G. (1963). Group therapy with father and son as co-therapists: Some dynamic considerations. *International Journal of Group Psychotherapy, 13,* 133–140.

Spitz, H. I. (1978). Structured interactional group psychotherapy with couples. *International Journal of Group Psychotherapy, 28,* 401–409.

Sptiz, H. I. (1979). Group approaches in treating marital problems. *Psychiatric Annals, 9,* 318–330.

Spotniz, H. (1952). Group therapy as a specialized technique. In G. Bychowski & J. L. Despert (Eds.), *Specialized techniques in psychotherapy* (pp. 85–101). New York: Basic Books.

Stahmann, R. F., & Hiebert, W. J. (1980). *Premarital counseling.* Lexington, MA: Lexington Books.

Star, B. (1978). Comparing battered and non-battered women. *Victimology, 2,* 499–510.

Stein, T. S. (1983). Men's groups. In K. Solomon & N. B. Levy (Eds.), *Men in transition: Theory and therapy* (pp. 275–307). New York: Plenum.

Steinglass, P. (1979). The alcoholic family in the interaction laboratory. *Journal of Nervous Mental Disorders, 167,* 428–436.

Steinglass, P. (1989). Alcohol and the family system. In C. N. Ramsey Jr. (Ed.), *Family systems in medicine.* New York: Guilford.

Steinmetz, S. K. (1978). Violence between family members. *Marriage and Family Review, 1*(3), 1–16.

Stoute, A. (1950). Implementation of group interpersonal relationships through psychotherapy. *Journal of Psychology, 30,* 145–156.

Strauss, M. A. (1991). New theory and old canards about family violence research. *Social Problems, 38*(2), 180–197.

Strauss, M. A., & Gelles, R. C. (1986). Societal change and change in family violence from 1975 to 1985 as revealed in two national surveys. *Journal of Marriage and the Family, 48,* 465–479.

Strauss, M. A., & Gelles, R. C. (1990). *Physical violence in American families: Risk factors and adaptation to violence in 8145 families.* New Brunswick, NJ: Transition.

Strauss, M. A., & Kurz, D. (1997). Domestic violence: Are women as likely as men to initiate physical assaults in partner relationships? In M. R. Walsh (Ed.), *Women, men and gender: Ongoing debates* (pp. 207–231). New Haven, CT: Yale University Press.

Sue, S. (1984). Psychotherapeutic service for ethnic minorities. *American Psychologist, 43,* 301–308.

Sue, S., & Sue, D. W. (1971). Chinese American personality and mental health. *Amerasia Journal, 1,* 36–49.

Sue, D., & Sue, D. W. (1990). *Counseling the culturally different: Theory and practice* (2nd ed.). New York: Wiley.

Sugar, M. (1975). The structure and setting of adolescent therapy groups. In M. Sugar (Ed.), *The adolescent in group and family therapy.* New York: Brunner/Mazel.

Thompson, C. (1941). The role of women in this culture. *Psychiatry, 4* 1–8.

Thompson, C. (1942). Cultural pressures in the psychology of women. *Psychiatry, 5,* 331–339.

Thornton, L., & DeBlassie, R. (1989). Treating bulimia. *Adolescence, 24,* 95.

Toseland, R., Kabat, D., & Kemp, K. (1983). An evaluation of a smoking cessation group program. *Social Work Research and Abstracts, 19*(1), 12–19.

Toseland, R. W., & Rivas, R. F. (1984). *An introduction to group work practice.* New York: Macmillan.

Trimprey, M. L. (1989). Self-esteem and anxiety: Key issues in an abused women's group. *Mental Health Nursing, 10,* 297–308.

Truax, C. B. (1966). Therapist empathy, warmth, and genuineness and patient personality change in group psychotherapy. *Journal of Clinical Psychology, 22,* 225–228.

Truax, C. B. (1971). Degree of negative transference occurring in group psychotherapy and client outcome in juvenile delinquents. *Journal of Clinical Psychology, 27,* 132–136.

Truax, C. B., & Carkhuff, R. R. (1967). *Toward effective counseling and psychotherapy.* Chicago: Aldine.

Truax, C. B., Carkhuff, R. R., Wargo, D. G., & Kodman, F. (1966). Changes in self concepts during group psychotherapy as a function of alternate sessions and vicarious therapy pretraining, institutionalized mental patients and juvenile delinquents. *Journal of Consulting Psychology, 30,* 309–392.

Tuckman, B. W. (1965). Developmental sequences in small groups. *Psychological Bulletin,* 63, 384–399.

Tuckman, B. W., & Jenson, M. A. (1977). Stages of small group development revisited. *Journal of Counseling and Development, 64*(1), 52–58.

Turner, S. (1993). Talking about sexual abuse: The value of short term groups for women survivors. *Journal of Group Psychotherapy, Psychodrama and Sociometry, 46*(3), 110–121.

Vachss, A. (1994, August 28). *Parade magazine,* pp. 4–6.

Vandereycken, W., Depreitere, L., & Probst, M. (1987). Body-oriented therapy for anorexia nervosa patients. *American Journal of Psychotherapy, 41*(2), 161–169.

Vander Kolk, C. J. (1985). *Introduction to group counseling and psychotherapy.* Columbus: Bell & Howell.

Van Emde Boas, C. (1962). Intensive group psychotherapy with married couples. *Journal of Group Psychotherapy, 12,* 142.

Vanicelli, M. (1982). Group psychotherapy with alcoholics: Special techniques. *Journal of Studies on Alcohol, 43,* 17–37.

Vanicelli, M. (1987). Treatment of alcoholic couples in outpatient group therapy. *Group, 11*(4), 247–257.

Vanicelli, M. (1989). *Group psychotherapy with adult children of alcoholics.* New York: Guilford Press.

Van Wormer, K. (1989). The male specific group in alcoholism treatment. *Small Group Behavior, 20*(2), 228–242.

Vinogradov, S., & Yalom, I. D. (1990). *Concise guide to group psychotherapy.* Washington, DC: American Psychiatric Press.

Voigt, H., & Weininger, R. (1992). Intervention style and client progress in time limited group psychotherapy for adults sexually abused as children. *Psychotherapy, 29*(4), 580–585.

Wagar, J., & Rodway, M. (1995). An evaluation of a group treatment approach for children who have witnessed wife abuse. *Journal of Family Violence, 10,* 295–305.

Wagner, B. M., Compass, B. E., & Howell, D. C. (1988). Daily and major life events: A test of an integrative model of psychosocial stress. *American Journal of Community Psychology, 16*(2), 189–205.

Walker, L. S. (1987). Women's groups are different. In C. M. Brody (Ed.), *Women's therapy groups: Paradigms of feminist treatment* (pp. 3–12). New York: Springer.

Washington, C. S. (1979). Men counseling men: Redefining the male machine. *Personnel and Guidance Journal, 57*(2), 462–463.

Washington, C. S. (1982). Challenging men in groups. *Journal of Specialists in Group Work, 7*(2), 132–136.

Webb, W., Jr. (1988). A clinical review of developments in the diagnosis and treatment of anorexia nervosa and bulimia. *Psychiatric Medicine, 6*(2), 25–39.

Wegsheider-Cruse, S. (1985). *Choice-making for co-dependents, adult children and spirituality seekers.* Pompano Beach, FL: Health Communications.

Weinstein, H., & Richman, A. (1984). The group treatment of bulimia. *Journal of American College Health, 32,* 208–215.

Wender, L. (1936). The dynamics of group psychotherapy and its application. *Journal of Nervous and Mental Diseases, 84,* 54–60.

Whitaker, C. A. (1949). Teaching the practicing physician to do psychotherapy. *Southern Medical Journal, 42,* 899–904.

Whitaker, D. S. (1982). A nuclear conflict and group focal conflict model for integrating individual and group level phenomena in psychotherapy groups. In M. Pines & L. Rafaelson

(Eds.), *The individual and the group: Boundaries and interrelations* (Vol. 1). New York: Plenum.

Woititz, J. (1983). *Adult Children of Alcoholics.* Pompano Beach, FL: Health Communications.

Wolman, C. S. (1976). Therapy groups for women. *American Journal of Psychiatry, 133,* 274–278.

Wright (1987). Men, shame and antisocial behavior: A psychodynamic perspective. *Group, 11,* 238–246.

Yalom, I. D. (1970). *Theory and practice of group psychotherapy.* New York: Basic Books.

Yalom, I. D. (1975). *The theory and practice of group psychotherapy* (2nd ed.). New York: Basic Books.

Yalom, I. D. (1980). *Existential psychotherapy.* New York: Basic Books.

Yalom, I. D. (1985). *The theory and practice of group psychotherapy* (3rd ed.). New York: Basic Books.

Yalom, I. D. (1990). *Understanding group therapy.* (Video.) Pacific Grove, CA: Brooks Cole.

Yalom, I. D. (1995). *The theory and practice of group psychotherapy* (4th ed.). New York: Basic Books.

Yalom, I. D., Houts, P. S., Newell, G., & Rand, K. H. (1979). Preparation of patients for group therapy. In H. B. Roback, S. I. Abramovitz, & D. S. Strassberg, *Group psychotherapy research: Commentaries and selected readings.* Huntington, NY: Krieger.

Yalom I. D., & Lieberman, M. A. (1971). A study of encounter group casualties. *Archives of General Psychiatry,* 16–20.

Yates, A., & Sambrailo, F. (1984). Bulimia nervosa: A descriptive and therapeutic study. *Behavior Research and Therapy, 22*(5), 503–519.

Yeary, J. R., & Heck, C. L. (1989). Dual diagnosis: Eating disorders and psychoactive substance dependence. *Journal of Psychoactive Drugs, 21*(2), 239–249.

Zimpfer, D. G. (1988). Marriage enrichment programs: A review. *Journal for Specialists in Group Work, 13*(1), 44–53.

Index

Ackerman, N. W., 192, 203, 208, 265
acting out, 189, 205, 206, 209, 239, 251
addiction, 23, 31, 190, 191, 197, 200,
    215, 216, 219, 238
Addicts' Bargain, 197
adolescents, 17, 75, 189, 201–209, 210,
    213, 246, 258
Adult Children of Alcoholics (ACA,
    ACoA), 23, 28, 190–200
Alcoholics Anonymous (AA), 191, 197
Alonso, A., 170, 171, 265, 269, 272, 273,
    274
ambiguity, 49, 50–53, 58, 59, 123–124,
    134, 239
announcements, 19–29
anorexia, 211, 212, 214, 216
anxiety, 6, 24, 33, 38, 47, 48, 49–51, 52,
    53, 55, 56–61, 134, 139, 157,
    204–206, 226–228, 239, 251
authority, of leader, 63, 72–74, 134, 194,
    203

Bernadett-Shapiro, S. T., 3, 74, 233, 277
Black, C., 192, 193, 197, 266
Bowen, M., 222, 266
Brown, S., 190, 191, 192, 197, 198, 199,
    245, 265, 266, 267
Bruch, H., 212, 217, 244, 266
Budman, S., 3, 5, 267
bulimia, 211, 212, 214, 216

catalyst, 90, 96, 124, 126–134, 139, 157
ceiling, 48, 71–74, 77
Cermak, T. L., 190, 191, 192, 198, 199,
    267
characteristics of leadership, 115–119, 135
closing, 98, 100, 105–110
Coche, E., 124, 223, 225, 226, 245, 267
Coche, J., 124, 223, 225, 226, 245, 267
co-leader, 18, 33, 35, 50, 51, 54, 75, 77,
    180, 181–185, 223, 260, 263

confidentiality, 18, 36, 40, 41–43, 48, 51,
    161, 162, 166, 178, 223, 226, 231,
    238,
Corey, G., 6, 14, 30, 36, 48, 98, 109,
    120, 174, 180, 181, 205, 224, 260,
    268
Corsini, R., 113, 114, 162, 268
costs, 162, 165
co-therapy, 180-185
    dangers, 184
couples, 7, 36, 52, 89, 106, 167, 221–234
    cross-cultural, 233
credentials, 16, 19, 164
cultural factors, 16, 19, 233, 261–263

Diamond, M. J., 5, 124, 181, 252, 253,
    268, 277
Dies, R. R., 5, 48, 124, 170, 264, 279
diversity, 188, 189
domestic violence, 235–243
DSM-IV, 211, 246
dyadic
    interactions, 48, 95
    level of intervention, 7, 88, 89
dysfunctional family, 191, 192

eating disorders, 25, 211–220, 244
efficacy, 5
ethics, 119, 158–168, 174, 257, 260
extragroup relationship, 40

fatherhood, 251, 252
fees, 8, 16–17, 165
floor, 48, 64–67, 74
follow-up, 109–110, 126, 162, 163, 166,
    199, 217, 232, 240

Gelles, R. C., 235, 244, 278
Grotjahn, M., 114, 116, 181, 221, 270,
    272
ground rules, 49-54, 126, 205, 238, 251

group goals, 5, 10, 16, 19, 23, 29, 30, 32, 40, 59, 89, 110, 113, 116, 122, 162, 166, 168
groups as treatment of choice, 3–5, 213, 222, 259

health maintenance organization (HMO), 7, 16–17, 18, 23, 26, 165, 168
help-rejecting complainer, 64–67
here-and-now, 6, 48, 50, 51, 58, 77, 78, 80, 81, 84, 122, 213, 230
heterogeneous membership, 30, 31, 32, 188–189, 244
homogeneous membership, 30, 188–189, 226, 239, 244

inclusion, 85–88, 92, 107, 188, 195, 216, 225, 241
information disseminator, 124, 126–127, 131, 135, 157, 241
information systems, 135–145
interpersonal interventions, 6, 10, 22, 38, 40, 48, 79, 88, 89, 93, 122–126, 145, 157, 185, 222
intrapsychic interventions, 7, 10, 72, 79, 88–89, 93, 121–126, 128, 145, 231–232
introductions, 27, 33, 54–55
isolates, 31–32, 225
involuntary groups, 26–28

Kraft, I. A., 204, 207, 272

Lakin, M., 114, 162–163, 260, 273
leadership
  challenge, 6, 62–79, 173, 194, 204, 206–207, 217, 241, 246, 251
  focus, 121–126, 231–232
  tests, 70, 77–79, 231, 233, 247, 251
  types, 120–121
length of group, 16, 18–19, 97, 214, 220
levels of intervention, 88–89, 185
location, 16, 17–18, 165
logistics, 16–19, 36, 40

MacKenzie, K. R., 14, 48, 57, 124, 267, 268, 273, 274
managed care, 3, 7–9, 16, 17, 18, 23, 31, 59, 93, 158, 165, 220, 257, 259

Mellody, P., 193, 199, 239, 274
members apply, 16, 19, 22, 27, 37
minority members, 85–88, 96
model, 116, 124–126, 131–134, 157, 160, 161, 183, 207, 217, 224, 231, 248, 250, 252
Moreno, J. L., 119, 202, 255, 274

nonverbal communication, 48, 55, 57, 58, 62, 88, 127, 129, 132, 135, 136–139, 207–208

open groups, 18, 107
orchestrator, 126, 128–131, 135, 139, 207

parallel process, 171, 197
participant (leader), 93, 124, 126, 131–135
perpetrators, 235–240, 243
personal group experience, 170, 172–174, 179, 261
personality, 112–113, 115–120, 125, 157, 182
Pratt, J. H., 4, 115, 119, 255, 275
premarital groups, 229–232, 233
preferred provider organization (PPO), 16, 17, 165
problem solving, 81, 84, 93, 145, 229, 231
process, 3, 5–7, 9, 10, 12–16, 31, 32, 33, 34, 36, 40, 41, 43, 48–49, 53, 54, 55, 58, 62-67, 70, 71, 74, 78, 79, 92–96, 100–101, 107, 110, 112, 123, 126–128, 145, 157, 168, 196, 203, 224, 226, 246–247, 250, 256, 260–261
publicity, 19

qualifications, 113, 161, 168

Rachman, A., 202, 205, 206, 207, 275–276
resistance, 98, 114, 195, 217, 228
rituals, 110–111
roles, 89–93, 112, 115, 124–126, 133–135, 145, 157, 183–184
Rosenbaum, M., 32, 180, 181, 182, 184, 276

Scheidlinger, S., 120, 276

screening, 23, 28–38, 40, 162, 163, 165, 168, 194–196, 205, 216, 225–226, 230, 238, 241, 246, 251

secret motivations, 34–35

self-esteem 4, 38, 192, 193, 196, 214, 218, 236, 237, 239, 240, 245, 246, 247

Shapiro, J. L., 3, 4, 5, 6, 14, 30, 35, 37, 54, 59, 91, 106, 114, 124, 163, 164, 169, 174, 181, 205, 207, 233, 252, 263, 268, 276, 277

silence, 34, 47, 54, 55–61, 62, 63, 71, 196

Slavson, S. R. 32, 116, 181, 202, 207, 277

Spotnitz, H., 113, 119, 277

stages of groups, 12–15, 93, 100, 122, 157

Strauss, M. A., 235, 244, 278

structure, 45, 49, 50, 52, 53–55, 56, 63, 71, 72, 131, 134–135, 157, 251

supervision, 170–171, 177–178, 260

survivors, 191, 240–244, 246, 247

symbiotic relationship, 32–33

termination, 97–110, 198–199, 209, 219–220, 229, 232, 240, 242, 248, 253
  early, 108
  obstacles, 98
  sudden, 109

there-and-then, 50, 56

time of session, 18, 19, 37,

training, 3, 7, 9, 14, 17, 40, 41–46, 51, 54, 56, 62, 71, 72, 100, 112–115, 159–164, 168, 169–179, 200, 259–264
  group, 40, 54, 113, 163, 172–174, 179
  programs, 169, 171–172
  transfer, 14, 98–102, 105, 111, 204, 218, 229, 232, 240, 242, 248

transference, 4, 7, 12, 24, 74, 105, 122, 127, 163, 180–181, 185, 197–198, 207, 258

trust, 84, 90, 93, 102, 116, 226, 228

twelve-step programs, 31, 197

unsolvable problem, 64–67, 70–71, 196, 227

Vanicelli, M., 192, 196, 279

victims, 236, 240–243, 244, 247

Wegscheider-Cruse, S. 192, 279

women, 18, 23, 24, 25, 28, 31, 32, 212, 240–241, 244–248

Yalom, I., 5, 11, 12, 14, 30, 32, 35, 40, 51, 78, 108, 114, 120, 123, 125, 162, 171, 173, 174, 181, 184, 201, 266, 273, 279, 280

TO THE OWNER OF THIS BOOK:

We hope that you have found *Brief Group Treatment: Practical Training for Therapists and Counselors* useful. So that this book can be improved in a future edition, would you take the time to complete this sheet and return it? Thank you.

School and address: ⸺⸺⸺⸺⸺⸺⸺⸺⸺⸺⸺⸺⸺

Department: ⸺⸺⸺⸺⸺⸺⸺⸺⸺⸺⸺⸺⸺⸺

Instructor's name: ⸺⸺⸺⸺⸺⸺⸺⸺⸺⸺⸺⸺⸺

1. What I like most about this book is: ⸺⸺⸺⸺⸺⸺⸺⸺

2. What I like least about this book is: ⸺⸺⸺⸺⸺⸺⸺⸺

3. My general reaction to this book is: ⸺⸺⸺⸺⸺⸺⸺⸺

4. The name of the course in which I used this book is: ⸺⸺⸺⸺

5. Were all of the chapters of the book assigned for you to read? ⸺⸺⸺

   If not, which ones weren't? ⸺⸺⸺⸺⸺⸺⸺⸺⸺⸺

6. In the space below, or on a separate sheet of paper, please write specific suggestions for improving this book and anything else you'd care to share about your experience in using the book.

Optional:

Your name: _____ Date: _____

May Brooks/Cole quote you, either in promotion for *Brief Group Treatment: Practical Training for Therapists and Counselors* or in future publishing ventures?

Yes: _____ No: _____

Sincerely,

Jerrold L. Shapiro
Lawrence S. Peltz
Susan Bernadett-Shapiro

FOLD HERE

NO POSTAGE
NECESSARY
IF MAILED
IN THE
UNITED STATES

BUSINESS REPLY MAIL

FIRST CLASS   PERMIT NO. 358   PACIFIC GROVE, CA

POSTAGE WILL BE PAID BY ADDRESSEE

ATT:  *Jerrold L. Shapiro, Lawrence S. Peltz, Susan Bernadett-Shapiro*

Brooks/Cole Publishing Company
511 Forest Lodge Road
Pacific Grove, California 93950-9968

FOLD HERE

Brooks/Cole is dedicated to publishing quality books for the helping professions. If you would like to learn more about our publications, please use the mailer to request our catalog.

Name: _____

Street Address: _____

City, State, and Zip: _____

FOLD HERE

NO POSTAGE
NECESSARY
IF MAILED
IN THE
UNITED STATES

BUSINESS REPLY MAIL
FIRST CLASS   PERMIT NO. 358   PACIFIC GROVE, CA

POSTAGE WILL BE PAID BY ADDRESSEE

ATT: *Human Services Catalogue*

Brooks/Cole Publishing Company
511 Forest Lodge Road
Pacific Grove, California 93950-9968

FOLD HERE

WARNER MEMORIAL LIBRARY
EASTERN COLLEGE
ST. DAVIDS, PA. 19087